Compendium
Volume Five
to
Commentary
on
The Book of Mormon

Philip M. Hudson

My own
weak attempts to
unlock the mysteries
of The Book of Mormon
in this volume remind me
of the Amish, who make some
of the finest quilts in the world.
On purpose, they build mistakes into
their projects, because they believe that
any attempt on their part to design
and produce a flawless creation
would be a mockery of God,
Who alone is perfect.

Copyright 2024 by Philip M. Hudson.
Published 2024.
Printed in the United States of America.
All rights reserved.

No portion of this book may be reproduced,
stored in a retrieval system, or transmitted
in any form or by any means, mechanical,
electronic, photocopy, recording, scanning,
or other, except for brief quotations in
critical reviews or articles, without
the prior written permission
of the author.

ISBN 978-1-957077-76-5
llustrations - Google Images.

This book may be ordered from
online bookstores.

Publishing Services
by BookCrafters, Parker, Colorado.
www.bookcrafters.net

Whether we are professional athletes or practiced panhandlers, living in the fast or the slow lane of life, whether we have rags or riches, are leaders or lepers, are early prodigies or late bloomers, venture capitalists or welfare recipients; no matter our circumstances, The Book of Mormon entrusts us with the responsibility to build bridges over troubled waters to those whose tentative steps betray their faltering faith.

Index
to
Compendia
Volumes 3-7

If we refuse
to let ourselves be
guided by The Book
of Mormon, and instead
we submit to blind guides,
we deny not only God's power
to transform our lives, but also
His grace. If we turn our backs on
the habitation of the Lord, we place
ourselves at risk of dismissing the
sacrifice of His Son, and esteeming
as a thing of naught His suffering.
When we close our minds to the soul
expanding opportunities afforded by
that book, and we are snared by the
wiles of Satan, we'll find that we
have been bound by his strong
chains. And we thought it
just a flaxen cord that
was around our
necks!

Volume 3 Essays

Abstinence in a Permissive World
Additional Scripture
Addressing Deity
Agency
Agency and Opposition
Agency and Youth
Age of Accountability
Alma's Discourse on Faith
And it Came to Pass
And Thus We See
Angels
Are Mormons Christian?
Are We Alone in The Universe?
(The) Atonement
Bah Humbug!
Baptism
Batteries are Not Included
Become as Little Children
Before a Wound Can Heal
Behold
Being Well Grounded
(The) Bible
(The) Biggest Loser
Blood, Covenant, and Land Israel
(The) Book of Mormon as History
Book of Mormon Strengths

(The) Book of Mormon was Preserved for our Day
Born Again Christians
Brevity)
Buddy Can You Spare a Dime?
Caesar
(A) Change of Heart
(The) Character of God
Choose the Harder Right
Choose ye This Day
Christians
(A) Christmas Miracle
Christ's Church is Restored
(The) Church
(The) Church of Jesus Christ in Former Times
Circle of Knowledge
Citizenship in The Church and Kingdom
Civil Liberties
(A) Coat of Many Colors
Cogito Ergo Sum
Cognates in The Book of Mormon
Combatting Evil
Commitment
Conditional Sentences in The Book of Mormon
Connections
Construction Zone: Proceed with Caution
Conversion

The teachable Lamanites who were converted by the power of the preaching of the word by The Sons of Mosiah came out of the world and left the loneliness of a fallen creation to enter the realm of divine experience. They had forsaken the orphanage of spiritual alienation, and were welcomed into the household of God. Today, we do the same thing. We leave the ranks of the nameless and take upon ourselves another name, that of Jesus Christ, becoming, in time, joint-heirs of all that our Father has.

Volume 4 Essays

- Courage
- Covenant Consciousness
- Covenants
- (The) Creation of The World
- Dancing With the Stars
- (The) Desert Shall Rejoice
- Diversity
- Doctrine – The Meaning of
- (The) Door Swings Both Ways
- Dry Humor in The Book of Mormon
- (The) Dust of The Earth
- (The) Duty of The Priest
- Education
- (The Best) Education
- Enduring to The End
- Entropy in The Physical and Eternal Worlds
- Environmental Concerns: An Eternal Perspective
- Establishing the Word
- (Our) Eternal Nature
- Eternal Progression in a Dynamic Universe
- Everyone Wants to Go to Heaven
- Evidences of God
- Faith and Knowledge
- Faith Building
- Faith is a Principle of Power
- (The) Fall
- Fasting
- Fate
- Father Forgive Them
- Finding Balance in Our Lives
- Friendship
- Focus
- Follow the Prophet
- Forgiveness
- For Unto Us a Child is Born
- (The Importance of) Friends
- Friendship
- Gathering of Israel
- General Conference
- (The) Germination of our Faith
- Gifts of The Spirit
- God is NowHere
- Godly Qualities
- God's Tactical Flashlight
- Gold – The Appearance of
- Grace
- Gratitude

At Cumorah, Mormon attempted to prick the hearts of his people with the word, continually stirring them up to purposeful repentance. He felt it was his responsibility to heal their deafness and blindness by applying a healing balm to their spiritual muscles and joints. But it was to no avail. He wrote to Moroni: "I am laboring with them continually, and when I speak the word of God with sharpness, they tremble and anger against me; and when I use no sharpness they harden their hearts against it, wherefore I fear, lest the Spirit of the Lord hath ceased striving with them." (Moroni 9:4).

Volume 5 Essays

Happiness
Happiness and Sharing the Gospel
Happiness / Wickedness
Having Been Commissioned of Jesus Christ
Heaven Can Wait
Heavenly Father Knows Us
(The) Heavens Were Opened
Higher Dimensional Realities
(The) Holy Ghost
(The) Holy Grail of Religious Doctrine
Honesty
(The) Hourglass of Life
How Does God Get Things Done?
Huckleberries and Chokeberries
Humility
Hypocrisy
I am a Child of God
I Have Fought a Good Fight
I Have Overcome the World
Isaiah in The Book of Mormon
Is Heaven Hotter Than Hell?
It's Our Book
Joseph Smith: A Rough Stone Rolling
Joseph Smith History
Joseph Smith's World

Jumping Out of Our Skin
Just Get Back on The Bike
Justice
Justice and Mercy
Keep Smiling
Labels
Lamanites by The Waters of Sebus
(The) Last Judgment
Life is a Three Act Play
Life or Death?
Life's Greatest Questions
Life's Important Decisions
Light
Light and Darkness
Light and Truth
(The) Light of Christ
(The) Light of The World
Limiting Beliefs
Living Water
Look Who's Coming to Town
Lost Books of The Bible
(The) Lost Manuscript
(The) Lost Ten Tribes
Lucifer

The Book of Mormon is in harmony with the principles of the gospel and the doctrine of Christ. When reviewing that doctrine, it is important to remember that God's work is progressive. It may change its appearance, but never its principles. Practices may change with circumstances, but doctrine remains constant. This doctrine draws attention to the issue of continuing revelation from God. "We believe all that God has revealed, all that he does now reveal, and we believe that he will yet reveal many great and important things pertaining to the Kingdom of God." (Ninth Article of Faith).

Volume 6 Essays

(A) Mailbox Marked With an "X"
Management by The Spirit
(The) Manifestation of Spirits
May the 4th Be With You
(The) Millennium
(The) Mind of God
Missing Scripture
Missionary Work
Moral Discipline
Mothers
Multi-tasking
(The) Name of Christ in The Book of Mormon
(The) Nature of God and Our Covenants
(Our) Neighbors
No Greater Call
(The) Number of Disciples Was Multiplied
Obedience
One Lord, One Faith, One Baptism
Persecution
Personal Revelation
(The) Plan of Salvation
(The) Plan of Salvation 15 Names
(A) Positive Mental Attitude
Power: The Ultimate Test of Character
Pragmatism in The Book of Mormon
Premortal Life
Preparation
Pride

(The) Priests of Baal in Our Lives
(The) Prime Directive
Professors
Proper Prior Preparation
(The) Prophet Joseph Smith
Prophet, Seer, and
(The) Q Continuum
Quorum Sensing
Receiving Revelation
Recognizing the Church of Christ
Removing the Barnacles of Life
Restoration – The Early Days
Revelation
Reverence
(The) Sabbath
(The) Sacrament
Sacramental Waters
Satan
(The) Scope of Our Decisions
(The) Second Mile
Service
Set Apart
Sharing the Gospel
Sharper Than a Two-edged Sword
(The) Sons of Mosiah
Speak Kind Words to Each Other
(The) Spirit of Revelation

Employing rhetoric that sounds as if it could have been lifted out of the pages of The Book of Mormon, Abraham Lincoln declared: "It is the duty of men as well as nations to owe their dependence upon the over-ruling power of God, to confess their sins and transgressions in humble sorrow. Yet, with assured hope that genuine repentance will lead to mercy and pardon, (we must) recognize that those nations only are blessed, whose God is the Lord."

Volume 7 Essays

- Spiritual Calisthenics
- Spiritual Gifts
- Spiritual Identity Theft
- (A) Standard of Excellence
- Strangers in The Land
- Strengths and Weaknesses
- Studying the Scriptures
- Success Strategies
- Symbols
- Talents
- Teaching in The Church
- Teaching Key Doctrine
- Technological Traps
- (A) Testimony of Christ
- (A) Thirty Day Spiritual Fitness Program
- Thou Hast Done Wonderful Things
- (The) Thrill of Victory / Agony of DeFeet
- Tithing
- Too Good to Be True
- (The) Tools of The Trade
- Touching His Garment
- Tough Questions
- Travel at The Speed of Thought
- (The) Twelve Tribes of Israel
- Types, Rites, Ceremonies, and Symbols (Alma Unity
- Updates are Ready
- Walk in The Light of The Lord
- (Our) Weaknesses
- Were There Two Cumorahs?
- What Think Ye of Christ?
- Wherefore and Therefore in The Book of Mormon
- (A) Whirlwind into Heaven
- Who is Packing Your Parachute?
- Why We Laugh
- Words of Mormon
- Work and Personal Responsibility
- Worship in Music
- Writing on Metal Plates Was a Pain
- Zion

In addition to the obvious reference to the plates deposited at the Hill Cumorah, "out of the ground" and "low out of the dust" could also refer to ancient records of lost civilizations known only to God. Of one such empire of antiquity, an Israeli archaeologist who oversaw the excavation of Masada observed: "Nothing remains here today of the Romans, but a heap of stones in the desert."

Compendium Volume 3-7 Scriptures

Introduction - Look Who's Coming to Town
1 Nephi 1:20 - Follow the Prophet
2 Nephi 1:30 - Friendship
1 Nephi 2:1-3 - Life's Important Decisions
1 Nephi 3:7 - Obedience
1 Nephi 3:15-16 - Just Get Back on The Bike
1 Nephi 8:2 - Cognates in The Book of Mormon
1 Nephi 8:20 – (The) Hourglass of Life
1 Nephi 8:24 & 11:25 - Being Well Grounded
1 Nephi 9:5-6 – (The) Lost Manuscript
1 Nephi 11:6 & 8 – Jumping Out of Our Skin
1 Nephi 11:25 - Living Water
1 Nephi 13:26 – (The) Lost Books of The Bible
1 Nephi 14:7 - Book of Mormon Strengths
1 Nephi 14:10 – (The) Church
1 Nephi 15:14 – Teaching Key Doctrine
1 Nephi 15:20 - Gathering of Israel
1 Nephi 15:30 - God's Tactical Flashlight
1 Nephi 17:22 - Speak Kind Words
1 Nephi 17:50-51 - Multi-tasking
1 Nephi 19:12 - Environmental Concerns
1 Nephi 20:6 - Circle of Knowledge
1 Nephi 21:25 - Combatting Evil
2 Nephi 1:30 - Friendship
2 Nephi 2:4 – (The) Fall
2 Nephi 2:11 - Entropy
2 Nephi 2:15-16) - Work & Responsibility
2 Nephi 2:16 & 27 - Agency
2 Nephi 2:2 &, Alma 42:8 - Why We Laugh
2 Nephi 2:27 - Fate
2 Nephi 2:28 - Cogito Ergo Sum
2 Nephi 3:7 - Joseph Smith: A Rough Stone
2 Nephi 3:7 & 15 – (The)Prophet Joseph Smith
2 Nephi 31:16 & 18, & Moroni 10:5 - Joseph Smith

2 Nephi 4:35 - Life's Greatest Questions
2 Nephi 9:13 - Plan of Salvation Names
2 Nephi 9:13 - Holy Grail of Religious Doctrine
2 Nephi 9:18 – (The) Church in Former Times
2 Nephi 9:29 - Agency and Opposition
2 Nephi 9:29 - Education
2 Nephi 11:7 – (The) Creation of The World
2 Nephi 12:5 - Walk in The Light
2 Nephi 15:20 - Light and Darkness
2 Nephi 21:6-9 – (The) Millennium
2 Nephi 21:22-23 – (The) Desert Shall Rejoice
2 Nephi 21:31 - Quorum Sensing
2 Nephi 21:31 – (The Meaning of) Doctrine
2 Nephi 24:1 - Strangers in The Land
2 Nephi 24:12 - Lucifer
2 Nephi 25:23 - Grace
2 Nephi 25:1 - Are Mormons Christian?
2 Nephi 26:14 – (The) Church in The Last Days
2 Nephi 26:16 – Book of Mormon Preserved
2 Nephi 26:16 - Establishing the Word
2 Nephi 26:29 – (The) Priests of Baal
2 Nephi 27:10-11 - Receiving Revelation
2 Nephi 27:26 – Wonderful Things
2 Nephi 28:3-4 – (The Best) Education
2 Nephi 28:12 - Pride
2 Nephi 28:20 - God is NowHere
2 Nephi 28:26 - Power: Ultimate Test of Character
2 Nephi 28:30 - Christ's Church is Restored
2 Nephi 28:30-32 - Updates are Ready
2 Nephi 29:3 – (The) Bible
2 Nephi 29:6 - For Unto Us a Child is Born
2 Nephi 29:7-8 - Additional Scripture
2 Nephi 30:2 & 2 Nephi 24:1-2 - Blood,
   Covenant, and Land Israel

Only when we enter into covenants with God can the bands of death be broken, and are we liberated from bondage to sin. "There is no other name given whereby salvation cometh," said Benjamin. "Therefore, I would that ye should take upon you the name of Christ, all you that have entered into the covenant with God." (Mosiah 5:8).

2 Nephi 31:16 & 18, & Moroni 10:5 - Joseph Smith History
2 Nephi 31:17-18 - Eternal Progression
2 Nephi 31:19-20 - (The) Prime Directive
2 Nephi 31:20 - Spiritual Calisthenics
2 Nephi 32:5-6 - Faith and Knowledge
2 Nephi 33:4 – (The) Second Mile
Jacob 1:6 - Revelation
Jacob 1:13-14 – (Our) Neighbors
Jacob 2:31 - Abstinence in a Permissive World
Jacob 4:6 – (The Spirit of) Revelation
Jacob 4:8 – (The) Mind of God
Jacob 4:11 - Faith Building
Jacob 4:13 - Too Good to Be True
Jacob 5:10 - Is Heaven Hotter Than Hell?
Enos 1:27 - Spiritual Identity Theft
Jarom 1:4 - Godly Qualities
Jarom 1:5 – (The) Sabbath
Jarom 1:20 - Plan of Salvation
Omni 1:26 - Fasting
Words of Mormon 1:3 - Words of Mormon
Words of Mormon 1:5 - Brevity
Mosiah 2:1 - General Conference
Mosiah 2:17 - Service
Mosiah 2:25 – (The) Dust of The Earth
Mosiah 3:12-13 - Proper Prior Preparation
Mosiah 3:15 - Symbols
Mosiah 3:19 - (The) Atonement
Mosiah 4:9 - Are We Alone in The Universe?
Mosiah 4:19 - Buddy Can You Spare a Dime?)
Mosiah 4:20-21 - Batteries are Not Included
Mosiah 4:27 - Finding Balance in Our Lives
Mosiah 5:7 - I am a Child of God
Mosiah 5:7 - Born Again Christians
Mosiah 5:7 - A Change of Heart
Mosiah 5:8-10 - Huckleberries and Chokeberries
Mosiah 8:13 & 16-17 - Heavens Were Opened
Mosiah 8:16 - Prophet, Seer, and
Mosiah 15:14-18 – (The) Thrill of Victory &
   The Agony of DeFeet
Mosiah 18:20 - Before a Wound Can Heal
Mosiah 18:21 – (A) Positive Mental Attitude
Mosiah 23:16-17 & 25:29 - Having Been
   Commissioned of Jesus Christ
Mosiah 25:19-20 – (The) Duty of The Priest

Mosiah 26:22 - Father Forgive Them
Mosiah 27:3 - Teaching in The Church
Mosiah 27:8-9 - Agency and Youth
Mosiah 27:11 - Angels
Mosiah 29:2 - Caesar
Mosiah 29:12-13 - Citizenship
Alma 5:7 - Set Apart
Alma 5:26 - Worship in Music
Alma 5:46 - Personal Revelation
Alma 7:20 - How Does God Get Things Done?
Alma 9:19-23 - Talents
Alma 11:43 – (The) Biggest Loser
Alma 12:27 – (The) Last Judgment
Alma 13:3 - Life is a Three Act Play
Alma 13:3 - Premortal Life
Alma 17:2-3 – (The) Sons of Mosiah
Alma 17:4 - Sharing the Gospel
Alma 17:34-36 – Lamanites by The Waters of Sebus
Alma 22:18 - Removing the Barnacles of Life
Alma 26:8 - Gratitude
Alma 27:27 - Honesty
Alma 26:23-24 – (The) Scope of Our Decisions
Alma 29:1 - Happiness and Sharing the Gospel
Alma 29:1-2 - No Greater Call
Alma 29:4 - Life or Death?
Alma 30:7-9 - Choose Ye This Day
Alma 30:13 - Everyone Wants to Go to Heaven
Alma 30:13 - Evidences of God
Alma 30:41 – (A) Testimony of Christ
Alma 30:44 - Dancing With the Stars
Alma 31:5 - Studying the Scriptures
Alma 31:5 - (Spiritual Fitness Program
Alma 32:5 - Limiting Beliefs
Alma 32:27 - Alma's Discourse on Faith
Alma 32:28 – (The) Germination of Our Faith
Alma 32:35 - Light
Alma 32:42-43 – (The) Tools of The Trade
Alma 34:32 - Preparation
Alma 36:12-14 - Bah Humbug!
Alma 36:19 - I Have Overcome the World
Alma 37:45 - Types, Rites, Ceremonies,
   and Symbols
Alma 40:20 - Construction Zone

As we read The Book of Mormon, we pray for unity in the faith, and for a time when all might worship the Lord in plainness and in truth. As did Nephi, and to that end, "we talk of Christ, we rejoice in Christ, we preach of Christ, we prophesy of Christ, and we write according to our prophecies, that our children may (confidently) know to what source they may look for a remission of their sins." (2 Nephi 25:16).

Alma 40:23-24 - (Our) Eternal Nature
Alma 41:10 - Happiness
Alma 41:13 - Justice
Alma 42:13-15 - Justice and Mercy
Alma 42:26 - (The) Character of God
Alma 46:12 - A Coat of Many Colors
Alma 46:15 - Christians
Alma 46:20 - May the 4th Be With You
Alma 48:7 - Courage
Alma 48:19 - Choose the Harder Right
Alma 50:23 - Happiness / Wickedness
Alma 51:5-6 - Civil Liberties
Alma 56:47-48 - Mothers
Alma 60:6-7 - Focus
Helaman 3:25-28 - The Number of Disciples Was Multiplied
Helaman 3:33 - Professors
Helaman 3:35 - Touching His Garment
Helaman 3:35 - Humility
Helaman 5:12 - Covenant Consciousness
Helaman 6:37 - Missionary Work
Helaman 10:6 - Heavenly Father Knows Us
Helaman 12:7-10 - Sharper Than a Two-edged Sword
Helaman 16:23 - Satan
Helaman 18:19-20 - Missing Scripture
Helaman 13:38 - Heaven Can Wait
3 Nephi 1:12-13 - (A) Christmas Miracle
3 Nephi 9:33 - Conversion
3 Nephi 11:10-11 - (The) Light of the World
3 Nephi 12:2 - What Think Ye of Christ?
3 Nephi 12:10 - Persecution
3 Nephi 12:48 - Nature of God and Covenants
3 Nephi 13:9 - Addressing Deity
3 Nephi 13:14 - Forgiveness
3 Nephi 13:14-15 - Door Swings Both Ways
3 Nephi 13:22 - (The) Q Continuum
3 Nephi 14:5 - Hypocrisy
3 Nephi 14:11 - Spiritual Gifts
3 Nephi 14:22-23 - (A) Mailbox Marked With an "X"
3 Nephi 15:9 - Enduring to The End
3 Nephi 16:1-3 - (The) Twelve Tribes of Israel
3 Nephi 17:4 - (The) Lost Ten Tribes
3 Nephi 19:30 - Keep Smiling
3 Nephi 23:1 - Isaiah in The Book of Mormon

3 Nephi 24:8-10 - Tithing
3 Nephi 26:14 - Become as Little Children
3 Nephi 27:5 - (The) Name of Christ in The Book of Mormon
3 Nephi 27:8 - Recognizing the Church of Christ
3 Nephi 27:13-20 - Baptism
3 Nephi 27:22 - Restoration, The Early Days
3 Nephi 27:28-29 - Tough Questions
3 Nephi 28:6 - Travel at The Speed of Thought
3 Nephi 28:13-15 - Higher Dimensional Realities
3 Nephi 28:13-15 - (A) Whirlwind into Heaven
3 Nephi 29:3 - Covenants
4 Nephi 1:17 - Labels
4 Nephi 1:17-18 - Unity
Mormon 1:3-4 - Book of Mormon as History
Mormon 3:20-22 - It's Our Book
Mormon 6:2 - Were There Two Cumorahs?
Mormon 8:5 - (The Importance of) Friends
Mormon 8:8 - Age of Accountability
Mormon 8:35 - Connections
Mormon 8:35 - Joseph Smith's World
Mormon 8:38 - (Our) Neighbors
Mormon 8:38 - Technological Traps
Mormon 9:6 - Who is Packing Your Parachute?
Mormon 9:32-33 - And it Came to Pass
Ether 4:12 - Light and Truth
Ether 12:24-25, Jacob 4:1 & Mormon 8:17 - Writing on Metal Plates Was a Pain
Ether 12:26 - (Our) Weaknesses
Ether 12:27 - Strengths and Weaknesses
Ether 15:11 - Gold - The Appearance of
Moroni 2:2 - (The) Holy Ghost
Moroni 4:1 - (The) Sacrament
Moroni 5:1-2 - Sacramental Waters
Moroni 6:9 - Reverence
Moroni 7:13 - Management by The Spirit
Moroni 7:19 - (The) Light of Christ
Moroni 7:24 - Diversity
Moroni 7:33 - Moral Discipline
Moroni 7:41 - Success Strategies
Moroni 7:44 - Faith is a Principle of Power
Moroni 8:8 - Commitment
Moroni 8:25-26 - One Lord, One Faith, One Baptism

Although the world measures success by telestial standards, The Book of Mormon reveals that we came from a more noble realm in which we were taught that accomplishment would be determined by the building of character. As we continue our investigation of truth, we discover that religious recognition is just that, a re-cognition or re-knowing of the principles of provident living that touch our spirits because they are inherently treasured, true, and trustworthy.

Moroni 10:8 - Gifts of The Spirit
Moroni 10:8 – (The) Manifestation of Spirits
Moroni 10:31 - Zion

Moroni 10:31 – (A) Standard of Excellence
Moroni 10:34 - I Have Fought a Good Fight

We were foreordained in heaven, even before the world was, to have glory added upon our heads forever, on the condition of our faithfulness to God, as we support Him in His great work by our actions. We are better able to do so, if we listen intently, as Book of Mormon prophets explain the power of the covenants to their people.

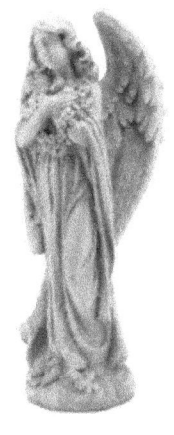

If you don't find what you are looking for in the Index of Volumes 3 – 7, check out this list of topics with related essay references.

- Abstinence – Abstinence in a Permissive World
- Accountability – Age of Accountability
- Adaptivity – Updates are Ready
- Apocrypha – Additional Scripture
- Apocrypha – Lost Books of The Bible
- Apocrypha – Missing Scripture
- Apostolic Church – (The) Church of Jesus Christ in Former Times
- Are We Alone in The Universe? – Dancing With the Stars
- Attitude – Just Keep Smiling
- Authority – Having Been Commissioned of Jesus Christ
- Born Again – A Change of Heart
- Ceremonies – Types, Rites, Ceremonies, and Symbols
- Character – Our Eternal Nature
- Charity – Buddy Can You Spare a Dime?
- Charity – A Mailbox Marked With an X
- Chastity – Abstinence in a Permissive World
- Christians – Are Mormons Christians
- Christ – What Think Ye of Christ?
- Church – Recognizing The Church of Christ
- Consequences – The Scope of Our Decisions
- Corrections – Writing on Metal Plates Was a Pain
- Covenants – Covenant Consciousness
- Covenants – The Nature of God and Our Covenants
- Cumorah – Were There Two Cumorahs?
- Darkness – Light and Darkness
- Death – Everyone Wants to Go to Heaven
- Dependency – Who is Packing Your Parachute?
- Devil – Lucifer
- Discipline – Moral Discipline
- Doctrine – Teaching Key Doctrine
- Evangelicals – Born Again Christians
- Evil – Combatting Evil
- Excellence – A Standard of Excellence
- Faith – Alma's Discourse on Faith
- Faith – The Germination of our Faith
- Faith – Alma's Discourse on Faith
- Feet – The Thrill of Victory / The Agony of DeFeet
- Forgiveness – The Door Swings Both Ways
- Forgiveness – Father Forgive Them
- Freedom of Choice – Agency
- Free Will – Agency
- Gathering of Israel – The Desert Shall Rejoice
- Gifts of The Spirit – Spiritual Gifts
- Government – Caesar
- Government – Management by The Spirit
- Great Apostasy – Apostasy
- Heaven – Higher Dimensional Realities
- Holy Ghost – Batteries are Not Included
- Holy Ghost – God's Tactical Flashlight
- Humility – The Dust of The Earth
- I Am a Child of God – Spiritual Identity Theft
- Immorality – Abstinence in a Permissive World
- I Think, Therefore I Am – Cogito, Ergo Sum
- Joseph's Technicolor Dream Coat – A Coat of Many Colors
- Kindness – Speak Kind Words to Each Other
- Knowledge – The Circle of Knowledge
- Last Days – The Church in The Last Days
- Laughter – Why We Laugh
- Light – Walk in The Light
- Mercy – Justice and Mercy
- Missionary Work – Happiness and Sharing The Gospel
- Missionary Work – No Greater Call
- Missionary Work – The Number of Disciples Was Multiplied
- Missionary Work – Sharing The Gospel
- Missionary Work – The Sons of Mosiah
- Missionary Work – Strangers in The Land
- Music – Worship in Music
- Non-members – Strangers in The Land
- Omniscience – (The) Q Continuum
- One Way – One Lord, One Faith, One Baptism
- Opposition – Agency and Opposition
- Opposition – Lamanites by The Waters of Sebus
- Optimism – Huckleberries and Chokeberries

The Book of Mormon teaches that the Merciful Plan of our Father requires us to give up only our sins to merit salvation thru His boundless grace. It is axiomatic that our exercise of free will must be carried out in an atmosphere that is fraught with danger. Unfortunately, with a frequency that is frustrating, there are undesirable consequences that must inevitably fall on the heels of the exercise of our agency. Because this must be so, it was ordained in heaven before the creation of the world that their effects would be mitigated by the power of the Atonement of Jesus Christ.

Peer Pressure – (The) Priests of Baal in Our Lives
Permissiveness – Abstinence in a Permissive World
Perseverance – Just Get Back on The Bike
Personal Responsibility – Work and Personal Responsibility
Plan of Salvation – (The) Hourglass of Life
Plan of Salvation – Life is a Three Act Play
Plates – Writing on Metal Plates Was a Pain
Power – May the 4th Be With You
Preaching the Gospel – Establishing the Word
Preparedness – Spiritual Calisthenics
Priest's Duty – (The) Duty of The Priest
Primitive Church – (The) Church of Jesus Christ in Former Times
Pseudepigrapha – Additional Scripture
Repentance – Before a Wound Can Heal
Repentance – Removing the Barnacles of Life
Responsibility – Work and Personal Responsibility
Restoration – Christ's Church is Restored
Revelation – The Heavens Were Opened
Revelation – Personal Revelation
Revelation – (The) Spirit of Revelation
Revelation – Receiving Revelation
Rites – Types, Rites, Ceremonies, and Symbols
Satan – Lucifer
Scripture Not in The Bible – Additional Scripture

Scriptures – Studying the Scriptures
Speed of Light / Thought – Travel at The Speed of Thought
Spirits – (The) Manifestation of Spirits
Spiritual Fitness – (A) Thirty Day Spiritual Fitness Program
Spiritual Gifts – Gifts of The Spirit
Symbols – Types, Rites, Ceremonies, and Symbols
Technology – Technological Traps
Telestial / Celestial – Jumping Out of Our Skin
Ten Tribes – (The) Lost Ten Tribes
Translation – (A) Whirlwind into Heaven
Truth – Light and Truth
Types – Types, Rites, Ceremonies, and Symbols
Unity – Quorum Sensing
Weakness – Strengths and Weaknesses
Why Things Fall Apart – Entropy in The Physical and Eternal Worlds
Wickedness – Happiness and Wickedness
Wishful Thinking – Too Good to Be True
Word of God – Sharper Than a Two-edged Sword
Work in Progress – Construction Zone: Proceed With Caution
Worship – Worship in Music
Youth – Agency and Youth

The Plan of Salvation that is described in The Book of Mormon is so magnificent that when it was presented to those who had collectively assembled in the Council, "the morning stars sang together and all the sons of God shouted for joy." (Job 38:7-8). The principles of equality advocated by its prophets renders it inconceivable that a Plan of such unfathomable perfection would have been intentionally designed to save only a very small percentage of our Heavenly Father's children in His Celestial Kingdom. To believe such would effectively dismiss as a thing of naught His mission statement, which is to bring about the immortality and eternal life of His children, which includes both the Nephites and Lamanites of this world.

Table of Contents

"Scripture consists not in what we read,
but in what we understand."
(St. Hilary).

It's The Book of Mormon that generates repetitive opportunities to smell the delicious aroma of the bread of life that has been baking in a celestial oven. In anticipation of a buttered slice, we steadily move along upon the path that carries us closer to the window sill of the kitchen in our heavenly home.

Author's Note...1

Introduction...3

Essays..11

However we fit into the grand scheme of the cosmos, we do know this: God quickens life by providing the animation of a physical world within which we freely interact; He "lends (us) breath, that (we) may live and move and do according to (our) own will, and (He supports us) from one moment to another." (Mosiah 2:21).

Observations

Observations..245

Commentary, Compendia, & Observations Index

Commentary, Compendia, & Observations Index..365

It was at the
very instant when their
unsatisfied craving for the praise
and the popularity of the world began to
sway their behavior, that the Nephites found
themselves in the uncomfortable position of
bending their character, when they thought
they were only taking a bow. It was chiefly
at this time that they needed the soothing
inspiration of the Holy Spirit, and the
healing guidance of their Lord and
Savior Jesus Christ, and finally
the nurturing encouragement
of their Father, Who looked
down upon them every
day of their lives,
from heaven
above.

Author's Note

These Compendia have taken on a life of their own, expanding into a collection of eight volumes of detailed information about The Book of Mormon that supplement my three volumes of Commentary. In essence, they are a distillation of my feelings that relate to The Book of Mormon. Their content is more visceral that that of the Commentary, and perhaps it more accurately reflects my personal feelings about the monumental themes that run throughout all of scripture. They summarize the more comprehensive body of work in my Commentary and showcase my feelings, in the hope that they might become living documents that not only reflect my present understanding of The Book of Mormon, but also the paradigms that expand with the utilization of new tools of discovery. It's a good bet that there is more to come. As the adage encourages, we need to "Think ourselves empty, read ourselves full, write ourselves clear, pray ourselves hot, and let ourselves go!"

Only thru the phenomenon of the continuing, enduring, immeasurable, infinite, uncorrupted, unfathomable, uninterrupted, and unspoiled grace that is taught in The Book of Mormon, do we find ourselves swallowed up in the joy of God, even to the exhausting of our strength. (See Alma 27:17).

Introduction

The promise that
is made by Moroni (see
Moroni 10:4-5), draws upon
the magnificent power of all three
members of the Godhead, and blesses
us with increasing receptivity to flashes
of insight, intuition, and inspiration. Its
fulfilment will cast us off into streams of
revelation that will carry us along within the
quickening currents of direct experience
with our Heavenly Father, with Jesus
Christ, and with the Holy
Ghost.

Cicero wrote: "The first law for the historian is that he shall never dare utter an untruth. The second is that he shall suppress nothing that is true. Moreover, there shall be no suspicion of partiality or of malice in his writing." The accounts in The Book of Mormon written by the prophets Nephi, Jacob, Alma, Mormon, Moroni, and others, and abridged by the prophet-historian Mormon, were true to the mandate given by Cicero. Although, as Washington Irving brooded: "It is the rule that history fades into fable; fact becomes clouded with doubt and controversy; the inscription moulders, and columns, arches, and pyramids are but heaps of sand, and their epitaphs, nothing but characters written in the dust," yet The Book of Mormon stands as a shining example of the divine model.

It "is the witness that testifies to the passing of time. It illuminates reality, vitalizes memory, provides guidance in daily life, and brings us tidings of antiquity." It is the "evidence of time, the light of truth, the life of memory, the directress of life, committed to immortality." (Cicero, "De Oratore," ii, 36). In its pages, "the centuries roll back to the ancient age of gold." (Horace, "Odes," IV, ii, 39).

In one of the beautiful simplicities of the gospel, we are taught that the Plan allows all of us to enjoy the same access to the simplest, and yet most powerful, witness to the truth. In an inarticulate voice softer than the faintest whisper of sweet breath on the cheek, the Holy Ghost gently testifies, or bears witness, of truth. As Moroni 10:5 teaches (in a verse that is often overlooked, in favor of the previous verse): "By the power of the Holy Ghost ye may know the truth of all things."

The Holy Ghost has revealed all that is true, and has illuminated every eternal principle that has guided the minds of men and women since the dawn of history. We constantly benefit from that which He reveals. In the Last Days, when the Spirit is "poured out upon all flesh, and when "young men see visions, and old men dream dreams," (Joel 2:28), it will be the Holy Ghost Who provides the creative drive. The irony is that many will fail to recognize the source of their inspiration. Job did not. He wrote: "For God speaketh once, yea twice, yet man perceiveth it not. In a dream, in a vision of the night, when deep sleep falleth upon men, in slumberings upon the bed; then he openeth the ears of men, and sealeth their instruction." (Job 33:14-16). We cannot help but think of the experience of Joseph Smith in his bedchamber, when we read Job's description of how, at certain times, Heavenly Father chooses to communicate with His children.

All who desire to have a sure personal witnesses must carefully and prayerfully read The Book of Mormon, and then ask in faith if what they have studied is true. They will then receive the testimony of the Holy Ghost to motivate them to seek out the Priesthood and to enter into sacred covenants with God. It will be as it was on the Day of Pentecost, when Peter and others were preaching to a multitude whose hearts and minds were open and receptive to the truth. The words of the Apostles carried the weight of authority, and penetrated the hearts of their listeners to the end that they asked: "Men and brethren, what shall we do? Then Peter said unto them, Repent, and be baptized every one of you in the name of Jesus Christ for the remission of sins, and ye shall receive the gift of the Holy Ghost." (Acts 2:37-38). And on that day, there were about 3,000 souls added to the kingdom of God on earth. (See Commentary Reference to 3 Nephi 15:21-24).

A similar scenario exists today. Since the restoration of the gospel, there has been a Pentecostal outpouring of the Spirit, and those with a sincere desire to understand the will of God bring the same humble petition to the doorstep of the missionaries: "Now that we have heard your message, have put it to the test of prayerful inquiry, and have received a witness of the Spirit, what shall we do?" The response of the servants of the Lord is unequivocal: "You must exercise saving faith that leads to the waters of baptism and to continuing commitment, dedicated discipleship, selfless service, and sustained spirituality."

Shakespeare wrote: "The past is prologue." ("The Tempest," Act 2, Scene 1). The phrase was intended to imply that our

If the octane rating of the fuel firing our witness of The Book of Mormon, the Prophet Joseph Smith, and our Lord Jesus Christ is too low, we may be able to just barely get by, but only for a while. As we limp along with the engine of discipleship misfiring badly, the incessant knocking sound of fear will ultimately overpower us, until we deny the faith, and we are no longer valiant in the testimony of Jesus.

past is merely a prologue, or an introduction, to the great adventure upon which we will embark if we follow through on our plans. This original interpretation teaches that what has come before on our journey through life doesn't matter in the grand scheme of things, because a new future lies before us, subject to the choices we will yet make. The human condition does not change much over time, which is one reason why the Lord has revealed The Book of Mormon in the Last Days, so that we might profit from the experiences of the Nephites who are distant from us in time and yet are so like us.

Hugh Nibley observed: "Men fool themselves, when they think for a moment that they can read scripture without ever adding something to the text or omitting something from it." Therein lies the power inherent in its study. We glean insight and understanding every time we investigate the word of God. I have learned to love the scriptures, and I often think of St. Hilary, who wrote: "Scripture consists not in what we read, but in what we understand." In these Compendia, I have consistently tried to anchor to the scriptures the ideas swirling around in my head.

Utilization of commentaries and compendia does not replace personal scripture study. The spiritual awakening that accompanies prayerful efforts to understand the mysteries of God through the study of His word cannot be achieved through another person's interpretation. Perhaps, though, my own perspectives on the eternal themes expressed within The Book of Mormon will be helpful to you as you read and seek your own guidance. It is my hope that you will use these compendia only to assist you in your own personal journey to Christ.

Our challenge is to enlist the aid of the Holy Ghost as we undertake that journey. Many years ago, Dallin Oaks wrote: "Latter-day Saints know that learned or authoritative commentaries (and compendia) can help us with scriptural interpretation, but we maintain that they must be used with caution. (They) are not substitutes for the scriptures any more than a good cookbook is a substitute for food. When I refer to "commentaries," I mean everything that interprets scripture, from the comprehensive book-length commentary to the brief interpretation embodied in a lesson or an article, such as this one."

"One trouble with commentaries," he continued, "is that their authors sometimes focus on only one meaning to the exclusion of others. As a result, commentaries, if not used with great care, may illuminate the author's chosen and correct meaning but close our eyes and restrict our horizons to other possible meanings. Sometimes, those other less obvious meanings can be the ones most valuable and useful to us as we seek to obtain answers to our own questions. This is why the teaching of the Holy Ghost is a better guide to scriptural interpretation than is even the best commentary." ("Ensign," 1/1985).

Harold B. Lee taught: "We are convinced that our members are hungry for the gospel undiluted, with its abundant truths and insights. There are those who have seemed to forget that the most powerful weapons the Lord has given us against all that is evil are His own declarations – the plain and simple doctrines of salvation as found in the scriptures." (Regional Representatives Seminar, 10/1/1970).

Bruce R. McConkie explained that "revelation is necessary because … each pronouncement in the holy scriptures is so written as to reveal little or much, depending on the spiritual capacity of the student." ("A New Witness for The Articles of Faith," p. 71).

And so, as President Oaks continued, "the scriptures are not the ultimate source of knowledge, but what precedes the ultimate source. The ultimate source comes by revelation. We encourage everyone to make careful study of the scriptures and of prophetic teachings … and to prayerfully seek personal revelation to know their meaning for themselves … If we seek and accept revelation and inspiration to enlarge our understanding, we will have the mysteries of God unfolded to us by the power of the Holy Ghost."

Any progress that we might make in our lives centers around what we do with The Book of Mormon, and upon what the gospel that it contains and explains does for us. Ideally, they will create a connection of understanding with the ability to bridge the gap that might otherwise exist between heaven and ourselves.

Elder McConkie also said: "I sometimes think that one of the best kept secrets of the kingdom is that the scriptures open the door to the receipt of revelation." ("Doctrines of The Restoration," p. 243). And President Oaks reaffirmed: "We do not overstate the point when we say that the scriptures can be a Urim and Thummim to assist each of us to receive personal revelation."

President Oaks enlarged upon the perspective of the young prophet: "Joseph was, by his own admission, no writer. He felt imprisoned by what he called the 'total darkness of paper, pen, and ink." (Joseph Smith to William W. Phelps, 11/27/1832, B.Y.U. Press, 2002, p. 287). He thus considered it 'an awful responsibility to write in the name of the Lord'. (Joseph Smith Papers, 1:367).

He did not suppose that he could receive the revelations perfectly, nor did the Lord ever set that standard. Joseph and his appointed brethren edited the revelations (see D&C 70:1-4) based on (that) same premise … namely, that he represented the voice of God as he spoke in what he characterized as his own 'crooked, broken, scattered, and imperfect language'. (Joseph Smith to William W. Phelps, 11/27/1832, quoted in "Making Sense of the Doctrine & Covenants, a Guided Tour Through Modern Revelation," Steven Harper. "Personal Writings of Joseph Smith," p. 186-187).

President Oaks concluded his own epistle by stating a simple truth: "Latter-day Saints know that true doctrine comes by revelation from God, and not by worldly wisdom." (See Moses 5:58). He was in good company, for the Apostle Paul wrote that we are not capable of thinking any thing of ourselves; but we look to God for our wisdom. (See 1 Corinthians 3:5).

I could not agree more heartily with these wise words of counsel. As a matter of fact, every time I proofed my compendium (and I did this many times) I found myself scribbling additional notes in the margins and thinking to myself, "Why didn't I see that before?." That is precisely what I hope will be the experience of everyone who takes the time to read my compendia. I trust the process will motivate you to search the scriptures more carefully and to be instructed by the Spirit, as you do so, that you might be led in directions that will prove to be personally illuminating.

I would expect that my older grandchildren who read this compendium will be impacted in ways that are different from my adult children or my contemporaries. I hope that my observations will touch you differently each time you read them. When I am long-gone, perhaps the considerable thought that went into its production will generate a palpable bond that will span the years separating us. Maybe, the gulf that then divides us will not be as great, and our shared energies will pave the way to an eventual joyous reunion.

A coat of many colors (see Genesis 37:3), was a gift from Joseph's father Jacob, or Israel. So too, those who have sought a similar blessing, as they've studied The Book of Mormon, have received the fabric of faith as a gift from our Father in Heaven. We can be certain that He has selected every bolt of cloth, that He has thoughtfully harmonized their hues, shades, and blushes, to accommodate the design He has planned for our lives, and that its dominant, recurring pattern is one that facilitates our easy recognition of the divinity of His Only Begotten Son.

Essays

When
the Nephites
were righteous, they
seldom forgot to call upon
God to protect them from worldly
influences, and from that old serpent
Beelzebub. They were acutely aware that
Satan was abroad in the land, for they had
often heard, and sometimes responded to, his
siren call coming from Babylon, that rang
loudly in their ears, even as they sought
"to sing the song of redeeming love."
(Alma 5:26).

Happiness

"Behold, there never was a happier time
among the people of Nephi, since the
days of Nephi, than in the days of
Moroni; yea, even at this time, in
the twenty and first year of
the reign of the judges."
(Alma 50:23).

Why is true happiness so elusive? Perhaps one reason is that we try very hard to create an environment that is free from care, and when we fail, as we inevitably do, we try even harder. We never come to the realization that happiness is born of contrast. Our natural inclination is to seek relief from discomfort, and we are quick to petition God for deliverance. But when Eve reasoned with Adam that he must partake of the forbidden fruit, she had already come to the realization that in order to experience happiness, they must also experience its opposite. Her eyes had indeed been opened. Too frequently, ours seem to be closed.

When people don't believe they have opposition in their lives, and frantically try to buy their way to happiness, they may be particularly vulnerable to depression and unhappiness. These are the very things they seek so desperately to avoid. Opposition is necessary to happiness. If we homogenize our mortal experience by smoothing out all the rough edges, we may inadvertently be neutralizing the very things that would have contributed most significantly to our happiness. If we have a one-dimensional view of life, we might find ourselves "running to and fro and never coming to a knowledge of the truth. We may come face to face with the stark reality that "wickedness never was happiness." Distorted perceptions may influence us to use mind-altering drugs in a desperate attempt to interface with reality. Chemicals cooked up in a meth lab will definitely change our perception of reality, but endorphins are a better choice.

Happiness also stems from want. If someone continually gluts himself in order to experience gratification, he will eventually diminish his capacity for enjoyment. Progressively greater enhancements will be required for the same level of satisfaction. Perhaps this is why happiness cannot be found in serial relationships that focus on physical attraction but have no emotional connection. As with the adulterer, greater and greater stimulation is necessary to achieve the same level of excitement, until there is a final retreat into the hollow core of oneself.

"Aha!" said the cartoon philosopher Pogo. "Here we have someone paying for the sin of excess. The hobnailed boots of indiscretion's marathon dancer tap a rowdy two-step across the terracotta of his consciousness. Excess was his master. Reason was cast into the rumble seat of his libidinous juggernaut. Now the piper must be paid!"

Well did Solzhenitsyn have his prison philosopher, Nerzhin, expound, "Happiness: When things are going very well, that's happiness. Everyone knows that. Thank God for prison! It gave me the chance to think. in order to understand the nature of happiness, we first have to analyze satiety. Remember that thin, watery barley or the oatmeal porridge without a single drop of fat? Can you say that you eat it? No. You commune with it; you take it like a sacrament. You eat it slowly; you eat it from the tip of the wooden spoon; you eat it absorbed entirely in the process of eating, in thinking about eating, and it spreads through your body like nectar. You tremble at the sweetness released from those overcooked little grains and the murky liquid they float in. And then, without hardly any nourishment, you go on living for six months, twelve months. Can you really compare the crude devouring of a steak with this?"

One of the greatest challenges faced by our society is the insatiable desire for pleasure, immediate gratification, and repetitive waves of greater and greater stimulation. We are frustrated by the limitations of our RAM, the horsepower of our automobiles, the capacity of our iPods, the features of our cell phones, and the speed of our micro-processors. We have only a dim recollection of operator assistance, two-lane country roads, typewriters, and white-out. As society demands escalating requirements to maintain a false standard of comfort and entertainment, we are blinded to the sobering comparison to a heroin addict's progressive tolerance and destructive reliance on his own false gods of wood and stone.

Twenty First century Americans "tend to fill space, as if what we have, what we are, is not enough. Being affluent, we strangle ourselves with what we can buy, things whose opacity obstructs our ability see what is really there." (Gretel Erlich, Under Wyoming Skies, Atlantic Magazine).

Happiness is like a butterfly. The more you chase it, the more it eludes you. But if you turn your attention to others, it will come and rest quietly on your shoulder.

Happiness and Sharing the Gospel

"O that I were an angel, and could have the wish of mine heart, that I might go forth and speak with the trump of God, with a voice to shake the earth, and cry repentance unto every people." (Alma 29:1).

Before Fiorello La Guardia became mayor of New York City, he was a magistrate. One day there appeared before him a man accused of stealing a loaf of bread. Upon questioning, he confessed that he'd committed the crime because his family was starving. Whereupon, La Guardia suspended his jail sentence, and instead fined everyone in the courtroom $5.00 for living in a city where a man must steal bread to feed his family. It was the Savior Who said: "I am the bread of life: He that cometh to me shall never hunger." (John 6:35). In the Eternal Court of Justice, then, what do you suppose will be the penalty for our failure to have fed others the bread of life?

Our first interest as a missionary-oriented church, said Ezra Taft Benson, is "to save and exalt the souls of the children of men." (C.R., 4/1974). The scriptures abound in exhortations to perform missionary work. Perhaps the most familiar is: "Go ye into all the world, and preach the gospel to every creature." (Mark 16:15). Thus, it "began to be preached, from the beginning," (Moses 5:58) until "every nation, and kindred, and tongue, and people" would hear the message of hope. (D&C 133:7). The missionaries now go "from land to land, and from city to city" to "bear testimony in every place." (D&C 66:5 & 7). These efforts have been made to give the world the supernal gift of happiness that is "is the object and design of our existence, and will be the end thereof, if we pursue the path that leads to it, and this path is virtue, uprightness, faithfulness, holiness, and keeping all the commandments of God." (Joseph Smith, "Teachings," p. 255).

Frequently, however, giving others this priceless gift is not easy, because salvation does not come cheaply. Nevertheless, we must persist in our efforts, because we can sin by silence when words should be spoken. (Original quotation by Ella Wheeler Wilcox). Of those who will not open their mouths because of the fear of man, the Savior warned: "Wo unto such, for mine anger is kindled against them." (D&C 60:2-3).

To paraphrase Tom Paine, these Last Days are the times that try our souls. Summer soldiers and sunshine patriots, when given the chance to share their testimonies with others, will recoil at the opportunity that is before them, but those witnesses who boldly declare their faith deserve the love and thanks of their neighbors. Our timidity is not easily conquered, yet we have the consolation that the harder the challenge, the more glorious is the triumph. What we obtain cheaply, we esteem lightly. 'Tis dearness only that gives everything its value. Heaven knows how to put a proper price upon its goods, and it would be strange, indeed, if so celestial an article as a vibrant, vital, humbly borne and eagerly shared testimony should not be highly rated. ("The Political Works of Thomas Paine," p. 55).

We pay dearly for our secular education and expect a return on our investment. But missionary work is a far more valuable tutorial experience. From the moment of our baptism, each of us is called and chosen to enroll in the Lord's university. Being given the opportunity to share the gospel is equivalent to being extended an offer to participate in a Bachelor of Independent Study Fine Arts program that demands no temporal tuition for enrollment. The only entrance requirement is a ready heart and a willing mind. Its far-reaching design is intended solely to expand the scope of our Father's Plan to all of His children. It is variously called The Plan of Salvation (Alma 24:14), The Plan of Salvation Unto all Men, (Moses 6:62), The Great Plan of Salvation (Alma 42:5), The Plan of Our God (2 Nephi 9:13), The Plan of Restoration, (Alma 41:2), The Great Plan of the Eternal God, (Alma 34:9), The Plan of Redemption (Alma 29:2), The Great Plan of Redemption, (Alma 34:31), The Great and Eternal Plan of Redemption, (Alma 34:16), The Plan of Mercy (Alma 42:15), The Great Plan of Mercy (Alma 42:31), The Great and Eternal Plan of Deliverance from Death (2 Nephi 11:5), The Merciful Plan of The Great Creator (2 Nephi 9:6), and my favorites, The Plan of Happiness (Alma 42:16), and The Great Plan of Happiness (Alma 42:8). Whatever its name, the Plan overshadows His ordained core curriculum of universal missionary work by those who have matriculated into His program. The Plan is a diagram to follow that illustrates how to pick our way through mortality, a map to guide us Home, a table that documents the perils and pitfalls we must avoid, a chart to fall back on when tempests beset us, and a graph that outlines and defines our progress on the pathway to perfection. Like the World Wide Web that requires only computer literacy, access to a network with an I.P address, and relevant hardware and software, the elements of the Plan provide the essentials and have the potential to bring meaning to a chaotic world and fluency to the spiritually illiterate. In simple terms, the Plan is our key to happiness.

Its blueprints suggest that sharing the gospel is related to happiness. The first page of the Plan reviews our life in the pre-earth existence, page two explains the purpose of mortality, while page three opens our hearts and our minds to the expanding opportunities that will be ours after we pass into eternity. When we conform to the Plan's overall formula for success, we are better friends, neighbors, and missionary representatives of Christ, and we are also better able to find true happiness. It is within the elements of the Plan that we discover that "thousands of candles can be lighted from a single flame, but the life of the candle will not be shortened. Happiness never decreases by being shared." (Buddha).

In our busy and complex world, however, we often see through a glass darkly which makes it very difficult to discern how to commit to memory and to life the elusive equations found within the Plan. We cannot tell, and it does not reveal, if we will find happiness through fame or anonymity, poverty or wealth, sickness or health, worldly influence, or obscurity, or if it is found in beauty or the beast. We sometimes forget that it promises both nurturing rain and the mud that inevitably follows, and that it is our lot in life to dutifully trudge along past potholes and other obstacles on rocky roads that are uphill most of the way. Within our Father's Plan, we are sometimes surprised to discover that "the dark threads are as needful in the weaver's skillful hand as the threads of gold and silver, in the pattern he has planned." (Benjamin Malachi Franklin).

None of us can hope to find meaning in our lives if we ignore the Plan or treat its integral element of happiness superficially or carelessly. A conscious appreciation of its value must be earned. If we take The Plan of Happiness for granted or if we abandon the principles upon which it is founded, its companion virtues may slip between our fingers and be lost forever. Sometimes, we use our free will inappropriately and make poor investment choices with our time and talents. Frequently, we are left with only a wad of counterfeit currency with which we must make late payments with interest tacked on for bad behavior. And still, in our efforts to gain, we seldom obtain, and more rarely retain feelings of true happiness. Never learning the hard lessons of life, we continually look to gods of wood and stone that cannot ransom us from our misery. Our worldly ways leave us vulnerable to a spiritual sickness that mimics the symptoms of those with advanced diabetes whose peripheral circulation has been compromised. We become numb to "the better angels of our nature." (Abraham Lincoln). As we lose the capacity to touch and feel, we become more and more isolated from the sensitivity to our surroundings that is critical to the success of the Plan. We may become inured to our condition in the sense that we are "past feeling," even as we develop a "lead foot" and we put the pedal to the metal. Although life in the fast lane may be thrilling, when it "takes our breath away" we may not realize that our reduced lung capacity has robbed us of vibrancy and joie de vivre that could have been ours. Cheap thrills can never replace the lofty rewards of The Plan. They are counter-productive and defeat the noble objectives of the Plan that would have allowed us to become engaged by our expedition, captivated by its complexity, immersed in its intricacies, riveted by its rewards, and wrapped up in its wonders at an unhurried pace.

In contrast to the hectic pace of supposed progress in our technologically oriented world, the elements of the Plan generate repetitive opportunities to stop and smell the roses along the way. In fact, Heavenly Father created the roses in the first place, as love letters to His children. Of these subtle elements of the Plan, the poet wrote: "Earth is crammed with heaven, and every bush with fire of God. But only those who see take off their shoes. The rest stand around picking blackberries." (Elizabeth Barrett Browning, "Aurora Leigh," Book Seven, 1856). The ingenuity, originality, and resourcefulness of the Plan are such that they create redundant mechanisms designed to give us repetitive opportunities for self-reflection, self-analysis, self-renewal, self-commitment, and self-actualization. When we conform our lives to its principles, we find our greatest expression. The Plan sets us free to be creative, and our creativity sets us free to plan properly prior to the time when we come face to face with the crises of life, so that we can prevent poor performance when we do. When we are completely reliant and utterly dependent upon the elements of the Plan, we find our greatest individuality and personal expression, and our happiness can be self-supporting and self-sustaining. One of the core principles of the Plan is the perfect law of liberty found in the gospel of Jesus Christ.

Those of weak character frequently think that they have found happiness in worldly pleasures, but this is because they have not learned to recognize, nor have they ever experienced, the real thing. They mistake wickedness for happiness, confusing nature with nobility. When their behavior reflects worldliness rather than illumination from the Source of all light, when their activities harmonize more with secular standards and less with spiritual sureties, or when they are with their peers but without God, the resulting false sense of security is unsustainable. Young people talk about Best Friends Forever, but Heavenly Father would rather have us Be Forever Faithful through a bond of obedience to the principles of the Plan.

Opposition in all things is a condition for the operation of the Plan of Happiness, so we need to be consciously, actively, and energetically participating in purposeful programs of personal progress to carry us forward on proven paths. Without this quality of sustainable support, our lives become cruel jokes with pitiless punch lines that will pierce our hearts when we are finally confronted by the utter futility and hopelessness of lives that lack the upward reach toward happiness that is the reward of faith which is itself integral to the successful implementation of the Plan.

Without light, some live their lives in shadows that are only illusions and caricatures of reality. The discrepancy between their marginalized behavior and gospel ideals becomes so great that their short-lived pleasure in worldly ways evaporates as the morning dew in the full light of day. The Lord will not always suffer the wicked "to take happiness in sin." (Mormon 2:13). Sooner or later, when depravity reaches critical mass, the requisite readjustment tears down the façade of corruption and hypocrisy to allow the cultivation within errant individuals of a more nurturing lifestyle.

We see this happening quickly in scripture, because historical narrative seems to compress the passage of time. In reality, the obligatory alterations occur more gradually. Reclaiming lost souls can take time and can be frustratingly difficult. But a major provision of the Plan is that our lives are times of probation, or of putting to the proof. There is enough time for correction, repentance, forgiveness, renewal, and recommitment. Because the fire of faith changes lives, sharing the gospel is part of the formulaic equation integral to the Plan. The Lord told Joseph Smith: "The thing which will be of the most worth unto you will be to declare repentance unto this people, that you may bring souls unto me, that you may rest with them in the kingdom of my Father." (D&C 15:6). When we conform our behavior to the elements of the Plan and begin to appreciate His divine nature, we recognize happiness for what it really is. Our capacity for happiness is a celestial barometer that measures our conformity to the principles of the Plan and introduces us to the refreshing breeze of celestial air. Happiness prepares us to be comfortable in God's company. Because the Plan is for all of His children: "It becometh every man who hath been warned to warn his neighbor." (D&C 88:81).

None of us wants to miss the "Glory Train" that has been provided by the Plan. We all want to be happy. We all want to "hear the whistle sound, for those souls heaven bound?" We are all eager to "climb onboard the glory ride and set our earthly bonds aside." Most assuredly, "this old train will leave someday boarding Christians along the way." We can see it now in our mind's eye, "roaring down those one-way tracks, and bound for heaven, it won't be back." We can hear the urgent call now: "Get your ticket while you can. If you want a ride to glory land, we'll meet at the Lord's station. There's no time left for hesitation." When we climb on board, we'll be in for the ride of our lives, because "this long black train has no gears. It's full throttle ahead leaving here." We'll be in good company, for "the archangel will be our engineer. We'll depart amidst angelic cheers." All Christians of conscience realize "the price of the ticket is paid for you. Jesus died on the cross for sins you do. Surrender to the Good Shepherd your all, before you miss that last boarding call." The promise is: "We'll glide on the ride to heavens' shore, where you will endure troubles no more. So shed your shackles. There's no need to pack. Board that glory train with one-way tracks!" (Kenneth Ellison, "Glory Train").

Our eternal welfare is so thoroughly integrated with happiness that the Lord has made an astounding promise: "I will forgive you of your sins with this commandment – that you remain steadfast in your minds in solemnity and the spirit of prayer, in bearing testimony to all the world of those things which are communicated unto you." (D&C 88:61). "For if you will that I give unto you a place in the celestial world, you must prepare yourselves by doing the things which I have commanded you and required of you." (D&C 78:7).

Spencer W. Kimball recognized the promise associated with this eternal principle when he urged members of the Church to lengthen their stride. In doing so, "he knew that the spirituality of the members would be intensified. Christ urged the man in bondage to go the second mile, to double his stride. The second mile is a gift of spiritual independence." (Richard L. Gunn, "Sensitivity and Spirit." p. 197). It is in the second mile that natural endorphins kick in to give us a natural "high." It is then that we are genuinely and intrinsically "happy" without the influence of chemical stimulants that pollute our state of mind and compromise our long-term emotional and physiological health. The prescription for happiness cannot be found in a pill bottle.

Our duties and responsibilities are clear: "If ye have desires to serve God ye are called to the work." (D&C 4:3). "My understanding," declared George Albert Smith, "is that the most important mission that I have in this life is first, to keep the commandments of God, and second, to teach them to my Father's children who do not understand them." (C.R., 10/1916). This two-fold undertaking sets us squarely on the path of happiness. But it is not in the first mile of the race that we get our second wind, for we have only just begun our journey. It is only after we have warmed up our muscles with spiritual aerobic exercise, when we have loosened up in comfortable interactions with others, when we have established a reasonably comfortable pace to see ourselves through, when we have cleared our vision to see beyond our limitations and have fixed our mind's eye on the finish line, that we become powerful vessels through which rejuvenating energy flows to our friends and neighbors.

What is involved in creating this spiritual interdependence that removes the veil of insensitivity to our destiny? If we are focused on latter-day idols of any kind, we will neither be happy, nor will we have the means to further the work. If our faith is flawed, we will be blinded to the reality that the objects of our desires are impotent. Sooner or later, our misery will catch up to us, and our souls, and the souls of those whom we might have saved had we done our duty, will be lost. When "the blind lead the blind, both shall fall into the ditch." (Matthew 15:14).

Those who feel confused, abandoned, disillusioned, or despair as a consequence of their focus on worldly pleasure, are like those of whom the Savior declared: "They seek not the Lord to establish his righteousness, but every man walketh in his own way, and after the image of his own god, whose image is in the likeness of the world, and whose substance is like that of an idol, which waxeth old and shall perish in Babylon, even Babylon the great, which shall fall." (D&C 1:16).

If we want to be happy, we cannot take a vacation in Idumea as a respite from life on the strait and narrow path. Such diversions are only detours from life's journey that inevitably delay our progress toward our determined destination, cause us to lose traction and forward momentum, and derail us from our sure footing on the rod of iron. When we delve into these distractions, we lose power, purpose, and focus. For example, if we depend more on economic security than on spiritual preparedness, we are more inclined in times of crisis to grasp at the world's goods rather than to drop to our knees, hold tightly to our faith, and with the help of our Father in Heaven work our way out of our problems. If we put our trust in "idea gods," where will look for help when the winds of change erode the foundations of our misplaced faith in the "flavor of the day?"

Why is there so much unhappiness in the world? It is easy to be infected by the desire to obtain what we do not need, what we have not earned, what we do not deserve, and what we cannot ultimately control. Each fall and winter, several million people worldwide succumb to the effects of an influenza virus in frustratingly mutated forms, but more die spiritually because they are infected by avarice and greed, covetousness and lust, and pride and prejudice. People think that they will be happy if they wander and play, never considering that the key to happiness is to ponder and pray.

The deception is compounded by activities that dull our senses and make us even more vulnerable to Satan's enticements. If we persist in behavior that is in opposition to the laws relating to happiness, we may even ask the Lord, as did Malachi rhetorically: "What have we spoken against thee?" Is our lifestyle really so bad? We are inclined to believe that "it is vain to serve God, and what doth it profit that we have kept his ordinances and that we have walked mournfully before the Lord of Hosts?" We haven't immediately seen the rewards that come from righteousness, and since we've never really been converted, it doesn't seem profitable to keep the commandments. It seems only natural then for us to deny the faith. From our perspective, "we call the proud happy." It seems to us that "they that work wickedness are set up; yea, they that tempt God are even delivered." From all outward appearances, our worldliness doesn't seem to make any difference. The wicked around us seem to be cheerful enough. In our view, black is white, and white is black, and who can really tell the difference? Anyway, who really cares? (Malachi 3:13-15). The distinction, however, is clear to those who have tried the virtue of the word of God, and who can "discern between the righteous and the wicked, between him that serveth God and him that serveth him not." (Malachi 3:18).

Life is all a stage, but when the bouquets are thrown at the feet of the cast and they are summoned for a final curtain call after the last act, it will only be the faithful and true who receive a standing ovation. This is why Samuel the Lamanite charged the people of Zarahemla: "Ye have sought all the days of your lives for that which ye could not obtain, and ye have sought for happiness in doing iniquity, which thing is contrary to the nature of that righteousness" which is in God. (Helaman 13:38).

The adversary finally betrays his followers because they can only mimic his behavior, sustain his lifestyle, and live after the manner of happiness for so long, and because Satan ultimately cannot deliver on his promises. He betrays them because his enticements lead those who are careless, or who have lost their covenant consciousness, into conceptual cul de sacs from which all exits lead to confusion, doubt, uncertainty, ambiguity, hesitation, and retreat. The defeat of the weak-willed is total and complete because his cunning caresses persuade them to plunge headlong into a perceived freedom that is on closer inspection a bottomless pit of misery.

In a perverted, twisted way, "the devil seeks that all men might be miserable like himself." (2 Nephi 2:27). Never does he promise happiness, perhaps because it is intrinsic to the merciful Plan of the Great Creator, and he is prohibited from employing it as an enticement. Instead, he influences us to engage in a warped reasoning that encourages rationalization in our quest for the Holy Grail of power, authority, control, wealth, dominion, affluence, fashion, style, comfort, position, and influence, that are only poor substitutes for happiness.

Winston Churchill said: "Men's and nations' finest hours are those when extraordinary challenge is met with extraordinary response." We live in such a day. After the close of World War II, he said: "It was the nation that had the lion's heart. I had the luck to be called upon to give the roar." In the challenging Last Days, the army of Israel will thunder in a voice of warning tempered by "faith, hope, charity, and love, with an eye single to the glory of God." (D&C 4:5). In our preparations for battle, we will "strengthen (our) "brethren in all (our) conversation, in all (our) prayers, in all (our) exhortations, and in all (our) doings." (D&C 108:7). Like the Seven Dwarfs, we will whistle while we work, because "all our doings" will become the seeds or genesis of happiness.

To "this end was the law given." The Restoration prepares us to believe in God, "and we are made alive in Christ because of our faith." (2 Nephi 25:25). The virtue of the word is its incredible power to touch our hearts. Many years ago, Leo Tolstoy said: "If Mormonism could be true to its foundations and remain unchanged for four generations, it might well become the most powerful social influence in the world," to change our nature, to soften us and to humble us, to make us as pliant clay in the hands of the Master Potter, to mold us as children, and to secure us in happiness while we safely dwell in Zion. Happiness is like a breathtakingly beautiful butterfly. The more we chase its caricatures, the more it eludes us. But if we plan our work and work the Plan, it will come and sit softly on our shoulders. (Henry David Thoreau).

Lehi simply stated: "If there be no righteousness there be no happiness." (2 Nephi 2:13). Later, the Lord confirmed: "If it be so that you should labor all your days in crying repentance unto this people, and bring, save it be one soul unto me, how great shall be your joy with him in the kingdom of my father." (D&C 18:15). It is quite clear that the provision built into the Plan relating to sharing the gospel is a key element of happiness.

Because misery loves company, Satan has launched a direct frontal assault on happiness, creating many social conventions to sabotage our efforts. Customs, rituals, traditions, and institutions work tirelessly to destroy any chance we may have. Even technology gets in the way, substituting the electronic media for direct interpersonal relationships that are fundamental to happiness. "Reach out and touch someone" becomes a euphemism for "Use technology to isolate yourself from others."

It is precisely because our capacity for happiness is so frequently threatened that we need the power of covenants to provide the opportunity for recommitment to a behavioral lifestyle that not only directly pertains to righteousness but also indirectly relates to happiness. So that we may make a connection with the events in which we are swept up, to the people who influence us, and to the environment that impacts us, we need unequivocal understanding and clear definitions of eternal truth, both of which are found in the Plan and are revealed by the Holy Ghost. These will protect us from the worldly influences that encroach on the fortress of our spiritual security, sanctuary, and symmetry that are essential to happiness. It becomes a question of context.

Internalizing gospel principles softens our telestial tendencies and making covenants creates an impenetrable shield of faith. As we gain eternal perspective, then, we will be able to discern between the polarized opposites that are essential to the Plan and so prevalent in the world. We will be able to tell the difference between happiness and its worldly counterfeits. The message of the Restoration will strike familiar chords within us, even as Satan's fingerprints will be more easily distinguished on the idols with which he tempts us to keep us from the truth.

Little wonder that the Master said His sheep would recognize His voice and follow Him. (John 10:27). The sturdiest plants that bear the best fruit are those that have deep roots in good, rich, nurturing soil. So, to be truly happy, and to share our happiness with others, we must surround ourselves with the best that can be provided in music and art, conversation, example, decency, virtue, and honor. This will allow our spirits to grow freely, even as we send down taproots into gospel soil to anchor ourselves to the Infinite.

As we do so, we will commit the Thirteenth Article of Faith to memory as well as to our lifestyle. "If there is anything virtuous, lovely, or of good report or praiseworthy, we seek after these things." To the extent that we do this, we may expect to be ignited with the "fire of God." (2 Kings 1:12). If we don't, we may experience hell while yet on earth, for that mental anguish may simply be the conscious recognition of lost opportunities and the unconscious sense of dread that accompanies the stupor of thought when we have made imprudent choices.

Knowledge is power, and members of the church have an advantage because they see the big picture, and understand that Adam fell so that we might live in a state of happiness on earth and have eternal joy in heaven. When his Fall is considered in conjunction with the Atonement of Christ, it is clear that both are critical to the success of the Great Plan of Happiness, for we can only attain a fulness of joy in a personal, tangible, perfected resurrection in the I, made possible by the One Who suffered for our sins. (See Alma 42:8). For we are "spirit, the elements are eternal, and spirit and element, inseparably connected (by the power of the Atonement) receive a fulness of joy." (D&C 93:33).

In the end, we will find happiness when we have so valued our spiritual welfare that we have loved the Lord, kept His commandments, and shared our testimonies with others. Heber J. Grant once said: "I bear witness to you as an Apostle of the Lord Jesus Christ, that material and spiritual prosperity is predicated upon the fulfillment of these duties and responsibilities that rest upon the Latter-day Saints." (C.R., 10/1889).

As we keep the laws of God, we experience the "happiness which is prepared for the saints." (2 Nephi 9:43). The Savior revealed: "Abundance is multiplied unto (the Saints) through the manifestations of the Spirit." (D&C 70:13). In other words, so profound will be the spirit that it will be overflowing. The Saints will realize that their righteous objectives stay in focus because they have paid constant attention to spiritual guideposts, and they will realize that the only true perspective of mortal experience is the one that is viewed from a gospel-centered orientation.

The Plan of Happiness is within the reach of every one of us, no matter what our cultural, social, political, or economic circumstances might be. The portals to the Plan are found in every gospel teaching and are interwoven into every gospel principle. On our own, we can do pitifully little to feather our nests, influence our circumstances, craft our environment, create opportunities, or generate conditions that would spontaneously and effortlessly lead to happiness. It is only through the miracle of the infinite, continuing, uninterrupted, unspoiled, uncorrupted, enduring, unfathomable, and immeasurable grace of God that we are "swallowed up in the joy of (our) God, even to the exhausting of (our) strength." (Alma 27:17). When we reach that epiphany, our hearts will "brim with joy." (Alma 26:11). Even the earth will be full of the spirit of God. She will have "travailed and brought forth her strength; and truth (will have been) established in her bowels; and the heavens (will) have smiled upon her; and she (will be) clothed with the glory of her God; for he (will stand) in the midst of his people." (D&C 84:101)

Alma's plea to "try the virtue of the word of God" was an invitation for us to enjoy the fruit of the tree of life and to open our senses to the matchless realm of joy available only through obedience to gospel principles embedded within the Plan. As we share the fruit with our friends and neighbors we will find that it is these divine characteristics, after all, that are the very keys to happiness.

Happiness / Wickedness

"Do not suppose, because
it has been spoken concerning
restoration, that ye shall be restored
from sin to happiness. Behold, I
say unto you, wickedness
never was happiness."
(Alma 41:10).

In our busy and complex world, it is very difficult to tell just what brings us happiness. Neither fame nor anonymity holds the key. Both poverty and wealth have failed miserably. Neither sickness nor health has the ability. Both principalities and the absence of worldly influence are inadequate. Neither beauty nor the beast has the advantage. In their quest for happiness, people sometimes forget that with nurturing rain they are also going to have to deal with some mud, that the road is rocky with potholes and other hidden obstacles, and that it is uphill most of the way. After all, "the dark threads are as needful in the weaver's skillful hand as the threads of gold and silver, in the pattern he has planned." (Anonymous). People can never hope to find meaning if they view life superficially, and they will not find happiness without first comprehending its price and then steadfastly seeking its reward. When our quest is casual, we are as vain imposters, and our experiences can be false and misleading and without the anticipated long-term effects. We generally do not value that which we do not deserve. In the Savior's parable, it was a wise merchant who, when he found one pearl of great price, "went and sold all that he had" in order to possess it. (Matthew 13:46).

Satan uses telestial trivia that rely on the treasures of the earth as counterfeit pleasures for the blessing of happiness that our Father in Heaven reserves for the faithful. He knows how easy it is to fashion gods of wood and stone to satisfy the vanities, passions, conceit, and appetites of man. Those of weak character may think that they have found happiness in these pleasures, because they have not learned to recognize and have never experienced the genuine article. In fact, they may even live "after the manner of happiness for a season," because both their level of understanding and their behavior harmonize with worldly standards. As long as they can shut out the light of Christ, they may live in that fantasy world. But sooner or later the discrepancy between their behavior and gospel ideals will become so great that their short-lived pleasure in their worldly ways will be destroyed. The Lord will not always suffer the wicked "to take happiness in sin." (Mormon 2:13). One can only conduct one's life in opposition to the laws of heaven for so long, before "critical mass" is reached. At that point, a readjustment is required, bringing the errant individual back into harmony with nature.

Worshipping idols of any kind blinds men to the recognition that their faith is flawed, and that the objects of their desires have no power to deliver on their promises. Sooner or later, the master pretender reveals his true character as the father of lies. Of the confused, abandoned, and disillusioned disciples who lie in his wake and litter the broad boulevards of the twin cities of worldliness and pleasure, the Savior declared: "They seek not the Lord to establish his righteousness, but every man walketh in his own way, and after the image of his own god, whose image is in the likeness of the world, and whose substance is like that of an idol, which waxeth old and shall perish in Babylon, even Babylon the great, which shall fall." (D&C 1:16). The blueprints of Babylon are always drawn with a stylus moved by the unsteady hand of man's own might. But we are put on notice as we remember that even though Babylon was for a time the greatest city of the ancient world, when it grew weak because it was rotten from within, it was conquered from without, and was left desolate and forgotten.

The world has always been mesmerized by an endless stream of illusions of influence, even though each is only a caricature of happiness. Because the world is wealthy and her telestial treasures provide what appears to be an overflowing cornucopia of comfort, it is all too easy for those who make their home in Babylon to put their trust in material resources, rather than in God. When people are seduced by a siren song that creates an insatiable desire for the world's goods, it is easy for their priorities to be out of order. As their vision blurs, they confuse a vacation in Idumea with life on the strait and narrow path. When that happens, they lose power, purpose, and focus. People who have grown to depend more on a secular safety net than on spiritual preparedness are more inclined in times of crisis to grasp at the world's goods, rather than to drop to their knees, hold tightly to their faith, and with the help of their Father in Heaven work their way out of their problems.

When the world becomes distracted by pagan gods of its own invention and construction, it allows itself to be led into spiritual bondage, until it is "as the heathen, as the families of the countries, to serve wood and stone." (Ezekiel 20:32). Jeremiah asked: "Shall a man make gods unto himself, and they are no gods?" (Jeremiah 16:20). If we unwisely set our hearts on the vain things of the world, those things that cannot deliver on their promises, we are infected by the desire to obtain that which we have not earned, that we do not deserve, and that we cannot ultimately control. Then, the treasures of spiritual insight and understanding lose the power to change and perfect our lives. It is little wonder that God set the standard in the Decalogue, when He warned His children about the virus of covetousness. One of the seven deadly sins, it is a communicable disease that is dangerously self-serving, decidedly unproductive, doggedly virulent, and deceptively unsatisfying. The antidote is clear: "Look to God, and live" abundantly. (Alma 37:47).

In the Last Days, Nephi warned, "the lofty looks of man shall be humbled." (2 Nephi 12:11). His mentor Isaiah urged Israel not to trust in man, whose power is impotent, and "whose breath is in his nostrils," but rather to trust in God who has given man "the breath of life," that he might become "a living soul," capable through divine intervention of experiencing unspeakable joy. (2 Nephi 12:22). It is easy to see why the mission of The Church of Jesus Christ of Latter-day Saints is simply to teach the principles associated with true happiness, for when people have abandoned or can no longer recognize their core values, they characteristically succumb to an obsession for that which can never satisfy their appetites. Such shifting sands cannot provide the solid foundation necessary to launch one on an eternally escalating course. With vivid imagery, the scriptures instead encourage the faithful to "increase in beauty, and in holiness," and Zion to "arise and put on her beautiful garments" in preparation for her happy reunion with her Creator. (D&C 82:14).

Men never do evil so cheerfully as when they think they are doing good. To compound the deception, Satan's substitutes for joy actually dull the senses and make man even more vulnerable to his enticements. As they persist in behavior that is in opposition to the laws relating to happiness, they may even ask the Lord "What have we spoken against thee?" "Is our lifestyle really so bad? We are inclined to believe that] "it is vain to serve God, and what doth it profit that we have kept his ordinances and that we have walked mournfully before the Lord of Hosts?" We haven't immediately seen the rewards that come from righteousness, and since we've never really been converted, it doesn't seem profitable to have "kept the commandments. It is only natural then for us to deny the faith. From our perspective, "we call the proud happy." It seems to us that they "they that work wickedness are set up; yea, they that tempt God are even delivered." "To us, black is white, and white is black, and so does it really matter?" (Malachi 3:13-15).

The distinction is clear, however, to those who have tried the virtue of the word of God, and who can "discern between the righteous and the wicked, between him that serveth God and him that serveth him not." (Malachi 3:18). Life is all a stage, but when the bouquets are thrown at the feet of the players, and they are summoned for a curtain call after the final act, it will only be the faithful and true who will, with joy, receive a standing ovation.

As the Saints endure to the end, they must be especially vigilant; they must avoid embracing "idea-gods" that rivet their attention, consume their energies, demand their devotion, divert their direction, obscure their objectivity, and dilute their capacity for happiness. Sitting with the engine idling while wasting time in telestial traffic jams can damage our ability and desire to move forward. Overzealously pursuing caricatures created with smoke and mirrors, or by jousting with windmills, is ultimately delusional and self-destructive.

As Saints embrace the principles of the gospel, their path is clear, and their destination is well defined. They do not confuse knowledge for intelligence, nor think that when they are learned they are wise. They understand that to be learned is good, but only if they are humble and obedient. When individuals are grounded in the bedrock of the gospel, testimonies are protected, souls are saved, and the work and the glory of God move forward as men approach a fulness of joy.

Samuel the Lamanite charged the people of Zarahemla: "Ye have sought all the days of your lives for that which ye could not obtain, and ye have sought for happiness in doing iniquity, which thing is contrary to the nature of that righteousness" which is in God. (Helaman 13:38). The Adversary finally betrays his followers, because he cannot deliver on his promises. His enticements lead Father's children into conceptual cul de sacs, from which there is no exit except rationalized retreat, frantic flight from responsibility, shifting stammering of blame, brazen back-pedaling, and confused complacency leading to senseless stupor of thought and total defeat. His cunning caresses entice the weak to plunge into a perceived freedom, which is really a bottomless pit of misery. In a perverted way, "the devil seeks that all men might be miserable like himself." (2 Nephi 2:27). Never does he dare to promise that his followers will be happy. Instead, he influences his disciples to engage in the twisted reasoning that allows them to rationalize their quest for the Holy Grail of power, wealth, dominion, position, and influence, that are, at best, poor substitutes for happiness.

"There are many spirits which are false spirits, which have gone forth in the earth, deceiving the world." They would entice man to persist in wickedness, relying on the quick fix of pleasure as a mean substitute for happiness. They have "sought to deceive you," cautioned the Lord, "that (they) might overthrow you." (D&C 50:2-3). They do this with cunning and guile, and often with genuine sophistication, for as Shakespeare wrote, even "the devil can cite Scripture for his purpose." (The Merchant of Venice, Act 1, Scene 3).

Among his many counterfeits, the Adversary often uses pride as a poor excuse for happiness. This is one reason why the world is in such a frenzied pursuit of material gain. As it accumulates more and more, in an endless quest for "enough," many are puffed up with inflated egos in a race that may not be well defined, will never be over, and certainly can never be won. There is no "exit strategy" because there is no conscious recognition that a personality disorder even exists. There is no one left to shout, "Stop the insanity" because everyone who had been waiting for the train bound for glory has instead clamored aboard the Excess Express.

He worked out for years to reduce all his fat. His muscles were firm, and his stomach was flat. He jogged day and night to keep himself trim, and still found time to play tennis and swim. He drank protein drinks, and ate health food galore, then lifted, stair-climbed, and lifted some more. He told family and friends that it gave him a 'high,' They encouraged him on as he waved them good-bye. 'If things work out,' he yelled back from afar, 'I'll be a great athlete, I'll be a big star!' But how could he miss the big truck up ahead? One thud, and his beautiful body lay dead. And then, he saw something that filled him with fright. His spiritual body was one sorry sight! No more than a skeleton, covered with skin. He got up to heaven, but didn't get in! 'Another soul's mine!' Satan started to scream. 'Give man something nice, and he'll take the extreme!' OK, I'll admit it; I'll outright confess. For the fast way to hell, take the excess express. ("The Excess Express," Anonymous).

The only refuge possible is the fortress of a perceived satisfaction in one's own accomplishments, and that requires inordinate attention to trivial detail and continual cosmetic re-construction to prevent it from self-destructing with either a slow leak or a blowout into oblivion. President Ezra Taft Benson called pride "the universal sin, the great vice" and identified its central feature as "enmity toward God and enmity toward our fellowmen." The insidiously evil and destructive quality of pride is that it "is essentially competitive in nature, arising when individuals pit their will against God's, or their intellects, opinions, works, wealth, and talents against those of other people." President Benson warned the Latter-day Saints that "pride is a damning sin" for "it adversely affects all our relationships and limits or stops progression." It is contrary to the nature of happiness. When pride swells in our bosom, it occupies such a volume that it squeezes out our capacity for meaningful happiness. Elder N. Eldon Tanner observed that "the craving for praise and popularity too often controls actions, and as a people succumb, they find themselves bending their character, when they think they are only taking a bow." As a result, many become disillusioned when their search for happiness through acquisition, accumulation, and gain rings hollow and leaves a sour aftertaste imprinted on the spirit. Such individuals never learned that "happiness is like a butterfly. The more you chase it, the more it eludes you. But if you turn your attention to service on behalf of others, it will come and sit softly on your shoulder." (Anonymous).

Joseph Smith declared that happiness "is the object and design of our existence and will be the end thereof, if we pursue the path that leads to it; and this path is virtue, uprightness, faithfulness, holiness, and keeping all the commandments of God." (Teachings, p. 255). Pursue it we must, for God will always grant to His children agency to choose their own path, "for behold, they are their own judges, whether to do good or do evil." (Alma 41:7). Although we may choose our own actions, we cannot choose to escape the resulting consequences. On the one hand are happiness and well-being. On the other are misery and despair. "The decrees of God are unalterable; therefore, the way is prepared that whosoever will, may walk therein and be saved" from the pain and anguish that follow poor choices. (Alma 41:8). Mortality's most valuable lessons come through our direct experience. One is the realization that "wickedness never was happiness." When we recognize that truth, its corollary snaps into focus: We cannot "be restored from sin to happiness." (Alma 41:10). Lehi put it this way: "If there be no righteousness there be no happiness." (2 Nephi 2:13).

Sometimes, with a gut-wrenching sense of hopelessness that comes "because of iniquity," we learn that despair fills a vacuum created by sin and is the antithesis of happiness. (Moroni 10:22). The wicked learn too late that every law has both a blessing and a punishment affixed to it. When the law is obeyed, a blessing is given that results in happiness, or joy. When that law is disobeyed, punishment follows that results in unhappiness, or misery. Despair is the feeling of abandonment and isolation that accompanies disobedience. Sooner or later, it will bear down heavily on every person who has adopted a lifestyle at odds with the Plan of Happiness. When one succumbs to such feelings, subsequent behavior tends to be reinforcing and the person spirals downward in an accelerating free-fall.

Alma explained that "all men that are in a state of nature, or I would say, in a carnal state, are in the gall of bitterness and in the bonds of iniquity; they are without God in the world, and they have gone contrary to the nature of God; therefore, they are in a state contrary to the nature of happiness." (Alma 41:11). The Savior taught that if men lack vision, and build "upon the works of men, or upon the works of the devil ... they (may) have joy in their works for a season." They may briefly enjoy the fruits of their labor, however ill-gotten is their gain, because eternal law obeys no man's timetable. In fact, were every act of obedience immediately rewarded, and every act of disobedience immediately punished, all would do right, but for the wrong reasons. Faith is developed by degrees, as we take baby steps into the unknown. Some of the blessings associated with faith are literally out of this world, for a fulness of joy can come only in the resurrection. (D&C 93:33, 101:36). However, we can now be certain that for the wicked, "by and by the end cometh, and they are hewn down and cast into the fire, from whence there is no return." (3 Nephi 27:11).

As we begin to understand how the Plan of Happiness operates, we realize that "the meaning of the word restoration is to bring back again .. good for that which is good; righteous for that which is righteous; just for that which is just; merciful for that which is merciful." (Alma 41:13). In other words, if we consistently conduct our lives in harmony with the Plan, the Law of Restoration assures us of happiness. Meanwhile, the world has done a remarkable job of rationalizing its predictably wicked behavior and redefining in double-speak the legitimacy of its ways in an effort to circumvent the Law of Just Compensation. In such jargon, wickedness takes on an air of respectability in an attempt to circumvent the pain that is the natural consequence of poor choices. Public drunkenness is rationalized as "social drinking." "Obscenity" matures to "adult content," and "sexual deviancy" is transformed to an "alternative lifestyle." "Pro-choice" puts a positive spin on "abortion." the "Holy Sabbath" morphs into "the weekend," and lying becomes "hyper-exaggeration." Stealing becomes "the involuntary redistribution of wealth."

But life has no coherence, and is in fact, a cruel joke, without the spiritual symmetry and balance that the Lord's fitness program can bring. Alma applied the principle of restoration to Corianton when he explained: "Therefore, my son, see that you are merciful unto your brethren; deal justly, judge righteously, and do good continually; and if ye do all these things then shall ye receive your reward; yea, ye shall have mercy restored unto you again; ye shall have justice restored unto you again; ye shall have a righteous judgment restored unto you again; and ye shall have good rewarded unto you again." (Alma 41:14). In short, such conduct guarantees the restoration and perpetuation of happiness, for, as Alma taught, "that which ye do send out shall return unto you again." (Alma 41:15). Perhaps this is why Paul warned, "the wages of sin is death, but the gift of God is eternal life." (Romans 6:23).

Because our capacity for happiness is so frequently threatened, we need the power of covenants to provide the opportunity for recommitment to those behavioral lifestyles that pertain to righteousness. So that we may correctly respond to the circumstances in which we find ourselves and to the events that affect us, we need unequivocal understanding and clear definitions that come from the Holy Ghost. These will protect us from the worldly influences that encroach on the fortress of our spiritual security, symmetry, and stability. Internalizing gospel principles creates an impenetrable shield of faith. As we gain eternal perspective, then, we can discern between the polarized opposites that are so prevalent in our world today. We can discern between happiness and its worldly counterfeits. The counsel of our Heavenly Father will strike familiar chords within us, even as Satan's fingerprints are more easily distinguished on the profane idols with which he tempts us. Little wonder that the Master said that His sheep would recognize His voice, and follow Him. (John 10:27).

The sturdiest plants that bear the best fruit are those that have deep roots in good, rich, nurturing soil. So, to be truly happy, we must surround ourselves with the best that can be provided in music and art, conversation, example, decency, virtue, and honor. Then our spirits will grow freely, even as we send down taproots in gospel soil to secure a solid footing. In so doing, we commit the 13th Article of Faith to our lifestyle as well as to our memory. "If there is anything virtuous, lovely, or of good report or praiseworthy, we seek after these things." To the extent that we do this, we may expect to blossom enthusiastically with the "fire of God."

If we don't, we may experience hell while yet on earth, for that mental anguish may simply be the recognition of lost opportunities. It can also be felt as the guilt and pain of unresolved sin, which is "like an unquenchable fire" that can leave our hope for happiness in ashes. (Mosiah 2:38). Mercy can have "no claim on that man," and Justice demands a never-ending torment. (Mosiah 2:39). Individuals in these circumstances are most profoundly on their own, in a state of eternal unhappiness, for it is as if no Atonement for sin had been made. To avoid such a fate, Benjamin urged that we awaken "to a remembrance of the awful situation of those that have fallen into transgression." (Mosiah 2:40). In contrast, he portrayed in his sermon "the blessed and happy state of those that keep the commandments." (Mosiah 2:41).

An understanding of the very foundations for happiness requires knowledge of the Fall of Adam. It is the doctrine of the church that there was opposition from the beginning, but that in the Garden of Eden, Adam and Eve did not have true moral agency; therefore, they could not be happy before the introduction of the enticements of Satan. The scriptures teach that "it must needs be that the devil should tempt the children of men, or they could not be agents unto themselves; for if they never should have bitter they could not know the sweet." (D&C 29:39). We know that Satan did not deceive Adam. Rather, his decision to partake of the forbidden fruit was intelligent and conscious, the result of a correct understanding of the requirements of the gospel Plan of Happiness. "Adam fell that men might be" eternally happy. (2 Nephi 2:25). Little wonder that "the morning stars sang together, and all the sons of God shouted for joy" when that same Plan was introduced to them. (Job 38:7).

Not knowing the mind of God, that there must needs be opposition in all things, Satan sought what he thought would be the end of happiness, or the misery of all mankind. With his congenital shortsightedness and his typical stratagem of promoting half-truths, he offered the forbidden fruit to Eve. "Ye shall be as God, knowing good and evil," he promised. (2 Nephi 2:18). He knew that we would then have the capacity for happiness, but he was confident that he could influence us to be miserable.

Our Father knew that life in Eden before the Fall was not an ideal existence. But with the temptation of Eve came our first parents' only opportunity to find eternal happiness. As Lehi clearly taught, had Adam not transgressed the Law in the Garden, he would have vegetated there forever in a morally static state. The Father knew that Adam must fall as a critically operative part of the Plan of Happiness.

One of the basic messages of the Restoration, then, is that Adam fell so that man might live in a state of happiness on earth and in eternal joy in heaven. When the Fall of Adam is considered in conjunction with the Atonement of Christ, it is powerfully clear that both are critical to the Plan of Happiness, for man can only attain a fulness of joy in a personal, tangible, perfected resurrection in the I, made possible by the Savior of the world Who suffered for our sins. "For man is spirit, the elements are eternal, and spirit and element, inseparably connected [by the power of the Atonement] receive a fulness of joy." (D&C 93:33).

It is Christ's way for men to act for themselves. (2 Nephi 2:26). It is Satan's way for them to be acted upon. The 'perfect law of liberty' requires that men be free according to the flesh. (2 Nephi 2:27, See James 1:25). The choice is between liberty, eternal life, and happiness, or captivity, spiritual death, and misery. But to earn these blessings, all action must be carried out within the context of the gospel and its laws; otherwise, unbridled freedom follows a slippery slope leading to oppression and tyranny. Men are free to choose the direction they will take, but they cannot choose to escape the consequences of their poor choices.

Satan's tactics rely on compulsion, deny agency, and require obedience. If we voluntarily give up our agency, we are trapped in the iron jaws of bad habits, and snared by Satan, we are bound by his strong chains. We ultimately feel those heavy cords around our necks that restrict our actions and drag us down to hell. It is very hard to break out of the grip of bad habits, because we have given up our agency in order to acquire them. Satan and all who follow him are miserable because, entrenched in sin, they no longer have the freedom to choose, and are powerless to change their circumstances. They know all too well where the exercise of their agency has taken them. Happiness is beyond their reach, and so their torment is excruciating. But misery loves company, and Satan desires that all men might be as he is. (2 Nephi 2:27). Giving up one's birthright of happiness for the mess of pottage characterized by the fleeting pleasures of the world leaves an empty, sick feeling in the pit of the stomach, as one realizes that one has been duped by the Destroyer.

Heavenly Father does not operate this way. He sees the eternal principle of agency differently. Agency does entail risk, because the element of failure is real, but it is the only way that we may justify our claim to unspeakable joy in our Father's kingdom. Rather than enslaving us in good habits, He repeatedly gives us the opportunity to recommit ourselves to our covenants of obedience to tried and true principles. At the same time, He promises that obedience to the laws that pertain to happiness will qualify us to receive that blessing. This is one of the most important reasons why church membership and activity are vital to one's spiritual well-being, inner peace, and happiness.

Brigham Young taught that "the Spirit is pure, and (is) under the special control and influence of the Lord, but the body is of the earth, and is subject to the power of the devil, and is under the mighty influence of that fallen nature that is of the earth. If the Spirit yields to the body, the devil then has power to overcome the body and spirit of that man, and he loses both." As he sinks into the quicksand of carnality and loses his wide-eyed innocence and purity, he forfeits the happiness that accompanies an untroubled soul. When we choose the good part, we elect to use our agency even as we yield our hearts to the Savior, ponder the great and terrible consequences of Gethsemane, travel with Him to Calvary, and enjoy the sweetness of the redeeming power of the Atonement, which is the keystone of the Plan of Happiness. "All things which pertain to our religion are only appendages to it," declared the Prophet Joseph Smith. These support and sustain the mission statement of the Savior" Who said that His work and glory was to bring about our immortality and eternal life in a state of perpetual and unmitigated happiness. ("Teachings," p. 127, See Moses 1:38).

If we value our spiritual welfare, love the Lord, and keep His commandments, we will find happiness. Heber J. Grant once said: "I bear witness to you as an Apostle of the Lord Jesus Christ, that material and spiritual prosperity is predicated upon the fulfillment of the duties and responsibilities that rest upon us as Latter-day Saints." (C.R., 10/1889). When we keep the laws of God, we will experience "that happiness which is prepared for the saints." (2 Nephi 9:43). Such happiness can transcend temporal security and worldly comforts.

Those teachings that give us insights into the spiritual roots of human relationships, or happiness based on the common bonds of spiritual interdependency, help us to live in the world without being tainted by it. In doing this, they illustrate the power of the ordinances of the gospel, that are not only essential to salvation, but have the capacity to make life on this telestial world sublime. As the Savior revealed: "Abundance is multiplied unto (the Saints) through the manifestations of the Spirit." (D&C 70:13). Our righteous objectives stay in focus only when we pay attention to the guideposts provided by our Heavenly Father and we enjoy the sustaining influence of His sweet spirit.

It is most remarkable that our opportunity for happiness is a gift from God that He weaves into every gospel teaching. It is by His infinite, continuing, uninterrupted and uncorrupted grace that we enjoy our mortal experience, after all we can do on our own. (2 Nephi 25:23). Brigham Young rightly observed, "There is no man who ever made a sacrifice on this earth for the kingdom of heaven except the Savior. I would not give the ashes of a rye straw for that man who feels he is making sacrifices for God. We are doing this for our own happiness." (J.D. 16:114). Alma's plea to the Saints in Zarahemla to "try the virtue of the word of God" was an invitation to enjoy the fruit of the tree of life and to open their senses to the matchless realm of joy available only through obedience to gospel principles. Today, we continue to seek after that which is virtuous, lovely, of good report and praiseworthy because these divine characteristics are the very things that will make us happy.

Having Been Commissioned of Jesus Christ
(D&C 22)

"And now, Alma was their high priest, he being the founder of their church. And it came to pass that none received authority to preach or to teach except it were by him from God. Therefore, he consecrated all their priests and all their teachers; and none were consecrated except they were just men ... and it came to pass that king Mosiah granted unto Alma that he might establish churches throughout all the land of Zarahemla; and gave him power to ordain priests and teachers over every church." (Mosiah 23:16-17 & 25:19).

"This revelation was given to the church in consequence of some who had previously been baptized desiring to unite with the church without rebaptism." (Superscript). When the first conference held in the Church convened at the home of Peter Whitmer, on June 9, 1830, those in attendance officially accepted this section and Section 20 as the "Articles and Covenants of the church of Christ." ("Far West Record," p. 1-2). The leaders used these two sections as a basic General Handbook of Instructions to help them establish the government of the church.

"Behold, I say unto you that all old covenants have I caused to be done away in this thing; and this is a new and an everlasting covenant, even that which was from the beginning." (V. 1). The new and everlasting covenant is the fulness of the Law of Christ and is composed of all covenants, contracts, bonds, obligations, oaths, vows, performances, connections, associations, and expectations that are sealed upon members of the church by the Holy Spirit of Promise, or the Holy Ghost. Those who conform their lives to every element of the New and Everlasting Covenant and follow the example of Christ in every whit will have their calling and election made sure.

The violation of the New and Everlasting Covenant affects everyone. Joseph Fielding Smith warned: "We should wake up to the realization that it is because of the breaking of covenants, especially the new and everlasting covenant, which is the fulness of the gospel as it has been revealed, that the world is to be consumed by fire and few men left. Since this punishment is to come at the time of the cleansing of the earth when Christ comes again, should not Latter-day Saints take heed unto themselves? We have been given the new and everlasting covenant, and many among us have broken it, and many are now breaking it; therefore, all who are guilty of this offense will aid in bringing to pass the destruction in which they will find themselves swept from the earth when the great and dreadful day of the Lord shall come." ("Deseret News," Church Department, p. 7, 10/17/1936).

When we conform our lives to the gospel principles, the earth obeys our commands, but if we alienate ourselves from God, all nature becomes our enemy. In the days of Enoch, when he spoke the word of the Lord by the power of the priesthood, "the earth trembled and the mountains fled, even according to his command; and the rivers of water were turned out of their course; and the roar of the lions was heard out of the wilderness." (Moses 7:13). However, in the Last Days, "plagues shall go forth, and they shall not be taken from the earth" until the Lord has completed His work. (D&C 84:97). "And thus, with the sword and by bloodshed the inhabitants of the earth shall mourn; and with famine, and plague, and earthquake, and the thunder of heaven, and the fierce and vivid lightning also, shall the inhabitants of the earth be made to feel the wrath, and indignation, and chastening hand of an Almighty God, until the consumption decreed hath made a full end of all nations." (D&C 87:6). As Brigham Young declared, when people refuse the gospel, their "land will eventually become desolate, forlorn, and forsaken," as nature refuses to share her bounties. ("Millennial Star," 38:344).

The church had been organized in the same month that this revelation was given, and the Lord took the opportunity to emphasize to Joseph Smith that old covenants had been done away with, and that he should now focus all his energies on bringing to the attention of a world in need the necessity of the saving ordinances of the New and Everlasting Covenant. "Wherefore, although a man should be baptized an hundred times it availeth him nothing," He explained, "for you cannot enter in at the strait gate by the law of Moses, neither by your dead works." (v. 2). "Faith and repentance lead to the strait gate of baptism. Those who pass through this gate, will obtain a remission of sins, gain membership in the church, and open the door leading to personal sanctification through repentance and receipt of the Holy Ghost. One may then find oneself on the path of eternal progression leading to the Celestial Kingdom. The way is strait and narrow. The gospel standard is undeviating, with no room for rationalization or compromise." (Stephen Robinson).

In the church, "we believe that a man must be called of God, by prophecy, and by the laying on of hands by those who are in authority, to preach the gospel, and to administer in the ordinances thereof." (Fifth Article of Faith). Before we can hope to administer these ordinances, however, we must receive our errand from the Lord. As the Savior explained to Hyrum Smith: "Behold, I command you that you need not suppose that you are called to preach until you are called." (D&C 11:15). "No man is authorized to act in the name of the Lord, or to officiate in any ordinance unless he has been properly called. For this reason, the priesthood was restored, and the church organized." (Joseph Fielding Smith, Jr., "Church History & Modern Revelation," 1:57). As Paul taught: "No man taketh this honour unto himself, but he that is called of God." (Hebrews 5:12). Therefore," said the Lord, "Let every man stand in his own office, and labor in his own calling, that the system may be kept perfect." (D&C 84:109-110).

The Savior led by example. When He submitted to baptism, He demonstrated that entrance into the church and kingdom is strait or narrowly defined, leaving no discussion or variance of opinion regarding the prescribed way. After He set the pattern, He said "Come ... follow me." (Matthew 19:21). He taught these principles to the Nephites with unmistakable clarity, saying to them: "On this wise shall ye baptize; and there shall be no disputations among you." (3 Nephi 11:22). There followed explicit instruction to the priesthood leaders of the Nephite church regarding the manner of baptism, for it was vitally important that His doctrine be clearly understood without ambiguity. "And there shall be no disputations among you," He cautioned, "concerning the points of my doctrine." (3 Nephi 11:28). As Nephi asked: "Wherefore, my beloved brethren, can we follow Jesus save we shall be willing to keep the commandments of the Father? And the Father said: Repent ye, repent ye, and be baptized in the name of my Beloved Son." (2 Nephi 31:10-11).

Joseph Smith's contemporaries who questioned the need for re-baptism by those who held the authority of the priesthood in the restored church did not yet have a clear understanding of the four purposes of baptism. 1). it allows us to receive a remission of sins. 2). it enables us to gain admission to the Church of Jesus Christ, "the only true and living church upon the face of the whole earth" with which the Lord is pleased. (D&C 1:31). 3). It provides us with access to personal sanctification through the Holy Ghost. 4). It is outwardly symbolic as the gateway to the blessings reserved for the faithful in the Celestial Kingdom of God. As members of the newly restored Church of Jesus Christ of Latter-day Saints grasped the concept that the purpose of baptism was not to make their lives better, but rather to enable them to enter God's Rest, they became anxious to enjoy that peace of mind born of a settled conviction of the truths of the gospel. Since April 6, 1830, the invitation has been extended to all to enter into God's Rest by abiding by the revealed celestial standard of baptism.

It is "because of your dead works," said the Lord, "that I have caused this last covenant and this church to be built up unto me." (V. 3). "Dead works" have no power to save our souls. As Benjamin taught, it is because of the covenant alone that we are called the children of Christ. It is only when we submit to the ordinances of His gospel that our hearts are changed, and we become His spiritual sons and daughters. (Mosiah 5:7). The ordinance of baptism is the earthly expression of the spiritual reality that we have been born again.

There are three frameworks within which we may develop saving faith in the doctrine of Christ: first, the scriptures, secondly, the inspired words of the prophet/teachers, and thirdly, the promptings of the Holy Ghost. The church of Christ that had so recently been organized would provide the broad organizational matrix within which its members could develop faith unto salvation.

Those who invited the Spirit to attend them as they submitted themselves to baptism were destined to have Pentecostal experiences. Their hearts would be changed, and they would have no more disposition to do evil. Of such, Joseph Smith observed: "The nearer a man approaches perfection, the clearer are his views, and the greater his enjoyments, 'til he has overcome the evils of his life and lost every desire for sin." ("Teachings," p. 51). As they walked into the light, the scales of darkness would fall from the eyes of all who embraced the gospel message.

"Wherefore, enter ye in at the gate, as I have commanded, and seek not to counsel your God." (V. 4). Baptism, properly administered, would be their gateway to the Celestial Kingdom, in the sense that those who had come up out of the world would be oriented onto the strait and narrow path leading to eternal life. This revelation teaches that it is ludicrous to attempt to question the wisdom or judgment of God, or to counsel Him, for He is "from everlasting to everlasting." (Moroni 7:22). His perfection renders us completely helpless to alter the progress or influence the outcome of any activities in which He is engaged. It was when Moses realized his utter dependence upon God that he exclaimed: "Now, for this cause I know that man is nothing, which thing I never had supposed." (Moses 1:10). In their utter dependence upon God to redeem them from their fallen and hopeless state, these early Saints recognized baptism as a portal that would open onto a panorama of infinite possibilities.

To paraphrase Tom Paine, these Last Days
are the times that try our souls. Summer soldiers
and sunshine patriots, when given the chance to share
their testimonies, will recoil at the opportunity that is before
them, but those who boldly declare their faith deserve the love and
thanks of their neighbors. Our timidity is not easily conquered, yet
we have the consolation that the harder the challenge, the more glorious
will be the triumph. What we obtain cheaply, we esteem lightly. 'Tis
dearness only that gives everything its value. Heaven knows
how to put a proper price upon its goods, and it would
be strange, indeed, if so celestial an article as a
vibrant, vital, humbly borne, and eagerly
shared testimony should not
be highly rated.

Heaven Can Wait

"Your days of probation
are past; ye have procrastinated
the day of your salvation until it is
everlastingly too late, and your destruction
is made sure; yea, for ye have sought all the days
of your lives for that which ye could not obtain; and
ye have sought for happiness in doing iniquity, which
thing is contrary to the nature of that righteousness
which is in our great and Eternal Head."
(Helaman 13:38).

In the 1970s, a motion picture entitled "Heaven Can Wait" was produced, that told the story of a man who cheated death, in a way, because he was allowed a second chance to live his life. As I have thought about the film, it strikes me that today I celebrate a milestone in my own life. I've lived one day longer than ever before, and in so doing have set a new personal record for longevity. At least for now, or so it seems, heaven can wait!

But, even as I rejoice, I come to the sobering realization that there is a price to be paid, for I am also one day closer to eternity. I'm okay with that, because I understand that "to everything there is a season, and a time to every purpose under the heaven: A time to be born," as well as "a time to die." (Ecclesiastes 3:1-2). Addressing that subject, Spencer W. Kimball said: "I am confident that there is a time to die, but I also believe that many people die before 'their time' because they are careless, abuse their bodies, take unnecessary chances, or expose themselves to hazards, accidents, and sickness. God controls our lives, and guides and blesses us, but He gives us our agency. We may live our lives in accordance with His Plan for us or we may foolishly shorten or terminate them." ("Teachings of Presidents of the Church," p. 11-21).

What really struck me as I read his observation, however, was the phrase that "God controls our lives" in the sense that He "guides and blesses us," with the qualifying modifier thrown in that He still "gives us our agency." At first glance, control and agency would appear to be antithetical, but they actually do no violence to harmony if we think of them as dynamic counterparts that are the fundamental elements of a process that leads us through a twisted temporal matrix toward the expansive, unrestrained, and seamless reality of "immortality and eternal life." (Moses 1:39). To put it another way, we realize that control and agency are part of the "opposition in all thing" described by Lehi, that are necessary for the Plan of Salvation to work, and that "if these things are not, there is no God." (2 Nephi 2:11 & 13).

He knew beforehand that when we left our first estate, we would be confronted with seemingly contradictory principles relating to His never-ending Parental concern on the one hand, and our promised birthright of agency or free will on the other. To resolve this conundrum, He created the gift of time and stitched it into His Plan as a dimension unique to mortality. By doing so, He was able to powerfully address His own worry for His children without violating His Prime Directive relating to the preservation of their free will.

The imaginative device of time made it possible for us to have experiences similar to His own, to appreciate both vicariously and up close and personally the delight as well as the anxiety that accompany parenthood, and to grow in gratitude for the grounded approach to rearing children that is at the very core of His Plan and our Divine Center. Best of all, His design allowed us to acquire nurturing parenting skills without experiencing the heartbreak of losing our little ones through the friendly fire of either overprotection or indifference. With time on their side, as our children negotiate the minefields of mortality, collateral damage may be kept to a minimum.

You see, God has given us the gift of time that we may have the opportunity to take upon ourselves His armour; our loins girt about with truth, and the breastplate of righteousness, and our feet shod with the preparation of the gospel of peace, above all, taking the shield of faith, the helmet of salvation, and the sword of the Spirit. (See Ephesians 6:13-17). As we inexorably move through time, these noble qualities facilitate our transition from mortal clay to the eternal element of the spirit, without the exercise of inappropriate or misguided control on His part that would have stifled our development from dependency as little children, through independency as self-actualized young adults, and finally to interdependency as committed disciples of Christ. All of the elements of the principles of the Pan work in concert with each other, to complete His grand design.

Our Heavenly Father did all of this seamlessly, and yet "when the veil which encloses us is no more, time will also be no more. (See D&C 84:100). Even now, time is clearly not our natural dimension. Thus it is, that we are never really at home in time. Alternately, we find ourselves impatiently wishing to hasten its passage or to hold back the dawn. We can do neither, of course. We are clearly not at home in time, because we belong to eternity. Time, as much as any one thing, whispers to us that we are strangers here. If time were natural to us, why is it that we have so many clocks and wear wristwatches?" (Neal A. Maxwell, B.Y.U. Devotional Address, 11/27/1979).

The scriptures suggest that time commands a high priority on God's agenda, as evidenced in His handbook of instructions that unfolds the details of the Plan of Salvation. There are 1,381 references to "time" in the scriptures, and 2,749 references to "now." Surprisingly, "eternal life" and "eternal lives" are mentioned only 113 times, and "eternity" just 38 times. Perhaps, it is only for our convenience that we are left with the easily recognizable, manageable, and savory reduction sauce of time. For the moment, at least, we are comfortable living in a linear temporal dimension from which there seems to be only one exit. Our only possible liberation from the arrow of time will come when we lay aside our mortal clay, clothed in the garments of immortality and eternal life. It is in that state of existence when we will finally and fully comprehend His work and glory. (See Moses 1:39).

God's stroke of genius in harnessing the quixotic element of time, by apportioning it in discrete increments of seconds, minutes, hours, and so on, allows thought, feeling, and spontaneity to germinate within the fertile matrix of agency. The scriptures record that before the dawn of creation: "The Lord said: Let us go down. And they went down at the beginning, and they, that is the Gods, organized and formed the heavens and the earth." (Abraham 4:1). From an eternal vantage point, the celestial clock was reset. It was calibrated to a temporal scale by omniscient, omnipotent, and omnipresent Beings, whereas the reckoning had been beforehand "the Lord's time, according to the reckoning of Kolob." (Abraham 3:4).

In a process that is far beyond our comprehension, the earth literally fell from Kolob into time as we know it. Its arrow, that had heretofore traveled in all directions simultaneously, was now locked into just one forward track. At that pivotal moment, a "majestic clockwork" was introduced that set in motion an evolution in thought culminating in Newton's "Principia," and Einstein's Theories of Relativity, ideas that have shaken the foundations of our understanding of physics, or broadly speaking, have mathematically wrestled with the concept of time in the natural world.

In 1916, Einstein unlocked the mercurial side of the nature of time. In a sense, he let the genie out of the bottle. Common folk like us, who are now comfortable with the phrase "It's all relative," seldom recognize the intimate association that expression shares with our exercise of free will, and with our comprehension of God. The truth is, that with our greater appreciation for the relationships between time and space, has come a sense of relief that, in order to honor the principle of agency, God does not have to cease to be, nor is He required to relinquish, His omniscience and omnipotence. This is the only explanation that makes sense of President Kimball's aforementioned declaration that God controls our lives, and guides and blesses us, while at the same time preserving our agency.

We have been able to do wonderful things with the gifts of time, space, and free will, while simultaneously keeping Heavenly Father firmly in the driver's seat. He is still in control, but the key element relating to His children is that "the power (remains) in them, wherein they are agents unto themselves." (D&C 58:28, underlining mine). We use action verbs to describe just how empowering is this gift. Action verbs describe things that we "do." and they presuppose motion in multiple dimensions across a temporal spectrum. We press forward with steadfastness, we feast upon the words of eternal life, we read, we fear, we ponder and pray, we lift the latch, and we force the way. We are bathed in vitality, and we are empowered with an otherworldly serenity. As Bagheera, the powerfully built black panther confided to Mowgli the man-cub: "I had never seen the jungle. They fed me behind bars from an iron pan until one night I felt that I was Bagheera the Panther, and no man's plaything, and I broke the lock with one blow of my paw, and I came away." (Rudyard Kipling, "The Jungle Book").

Our normal lifespan gives us ample opportunity to develop patience as we bide our time, mature in discipline as we take time, delight in diligence as we make time, expand our care and concern as we find time, enhance our thoughtfulness as we spend time, cultivate wisdom as we invest time, and experience pleasure as we share time. It is time that becomes our steady schoolmaster, and when we use it wisely, we do so to engage the curriculum of Christ. (See Galatians 3:24).

Under normal circumstances, heaven can wait, in order to allow us to enjoy the gift of time and to use it with responsibility. In the motion picture, "Indiana Jones and The Last Crusade," the Grail Knight told Indie: "You must choose. But choose wisely, for as the true Grail will bring you life, the false Grail will take it from you." The gospel Plan teaches us how to choose wisely, because it identifies the Holy Grail that must be our quest. Spencer W. Kimball urged: "Do it! Do it right! Do it right now!" because "there's no time like the present; no present like time, and life can be over in the space of a rhyme." (Georgia Byng). Even the rabbit in Alice's "Wonderland" recognized the value of time well-spent, when he exclaimed to no one in particular: "I'm late! I'm late! For a very important date! No time to say 'Hello!' 'Good-bye!' I'm late, I'm late, I'm late!"

As time is measured by The Science and Security Board of The Bulletin of Atomic Scientists, it is 11:55 p.m. on the Doomsday Clock, which represents a countdown to global catastrophe. Since 1947, the Board, including 18 Nobel Laureates, has maintained the clock and pessimistically adjusted its hour and second hand closer and closer to the apocalyptic hour of midnight. With just five minutes left until the clock strikes twelve, we can be sure that the angels in heaven have already raised their swords, and are only waiting upon the Lord's command to let them fall.

With so little time left, what does prudence dictate that we do? We could roll the dice on the assumption that heaven can, and will, wait. We could put the inevitable out of our minds, and dull our senses with the narcotics of immediate gratification and the hope and expectation of deferred consequences. The problem with that flawed perspective is that it leads to faulty perception, impaired judgment, and unfortunate and unanticipated consequences. In real life, things don't end well if we eat, drink, and make merry. The older we get, the more we realize that heaven can't wait, because we are already living in eternity.

Both Newton and Einstein, who, as noted above, toyed with the equations defining the arrow of time, may have been on to something. One or both may have been right, or both could be equally wrong. Time may be absolute in a relative sense, but not necessarily in the way those two pillars of physics would have defined it. Maybe God is the only One that can have it both ways, and Who can tinker with time without paying homage to the laws of physics. He may have found a way to slow down the hectic pace of our lives, in order to allow us to ponder the solemnities of eternity and to engage our agency in ways that only He could envision. In any event, we can be sure that His learning style is the only one that is expansive enough to accommodate the concept of eternal progression, as we view it from a temporal perspective.

If the time space continuum is thought of as a temporal and spatial matrix conceived by God to allow us to be free agents, then the distractions we have learned to throw up may be nothing more than coping mechanisms to help us deal with the day-to-day minor emergencies of mortality. If they are distortions in the fabric of time and space, they will require mending to restore equilibrium in the cosmos. These repair processes might take shape as the laws governing faith, repentance, forgiveness, mercy, justice, and atonement. These laws of the gospel might be more fundamental to our living, moving, and being while living in mortality than most of us realize.

Time and space, with the catalyzing influence of agency, are in perfect balance when they allow us to regroup, reassess, repent, and take purposeful action. Thanks to Heavenly Father's omniscience, the observable elements of time and space, and the immaterial element of agency combine into a single clarifying creation that coalesces to give us a swift kick in our complacency, bringing us to the realization that heaven really can't wait. That comprehension, and that acknowledgement, may be the unified field theory of purposeful action that is the Holy Grail to which the Knight was referring. When we realize that heaven can't wait, our Quest takes on its deserved sense of urgency.

When these elements of the Plan operate in perfect harmony, there is still plenty of wiggle-room within which we may make choices that are refreshingly unhampered by coercion. Free will remains untarnished. The Plan provides us with currency sufficient to satisfy our needs, but also allows us to substitute for legal tender wads of counterfeit cash with which we may attempt to make late payments, with interest tacked on for bad behavior. Remember, the kicker in the aforementioned quotation from the teachings of Spencer W. Kimball is that "God controls our lives, guides and blesses us, but gives us our agency." If we try to subvert the Plan with futile efforts to gain, obtain, and retain blessings we do not deserve, our destabilizing efforts will reward us with nothing more than a pyrrhic victory. Time will grind on, but if we have sown the wind, we will reap the whirlwind.

Heaven cannot wait. The idea that it can is a subtle tactic of the devil, designed to lull us into a false sense of complacency. The idle use of our time is the devil's workshop. Surely, we must be living in heaven right now. We feel each other's pain and loss, as well as pleasure and gain. One of the compelling evidences that heaven cannot wait is our abundant blessing of concern, consideration, kindness, compassion, and empathy. These are qualities that remind us of our former life, and that propel us on the path of progress leading back home. Heaven cannot wait because its benign benevolence is blind to hypocrisy, and demands that we address principles and doctrines that resonate with truth. It is precisely because heaven cannot wait that we "never send to know for whom the bell tolls," because it tolls for each of us. (John Donne, "Meditation 17").

Heaven can't wait, because it is all around us, clamoring for our attention. It begins even "in our infancy! (But then), shades of the prison-house begin to close upon the growing boy, (and) he beholds the light, and whence it flows; he sees it in his joy. The youth, who daily farther from the east must travel, still is nature's priest, and by the vision splendid is on his way attended. At length, the man perceives it die away, and fade into the light of common day." (William Wordsworth, "Ode: Intimations of Immortality from Reflections of Early Childhood").

Heaven is our natural element. It is the ether that fills our lungs with celestial air, and is the state of being to which we all intuitively aspire. God created the physical world, and established laws to govern it that were designed to lead us back into His presence. Because we are spiritual beings having mortal experiences, we sometimes feel that we are not synchronized with our natural element. If that is so, our true greatness, and our power, will only be manifest when "the stars fade away, the sun himself grow dim with age, and nature sink in years." Then, we "shall flourish in immortal youth, unhurt amidst the war of elements, the wreck of matter, and the crash of worlds." (Joseph Addison, "Cato" Act 5, Scene 1).

What are we, that God is mindful of us? For He has made us a little lower than the angels, and has crowned us with glory and honour. (See Psalms 8:14-15). His work and His glory is to bring to pass our immortality and our eternal life. (See Moses 1:39). Just as our earthly fathers would do, He invests time and effort doing things in our behalf, because we are His sons and daughters.

Heavenly Father Knows Us

"Behold, thou art Nephi,
and I am God."
(Helaman 10:6).

"What is man, that thou art mindful of him? And the son of man, that thou visitest him? For thou hast made him a little lower than the angels, and hast crowned him with glory and honour." (Psalms 8:14-15). "For this is my work and my glory, to bring to pass the immortality and eternal life of man." (Moses 1:39). Heavenly Father invests His time and effort doing things for us because we are His sons and daughters, just as our earthly fathers would do.

1. Fathers show their love for us by taking the time to talk with us. There was once a little boy who, before going to bed, was saying his prayers, in a very low voice. His mother gently chided him: "I can't hear what you're saying, son." "I wasn't talking to you, Mom," said the small child. (Mosiah 4:21).

Fathers avoid vain repetition, as should we. For example, a visitor was once invited to offer the invocation for a congregation of L.D.S. inmates at the Utah State Prison. As he was praying, he asked: "Bless all those who could not be here, that Thou might make it possible for them to be here next time."

On another occasion, members of the ward brought their non-member neighbors to a Church meeting, and then to several activities. At the conclusion of each, in the benediction, supplication was made that "no harm or accident might befall us." Finally, the neighbors asked, "Do a lot of Mormons die on the way home from meetings?"

2. Fathers listen to our problems. When we pray, our supplications are often independent of circumstances. One morning, as a family began to eat breakfast, it was Tommy's turn to ask the blessing. He asked Father in Heaven to bless the food, and then he thanked Him for the beautiful day. When the prayer was finished, his mother reminded him that it was 33° outside and freezing rain was falling from the dreary sky. She asked him why he had thanked Father for the beautiful day. Tommy replied: "Mommy, you can't judge the day by the weather."

Faith is fear that has said its prayers. Faith is incompatible with fear. Dozens of times, the scriptures admonish us: "Ask, and ye shall receive." The Lord said: "Now after I have spoken these words, if ye cannot understand them it will be because ye ask not, neither do ye knock, wherefore, ye are not brought into the light, but must perish in the dark." (2 Nephi 32:5). We must persistently, insistently, actively, and consistently solicit the attention of the Lord. But we cannot hope to receive a $10,000.00 answer after offering a 10-cent prayer.

A man was walking along the edge of a steep cliff, when he lost his footing and tumbled off into space. On the way down, he cried to God: "Save me, save me!" Just then, his pant leg snagged a root sticking out of the face of the cliff, and he was jerked to a stop. As he looked around himself to survey his situation, he muttered: "Never mind, God. I'm all right now." We must "pray always, and not faint (and He will) consecrate (our) performance unto (us), that (our) performance may be for the welfare of (our) soul." (2 Nephi 32:9).

But our prayers must be well-intentioned. We should avoid vain repetition that is not so much saying the same thing, as not praying from the heart. A man drowning sputters the word "Help!" once, twice and a third time. The word that he uses over and over again may be the same, but it's coming from his heart.

3. Fathers provide wise counsel. Their best guidance comes from a rapport with the Spirit, that allows our powers expand as we become receptive to flashes of insight as we are cast off into a stream of revelation and carried along in the quickening currents of direct experience with God. The Holy Ghost introduces us to a Plan that releases our energies to be creative, and that fosters freedom. in its design is the perfect law of liberty.

We see that the mysteries of the kingdom as windows of opportunity to better understand prayer, revelation, priesthood authority, baptism, living prophets, the Godhead, the Atonement, repentance, forgiveness, the Sacrament, the endowment, celestial marriage, eternal progression, and exaltation. The Lord has assured us: Ye "shall know of a surety that these things are true, for from heaven will I declare it unto (you)." (D&C 5:12).

4. Fathers provide for our needs. They teach us that wealth is not measured by the quantity, or even by the quality, of our possessions, but by our attitude toward our possessions. "Seek not for riches but for wisdom, and behold, the mysteries of God shall be unfolded unto you, and then shall you be made rich." (D&C 6:7). We cannot escape the fact that we generally obtain those things upon which we focus our attention, for "the soul attracts that which it secretly harbors; that which it loves." (James Allen, "As a Man Thinketh"). That is a good thing, as long as we keep our priorities straight.

5. Fathers teach us to save money for a mission, but also to establish a spiritual bank account. We need to make regular deposits to that account, so that when we need to make a withdrawal, there will be sufficient means to do so. We cannot, in the day of adversity, expect to write checks that cannot be cashed.

6. Fathers provide a nurturing atmosphere in which we can grow to reach our potential. The sturdiest plants that bear the best fruit are those that have deep roots in rich gospel soil. So should it be with all of Heavenly Father's children. They should be provided the mulch of music and art, and the mossy loam of conversation, example, decency, virtue, honor, and spirit in order to give them room to grow freely. Their topsoil must be deep and sustaining and nourishing. We cannot allow it to blow away in a dust bowl of depravity, a tornado of travesty, or a hurricane of hubris, or to be inundated by ignorance, compounded by confusion, or to suffer the anorexia of apathy.

The spirit of the Thirteenth Article of Faith should be always manifest in our homes. "If there is anything virtuous, lovely, or of good report or praiseworthy, we seek after these things." To the extent that we do this, we may expect to see our children blossom as creative individuals who stand out as champions for righteousness. "Train up a child in the way he should go, and when he is old, he will not depart from it." (Proverbs 22:6).

7. Fathers bless us with their wisdom. Letting up when we should be pressing forward can spell the difference between victory and defeat. Keeping our wits about us in challenging situations is crucial, because falling apart is more a mental meltdown than a physical collapse. Proverbs tells us that we should "keep sound wisdom and discretion" in such circumstances. (Proverbs 3:21). It also admonishes us: "Incline thine ear unto wisdom, and apply thine

heart to understanding." (Proverbs 2:2). "For the Lord giveth wisdom: out of his mouth cometh knowledge and understanding. (Proverbs 2:6). "Be ye therefore wise as serpents," counseled the Master. (Matthew 10:16).

8. Fathers create happy memories. When the Lord was ministering ever so briefly among the Nephites following His resurrection, He knew that it would be important for the people to have time to absorb His teachings, that they might have "happy memories." After an exhausting and yet spiritually stirring day, His disciples were told: "Go ye unto your homes, and ponder upon the things which I have said, and ask of the Father, in my name, that ye may understand, and prepare your minds for the morrow, and I come unto you again." (3 Nephi 17:3).

9. Fathers build faith. The highest pinnacle of our spiritual life is the unbroken sunshine of absolute and undoubting faith in God's love. It was in this sense that Helen Keller wrote: "I believe that no good shall be lost, and that all man has willed or hoped or dreamed of good shall exist forever. I believe in the immortality of the soul because I have within me immortal longings. I believe that the state we enter after death is wrought of our own motives, thoughts, and deeds. I believe that my home there will be beautiful with colour, music, and speech of flowers and faces I love. Without this faith, there would be little meaning in my life. I should be a mere pillar of darkness in the dark. Observers in the full enjoyment of their bodily senses pity me, but it is because they do not see the golden chamber in my life where I dwell delighted; for dark as my path may seem to them, I carry a magic light in my heart. Faith, the spiritual strong searchlight, illuminates the way, and although sinister doubts lurk in the shadow, I walk unafraid towards the Enchanted Wood where the foliage is always green, where joy abides, where nightingales nest and sing, and where life and death are one in the presence of the Lord." ("Midstream").

10. Fathers build character. They know that "fame is a vapor, and popularity is an accident, ad that those who cheer you today may curse you tomorrow. In the end, the only thing that endures is character." (Anonymous). Woven throughout the teachings of fathers of all ages is the desire to instill in people a sense of integrity, of character, of honesty, that shines like a light through the eyes. George Washington wrote: "I hope I shall always possess firmness and virtue enough to maintain what I consider the most enviable of all titles, the character of an 'Honest Man.'"

11. Fathers teach us how to respect our bodies and each other, especially within the sacred bounds of marriage and family. "There are but a very few beings in the world who understand rightly the nature of God, and if men do not understand the character of God they do not comprehend themselves." (Joseph Smith). One of the blessings associated with the Restoration of the gospel is the knowledge that the purpose of mortality is to give us the opportunity to develop qualities and character traits that are consistent with the divine nature of our Father in Heaven. Because of the Restoration, ordinances are now available that bind us to receive the blessings of the gospel by means of covenants of action between ourselves and God. These bring us to a greater understanding of His nature. The marriage covenant lies at the apex of these ordinances of exaltation.

Marriage is the most sacred relationship that can exist between a man and a woman. "Marriage is perhaps the most vital of all the decisions and has the most far-reaching effects. Of all the decisions, this one must not be wrong," because our exaltation hinges upon it. (Spencer W. Kimball). Heavenly Father would not have given us the Law of Eternal Marriage were it not possible to become as He is, to internalize His divine nature and develop His character, within the bonds of holy matrimony.

12. Fathers teach us how to show gratitude. Because God "giveth to all men liberally," one of our greatest challenges is to muster the capacity to express real and continuous appreciation. (James 1:5). We who have no resources will be forever in His debt, and yet, we may still "buy wine and milk without money and without price." (Isaiah 55:1). Perhaps it is in a multitude of our expressions of gratitude that we best communicate to our Heavenly Father our love. With the cultivation of gratitude, wonderful things happen. Good eclipses evil. Love overpowers jealousy, hate, and

prejudice. Light drives away darkness. Knowledge banishes ignorance. Humility overwhelms pride. Courtesy checks rudeness. Appreciation overcomes thanklessness. Abundance overshadows poverty. Well-being replaces weakness. Simplicity supplants perplexity. Harmony displaces discord. Faith controls fear. Hope casts out despair. Charity subdues selfishness. Joy deposes unhappiness, sadness, dejection, and misery. Confidence is substituted for timidity. Certainty dethrones bewilderment. Assurance dislodges discouragement and even despair.

13. Fathers provide us with experience in the learning laboratory of life. Most young people in the United States spend twelve years gaining what some people call "an education." But for some, the process is sporadic at best. Often it is put on hold, or worse, it stops altogether. All of us remember in elementary school going back in September and writing an essay entitled: "How I spent my summer." So, the real questions may be: "Does education continue even when we are not in school? Does education cease during our undisciplined free time? Does eternal progression relate to education? Does the Latter-day Saint tradition relating to education have a foundation in gospel principles? Is improvement through education a key to successful living?" Our fathers can help us to develop perspective as we ponder these questions, and act upon our promptings.

14. Fathers teach us how to focus on the important things. While they drew, a kindergarten teacher walked up and down the rows of desks in her classroom of children, observing their work. She stopped beside one little girl and asked what her drawing was. She replied, "I'm drawing a picture of God." The teacher paused, and then said, "But no one knows what God looks like." Without missing a beat or looking up from her paper, the little girl replied, "They will in a minute." Though tender in years, this child had what we might call "focus."

If we ignore this innate urge to focus, and allow ourselves to be habitually distracted by trivial concerns, we sin by omission and risk settling for a life in a "second-class hotel" of our own making. There is, after all, "a tide in the affairs of men, which, taken at the flood, leads on to fortune. Omitted, all the voyage of their life is bound in shallows and in miseries." (Shakespeare, Brutus, in "Julius Caesar," Act 4, Scene 2).

15. Fathers help us to multiply our talents. A talent is a stewardship or responsibility in the Kingdom of God. Paul taught that under the best of circumstances, we "are one body in Christ" with individual gifts. (Romans 12:5-6). After we have linked our fortunes to the church, we "are no more strangers and foreigners, but fellowcitizens with the saints, and of the household of God." (Ephesians 2:19-20). Within this vast congregation "are diversities of gifts." (1 Corinthians 12:4-31). The implication is that every member of the flock has talents that may be used to bless the lives of others living within the household.

As we discover our talents and make efforts to improve and develop them, we would do well to remember the law of inertia. We need to get moving and sustain our momentum, remembering that if we always do what we always did, we'll always get what we always got. Even if we are on the right road, we're going to get run over, if we just sit there. Those who seek to improve their talents have high ideals, which "are like stars. We will not succeed in touching them with our hands. But, like the seafaring man in the desert of waters, we choose them as our guides, and following them, we will reach our destiny." (Carl Shurz, BYU Studies 16:40.

We must share our talents with others, and not be like the "very cautious man who never laughed or played; who never risked and never tried; who never sang or prayed. And when, one day, he passed away, his insurance was denied. For since he never really lived, they claimed he never died." (Anonymous).

16. Fathers teach us how to multi-task. We can even learn how to multi-task righteousness. At the beginning of each day, we can wake up with a prayer in our hearts even as, in other ways, we prepare for the day. While attending to a host of responsibilities, Harold B. Lee was often asked difficult ecclesiastical questions. He often answered: "In the

early hours of the morning, while I was pondering that very question," Multi-taskers like him seize every opportunity to ponder the important questions of life. While brushing our teeth at the break of day, we keep pads of paper and pencils on the counter, because thoughts pop into our minds relating to the complexities that lie before us. Whoever invented 3 M sticky notes had multi-tasking in mind. When we multi-task, the capabilities of our minds are more breathtaking than the most sophisticated computer that can "think" only in a linear fashion.

We face new challenges every day, and conflicts inevitably begin to pile up, but using gospel principles as multi-tasking tools helps us to successfully cope. At one and the same time, as we deal with issues that demand our conscious attention, there are underlying currents of honesty, benevolence, patience, courage, and virtue that define our behavior, focus our energy, and give coherence to our actions. How we comport ourselves is, essentially, a witness of our faith and testimony. Our charity, compassion, and tolerance are silent evidence of our core values. A harmonic resonance of the Spirit within us allows our character to run on cruise-control even as we multi-task.

17. Fathers teach us things we could not otherwise know. Without such revelatory guidance, we cannot comprehend the two great opposites that are at work in the universe, nor can we create order in the seeming chaos of existence. We cannot enjoy the holy and exalted state of happiness unless we are in harmony with gospel principles and in opposition to satanic forces. They teach us that there was opposition from the beginning, and that we cannot enjoy moral agency that leads to happiness unless we learn to reject the enticements of Satan, whom God has allowed for a wise purpose to encroach upon the fortress of our spirituality. Mortality thus becomes a time of testing and of putting to the proof. Agency and opposition are powerful forces that constantly refine us in the fiery blast furnace of experience. We can never eliminate the consequences that hang over our heads as the dangling Sword of Damocles. Always at issue is the question whether we will repent and take advantage of the Atonement of the Savior.

18. Fathers provide a nurturing atmosphere in which we can grow. Even the best athletes cannot hope to compete competitively, much less have podium finishes, unless they understand the rules of the game and have been provided a foundation upon which to build winning strategies. No one can reasonably expect to be able to successfully engage in the game of life, unless they possess the rule book and comprehend the guidelines that governs our existence. As Alma said: "God has had mercy on us, and made these things known unto us that we might not perish; yea, and he has made these things known unto us beforehand, because he loveth our souls as well as he loveth our children; therefore, in his mercy he doth visit us by his angels, that the plan of salvation might be made known unto us as well as unto future generations." (Alma 24:14).

19. Fathers teach us how to set realistic goals. Often, our problem is not that we set our goals too high and fail to reach them. Rather, it is that we set them too low, and we do reach them, far too easily and with minimal effort. The masses settle for mediocrity, while once in a while, one or two souls forget themselves through service right into heaven. Calvin Coolidge said: "We cannot do everything at once, but we can do something at once." While still a young man, Abraham Lincoln, declared: "I will prepare myself, and someday my chance will come." Making the effort, however small, is the critical element that initiates the undertaking of successful endeavors. It may be too late to write a new beginning to our life story, but it is never too late to begin a new ending.

If we work without vision, we will become mired in details, and conceptually punch a time clock, work for pay, and be satisfied with an hourly wage. If we have vision, but don't understand that inspiration and perspiration are inseparably interrelated, we will be living in a dream world. But if we have both vision and the determination to work to achieve our goals, it will be our destiny to soar with eagles.

20. Fathers teach us not only how to endure, but to do so in righteousness. When we are on the path leading to eternal life, it is important to move forward with purpose. It is not enough to have been baptized and to have received the Holy

Ghost. We must not camp out on the path and remain in a passive or vegetative state. The dictionary is the only place where success comes before work. Hence, the Savior's observation: "Many will say to me in that day, Lord, Lord, have we not prophesied in thy name, and in thy name have cast out devils, and in thy name done many wonderful works?" (3 Nephi 14:22).

The scriptures teach about come-from-behind victories, for "the race is not to the swift, nor the battle to the strong, neither yet bread to the wise, nor yet riches to men of understanding, nor yet favour to men of skill; but time and chance happeneth to them all." (Ecclesiastes 9:15). When we believe that we are winners, anything can happen.

21. Fathers instill in us an appreciation of the principles that relate to happiness. If we take it for granted or if we abandon the principles upon which it is founded, happiness may slip between our fingers and be lost forever. Sometimes, we use our agency inappropriately and make poor investment choices with our time and talents. Frequently, we are left with only a wad of counterfeit currency with which we must make late payments with interest tacked on for bad behavior. And still, in our efforts to gain, we seldom obtain, and more rarely retain feelings of true happiness. Never learning the hard lessons of life, we continually look to gods of wood and stone that have no power to redeem us from our misery. Our worldly ways leave us vulnerable to a spiritual sickness that mimics the symptoms of those with advanced diabetes whose peripheral circulation has been compromised. We become numb to "the better angels of our nature." (Abraham Lincoln). As we lose the capacity to touch and feel, we become more and more isolated from the sensitivity to our surroundings that is critical to the success of the Plan. We may become inured to our condition, overcompensate with a knee-jerk reaction, and develop a "lead foot" as we put the pedal to the metal. Although life in the fast lane may be thrilling, when it "takes our breath away" we may not realize that our reduced lung capacity has robbed us of what could have been ours. Cheap thrills can never replace the lofty goals of the Plan. They are counter-productive and defeat its objectives that would have allowed us to enjoy our journey at an unhurried pace.

22. Fathers sometimes have the means to provide for our secular education, but always plumb the depths of their reserves to provide for our spiritual education. We pay dearly for our secular education, and expect a return on our investment. But as we study the gospel, we obtain a far more valuable spiritual education. At the moment of our baptism, each of us is called and chosen to enroll in the Lord's university, to participate in a Bachelor of Independent Study Fine Arts program that demands very little temporal tuition for enrollment. The only entrance requirement is a ready heart and a willing mind. Its design is solely intended to expand the scope of our Father's Plan to all of His children. It is variously called The Plan of Salvation, The Plan of Our God, The Plan of Redemption, The Plan of Mercy, The Great and Eternal Plan of Deliverance from Death, The Merciful Plan of The Great Creator, and my favorites, The Plan of Happiness, and The Great Plan of Happiness. Whatever its name, the Plan overshadows His ordained core curriculum of universal missionary work by those who have matriculated into His program. The Plan is a diagram to follow, that illustrates how to make our way through mortality, a map to guide us Home, a table that documents the perils and pitfalls we must avoid, a chart to fall back on when tempests beset us, and a graph that outlines and defines our progress on the pathway to perfection. Like the World Wide Web that requires only computer literacy, access to a network with an I.P address, and relevant hardware and software, the elements of the Plan have the potential to bring meaning to a chaotic world and fluency to our spiritually illiteracy. In simple terms, the Plan is our key to happiness.

23. Fathers bless our lives with opportunities to experience opposition and disappointment. It is for our benefit that we become acquainted with evil as well as with good, with darkness as well as with light, with error as well as with truth, with sorrow as well as with happiness, and with punishment for the infraction of eternal laws as well as with the blessings that follow obedience.

24. Fathers help us to resist Satan. Satan wants us to believe that he does not exist, but our fathers know best. He

has always raged "in the hearts of men, and stir(ed) them up to anger against that which is good." (2 Nephi 28:20). Sometimes he pacifies us and lulls us into a false sense of worldly security, making us believe that we are gaining something when we are really losing. He does this very subtly, so as not to awaken our senses to the reality of what is happening. (2 Nephi 28:21). His favorite strategy is to move us from brilliant, dazzling white, through every shade of grey, to a fathomless black which, by subtraction, is the absence of worthy thoughts, words, deeds, and an unprincipled moral vacuum. He flatters us, and whispers that he does not exist, which leads us to judge ourselves to be deserving of peace and plenty, without having really earned the reward.

25. Fathers teach us about the consequences of sin. "Ye look upon me as a teacher," Jacob said to his people, many of whom were his own children, and so "it must needs be expedient that I teach you the consequences of sin. Behold, my soul abhorreth sin, and my heart delighteth in righteousness." (2 Nephi 9:48-49).

26. Fathers teach us how to repent. The Lord Himself told Adam, His first mortal child: "Wherefore, teach it unto your children, (His own grandchildren), that all men, everywhere, must repent, or they can in nowise inherit the kingdom of God, for no unclean thing can dwell there, or dwell in his presence." (Moses 6:57).

27. Fathers teach us about the nature of time. It seems to be human nature to want to hold on to it dearly, for the prospect of death is terrifying to those who think that time will grind to a halt, and the body will turn to dust. Heavenly Father looks at it differently. "Someone once said that time is a predator that stalks us all our lives. I prefer to think of it as a companion that accompanies us on the journey, reminding us to cherish every moment." (Captain Jean Luc Picard). Fathers teach their children to manipulate time and make the most of their gift of mortality, that they might insure their happiness and continued prosperity in eternity. They teach their children to give careful attention to the way in which they spend their time, and also the care with which they make time, the diligence with which they find time, and the discipline they exhibit in taking time. This process allows their children to create more time for accomplishment in their already busy lives! Only foolish people who have lost their focus on things of real worth would treat time so disdainfully that they would waste time, or would actually kill time.

28. Fathers give us responsibility, and the freedom to exercise our agency. They honor the eternal principle of free will. God counseled Adam: "Thou mayest choose for thyself, for it is given unto thee." (Moses 3:17). It is riskier, but it is the only way that eternal progress can be possible. "Behold," He declared in the Garden after the Fall, "the man is become as one of us to know good and evil." (Moses 4:28). It was obvious to Him that choices and opposites would be necessary if our immortality and eternal lives were to be made possible through the Atonement of Christ. In the process, rather than enslaving us in good habits, God would repeatedly give us the opportunity to voluntarily recommit ourselves to covenants of obedience to true and eternal principles.

29. Fathers provide us with experiences that allow us to develop trust in ourselves. It is educational to think of ourselves as disciples. Because we have learned to restrain ourselves through obedience to eternal principles, our choices expand exponentially to secure our freedom. Our education becomes a repetitively reinforcing pattern of behavior that creates a blueprint for success. "You may know me," said the personality trait. "I'm your constant companion. I'm your greatest helper; I'm your heaviest burden. I will push you onward or drag you down to failure. I am at your command. Half the tasks you do might as well be turned over to me I'm able to do them quickly, and I'm able to do them the same every time if that's what you want. I'm easily managed; all you have to do is be firm with me. Show me exactly how you want it done; after a few lessons I'll do it automatically. I'm the servant of all great men and women, and the servant of failures, too. But I work with all the precision of a marvelous computer. You may run me for profit, or you may run me to ruin; it really makes no difference to me. Work with me. Be easy with me and I will destroy you. Be firm with me and I'll put the world at your feet. Who am I? I'm Habit!" (Anonymous).

What if we committed ourselves to a perpetual program of self-improvement and looked upon "graduation" as a commencement or the beginning of a wonderful journey? Our formal education would prepare us how to think, how to process information, and how to act. If we were to approach our continuing education with an appreciation of the dynamic influence it could have in our lives, and if we were aware of its power to focus our energy and steady our course, it would become a vehicle to reach for the stars. "Of all the communities available to us," said Albert Einstein, "there is not one I would want to devote myself to, except for the society of the true searchers, which has very few living members at any time."

30. Fathers allow us to experience both the positive and the negative consequences of our own actions. The reality is that we miss 100% of the shots we don't take. We sometimes fail to appreciate that most of us also miss about 50% of the shots we do take. The Plan of Salvation operates roughly the same way. Earth life is a time to see if we will behave as we know we should. Because we often do not, "there was a time granted unto man to repent, yea, a probationary time, a time to repent and serve God." (Alma 42:4). And so, "the days of the children of men were prolonged, according to the will of God, that they might repent while in the flesh; wherefore, their state became a state of probation." (2 Nephi 2:21). If we become angry or frustrated with ourselves when we do not live up to our potential, and especially if we throw in the towel, call it a day, or give up entirely, our "days of probation are past; (because we) have procrastinated the day of (our) salvation until it is everlastingly too late, and (our) destruction is made sure." (Helaman 13:38).

31. Fathers sometimes intervene in our behalf, to spare us the unpleasant consequences of our foolish behavior. Fathers who have known hardship are usually much better able to help their children to face adversity. This principle may help to explain why so many church members, even after living Christ-like lives, are not spared such challenges in their mortal experiences.

32. Fathers sacrifice for us. They teach us about the ultimate sacrifice, the Atonement, that can save us from our natural state of carnality, sensuality, and devilish inclinations. They teach us how the Atonement triggers the Law of Mercy, which mitigates for those who conform to its requirements the effects of the first Law, which demands Justice. The Atonement lifts us to a state of holiness, spirituality, and angelic innocence. The Apostle Paul confirmed: "By grace ye are saved, thru faith, and that not of ourselves; it is the gift of God." (Ephesians 2:8).

33. Fathers provide role models to follow. Their example sets the moral and ethical standard upon which we can anchor our own belief systems. Others, who make value judgments based on endocrine secretions, rather than on the unchanging and eternally validated laws of the gospel, have no such foundation, but instead build their houses on the shifting sands of expediency and circumstance. Fathers now that should their children seek to be lights unto themselves, they will fail to improve the quality of their dispositions, because their intellects can never bridge the gap between rational behavior and faith, nor can they provide the mortar necessary to build character.

(The) Heavens Were Opened

"Now Ammon said unto him:
I can assuredly tell thee, O king, of
a man that can translate the records; for
he has wherewith that he can look, and translate
all records that are of ancient date; and it is a gift
from God ... And Ammon said that a seer s a revelator
and a prophet also; and a gift which is greater can no man
have ... But a seer can know of things which are past, and
also of things which are to come, and by them shall all
things be revealed, or rather, shall secret things be
made manifest, and hidden things shall come
to light, and things which are not known
shall be made known by them, and
also things shall be made known
by them which otherwise
could not be known."
(Mosiah 8:13 &
16-17).

"Thou shalt be called a seer, a translator, a prophet, an apostle of Jesus Christ, an elder of the church through the will of God the Father, and the grace of your Lord Jesus Christ." (D&C 21:1).

"This revelation was given at the organization of the church," April 6, 1830. (Superscript to Section 21). Although they had earlier been ordained to the Melchizedek Priesthood, Joseph Smith and Oliver Cowdery were told to defer ordaining each other to the office of Elder within the priesthood until the Church was formally organized. (H.C., 1:61). Now, with the foundation of the church in place, by "the laying on of hands, Joseph ... ordained Oliver an elder of the church; and Oliver similarly ordained Joseph." (Superscript).

A seer is an interpreter and clarifier of eternal truth who walks in the Lord's light with open eyes. (See Mosiah 8:13). "A seer is one who may see God, who may talk with God, who may receive personal instruction from God. Our prophet is a seer and a revelator. There must be someone to whom the people can turn and trust, who can speak for God. God must have someone on earth who can point the way and say: 'This is true.' God has given us a living seer and prophet (who) reveals personal testimony that Jesus is in very deed the Risen Savior, the Living God." (Theodore Burton, C.R., 10/1961). A seer is literally a 'see-er' who has the right to use the Urim and Thummim. (J.S.H. 1:35).

By seers "shall all things be revealed." (Mosiah 8:17). Helen Keller once remarked: "There is one tragedy in life worse than to be born without sight, and that is to be born with sight but without vision." A loving God has "provided a means that man, through faith, might work mighty miracles; therefore, he becometh a great benefit to his fellow beings." (Mosiah 8:18). A seer can see the storm clouds before they appear on the horizon.

A translator is one who converts the written language of one culture into another, or one who gives language a clearer meaning, or who preserves by revelation the thoughts and intent of original writers. Joseph would soon commence his work on the King James Version of the Bible. He called his work a translation. "This is apparently the sense in which he understood the work he was doing with the Bible. Since, in part, he was effecting a restoration of lost meaning and material, and since the Bible did not originate in English, his work to some degree would amount to an inspired, or revelatory, translation into English of that which the ancient prophets and apostles had written in Hebrew, Aramaic, and/or Greek." (Robert J. Matthews, "A Plainer Translation - Joseph Smith's Translation of The Bible," p. xxx).

A prophet is a teacher of the body of truth revealed by the Lord. Under inspiration, he explains it to the understanding of the people. The word "prophet" comes from the Greek "prophetes" that means, "inspired teacher." "He that prophesieth," wrote Paul, "speaketh unto men to edification, and exhortation, and comfort." (1 Corinthians 14:3). By scriptural definition, "the testimony of Jesus Christ is the spirit of prophecy. (Revelation 19:10). In Old Testament times, Moses exclaimed: "Would God that all the Lord's people were prophets, and that the Lord would put his spirit upon them!" (Numbers 11:26-29). To that end, schools of prophets existed in Old Testament times that were the pattern for the one started by Joseph Smith in 1832. (See D&C 88:127 & 136-37, & 90:7, 10 & 13).

Isaiah was a prophet of God, confirming to all Israel: "Behold, I have declared the former things from the beginning; and they went forth out of my mouth, and I showed them." (Isaiah 48:3). It is one thing to recount the dealings of God with His children from the beginning. Those events that have come to pass which were prophesied long ago serve to confirm our faith and strengthen our testimony that God maintains a close relationship with us. It is quite another thing to witness the prophetic power of the servants of God who reveal truths that have long been hidden from the world. "New things do I declare," wrote Isaiah, and "before they spring forth I tell you of them." (Isaiah 42:9). I declare "the end from the beginning, and from ancient times the things that are not yet done, saying, My counsel shall stand, and I will do all my pleasure. Yea, I have spoken it, I will also bring it to pass; I have purposed it, I will also do it. Hearken unto me, ye stouthearted, that are far from righteousness." (Isaiah 46:10-11).

This counsel from Isaiah is appropriate to all ages, and the similar word of the Lord has been reiterated in our day: "We believe all that God has revealed, all that He does now reveal, and we believe that He will yet reveal many great and important things pertaining to the Kingdom of God." (9th Article of Faith).

Continual guidance from the Spirit of God, known as revelation, is critical to vital religion, for it "cannot be maintained and preserved on the theory that God dealt with our human race only in the far past ages, and that the Bible is the only evidence we have that our God is a living, revealing, communicating God. If God ever spoke, He is still speaking. He is the great I Am, not the great He was." (Rufus Jones, "Time Magazine," 10/11/1948).

The Lord wanted to make very clear to the church that had on that very day (April 6, 1830) been restored to the earth, that Joseph Smith was His prophet. In ancient Israel, the Lord had repeatedly foretold events long before they came to pass, lest in the hardness and obstinacy of the people they should claim that it was their idols and images that had initiated the events. As Isaiah explained: "I showed them for fear lest thou shoudst say - Mine idol hath done them, and my graven image, and my molten image hath commanded them." (Isaiah 48:5).

Doctrine & Covenants Section 21 stands as a testimony against those who would take the credit for the fulfillment of prophecy. Speaking in the name of the Lord, Isaiah declared to an apostate world: "For mine own sake will I do this, for I will not suffer my name to be polluted, and I will not give my glory unto another." (Isaiah 48:11). Satan is a skillful imitator who relentlessly distorts our perception of events until even the very elect may be misled. "For there shall arise false Christs, and false prophets," warned Jesus, "and shall shew great signs and wonders; insomuch that, if it were possible, they shall deceive the very elect." (Matthew 24:24). When He taught this principle, the Savior did not say that there would be no-one to guide the people, but only made the distinction between true and false prophets.

An apostle is "a special witness of the name of Christ in all the world - thus differing from other officers in the church in the duties of their calling." (D&C 107:23). All men may, by virtue of the priesthood and the gift of the Holy Ghost, be witnesses for Christ. But only apostles hold the fulness of authority, keys, and priesthood to open the way to preach the gospel to every nation, kindred, tongue, and people.

The Lord told Joseph Smith: "To some it is given by the Holy Ghost to know that Jesus Christ is the Son of God, and that he was crucified for the sins of the world. To others it is given to believe on their words, that they also might have eternal life if they continue faithful." (D&C 46:13-14). "And by doing so, the Lord God prepareth the way that the residue of men may have faith in Christ, that the Holy Ghost may have place in their hearts." (Words of Mormon 1:32).

Consequently, as an Apostle of Jesus Christ, Joseph Smith was commissioned to declare with boldness his witness of the truth, that faith might be developed in the hearts of those who heard his testimony. His was a unique perspective. He "was called of God, and ordained an apostle of Jesus Christ, to be the first elder of this church." (D&C 20:2). "I had actually seen a light," he said, "and in the midst of that light I saw two Personages, and they did in reality speak to me; and though I was hated and persecuted for saying that I had seen a vision, yet it was true ... and who am I that I can withstand God ... For I had seen a vision; I knew it, and I knew that God knew it, and I could not deny it, neither dared I do it." (J.S.H. 1:25).

Joseph also declared: "Could we read and comprehend all that has been written from the days of Adam on the relation of man to God and angels in a future state, we should know very little about it. Reading the experience of others or the revelation given to them can never give us a comprehensive view of our condition and true relation to God. Knowledge of these things can only be obtained by experience through the ordinances of God set forth for that purpose. Could you gaze into heaven five minutes, you would know more that you would by reading all that has ever been written on the subject." (H.C., 6:50).

In his history, Joseph repeatedly stated that he had been given instruction that the world was not yet prepared to receive: "And many other things did (the personage) say unto me, which I cannot write at this time." (J.S.H. 1:20). Moroni "quoted many other passages of scripture, and offered many explanations which cannot be mentioned here." (J.S.H. 1:41). On one occasion, Joseph Smith lamented; "Would to God I could tell you what I know. But you would call it blasphemy, and there are men upon this stand who would want to take my life. if the church knew all of the commandments, one half they would reject through prejudice and ignorance." (Ivan J. Barrett, "Joseph Smith & The Restoration," p. 522).

Elder is the general title used to address one who holds the Melchizedek Priesthood. "An individual who holds a share in the priesthood and continues faithful to his calling will secure to himself not only the privilege of receiving, but the knowledge how to receive the things of God, that he may know the mind of God continually; and he will be enabled to discern between right and wrong, between the things of God and the things that are not of God. And the priesthood, the spirit that is within him, will continue to increase until it becomes like a fountain of living water; until it is like the tree of life; until it is one continued source of intelligence and instruction to that individual." (Brigham Young, J.D. 3:192).

Joseph Smith was "inspired of the Holy Ghost to lay the foundation" of the church, "and to build it up unto the most holy faith." (D&C 21:2). in the first decade of the Nineteenth Century, "men were following with bated breath the march of Napoleon and waiting with feverish impatience for news of the wars. And all the while in their homes babies were being born. But who could think about babies? Everybody was thinking about battles. (In that decade) there stole into the world a host of heroes: Gladstone was born in Liverpool; Tennyson at the Somersby Rectory; and Oliver Wendell Holmes in Massachusetts. Abraham Lincoln was born in Kentucky, and music was enriched by the arrival of Felix Mendelssohn in Hamburg." Joseph and Lucy Mack Smith welcomed the arrival of a son, and named him after his father and grandfather before him. "But nobody thought of babies; everybody was thinking of battles. Yet which of the battles mattered more than the babies? We fancy God can manage His word only with great battalions, when all the time, He is doing it with beautiful babies. When a wrong wants righting, or a truth wants preaching, or a continent wants discovering, God sends a baby into the world to do it." (Attributed to F.M. Bareham, but unverifiable).

"When theologians are reeling and stumbling, when lips are pretending and hearts are wandering, and people are running to and fro, seeking the word of the Lord and cannot find it, when clouds of error need dissipating and spiritual darkness needs penetrating and heavens need opening, a little infant is born." (Spencer W. Kimball, C.R., 4/1960).

There are "intelligences that were organized before the world was, and among all these there were many of the noble and great ones; (And God said) these I will make my rulers." (Abraham 3:22-23). Joseph Smith, who commenced the work of restoration and lay the foundation, was surely in this company. Even before he received the plates from which The Book of Mormon was translated, he went to the Hill Cumorah "at the end of each year, and at each time (he) found the same messenger there, and received instruction and intelligence from him at each of (his) interviews, respecting what the Lord was going to do, and how and in what manner his kingdom was to be conducted in the last days." (J.S.H. 1:54).

Today it is our habit in the church "to think of the restoration of the gospel as a past event," wrote Bruce R. McConkie. "It is true that we have the fulness of the everlasting gospel in the sense that we have those doctrines, priesthoods, and keys which enable us to gain the fullness of reward in our Father's kingdom. But the restoration of the wondrous truths known to Adam, Enoch, Noah, and Abraham has scarcely commenced. The sealed portion of The Book of Mormon is yet to be translated. All things are not to be revealed anew until the Lord comes. The greatness of the era of restoration is yet ahead. We are now making a beginning, but the transcendent glories and wonders to be revealed are for the future. Much of what Isaiah, prophet of the restoration, has to say is yet to be fulfilled." (Bruce R. McConkie, "10 Keys to Understanding Isaiah").

The "church was organized and established in the year of your Lord eighteen hundred and thirty, in the fourth month, and on the sixth day of the month which is called April." (V. 3). On that date, "Joseph Smith and others met at the Peter Whitmer home in Fayette, New York. On this momentous occasion, six brethren officially organized the church. The Lord also spoke through Joseph to the church, giving the revelation that is now D&C Section 21. The Prophet said of this occasion: "After a happy time spent in witnessing and feeling for ourselves the powers and blessings of the Holy Ghost, through the grace of God bestowed upon us, we dismissed with the pleasing knowledge that we were now individually members of, and acknowledged of God, 'The Church of Jesus Christ." (H.C., 1:79).

The Lord admonished those who had joined with the church: "Give heed unto all" of Joseph Smith's "words and commandments which he shall give unto you as he receiveth them. For his word ye shall receive, as if from mine own mouth." (V. 4-5). When the prophet of the Lord speaks when moved upon by the Holy Ghost, his words assume "the power of God unto salvation." (D&C 68:4). Joseph Smith taught: "Wherever there is a righteous man on the earth unto whom God revealed His word and gave power and authority to administer in His name, and wherever there is a priest of God, a minister who has power and authority from God to administer in the ordnances of the gospel and officiate in the Priesthood of God, there is the Kingdom of God." (H.C., 5:256).

"For by doing these things," the Lord will bless us in three distinct ways. (1) "The gates of hell shall not prevail against you; yea, and (2) the Lord God will disperse the powers of darkness from before you, and (3) cause the heavens to shake for your good, and his name's glory." (V. 6). The gates of hell are the entrance to the so-called 'spirit prison of the unjust,' where the wicked go to await the day when they come forth to participate in the second resurrection of the damned. (See D&C 76:13, 23, & 73, 138:8 & 28, Isaiah 61:1, 1 Peter 3:19, & Moses 7:57).

At the opening of every Dispensation of the gospel, Satan has made a frontal attack against the dissemination of truth. He deceived the sons and daughters of Adam and Eve in the First Gospel Dispensation. At the beginning of the Mosaic Dispensation, "Satan came tempting him saying: Moses, son of man, worship me." (Moses 1:12). In the Meridian of Time, Satan attacked the Master Himself. (Luke 4:1-13). We learn from the Prophet Joseph Smith that Satan also hotly contested the opening of the Dispensation of The Fulness of Times. (J.S.H. 1:15).

The cloak of darkness that he commands is the power of delusion, confusion, strife, bitterness, and class distinction that stirs the wicked up to anger and blinds their minds. "The devil has done very well in his various projects of distorting the truth or using a little truth to color lies and deceive people of the world. There is only one clear, bright light of truth, but there is a many faceted flickering, dancing light show of deceptive error with many shades of darkness engulfing the world. It is difficult sometimes to pick out truth and identify it amid its various counterfeits." ("Gospel Doctrine Teacher's Manual").

Truman Madsen observed of those groping about in spiritual confusion that, "in their efforts to clarify their consideration of Christ, they often simply multiply mirrors and study angles without increasing the light. The New Dispensation brought a flood of light that did not simply replace the darkness, but illuminated elements and principles and their relationships, that heretofore had been only dimly perceived." ("B.H. Roberts, "The Truth, The Way, The Life," p. 263).

Surely, the heavens will shake in defense of the righteous. Joseph Fielding Smith, Jr. declared: "No power on earth or hell can overthrow or defeat that which God has decreed. Every plan of the Adversary will fail; for the Lord knows the secret thoughts of men, and sees the future with a vision clear and perfect, even as though it were in the past." ("Church History and Modern Revelation," 1:26).

Joseph Smith explained to John Wentworth: "No unhallowed hand can stop the work from progressing. Persecutions may rage, mobs may combine, armies may assemble, calumny may defame, but the truth of God will go forth boldly, nobly, and independent, until it has penetrated every continent, visited every clime, swept every country, and sounded in every ear; till the purposes of God shall be accomplished, and the Great Jehovah shall say 'The work is done.'" (H.C., 4:540). "The truth is, that after the thousands of attacks, and scores of books that have been published, not one criticism has survived, and millions have borne witness that the Lord has revealed to them the truth of this marvelous work." (Joseph Fielding Smith, Jr., "Church History and Modern Revelation," 1:28-29). "To the Son is given the power of the resurrection, the power of the redemption, the power of salvation, the power to enact laws for the carrying out and accomplishment of the design. Hence, life and immortality are brought to light, the gospel is introduced, and He becomes the Author of eternal life and exaltation." (John Taylor, "Mediation and Atonement," p. 171-172).

"For thus saith the Lord God: (Joseph Smith) "have I inspired to move the cause of Zion in mighty power for good, and his diligence I know, and his prayers I have heard." (V. 7). Even though conditions in the world are degenerating and peace will be taken from the wicked, those in Zion will enjoy the safety and security that only righteousness can guarantee, and there will be such an outpouring of the Spirit that "the earth (will) be full of the knowledge of the Lord, as the waters cover the sea." (Isaiah 11:9).

We would do well to emulate B.H. Roberts, who had a great testimony of the prophet, and "having gone word by word and line by line through his writings, and having read everything he could find on his life, found Joseph Smith to be possessed of a deeper and richer comprehension of Christ than anyone he had read in the Christian tradition since the apostles. Through all Roberts' buffetings and his intellectual probings, honing his own mind with the major figures in the history of Western thought, this conviction never diminished. And as his extensive knowledge of the alternatives increased, his convictions deepened: Joseph Smith told the truth. Joseph Smith was a prism of the Lord Jesus Christ." (Truman Madsen, "Defender of The Faith," p. 93).

Higher Dimensional Realities

"And behold, the heavens were opened,
and they were caught up into heaven, and saw
and heard unspeakable things. And it was forbidden
them that they should utter; neither was it given unto them
power that they could utter the things which they saw and heard.
And whether they were in the body or out of the body, they could
not tell; for it did seem unto them like a transfiguration of
them, that they were changed from this body of flesh
into an immortal state, that they could behold
the things of God. (3 Nephi 28:13-15).

"And it shall come to pass in the last days, saith God, that I will pour out my spirit upon all flesh; and your sons and your daughters shall prophesy, and your young men shall see visions, and your old men shall dream dreams." (Acts 2:27 & Joel 2:28). Today, the Holy Ghost is being poured out in rich abundance, and to the Saints in particular. Joseph Smith promised: "God shall give unto you knowledge by His Holy Spirit, yea, by the unspeakable gift of the Holy Ghost, that has not been revealed since the word was until now." Ours is a time when "nothing shall be withheld ... All thrones and dominions, principalities, and powers, shall be revealed ... And also, if there be bounds set to the heavens or to the seas, or to the dry land, or to the sun, moon, or stars, (all this) shall be revealed." (D&C 121:26-31).

What are these boundaries that are to be erased, of which the Prophet spoke? Are they temporal and spatial? For all practical purposes, we live in a three-dimensional world and move through time in a forward direction at the rate of one day in every 24 hours. We can be certain that the boundaries of the seas, land, sun, moon, and stars will continue to be mathematically defined with greater and greater precision, even as they are esoterically debated by theologians and philosophers alike. But what about heaven? We have the assurance that the relationship between finite boundaries and the metaphysical thrones, dominions, principalities, and powers that relate to the eternal worlds will be revealed as well.

The Spirit will open the eyes of our understanding to undreamed of vistas of otherwise inaccessible experience. For example, we have yet to comprehend the scope of Moroni's promise that "by the power of the Holy Ghost ye may know the truth of all things." (Moroni 10:5). Understanding will set us free not only from the limitations of ignorance, but also from the constraints of mortality itself. (John 8:32). We will then be as one with the majestic clockwork, "like a bird that, pausing in her flight a while on boughs to light, feels them give way beneath her and yet sings, knowing that she hath wings." (Victor Hugo). The depth and breadth of our comprehension will finally put to rest the debates that have preoccupied us since the Age of Reason began. We will soar to new heights as the reconciliation between science and religion harmonizes and clarifies our understanding of our place both in the universe and in the eternities.

The scriptures testify that "eye hath not seen, nor ear heard, neither have entered into the heart of man, the things which God hath prepared for them that love him," meaning that He is eager to share the knowledge of His creations with those who are prepared to receive it. (1 Corinthians 2:9). Because encounters with the Spirit defy rational explanation, "no tongue can speak, neither can there be written by any man, neither can the hearts of men conceive (the) great and marvelous things" that are God's ever-present reality. (3 Nephi 17:7). These come only from extrasensory perceptions that have the capacity to carry us beyond the conventional boundaries of time, space, and the limitations of our five natural senses. The specialized nerve tissues designed by God to put us "in touch" with our physical surroundings, when combined with our previous experience, create the powerfully persuasive perceptions that form the basis of our understanding of the world around us but do little to prepare us for the solemnities of eternity.

Even our comprehension of the observable universe is at risk when we set our sights too low and edge into conceptual cul-de-sacs from which there is no retreat. Surely, those with a one-dimensional view of the world will see things not as they really are, but only as their limited vision permits. The inherent danger is: "Where there is no vision, the people perish." (Proverbs 29:18). The gospel endows us with a multi-dimensional view of existence that provides a much more accurate context in which to develop a construct of the universe in which we live. In this sense, "the glory of God is intelligence," or the ability to perceive both the physical and spiritual world around us, even the multi-dimensional world that we cannot see with our eyes. The "light and truth of intelligence" is a more precise representation of the Cosmos that affords us the opportunity to clarify our vision to better perceive reality. (D&C 93:36).

This experience transcends the world with which we are familiar in ways that are unfathomable to unenlightened minds. The rational approach is doomed to failure and can never hope to plumb the depths of spiritual experience because it is grounded so firmly in the temporal world, relies so heavily on the proofs of science, and requires experimental confirmation of observable phenomena. Its own logic is inherently self-defeating, because it denies the existence of the only power with the capacity to convey real understanding. Therefore, even as we make valiant efforts to focus the powers of our intellect on eternal elements, because we are bounded on all sides by a present reality, whenever our hearts have not been softened at the same time to relate to the things of the Spirit, we cannot hope to understand God or His creations except in the most abstract, obtuse, and academic ways. As Joseph Smith declared: "We must have a change of heart to see the kingdom of God." ("Teachings," p. 328).

When we think rationally, we are hedged in by the very things from which we yearn to be free - our mortal perspective and perceptions, that are, sadly as it may seem, the sum and substance of our temporal experience. We seek the right answers, but ask the wrong questions. Our efforts to construct a working definition of heaven and earth by subtraction, rather than by addition, are doomed to failure. God's reality is infinitely richer and more satisfying than any reality the rational approach grudgingly concedes could possibly exist. It is more than we could ever know by relying only upon the poor lenses of the body.

For example, if we visualize something as simple as the curvature of space, and then apply gospel principles to the concept, we can see how they resonate with reason and enlarge our understanding of reality itself to an unprecedented level, even as they coordinate with science. Let's begin with a piece of graph paper made of a rubber sheet, and then drop a steel ball bearing onto it. As a result of the mass of the ball and its kinetic energy and inertia, the surface of the graph paper will be deformed or puckered in spacetime. It may be thought of as a representation of two-dimensional space that has been warped by mass into a third physical dimension. By extrapolation on a larger scale, we can observe that the gravity caused by planets (that have large mass) is a distortion in the fabric of three-dimensional space. By applying the laws of physics applicable to the observable universe, we can deduce that under these conditions our familiar space will be curved and unbounded, with no edge and no center. This is about as far as we can go with the rational approach if we refuse the further light and knowledge that the Lord has promised to give us regarding the subject.

In fact, He does shed light on the basic principles uncovered by reason. "There are many kingdoms," He explained, "for there is no space in the which there is no kingdom, and there is no kingdom in which there is no space, either a greater or a lesser kingdom. And unto every kingdom is given a law; and unto every law there are certain bounds also and conditions." (D&C 88:37-38). In other words, there are many kingdoms or realities, and every one of them occupies space. But implied in the scriptural explanation is the suggestion that each space may be governed by certain bounds and conditions specifically tailored to its own individual and unique circumstances.

When Jehovah stood in the presence of God the Father at the time of the creation of the earth, He said to those assembled: "We will go down, for there is space there, and we will take of these materials, and we will make an earth." (Abraham 3:24). The three-dimensional space reserved for the earth already existed; all that was necessary was for Jehovah to "go" there and establish, or set in motion, the laws, bounds and conditions by which the earth could roll into existence as a temporal entity with the arrow of time moving forward. As Luke wrote, God "made the world and all things therein ... and hath determined the times ... and the bounds of their habitation." (Acts 17:24 & 26). He established both the temporal and spatial conditions that would define life on earth.

But what if each new dimension of space builds upon the previous one. The world we perceive exists in the three-dimensions of depth, width, and height. What if it were possible to locally distort that world into a fourth physical dimension that we cannot perceive directly, in much the same way that we have demonstrated that space may be distorted by mass? In three-dimensional space, a cube is created when we move a square five times at right angles to itself. The shadow of a cube is drawn in two dimensions as two squares with their vertices connected. In that representation of a cube, all the lines appear to be equal, but not all the angles are right angles. The cost of losing a dimension in the geometrical reduction is that the three-dimensional object has lost its dimensional accuracy in its representation in only two dimensions.

If we carry our three-dimensional cube at right angles to itself, through a fourth physical dimension, thereby creating new bounds and conditions for the 'kingdom' thus created, in what directions could we define that fourth physical dimension? It would not be left-right, not forward-backward, not up-down, but simultaneously at right angles to every one of those directions. We cannot demonstrate what direction that is, because it is outside our experience and may not even exist in our universe. Nevertheless, in such a scenario, a four-dimensional hypercube, also called a tesseract, is generated. Its proof lies beyond the laws, bounds, and conditions by which the earth, and for that matter our temporal universe, exists. We can only perceive the three-dimensional shadow of a tesseract resembling two nested cubes with all of the vertices connected by lines. A real tesseract, in four dimensions, would have lines of equal length at right angles to each other. The cost of losing a dimension in the geometrical reduction is that the four-dimensional object has lost its dimensional accuracy in its representation in only three dimensions. Nevertheless, it can be imagined to exist, and it can even be inferred from mathematical permutations as well as from a number of scriptures and from statements of church leaders.

For example, Lehi declared: "It must needs be that there is an opposition in all things." (2 Nephi 2:11). In addition to the familiar applications of this basic principle, what if Lehi also meant that our world itself has an isomer? What if the world as we know it has one particular molecular formula, but the world we cannot see, that is its mirror, has a different isomeric structural formula? Could Lehi have been saying that our world itself has its opposite, one that is described as being "without beginning of days or end of years, being prepared from eternity to all eternity, according to (God's) foreknowledge of all things?" (Alma 13:7).

It is anyone's guess if intellectual mind-games have anything to do with the gospel of Jesus Christ, but we have been admonished to grow "in the knowledge of that which is just and true" and that out of the mouth of the Lord "cometh knowledge and understanding." (Mosiah 4:12 & Proverbs 2:6). In any event, have you ever wondered, "Where is the center of God's universe? Is there an edge to it, and if so, what lies beyond?" Where is heaven? Where are the kingdoms of glory? Where is the spirit world? Where are the many mansions mentioned by the Savior? Where is outer darkness? How do those in one kingdom of glory move to another kingdom? What is translation? How can God instantly hear and respond to our prayers?" How can He move instantaneously from one part of His kingdom to another?

There are many intriguing questions relating to the gospel that defy simple explanation and can only be understood within the context of higher-dimensional realities. Joseph Smith once told a gathering of the Saints: "Would to God I could tell you what I know. But you would call it blasphemy." ("Joseph Smith and The Restoration," p. 522). On another occasion, he declared: "I could explain a hundred-fold more than I ever have of the glories of the kingdoms manifested to me in the vision (known as Doctrine & Covenants Section 76) were I permitted, and were the people prepared to receive them." He assured the Saints "that truth, in reference to these matters, can and may be known through the revelations of God in the way of His ordinances, and in answer to prayer." (C.R., 10/9/1843, "Times and Seasons," 4:331-332). Today we are better prepared than ever to explore the possibility that higher-dimensional realities are integral to the gospel Plan, and to deepen our understanding of the innumerable thrones, dominions, principalities, and powers that have been created to accomplish His mission statement. (See Moses 1:39).

This much seems reasonable: If our three-dimensional universe is actually curved through a fourth physical dimension that lies outside our spatial boundaries, the definitive answers to these and other equally provocative questions may lie beyond the horizon of our vision, inaccessible to us in that fourth dimension. Without the intervention of a higher power, these vistas might be forever inaccessible to our inquiry. The Prophet said: "The organization of the spiritual and heavenly worlds, and of spiritual and heavenly beings, was agreeable to the most perfect order and harmony (and) their limits and bounds were fixed irrevocably." (James Adams funeral sermon, cited above). Only if we subscribe to and embrace principles of eternal truth, use them as building blocks and steppingstones, work the pieces of the puzzle in all their permutations, and tirelessly wrestle with possibilities, will the more comprehensive matrix within which all mortal experience and our present reality are embedded snap into sharp focus.

"The Lord's throne is in heaven," wrote the Psalmist. (Psalms 11:4). In the beginning when God created the heaven and the earth, He made them temporally and spatially separate from each other. Their bounds and conditions were distinct. It was this stroke of genius on the part of our Father that allowed Him to manipulate the laws of physics to create a veil, as it were, so that we would forget all about our pre-mortal home in order to fulfill the mortal conditions of His Merciful Plan.

Nevertheless, we do know something about heaven, because according to the Book of Abraham's Facsimile #2, a place exists that is named Kolob, signifying the first creation, nearest to the celestial, or the residence of God. Of our relationship to that realm, William W. Phelps wrote: "No man has found pure space, nor seen the outside curtains, where nothing has a place." In the matrix of the dimensional reality in which he envisioned Kolob, "there is no end to matter, space, spirit, or race, virtue, might, wisdom, or light, union, youth, priesthood, or truth, glory, love, or being," because these are defined by different bounds and conditions. ("If You Could Hie to Kolob").

Ultimately, said the Lord, "there shall be the reckoning of the time of one planet above another, until thou come nigh unto Kolob, which Kolob is after the reckoning of the Lord's time; which Kolob is set nigh unto the throne of God, to govern all those planets which belong to the same order as that upon which thou standest." (Abraham 3:9). Somehow, it is from Kolob that the order of the other creations of God is temporally and spatially governed, and from there the boundaries of heaven are established in such a manner that it is beyond the reach of detection by even the most sophisticated and delicately calibrated instruments utilized by scientists. The Hubble telescope can see 10 or 15 billion light years into our past, almost back to the moment of creation at the Big Bang, but it cannot gaze into heaven five minutes. If we could do that, we "would know more than (we) would by reading all that has ever been written on the subject." (Joseph Smith, H.C. 6:50). Especially in the case of higher temporal and spatial dimensions, it would seem that some things need to be believed to be seen.

Isaiah confirmed that heaven and earth are spatially and temporally separate. "The heaven is my throne," the Lord revealed, "and the earth is my footstool." (Isaiah 66:1). It is the Spirit, however, that has the power to carry us beyond the perceptible confines of this world to a place where boundaries become blurred, the barricade of borders disappears, and reality resonates with crystal-clear clarity. As John the Revelator exclaimed when he received his apocalypse: "Immediately I was in the spirit, and, behold, a throne was set in heaven." (Revelation 4:2). Joseph F. Smith had a similar experience, when the eyes of (his) understanding were opened, and the Spirit of the Lord rested upon (him)," and he (too) saw into the eternal world. (D&C 138:11). Normally, the veil functions as an artificial horizon that permits our senses to have no hint of what lies beyond. It is only the Spirit that generates the power to see through that barrier that isolates us from the sum and substance of reality. It is the Spirit that will answer our questions: "O God, where art thou? And where is the pavilion that covereth thy hiding place?" (D&C 121:1).

In the beginning, it was "the Gods (who) organized and formed the heavens and the earth" by defining the boundaries of the temporal universe, not to mention the eternal world. (Abraham 4:1). They did this by the power of faith. They set the conditions "by which the worlds were framed, (and) all things in heaven, on the earth, or under the earth. (These) exist by reason of faith as it existed in (the mind of the Gods). Had it not been for this principle of faith, the worlds would never have been framed, neither would man have been formed of the dust. It is this principle by which Jehovah works, and through which he exercises power over all temporal as well as eternal things." (Joseph Smith, "Lectures on Faith," #1). Perhaps this is why it is only by exercising perfect faith that we can have a true understanding of God's creations and experience His reality. (James 2:22). After all, "truth is knowledge of things as they are, and as they were, and as they are to come." (D&C 93:24).

Physics tells us that there are no privileged frames of reference. The galaxies are imbedded in time and attached to a space whose fabric is constantly expanding. If we ask where and when the creation took place, the answer is everywhere and forever. If the universe is warped through time and space into a fourth dimension, it just might expand like a balloon, creating in every instant more space. It seems reasonable that God would utilize our everyday laws of physics to accomplish His purposes within the framework of the eternal thrones, dominions and principalities that are His higher-dimensional reality. This may explain why the Lord said to Moses: "As one earth shall pass away, and the heavens thereof even so shall another come, and there is no end to my works." (Moses 1:38). "For by him were all things created, that are in heaven, and that are in earth, visible and invisible, whether they be thrones, or dominions, or principalities, or powers: all things were created by him." (Colossians 1:16).

To understand our relationship to higher-dimensional beings who may live in those eternal realms, it is instructive to look into a two-dimensional world that is easy to visualize because it is comfortably within our experience. We are familiar with the laws, bounds, and conditions that would govern such a world. Thus, we perceive it as nothing more than a large, flat disk, with structures on its surface consisting of broad lines with gaps in them for entrances and exits. Trapped in the two dimensions of width and depth, inhabitants of such a world could move in only those two dimensions and could perceive nothing of a third dimension (height). Without assistance, they could not move into or appreciate the perspective of that third dimension that is so familiar to us. A two-dimensional being would be at a loss for words to describe a three-dimensional experience, for there would be nothing with which to compare it. Any feeble attempts would surely be met with skepticism, disbelief, or ridicule by others. Perhaps the best that could be expected would be to declare, as did Paul, "whether in the body, or out of the body, I cannot tell." (2 Corinthians 12:3).

When we view two-dimensional space from our three-dimensional perspective, we quickly see that everything is open to our inspection, because there is nothing to hide 'behind.' We see every element of every object in those two-dimensions. Regardless of how many obstacles lie in the way of beings moving about in that world, we have access to their every nook and cranny. We can even see inside two-dimensional objects, and can discern every particle therein, just as we might view every pigment on an expanse of canvas in a two-dimensional landscape portrait (that is the representation of three-dimensional objects) hanging on a wall. In effect, we can "enter" two-dimensional space at will. We can pop in and out anywhere and anytime on the canvas of two-dimensional space. By analogy, from a hyper-dimensional perspective, Heavenly Father has access to all three-dimensional space, and can view every particle of every object therein. Nothing is hidden or obscured from His view; for once again, from His perspective, there is nothing "behind" which one can hide in three-dimensional space. As Jeremiah asked: "Can any hide himself in secret places that I shall not see him? Saith the Lord. Do not I fill heaven and earth?" (Jeremiah 23:24).

Because they have no "thickness," or depth, an infinite number of two-dimensional worlds could be "stacked" on top of each other, like the ones and zeros of binary code on a digital video disk, but there would be absolutely no interaction between adjacent worlds. Perhaps this explains how there is no end to the works of God. "As one earth shall pass away, and the heavens thereof even so shall another come," in an unending succession of worlds, each oblivious to the existence of every other. (Moses 1:38).

So far, we have established basic relationships between a three-dimensional universe and the two-dimensional world layered within it. We have alluded to the possibility that our three- dimensional universe may be one of many that are nested within a four-dimensional universe. By extension, we have suggested that it might even be possible to stack an infinite number of three-dimensional worlds on top of one another within four-dimensions. These would be somewhat like the layers of an onion, separated by just enough space so that there could be no mutual interaction without the intervention of a higher-dimensional power or influence. These nested universes might more accurately be described as "pluriverses," or "multiverses." The multiverse (or meta-universe, metaverse) is the hypothetical set of multiple possible universes (including the historical universe we consistently experience) that together comprise everything that exists: the entirety of space, time, matter, and energy as well as the physical laws and constants that describe them. The term was coined in 1895 by the American philosopher and psychologist William James. The various universes within the multiverse are sometimes called parallel universes." (Wikipedia, "multiverse").

Just such an intercession may have taken place when Moses talked with God face to face. "The glory of God was upon Moses, therefore Moses could endure his presence" to better appreciate His eternal perspective. Thus prepared, he was commanded: "Look, and I will show thee the workmanship of mine hands." At the same time, however, The Lord said: "My works are without end, and also my words, for they never cease. Wherefore, no man can behold all my works, except he behold all my glory." God reminded Moses: "All things are present with me, for I know them all." (Moses 1:2-6). But to be aware of all things and to experience them as a present reality, Moses needed to receive the tangible element characterized as the glory of God.

It was by while under the influence of that spiritual element that Moses beheld "many lands, and each land was called earth, and there were inhabitants on the face thereof." Were these earths in parallel dimensions? Were they temporal and spatial realities stacked up like so many pages in a book? Then the Lord told Moses: "Worlds without number have I created ... for behold, there are many worlds that have passed away by the word of my power. And there are many that now stand, and innumerable are they unto man; but all things are numbered unto me, for they are mine and I know them." (Moses 1:29, 33 & 35).

"When I consider the heavens," wrote David, "the work of thy fingers, the moon, and the stars, which thou hast ordained; What is man, that thou art mindful of him? and the son of man, that thou visitest him? For thou has made him a little lower than the angels." (Psalms 8:3-5). Perhaps we are lower than the angels in the sense that their natural abode is within a higher dimensional reality. Perhaps the work of His fingers, even the moon and the stars, are ordained to exist in realities that are simply beyond our comprehension. But there will come a day when "he shall reveal all things - Things which have passed, and hidden things which no man knew, things of the earth by which it was made, and the purpose and the end thereof - Things most precious, things that are above, and things that are beneath, things that are in the earth, and upon the earth, and in heaven." (D&C 101:32-34).

For now, our poor lenses cannot discern what is really there. "No man hath seen God at any time in the flesh, except quickened by the Spirit of God?" (J.S.T. John 1:18). If it is true that "the light of the body is the eye," then, when the eye is single to faith, our "whole body shall be full of light." (3 Nephi 13:22). On one occasion after having received revelation, Joseph Smith confirmed the reality of that promise, and declared: "My whole body was full of light, and I could see even out at the ends of my fingers and toes." (N.B. Lundwall, "The Vision," p. 11). This may be why the angel Moroni hovered in the air during his visits to Joseph Smith in his chamber, and why his hands and his feet were naked. (J.S.H. 1:31). He could "see" with every part of his body. Every child of God potentially possesses this gift, and the Lord has promised that it only waits to be revealed. "If your eye be single to my glory," He said, "your whole bodies shall be filled with light, and there shall be no darkness in you; and that body which is filled with light comprehendeth all things." (D&C 88:67). There will come a day when "the sun shall no more go down; neither shall (the) moon withdraw itself: for the Lord shall be (our) everlasting light." (Isaiah 60:20).

Orson Pratt appreciated the ramifications of the truth that celestial beings have the ability to perceive with all parts of their bodies. "The spirit," he said, "is inherently capable of experiencing the sensations of light. I think we could then see in different directions at once. Instead of looking in one particular direction, we could then look all around us at the same instant." (J.D., 2:238-248).

When each of us comes face to face with eternity, as we surely will, the spiritual element will transform our mortal clay. Beforehand, while we tarry on the earth, we might ask under what circumstances does that element quicken us, and how is the pure knowledge that flows out of it vitalized? "A man's wisdom maketh his face to shine, and the boldness of his face shall be changed." (Ecclesiastes 8:1). When we are at one with God, when we have spiritually been born of Him and have internalized His divine nature, we will receive His image in our countenances. (Alma 5:14). That image and His likeness will bridge the barriers of time and space to leave their marks as reminders of our noble birthright. Our genetic code will be transformed to bless us with an endowment of unearthly powers.

Abinadi's "face shone with exceeding luster, even as Moses' did while on the mount of Sinai, while speaking with the Lord." (Mosiah 13:5, See Exodus 34:29). The features of the brothers Lehi and Nephi "did shine exceedingly, even as the faces of angels." (Helaman 5:36). Interestingly, to witnesses, it seemed "that they did lift their eyes to heaven; and they were in the attitude as if talking or lifting their voices to some being whom they beheld" from the unseen world. (Helaman 5:36). These observers were prompted to ask: "Who is it with whom these men do converse?" The answer could have been: "They do converse with the angels of God," who reside within the unseen world of a dimensionally superior reality. (Helaman 5:38-39).

Bathed in the glory of the Lord, Moses stood "in the presence of God, and talked with him face to face." (Moses 1:31). From that perspective, he was able to see "the inhabitants (of the earth), and there was not a soul which he beheld not; and he discerned them by the Spirit of God." (Moses 1:28). Clearly, "the Lord seeth not as man seeth; for man looketh on the outward appearance," while the Lord focuses on that inner vessel which is beyond the capacity of the five physical senses to detect. (1 Samuel 16:7). Thus, He is able to say: "I can stretch forth mine hands and hold all the creations which I have made; and mine eye can pierce them also." (Moses 7:36). We all live "under the glance of the piercing eye of the Almighty God." (Jacob 2:10). His voice "is unto all men, and there is none to escape, and there is no eye that shall not see, neither ear that shall not hear, neither heart that shall not be penetrated." (D&C 1:2). As Jacob said: "He can pierce you, and with one glance of his eye he can smite you to the dust!" (Jacob 2:15). Looking at it this way illuminates the scriptures with new meaning: "For the word of God is quick, and powerful, and sharper than any two-edged sword, piercing even to the dividing asunder of soul and spirit, and of the joints and marrow, and is a discerner of the thoughts and intents of the heart." (Hebrews 4:12).

The scriptures suggest that there is only a thin line between the temporal and spiritual worlds. Many have had near death experiences, during which they have been visited by a "being of light whose questions are the prelude to a moment of startling intensity during which the being presents to the person a panoramic review of his life. It is often obvious that the being doesn't need information for there is displayed before him the individual's whole life. His only intention is to provoke reflection. This review can only be described in terms of memory, since that is the closest familiar phenomenon to it, but it has characteristics that set it apart from any normal type of remembering. First of all, the remembrance is extraordinarily rapid. Everything appears at once, and can be taken in with one mental glance in an instant of earthly time. Yet, despite its rapidity, the review is incredibly vivid." (Raymond Moody, M.D., "Life After Life").

Mormon said: "The day soon cometh that your mortal must put on immortality, and these bodies which are now moldering in corruption must soon become incorruptible bodies." (Mormon 6:21). This may be accomplished as our Heavenly Father carries us into the greater light of His higher dimensional, or eternal, reality. Just as an ultraviolet light is used in sterilization, (ultraviolet germicidal irradiation – UVGI), could it be that it is the physical phenomenon of the unearthly light intrinsic to God that purifies and renews our sin-stained souls? "Though your sins be as scarlet," Isaiah promised, "they shall be as white as snow; though they be red like crimson, they shall be as wool." (Isaiah 1:18). If no unclean thing can enter the presence of God, it may be that it is the temporal and spatial transformation that takes place at the time of our resurrection that carries us from corruption to incorruption. Think of Paul's description: "There are also celestial bodies, and bodies terrestrial: but the glory of the celestial is one, and the glory of the terrestrial is another. There is one glory of the sun, and another glory of the moon, and another glory of the stars: for one star differeth from another in glory. So, also, is the resurrection of the dead. it is sown in corruption; it is raised in incorruption … It is sown a natural body; it is raised a spiritual body." (1 Corinthians 15:40-44). Maybe nothing really ever dies, and we are simply brought into the greater light of day after the spirit leaves our mortal clay. As Mormon explained: "The day soon cometh that your mortal must put on immortality, and these bodies which are now moldering in corruption must soon become incorruptible bodies." (Mormon 6:21). Maybe from the time of the formation of the world, when the light was divided from the darkness, it was always a question of dimension, and not just of time and place. "God saw the light" when the world was created, "and that light was good." (Moses 2:4)

It may be that we may receive unanticipated and unappreciated assistance from beings existing in higher temporal and spatial dimensions, even though we may be unaware of their close proximity, ready availability, and potentially protective influence. In the Old Testament, we read that when Elisha's servant "was risen early, and (had) gone forth, behold, a host compassed the city both with horses and chariots. And his servant said unto him, Alas, my master, how shall we do? And he answered, Fear not: for they that be with us are more than they that be with them. And Elisha prayed, and said, Lord, I pray thee, open his eyes, that he may see. And the Lord opened the eyes of the young man; and he saw: and, behold, the mountain was full of horses and chariots of fire round about Elisha." (2 Kings 6:15-17). They had been there the whole time, but it was only the prophet Elisha who had been aware of their presence. It was only when the Lord touched the eyes of the young man's understanding that he, too, was able to see what was really there. Certainly, there is more to the office of the prophet, seer, and revelator than superficially meets the eye. Joseph Smith wrote of the revelatory experience: "The Lord touched the eyes of our understandings and they were opened, and the glory of the Lord shone round about." (D&C 76:19).

In a related incident, after an angel announced to shepherds tending their flocks by night in the fields near Bethlehem that Christ the Lord had been born, "suddenly there was with the angel a multitude of the heavenly host praising God." (Luke 2:13). This manifestation of numerous beings from the unseen world prompted the shepherds to hurry to Bethlehem to see the things that had come to pass that the Lord had made known unto them. (Luke 2:15).

When the Apostles were gathered together with members of the church on the Day of Pentecost, "they were all with one accord in one place." The introduction of the Holy Ghost from the unseen world was accompanied by "a sound from heaven as of a rushing mighty wind, and it filled all the house where they were sitting." So dramatic was His appearance, that "there appeared unto them cloven tongues like as of fire, and it sat upon each of them." Its manifestation was so dramatic that "they were all filled … and began to speak with other tongues as the Spirit gave them utterance." (Acts 2:1-3).

On the Mount of Transfiguration, the Apostles Peter, James, and John had a higher-dimensional experience. Jesus led them up "into an high mountain apart by themselves: and he was transfigured before them. And his raiment became shining, exceeding white as snow; so as no fuller on earth can white them. And there appeared unto them Elias with Moses: and they were talking with Jesus … And there was a cloud that overshadowed them: and a voice came out of the cloud, saying, This is my beloved Son: hear him. And suddenly, when they had looked round about, they saw no man any more, save Jesus only with themselves." (Mark 9:2-8).

Perhaps, in the scriptures we should be alert to the use of the word "suddenly," for it often seems to presage a higher-dimensional experience. For example, the Lord said: "I am Jesus Christ, the Son of God; wherefore, gird up your loins and I will suddenly come to my temple. " (D&C 36:8, see Malachi 3:1, Numbers 12:4, J.S.H. 1:44, & 3 Nephi 24:1). Our awakening appreciation of higher dimensions allows us to more easily understand how He could do so. "For I am the Lord thy God; I dwell in heaven; the earth is my footstool; I stretch my hand over the sea, and it obeys my voice; I cause the wind and the fire to be my chariot; I say to the mountains—Depart hence— and behold, they are taken away by a whirlwind, in an instant, suddenly." (Abraham 2:7).

There is another possibility regarding planes of existence, raised by Carl Sagan. It is not suggested by scripture, and no church authority has advocated its plausibility. And yet it is "an idea, strange, haunting, evocative, one of the most exquisite conjectures in science or religion. It is entirely undemonstrated, and it may never be proven. But it stirs the blood. There is, we are told, an infinite hierarchy of universes, so that an elementary particle, such as an electron, in our universe, would, if penetrated, reveal itself to be an entire closed universe. Within it, organized into the local equivalent of galaxies and smaller structures, are an immense number of other, much tinier elementary particles, which are themselves universes at the next level, and so on forever, an infinite downward regression, universes within universes, endlessly. And upward as well. Our familiar universe of galaxies and stars, planets, and people, would be a single elementary particle in the next universe up, the first step of another infinite progress. This is the only religious idea I know that surpasses the endless number of infinitely old cycling universes in Hindu cosmology. What would those other universes be like? To enter them, we would somehow have to penetrate a fourth physical dimension … Poised at the edge of forever, we would jump off" into life's ultimate incredible journey. ("Cosmos," p. 262-267).

Wherever, whenever, or however we fit into the cosmos, we know this: God quickens life in the sense that He provides our spirits with an animated physical world with which we freely interact; He "lends (us) breath, that (we) may live and move and do according to (our) own will, and (He supports us) from one moment to another." (Mosiah 2:21). But, at the same time, we are cautioned that our world is only a shadow of that which is to come, and we cannot now expect to understand it at God's level of comprehension. As Paul wrote: "For now we see through a glass, darkly; but then face to face: now I know in part; but then shall I know even as also I am known." (1 Corinthians 13:12). "My thoughts are not your thoughts," said the Lord, "neither are your ways my ways ... For as the heavens are higher than the earth, so are my ways higher than your ways, and my thoughts than your thoughts." (Isaiah 55:8-9). His thoughts are loftier, broader, more visionary, and infinitely more expansive. His ways circumscribe the sum of our reality and encompass more than we have ever dared to dream.

Our own feeble attempts to describe God's reality utilize abstractions, for thoughts cannot be shaped, nor words formed, nor sentences framed that accurately articulate His glory. Figures of speech are employed because we would otherwise be at a complete loss for words when grasping for even a basic explanation of these most profound metaphysical realities. To Moses, "the presence of the Lord appeared (as) a flame of fire out of the midst of a bush: and he looked, and, behold, the bush burned with fire, and the bush was not consumed." (J.S.T. Exodus 3:2). That fire on Sinai burned all the way from the earth "unto the midst of heaven" itself. (Deuteronomy 4:11). Those who witnessed this manifestation thought they could see through a brilliant conduit, as it were, right into heaven itself.

Joseph Smith said: "Spirits can only be revealed in flaming fire and glory." (C.R., 10/9/1843, "Times & Seasons," 4:331-332). Paul wrote that God can be best described as "a consuming fire" in the sense that His hyper-dimensional Presence, His glory, is akin to fire and smoke and everlasting burnings. (Hebrews 12:29 & Deuteronomy 4:24). When He reveals Himself in our corruptible reality, or when He unveils the heavens and His glory fills the earth, the elements in our three-dimensional world will melt, mountains will flow like rivers, valleys will be exalted, and rough places will be made smooth. (D&C 109:74).

When Elijah did nothing more than simply speak with the Lord, that experience was so overwhelming that "a great and strong wind rent the mountains, and brake in pieces the rocks before the Lord ... and after the wind an earthquake ... And after the earthquake a fire." (1 Kings 19:11-12). The Lord's Presence was manifest in these representations of the most dramatic forces in nature. The Second Coming of The Lord will be similarly powerful insomuch that the Mount of Olives will be rent in twain, and later the whole earth will come together into one landmass as it was in the days before Peleg (Genesis 10:25, D&C 133:24, and the Tenth Article of Faith).

When Nephi and his brother Lehi were incarcerated by their enemies, they heard a voice "as it were above the cloud of darkness" that enveloped them, and they "beheld that it was not a voice of thunder, neither was it a voice of a great tumultuous noise, but behold, it was a still voice of perfect mildness, as if it had been a whisper (and yet) it did pierce even to the very soul." (Helaman 5:29-30). If this voice came from a higher dimension that envelops our world, no wonder that "notwithstanding the mildness of the voice, behold the earth shook exceedingly, and the walls of the prison trembled again, as if it were about to tumble to the earth." The natural order of our temporal and spatial reality was disrupted by the interjection of the voice of the Lord from another dimension in time and space. Evidently the conditions introduced into the world by God's Presence caused a rift, manifest to Nephi and Lehi as a disruption in the order of nature, so that when the voice did come, it spoke "unto them marvelous words which cannot be uttered." (Helaman 5:31 & 33).

In the Sacred Grove, Joseph Smith witnessed "a pillar of light exactly over (his) head, above the brightness of the sun, which descended gradually until it fell upon (him)." (J.S.H. 1:16). Latter-day Saints are so familiar with this description of the appearance of Heavenly beings from other temporal and spatial dimensions that they characteristically overlook the unusual language Joseph Smith employed to describe the event. It was not just a light that flashed on, but it was a veritable "pillar of light" or a column with distinct borders.

Stranger still was the fact that the light "descended gradually," entering the quiet grove slowly enough that Joseph was able to gauge the rapidity of its approach until it finally reached him and enveloped him within its dazzling brilliance. It was only then that he "saw two Personages, whose brightness and glory (defied) all description."

(J.S.H. 1:17). They were somehow standing in the air above him, within the encircling light. Finally, he heard the confirming voice speak peace, not only to his ears, but to his very soul as well: "This is my Beloved Son. Hear Him!" (J.S.H. 1:17).

The New Testament tells us that when Jesus was transfigured before Peter, James, and John, "his face did shine as the sun, and his raiment was white as the light." (Matthew 17:2). In the Old Testament, we read that when Elijah was translated, "there appeared a chariot of fire, and horses of fire … and Elijah went up by a whirlwind into heaven," there to witness unspeakable things within eternal realms. (2 Kings 2:11). We immediately think of the description provided by Joseph Smith of Moroni's temporal and spatial transference, when he "saw, as it were, a conduit open right up into heaven, and (he saw the angel who) ascended till he entirely disappeared." (J.S.H. 1:43). If there is a process by which mortals may move between dimensional realities, these scriptures may provide our best descriptions of the mechanism.

"Who among us shall dwell with the devouring fire?" asked Isaiah. "Who among us shall dwell with everlasting burnings?" What qualifies us to experience the far journey from our present three-dimensional reality to the higher-dimensional eternal world? Isaiah answered his own question: "He that walketh righteously, and speaketh uprightly; he that despiseth the gain of oppressions, that shaketh his hands from holding of bribes, that stoppeth his ears from hearing of blood, and shutteth his eyes from seeing evil. He shall dwell on high. (His eyes) shall behold the land that is very far off" in the higher-dimensional world that is the habitation of the Gods. (Isaiah 34:14-17).

That "land unpromised and unearned is a realm of spirit." Even as we dwell upon the earth, we can still appreciate that "it is the realm of sensory delight - of fragrance, sound, and form and color. It is the realm of human associations - of gratitude, loyalty, and appreciation, of selflessness, helpfulness, and forgiveness, of friendship, love, and compassion. It is the realm of human growth and transcendence and of truth discovered and accepted, of beauty created and enjoyed, of goodness deepened and made manifest in life. Most of us are more at home, more at ease, in the world of things, in the world of getting and spending. So, when conflicts arise between our spiritual and our material worlds, as they inevitably do, it is usually our spiritual world that suffers," and we end up retreating into the comfort zone of our familiar temporal and spatial reality. (P.A. Christensen, "The Realm of Spirit: A Land Unpromised and Unearned, B.Y.U. Studies, 16:1). Sooner or later, when we have conformed our lives to the character of God, we will enjoy that realm of spirit as our natural environment and we will understand that it is more vibrantly real than anything we have ever known. In the meantime, we continue to strangle ourselves with illusions of reality, and with "things whose opacity obstructs our ability to see what is really there." (Gretel Erlich, "Under Wyoming's Skies," The Atlantic Magazine).

To those who are prepared, however, the Lord "will shew wonders in the heavens and in the earth, blood, and fire and pillars of smoke." (Joel 2:30). When He revealed Himself to the prophet Isaiah, so powerful was the manifestation that "the posts of the door moved at the voice of him that cried, and the house was filled with smoke. Then (Isaiah) said, Woe is me! For I am undone." (Isaiah 6:4-5). His physical frame could barely tolerate the Presence of God. Even "the still small voice," wrote Joseph Smith, "whispereth through and pierceth all things, and often times it maketh my bones to quake while it maketh manifest." (D&C 85:6). The introduction into the world of higher temporal and spatial dimensional influences is disruptive to the status quo. When Belshazzar beheld no more than the fingers of a man's hand that wrote upon the wall of the palace, his "countenance was changed, and his thoughts troubled him, so that the joints of his loins were loosed, and his knees smote one against another." (Daniel 5:5-6).

Philo Dibble was an eyewitness to the influence of the spirit upon Joseph Smith and Sydney Rigdon when they received the Vision preserved as Doctrine & Covenants Section 76. He recorded in his journal: "Joseph sat firmly and calmly, all the time in the midst of a magnificent glory, but Sydney sat limp and pale, apparently as limber as a rag. Observing which, Joseph remarked, smilingly, "Sydney is not used to it as I am." ("Juvenile Instructor," 5/1892, p. 303-304).

The Psalmist described conditions on one occasion when the Lord introduced Himself into the everyday world: "Fire goeth before (Him), and burneth up his enemies round about. His lightnings enlightened the world: the earth saw, and trembled. The hills melted like wax at the presence of the Lord of the whole earth." (Psalms 97:3-5). As Mormon observed: "The dust of the earth moveth hither and thither, to the dividing asunder, at the command of our great and everlasting God. Yea, behold at his voice do the hills and the mountains tremble and quake. And by the power of his voice, they are broken up, and become smooth, yea, even like unto a valley. Yea, by the power of his voice doth the whole earth shake; Yea, by the power of his voice, do the foundations rock, even to the very center. Yea, and if he say unto the earth – Move - it is moved. Yea, if he say unto the earth - Thou shalt go back, that it lengthen out the day for many hours - it is done." (Helaman 12:8-14). Thus is manifest the awful power of God. It may not be so much that He commands the earth to tremble, but rather that His powerful influence from a higher dimensional reality causes the anatomic structure of our world to rock to the very center as it struggles to bring itself into harmony with His foreign nature. In fact, in the day that the Lord comes as a thief in the night, "the heavens shall pass away with a great noise, and the elements shall melt with fervent heat, (and) the earth also and the works that are therein shall be burned up." (2 Peter 3:10).

In the meantime, those who have claimed their birthright and have harnessed the awesome authority of the Melchizedek Priesthood, will "have power, by faith, to break mountains, to divide the seas, to dry up waters, to turn them out of their course; to put at defiance the armies of nations, to divide the earth, to break every band, to stand in the presence of God, to do all things according to his will, according to his command, subdue principalities and powers; and this by the will of the Son of God which was from before the foundation of the world. And men having this faith, coming up unto this order of God, were translated and taken up into heaven." (Genesis 14:30-32). It is God, after all, Who "hath given a law unto all things, by which they move in their times and their seasons," and it is He Who sets the bounds and conditions of every temporal and spatial dimension. (D&C 88:42). He is the Lord Omnipotent. We can know Him on the terms He has established, or we can know Him not at all.

Who knows what God is really like? Joseph Smith said: "There are but a very few beings in the world who understand rightly the nature of God (and) if men do not understand the character of God they do not comprehend themselves." ("Teachings," p. 343). When He manifested Himself on the earth, all that could be known of Him was the three-dimensional representation of a man that was discernible by our five natural senses. He told His disciples that of His Father: "Ye have neither heard his voice at any time, nor seen his shape." (John 5:37). But then He told Philip: "He that hath seen me hath seen the Father." (John 14:9). The Man Jesus was a comprehensible representation of His Father. Perhaps the Greeks of Paul's day were not too far from the mark when they erected "and altar with this inscription, To the Unknown God." (Acts 17:23). Only with a gospel perspective can we begin to fathom His nature.

We know by the description provided by John the Revelator that His higher-dimensional figure is striking: "His head and his hairs were white like wool, as white as snow; and his eyes were as a flame of fire; and his feet like unto fine brass, as if they burned in a furnace; and his voice as the sound of many waters." (Revelation 1:14-15). Joseph Smith said: "Under his feet was a paved work of pure gold, in color like amber. His eyes were as a flame of fire; the hair of his head was white like the pure snow; his countenance shone above the brightness of the sun; and his voice was as the sound of the rushing of great waters." (D&C 110:2-3).

In Sinai, the Children of Israel saw God, "and there was under his feet as it were a paved work of a sapphire stone, and as it were the body of heaven in his clearness … And the sight of the glory of the Lord was like devouring fire on the top of the mount in the eyes of the children of Israel." (Exodus 24:9 & 17). The Three Witnesses of The Book of

Mormon were also given powerful manifestations of His Presence, that it was "clear as the moon, and fair as the sun, and terrible as an army with banners." (D&C 5:12-14).

Following the destruction in Zarahemla at the time of the crucifixion, through the veil separating the survivors from higher temporal and spatial dimensions, "there was a voice heard among all the inhabitants of the earth, upon all the face of this land." (3 Nephi 9:1). It was not a deafening voice of a hundred decibel, but simply a quiet sound heard by everyone regardless of their physical location in the land. It was a voice unlike any sound that had ever before been heard, for it came from immortal lips with an effect on both heaven and earth that was profound.

At that time the promises were fulfilled, that when the Lord should utter "his voice out of heaven, the heavens (would) shake and the earth (would) tremble, and the trump of God (would) sound both long and loud." (D&C 43:18). To Joel, the Lord promised that He would "roar out of Zion, and utter his voice from Jerusalem, and the heavens and the earth (would) shake, (and) the sun and the moon (would) be dark, and the stars (would) withdraw their shining, (for) the day of the Lord (would be) great and very terrible, and who (would be able to) abide it?" (Joel 3:16, 2:10 & 12).

In Zarahemla, temporal and spatial harmony were so disjointed that "there was thick darkness upon all the face of the land, insomuch that the inhabitants thereof who had not fallen" during the destruction at the time of the crucifixion "could feel the vapor of darkness. And there could be no light, because of the darkness, neither candles, neither torches; neither could there be fire kindled with their fine and exceedingly dry wood, so that there could not be any light at all. And there was not any light seen, neither fire, nor glimmer, neither the sun, nor the moon, nor the stars, for so great were the mists of darkness which were upon the face of the land. And it came to pass that it did last for the space of three days that there was no light seen." (3 Nephi 8:20-23).

There had been such a distortion in the fabric of spacetime, that "the face of the whole earth became deformed." (3 Nephi 8:17). During the three hours of destruction, "it was said by some that the time was greater," so confused were the people by the temporal and spatial disturbances. (3 Nephi 8:19). The Spirit of Christ had been withdrawn, at least locally; thus, "there could not be any light at all." (2 Nephi 8:21). Truly, "the Spirit (which) giveth light to every man that cometh into the world," had been withheld. (D&C 84:46).

Zarahemla had been moved out of its place into a netherworld, as it were, to an unstable place within limbo, an indeterminate state somewhere outside the secure boundaries of our temporal and spatial dominion. Perhaps the Lord, who had established the laws and conditions by which the earth existed, was so intent on accomplishing the final details of the Atonement on the cross and in the tomb that His preoccupation momentarily compromised the divine concentration normally required to hold the elements together in harmony and cohesion. Perhaps this had been His design from the beginning.

In any event, there was a tangible element, a palpable feeling that could only be described by those who experienced it as "a vapor of darkness." As soon as it "dispersed from off the face of the land" when the Lord again focused His full attention on His creation, "the earth did cease to tremble, and the rocks did cease to rend, and the dreadful groanings did cease, and all the tumultuous noises did pass away, and the earth did cleave together again" as the fabric of time and space once again settled into the order of our familiar three-dimensional world. (3 Nephi 10:9-10). Normality had been re-established, at least for the time being, although "the whole face of the land was changed." (3 Nephi 8:12).

Then, from no particular direction, the inhabitants of Zarahemla "heard a voice as if it came out of heaven; and they cast their eyes round about, for they understood not the voice which they heard; and it was not a harsh voice, neither was it a loud voice; nevertheless, and notwithstanding it being a small voice it did pierce them that they did hear to the center, insomuch that there was no part of their frame that it did not cause to quake; yea, it did pierce them to the very soul, and did cause their hearts to burn." (3 Nephi 11:3).

Elijah had a similar experience, when "the Lord passed by, and a great and strong wind rent the mountains, and brake in pieces the rocks before the Lord; but the Lord was not in the wind: and after the wind an earthquake; but the Lord was not in the earthquake: And after the earthquake a fire; but the Lord was not in the fire: and after the fire a still small voice." (1 Kings 19:11).

From whence do these voices come? The scriptures may suggest a higher-dimensional source, a state of being natural to God but unfamiliar to us. As a mortal being, Jesus had a similar experience that was recorded by Matthew. "And Jesus, when he was baptized, went up straightway out of the water: and, lo, the heavens were opened unto him, and he saw the Spirit of God descending like a dove, and lighting upon him. And lo a voice from heaven, saying, This is my beloved Son, in whom I am well pleased." (Matthew 3:16-17). Whether or not others that were present experienced the manifestation is unclear. Suffice to say that the Mortal Messiah Himself had a higher-dimensional experience at the time of His baptism. Matthew might just as easily have recorded that "Jesus saw, as it were, a conduit open right up into heaven, and the Holy Ghost descended till he entirely appeared, manifesting Himself by the sign of the dove." (See J.S.H. 2:30).

When Saul was journeying to Damascus to persecute the Saints, "suddenly, there shined round about him a light from heaven. And he fell to the earth, and heard a voice saying unto him, Saul, Saul, why persecutest thou me? ... And he trembling and astonished said, Lord, what wilt thou have me to do? ...And the men which journeyed with him stood speechless, hearing a voice, but seeing no man." (Acts 9:3-7).

Zion is also susceptible to the influences of higher dimensions. Its inhabitants enjoy peace and rest from the cares of the world in a temporal and spatial reality that greatly enhances their power to preach the gospel, bring souls unto Christ, and build the kingdom of God. It was in this state of being that "Enoch beheld angels descending out of heaven, bearing testimony of the Father and Son; and the Holy Ghost fell on many, and they were caught up by the powers of heaven" through a portal of some type connecting our two dimensionally separate but adjacent realities "into Zion." (Moses 7:27). Enoch and the inhabitants of his city became the prototype for all who desire to enter into the state of translation in which people and entire cities are suddenly removed from the earth in a phenomenon of transference to another dimension. Where do they go and how do they get there? How long do they stay? Is their transference stable? Conventional space travel to another part of our universe seems to be out of the question, because of the limitations established by the cosmic speed limit. Nothing can move faster than the speed of light. So alternatively, could it be that translated beings simply have a change wrought upon their bodies giving them the capability to move at will both temporally and spatially between dimensions in the physical and eternal worlds that are sandwiched on top of each other?

Perhaps only millennial man will be able to make the transition back and forth from our every-day world to dimensionally superior realms while yet in the flesh, for they "will live in a state akin to translation." (Bruce R. McConkie, "The Millennial Messiah," p. 644). During the Millennium, the relationship between the eternal world and ours may be so well defined and stabilized that these transitions will be much more frequently, predictably, and easily accomplished.

At the Second Coming, all the Saints will experience spatial transference when they are "caught up together ... in the clouds, to meet the Lord in the air." (1 Thessalonians 4:17). When we leave this mortal clay to enter higher-dimensional realms, "we shall all be changed, in a moment, in the twinkling of an eye" enabling us to experience multiple realities as our natural states of being. (1 Corinthians 15:51-52).

Even now, we are occasionally privileged to see beyond our mortal horizons. We even have a name for these higher-dimensional states, calling them "the depths of eternity." The promise is that we "shall inherit thrones, kingdoms, principalities, and powers, (and) dominions, (of) all heights and depths." (D&C 132:19). The question is: In what direction are these 'depths?' We have determined that we cannot reach them by going to the left, or to the right, and not by going forward or backward, or up or down, but for argument's sake, simultaneously at right angles to every one of those directions. When John looked into those depths, he saw a door "opened in (into – J.S.T.) heaven: and the first voice which (he) heard was as it were of a trumpet talking with (him); which said, come up hither, and I will shew thee things which must be hereafter. And immediately (he) was in the spirit: and, behold, a throne was set in heaven, and one sat on the throne. And he that sat was to look upon like a jasper ... and there was a rainbow round about the throne, in sight like unto an emerald." (Revelation 4:1-3). John had been taken from his temporal and spatial surroundings into the presence of God, into the "depths of eternity," into the "hereafter," if you will. He was somehow at the same time both "here" and "after," which although vague is about as specific as we can get when referring to higher dimensional states. Thus, John described what he both saw and heard as "lightnings and thunderings and voices." (Revelation 4:5). To Joseph Smith, the voice of the Great Jehovah struck a similar chord "as the sound of the rushing of great waters." (D&C 110:3).

There have been a number of scripturally documented 'closed room' visitations by beings from the unseen world. For example, when the Apostles were gathered together shortly after Christ's death, the doors had been "shut where the disciples assembled for fear of the Jews. (Then) came Jesus and stood in their midst." (John 20:19). Because 'the doors were shut,' such an abrupt manifestation of His tangible presence can be explained if He came into the room from another dimension. Another 'closed room' event occurred as the resurrected Lord walked to Emmaus. (Luke 24:13-32). After stopping for the evening with two fellow travelers, the Savior was recognized as He blessed the meal, after which He abruptly disappeared from the closed room. "And it came to pass, while he blessed them, he was parted from them, and carried up into heaven." (Luke 24:51).

When Zacharias was alone in the temple, there suddenly "appeared unto him an angel of the Lord standing on the right side of the altar of incense. And when Zacharias saw him, he was troubled, and fear fell upon him." (Luke 1:11-12). After delivering his message, the angel explained that he was "Gabriel, that stand in the presence of God," and that he was sent to speak unto Zacharias, and to show him glad tidings. (Luke 1:19).

Alma the Younger with the Sons of Mosiah witnessed the appearance of an angel who "descended as it were in a cloud; and he spake as it were with a voice of thunder, which caused the earth to shake upon which they stood." (Mosiah 27:11). He asked Alma: "Can ye dispute the power of God? For behold, doth not my voice shake the earth? And can ye not also behold me before you?" Lest there be any confusion regarding where he had come from, he declared: "I am sent from God." (Mosiah 27:15). "These were the last words which the angel spake unto Alma, and he departed. And now Alma and those that were with him fell again to the earth...for with their own eyes they had beheld an angel of the Lord; and his voice was as thunder, which shook the earth; and they knew that there was nothing save the power of God that could shake the earth and cause it to tremble as though it would part asunder." (Mosiah 27:17-18).

Three times in one night, the angel Moroni visited the boy Joseph Smith's chamber. Without reservation or apology, Joseph gave in his history perhaps the most detailed description of the appearance of a being from another realm: "I discovered a light appearing in my room," he wrote, "which continued to increase until the room was lighter than at noonday, when immediately a personage appeared at my bedside, standing in the air, for his feet did not touch the floor ... The room was exceedingly light, but not so very bright as immediately around his person ... After this communication, I saw the light in the room begin to gather immediately around the person of him who had been speaking to me, and it continued to do so until the room was again left dark, except just around him; when, instantly, I saw, as it were, a conduit open right up into heaven, and he ascended till he entirely disappeared, and the room was left as it had been before this heavenly light had made its appearance." (J.S.H. 2:30, 32 & 43).

In that era without electricity and long before the wonders of Industrial Light and Magic and Computer-Generated Imagery (CGI), Joseph Smith witnessed his closed chamber gradually flood with blinding light, followed immediately by the appearance of an angel within an even brighter part of the room. That light later gathered around the angel as the rest of the room went dark. It defies logic and the laws of physics to suggest that a room would at first go dark only in the peripheries, and then gradually around some central object, until the light finally winked out! We can digitally recreate such a scenario, but we cannot duplicate it in the real world. When we flip an electric switch, the result is instantaneous and relatively uniform. If we think of an angel coming from the glory of God in an adjacent dimensionally superior realm, however, it is easier to conceptualize how the light might have first appeared and then disappeared gradually, as the angel entered and then departed a narrowly defined portion of three-dimensional space within Joseph Smith's bed chamber.

There have also been many open area visitations by beings from eternal realms. The day following the visit of an angel in Joseph's bedchamber, in broad daylight, he had another manifestation from the unseen world. While working in the fields, he said: "My strength entirely failed me, and I fell helpless on the ground, and for a time was quite unconscious of anything. The first thing that I can recollect was a voice speaking unto me, calling me by name. I looked up, and beheld the same messenger standing over my head, surrounded by light as before." (J.S.H. 1:48-49). He later asked: "Now, what do we hear" in our three-dimensional state? "Moroni (and) the voice of Michael ... of Peter, James, and John ... and again, the voice of God ... of Gabriel, and of Raphael, and of divers angels, from Michael or Adam down to the present time." (D&C 128:19-21).

A well-documented open area visitation occurred at the temple in Bountiful. The Nephites who had gathered there after the crucifixion "saw a Man descending out of heaven; and he was clothed in a white robe; and he came down and stood in the midst of them; and the eyes of the whole multitude were turned upon him, and they durst not open their mouths, even one to another, and wist not what it meant, for they thought it was an angel" from the unseen world "that had appeared unto them." (3 Nephi 11:8).

On at least one occasion during His mortal ministry, Jesus spatially transported Himself from one location to another. When He angered the Jews by suggesting that "Before Abraham was, I am," the Jews took "up stones to cast at him: but Jesus hid himself, and went out of the temple, going through the midst of them, and so passed by." (John 8:59).

Jesus was also spatially transported when the devil tempted him as He fasted in the wilderness of Judea following His baptism. Matthew recorded: "The devil taketh him up to the holy city, and setteth him on a pinnacle of the temple." (Matthew 4:5). Then, "the devil, taking him up into an high mountain, shewed him all the kingdoms of the world in a moment of time." (Luke 4:5).

The earth itself has been spatially transformed, as when Israel walked on dry ground over the bed of the Red Sea. "And Moses stretched out his hand over the sea; and the Lord caused the sea to go back by a strong east wind all that night, and made the sea dry land, and the waters were divided. And the children of Israel went into the midst of the sea upon the dry ground: and the waters were a wall unto them on their right hand, and on their left." (Exodus 14:21-22).

Perhaps the solar system itself experienced a temporal distortion, when "the sun stood still, and the moon stayed, until the people had avenged themselves upon their enemies. Is not this written in the book of Jasher? So, the sun stood still in the midst of heaven, and hasted not to go down about a whole day." (Joshua 10:13).

How do God and angels move around in this manner without violating the laws of physics? Even at the speed of light, it would take at least 10 or 15 billion years to traverse the known universe, so physically moving from one point to another within it seems unlikely because after we have captured the Lord's attention, His intercession can be instantaneous. Samuel was once moved to exclaim: "In my distress I called upon the Lord, and cried to my God: and he did hear my voice out of his temple, and my cry did enter into his ears. Then the earth shook and trembled; the foundations of heaven moved and shook," as God instantly responded to his entreaty in a powerful manifestation from a higher dimensional realm. (2 Samuel 22:7-8). The same thing happens when the faithful pray to Heavenly Father. As James declared: "The effectual fervent prayer of a righteous man availeth much." (James 5:16). God hears His children even as they cry out to Him, and He has the power to immediately respond to their needs. Existing in a higher spatial dimension also gives God the ability to hear all of His children's petitions simultaneously wherever and whenever they may be without the inherent limitations of three-dimensional space.

Additional insight into higher spatial dimensions comes from accounts of the creation of the earth. Brigham Young used very unusual language when referring to the earth as it was at the time of the Fall and when it receives its paradisiacal glory. He said: "When the earth was framed and brought into existence and man was placed upon it, it was near the throne of our Father in Heaven. And when man fell … the earth fell into space, and took up its abode in this planetary system, and the sun became our light. This is the glory the earth came from, and… it will return again unto the presence of the Father, and it will dwell there." (J.D. 17:143). This description of falling into space and then leaving to return to the presence of the Father suggests an adjacent spatial dimension. As Micah prophesied: "The Lord cometh forth out of his place, and will come down, and tread upon the high places of the earth." (Micah 1:3).

There may be lateral moves, as well. As the Savior explained to the Nephites: "I have other sheep, which are not of this land, neither of the land of Jerusalem, neither in any parts of that land round about whither I have been to minister. For they of whom I speak are they who have not as yet heard my voice; neither have I at any time manifested myself unto them." (3 Nephi 16:1-2). Those of whom the Lord spoke were the Lost Ten Tribes of Israel.

Going to visit "other sheep" may be a cognitively comfortable way of expressing how we may travel to other dimensions. Perhaps Alma meant it literally, when he explained in regard to the Spirit World: "There is a space between death and the resurrection of the body." (Alma 40:21).

Perhaps it is easy access to higher-dimensional states that allows 'restoration' itself. From that vantage point, looking down on all the seraphic host, not by going to the left, or to the right, and not by going forward or backward, or up or down, but simultaneously at right angles to every one of those directions, God is in an ideal position to bring to pass our immortality and eternal life. From that perspective, He can confidently promise: "The soul shall be restored to the body, and the body to the soul; yea, and every limb and joint shall be restored to its body; yea, even a hair of the head shall not be lost; but all things shall be restored to their proper and perfect frame." Perhaps this is the mechanism of "the restoration of (those things) which has been spoken by the mouths of the prophets." (Alma 40:22-24).

Yet another utilization of the ability to move between dimensions may relate to the Lost Ten Tribes of Israel. The apocryphal writer Esdras suggested that they entered another state when they were carried "over the waters, and so came they into another land. But they took this counsel among themselves, that they would leave the multitude of the heathen, and go forth unto a further country, where never mankind dwelt, that they might there keep their statutes, which they never kept in their own land. And they entered into Euphrates by the narrow passage of the river. For the most High then shewed signs for them, and held still the flood, till they were passed over. For through that country there was a great way to go, namely, of a year and a half: and the same region is called Arsareth. Then dwelt they there until the latter times; and now when they shall begin to come, The Highest shall stay the stream again, that they may go through." (Apocrypha, 2 Esdras 13:40-47).

The Holy Scriptures record: "They who are in the north countries shall come in remembrance before the Lord; and their prophets shall hear his voice, and shall no longer stay themselves; and they shall smite the rocks, and the ice shall flow down at their presence. And an highway shall be cast up in the midst of the great deep, like as it was in the day that (Israel) came up out of the land of Egypt." (D&C 133:26-17, see Isaiah 11:16). There was no literal highway for the Ten Tribes, but the Lord did prepare a way for them, that they might reach their destination. Perhaps He has also prepared a way for them to remain hidden from the world in another spatial dimension until they are prepared to fulfill their millennial destiny.

Latter-day Saints are familiar with the concept of the "spirit world" and recognize it as an adjacent state-of-being. It "is a tangible sphere where disembodied spirits live in one of several conditions according to what their mortal lives have merited." (Dale Mouritsen, "The Spirit World, Our Next Home," Ensign, 1/1977). The Prophet Joseph Smith said that we should focus our study on the spirit world "day and night." He declared: "If we have any claim on our Heavenly Father for anything, it is for knowledge on this important subject." ("Teachings," p. 324). He also said: "The spirits of the just are exalted to a greater and more glorious work; hence they are blessed in their departure to the world of spirits. Enveloped in flaming fire, they are not far from us, and know and understand our thoughts, feelings, and motions, and are often pained therewith. Flesh and blood cannot go there; but flesh and bones, quickened by the Spirit of God, can." ("Teachings," p. 326).

Brigham Young asked: "When you lay down this tabernacle, where are you going? Into the spiritual world. Where is the spirit world? It is right here. Do the spirits go beyond the boundaries of this organized earth? No, they do not. They can see us, but we cannot see them, unless our eyes are opened." ("The Contributor," 10:9, quoted in N.B. Lundwall, "The Vision," p. 55-56, see "Discourses of Brigham Young," p. 376). This only makes sense if they are in a higher spatial dimension that may be like our being in a room with a one-way mirror in which they can look down and witness our every-day world. But to those of us within the room, trapped in the here-and-now, trying to see what lies in the other "direction" beyond the mirror is fruitless. Bound by the laws and conditions of our temporal and spatial reality, all we can hope to gain by observation is a confirmation of the validity of that which we already know, that is only a reflection of our own experience.

Parley P. Pratt also taught that the spirit world "is here on the very planet where we were born. The earth and other planets of like sphere have their inward or spiritual spheres, as well as their outward, or temporal. The one is peopled by temporal tabernacles, and the other by spirits. A veil is drawn between the one sphere and the other, whereby all the objects in the spiritual sphere are rendered invisible to those in the temporal." ("Key to Theology," p. 126-7). In today's vernacular, he would have said that temporal and spiritual worlds exist in nested dimensions that are separate and distinct realities.

Another way of saying this is that "spirits are composed of matter so refined as not to be tangible to this coarser organization." (Brigham Young, "Discourses of Brigham Young," p. 379). Joseph Smith said: "There is no such thing as immaterial matter. All spirit is matter, but it is more fine or pure, and can only be discerned by purer eyes. We cannot see it, but when our bodies are purified we shall see that it is all matter." (D&C 131:7-8, See H.C. 5:392-3).

When we achieve that state of refinement, perhaps we will then be able to join with the Dead Sea Covenanter who declared: "Behold, for mine own part, I have reached the intervision, and through the spirit thou hast placed within me, come to know Thee, my God." (Eleventh Hymn, Quoted in Preston Robinson's "Christ's Eternal Gospel," p. 111).

Perhaps the "intervision" is the state of consciousness that enables us to see parallel universes and to embrace the sum of reality.

Ezra Taft Benson said in General Conference: "Sometimes the veil between this life and the life beyond becomes very thin." (C.R., 4/1971). The veil reduces death to a state of being wherein our existence simply continues in an adjacent but superior spatial and temporal dimension.

This doctrine suggests that in our future state we shall see from multiple perspectives, freed from the myopic vision that currently limits our sight to the physical and temporal present within a very narrow band of the electromagnetic spectrum. As Albert Einstein wrote of the passing of one of his old friends: "This death signifies nothing. For us believing physicists, the distinction between past, present, and future is only an illusion, even if a stubborn one." ("Einstein," NOVA, 1979, p. 18).

Those who have had near-death experiences confirm the presence of adjacent temporal and spatial dimensions. An individual teetering on the brink between this life and the next "feels himself moving rapidly through a long, dark tunnel. After this, he suddenly finds himself outside his own physical body, and sees his own body from a distance, as though he were a spectator. He notices that he still has a body, but one with very different powers from the physical body he has left behind. Soon, others come to meet and help him. He glimpses the spirits of relatives and friends who have died. At some point he finds himself approaching a sort of barrier or border. He finds that he must go back to the earth, that the time for his death has not yet come. At this point he resists, for by now he is taken up with his experiences in the afterlife and does not want to return. He is overwhelmed by intense feelings of joy, love, and peace. Despite his attitude, though, he somehow re-unites with his physical body. Later, he tries to tell others, but he has trouble doing so. He can find no words adequate to describe these unearthly episodes. He also finds that others scoff, so he stops telling them. Those who have had near-death experiences describe a spiritual body that is invisible to others and lacks solidity. Travel in this state, once one gets the hang of it, is apparently exceptionally easy. Physical objects present no barrier, and movement from one place to another can be rapid, almost instantaneous.

What we learn about death may make an important difference in the way we live our lives. If experiences of this type are real, they have profound implications for what every one of us is doing with his life. For then, it would be true that we cannot fully understand this life until we catch a glimpse of what lies beyond it." (Raymond Moody, M.D., "Life after Life"). Evidently, we cannot be complete or whole until we appreciate our potential as children of a God Who has sent us to earth to lead us, guide us, walk beside us, and help us find the way back home.

If this is the case, then, as Joseph Smith said: "The only difference between the old and young dying is, one lives longer in heaven and eternal light and glory than the other, and is freed a little sooner from this miserable wicked world." (H.C. 4:553-554). Clearly, he felt our next estate would be soul-expanding with virtually unlimited options, in contrast to the limited scope of our potential here on earth.

Notwithstanding the promise of this glory, we frequently lose sight of it, and mourn the loss of our departed loved ones. Stretching our minds in this way, however, "speaks volumes of happiness, of joy and gratitude to (the) soul. Thank the Lord he has revealed these principles to us." (Joseph Smith, "Teachings," p. 197).

A reminiscence by a friend and associate of Joseph Smith reflects the gossamer fabric of the veil separating the world we know from the world of spirits. "'I am getting tired and would like to go to my rest,' said Joseph. His words and tone thrilled and shocked me, and like an arrow, pierced my hopes that he would long remain with us, and I said, as with a heart full of tears: 'Oh, Joseph, what could we, as a people, do without you and what would become of the great latter-day work if you should leave us?' He saw and was touched by my emotions, and in reply he said, 'Benjamin,

I would not be far away from you, and if on the other side of the veil, I would still be working with you, and with a power greatly increased, to roll on this kingdom.'" (Benjamin F. Johnson, in N.B. Lundwall, "The Vision," p. 140-141). Did the Prophet mean that he would have increased power in the sense that he would possess the ability to freely move between temporal and spatial dimensions? Perhaps he shared the vision of Abraham, who said of the creations of God: "They existed before, they shall have no end, they shall exist after, for they are … eternal." (Abraham 3:18).

Wilford Woodruff related a personal experience that bears directly on the Prophet's assurance of his close proximity to us after his death. "While I was upon my knees praying," he said, "my room was filled with light. I looked and a messenger stood by my side. I arose, and this personage told me he had come to instruct me. He presented before me a panorama. He told me he wanted me to see with my eyes and understand with my mind what was coming to pass in the earth before the coming of the Son of Man. After this passed by me, he disappeared. It made an impression upon me that has never left me from that day to this. The next day I was a lost man. I hardly knew where I was, so enveloped was I in that which I had seen." (Wilford Woodruff, Weber Stake Conference, Ogden, Utah, 10/19/1896).

One day we will all "see the Son of man sitting on the right hand of power, and coming in the clouds of heaven." (Mark 14:62). The Savior will come "down from heaven, not to do (His) own will, but the will of" His Father. (John 6:38). Where is heaven? Jesus simply declared: "I proceeded forth and came from God." (John 8:42). We know that "every good gift and every perfect gift is from above, and cometh down from the Father of lights." God is the author, embodiment, and source of light, His presence is real, and in Him there "is no variableness, neither shadow of turning." (James 1:17). Evidently, a higher-dimensional state of being eliminates ambiguity and creates clarity in a flood of unearthly light of unimaginable intensity.

Prophetic visions also suggest the existence of higher spatial dimensions. For example: "Moses cast his eyes and beheld the earth, yea, even all of it; and there was not a particle which he did not behold, discerning it by the spirit of God. And he beheld also the inhabitants thereof, and there was not a soul which he beheld not; and he discerned them by the Spirit of God; and their numbers were great, even numberless as the sand upon the seashore." (Moses 1:27-29). He knew this only because he had received a spiritual confirmation. Without it, he would have been oblivious to these mysteries of the kingdom, for "no man" on his own merits "can find out the work that God maketh from the beginning to the end." (Ecclesiastes 3:11). They "have no end, neither beginning." (D&C 29:33).

In the first chapter of Ezekiel, the prophet wrote: "Now it came to pass … that the heavens were opened, and I saw visions of God … And I looked, and, behold, a whirlwind came out of the north, a great cloud, and a fire infolding itself, and a brightness was about it … Also, out of the midst thereof came the likeness of four living creatures. And this was their appearance: they had the likeness of a man. And every one had four faces, and every one had four wings … Their wings were joined one to another; they turned not when they went; they went every one straight forward … As for the likeness of the living creatures, their appearance was like burning coals of fire, and like the appearance of lamps … and the fire was bright, and out of the fire went forth lightning. And the living creatures ran and returned as the appearance of a flash of lightning. Now as I beheld the living creatures … they four had one likeness: and their appearance and their work was, as it were, a wheel in the middle of a wheel. When they went, they went upon their four sides; and they turned not when they went." (Ezekiel 1:16).

The language Ezekiel used to describe what he saw was complex, metaphorical, stylistic, symbolical, and, yes, confusing, and might well have been the result of his inability to describe higher-dimensional objects and events. In particular, his characterization of a "wheel in the middle of a wheel" could have been an attempt to describe a four-dimensional tesseract, just as a hypercube is often represented as a cube within a cube. His references to a fire infolding itself and to multiple-sided beings who went straight forward even though they were facing in different directions may be the best descriptions we have of a hyper-object entering our space.

This may not have been Ezekiel's only higher-dimensional experience. "I beheld, and lo a likeness as the appearance of fire," he wrote, "from the appearance of his loins even downward, fire; and from his loins even upward, as the appearance of brightness, as the colour of amber. And (God) put forth the form of an hand, and took me by a lock of mine head; and the spirit lifted me up between the earth and the heaven, and brought me in the visions of God to Jerusalem, to the door of the inner gate … And, behold, the glory of the God of Israel was there, according to the vision that I saw." (Ezekiel 8:2-4). Thus did Ezekiel recount how the Lord had brought him through both time and space to witness events in Israel.

In a similar vision, Ezekiel was carried "into the land of Israel, and set … upon a very high mountain." "Behold with thine eyes," he was told, "and hear with thine ears, and set thine heart upon all that I shall shew thee." (Ezekiel 30:2 & 4). The prophet was able to see and hear with his physical faculties, but with a power greatly increased because of the influence of the Spirit. It "took me up," he said, "and brought me into the inner court; and, behold, the glory of the Lord filled the (temple)." (Ezekiel 43:5). "There is no apparent limit," wrote Parley P. Pratt, "to the speed attainable by the body, when unchained, set free from the elements which now enslave it." ("Key to The Science of Theology," p. 162).

Brigham Young believed that "the brightness and glory of the next apartment" to a higher-dimensional temporal and spatial reality "is inexpressible." Those who reside there "move with ease and like lightning. If we want to visit Jerusalem, or this, that, or the other place, there we are. If we want to behold Jerusalem as it was in the days of the Savior, or if we want to see the Garden of Eden as it was when created, there we are. We may behold the earth as at the dawn of creation, or we may visit any city we please that exists upon its surface." (J.D., 4:231). It seems that temporal and spatial transportations were not unfamiliar concepts to the prophets, for whom the arrow of time moves in two directions.

Many of the higher-dimensional experiences of the personalities in the scriptures simply cannot be articulated. When Paul wrote of being "caught up to the third heaven," he deferred from a lengthy explanation by simply stating: "Whether in the body, I cannot tell, or whether out of the body I cannot tell. God knoweth." (2 Corinthians 12:2). When the Three Nephites "were caught up into heaven, (they) saw and heard unspeakable things. And it was forbidden them that they should utter; neither was it given unto them power that they could utter the things which they saw and heard." (3 Nephi 28:13-14).

Helen Keller, who was blessed with neither sight nor hearing, nevertheless very perceptively wrote: "Only He who made all things can gaze upon unveiled glory. We could not behold untempered splendour and live. That is why man is permitted to look at everything only as in a glass, darkly, and gaze only upon the shadows in one small, dimly lighted chamber. Why should he speak of the dim mysteries of heaven so doubtingly, when really he apprehends so little of earth, and that only with veiled senses? Why cannot the soul with equal freedom go forth from its dwelling place, and discarding the poor lenses of the body, peer thru the telescope of truth into the infinite reaches of immortality?" ("My Religion," p. 77).

Adjacent dimensional realities, or 'the infinite reaches of immortality,' may be the focus of The Pearl of Great Price wherein "many lands" were described, and each "was called earth, and there were inhabitants on the face thereof." (Moses 1:29). We gain additional insight by studying Abraham's similar vision, when the Lord "put his hand upon (his) eyes, and (he) saw those things which his hands had made, which were many, and they multiplied before (his) eyes, and (he) could not see the end thereof." (Abraham 3:12).

When we have accepted the possibility that there is a fourth spatial dimension, the next logical question is: "What about a fifth-dimension, or a sixth, or a tenth? Is there any end to the creations and adjacent spatial dimensions of

God? These inquiries relate to the doctrines of kingdoms of glory and eternal progression, for as Brigham Young declared: "How many kingdoms of glory there are, I know not; and how many degrees of glory there are in these kingdoms, I know not; but there are multitudes of them ... The kingdoms that God has prepared are innumerable." (J.D., 8:154 & 9:107).

Doctrine & Covenants Section 76 teaches that there are three kingdoms of glory, the celestial, the terrestrial, and the telestial, and that the inhabitants of a particular kingdom cannot visit higher kingdoms but can visit lower kingdoms. For example, the inhabitants of the telestial kingdom "shall be servants of the Most High; but where God and Christ dwell they (simply) cannot come." (D&C 76:112). It may be that this limitation exists because each higher kingdom has at least one more spatial dimension than the next lower kingdom. In this sense, those in a lower kingdom could no more move into a higher kingdom than we could, by our own efforts, move from our three-dimensional world into a four-dimensional world. It would take the intervention of a higher power for them, or us, to do so. At the same time, however, those inhabiting a higher dimensional world could freely move from there into a lower dimensional world, just as we can, from our three-dimensional perspective, interact with two-dimensional and one-dimensional space with ease.

Eternal progression can be thought of in much the same way. Joseph Smith asked: "What did Jesus do? Why, I do the things I saw my Father do when worlds came rolling into existence. My Father worked out his kingdom with fear and trembling, and I must do the same; and when I get my kingdom, I shall present it to my Father, so that he may obtain kingdom upon kingdom, and it will exalt him in glory. He will then take a higher exaltation, and I will take his place, and thereby become exalted myself. So, Jesus treads in the tracks of the Father, and inherits what God did before." ("Teachings," p. 347-348).

Once we have been resurrected to glory in the Celestial Kingdom of God, our eternal progression might then involve advancement to a dimensionally higher state of being as soon as we are prepared to take that giant leap. In this case, we might progress to have dominion over an infinite number of dimensionally inferior realms similar in make-up to our previous habitation. This would allow those under our stewardship to advance to the position that we had formerly occupied. Once again, consider this insight from the Doctrine and Covenants: "All kingdoms have a law given; And there are many kingdoms; for there is no space in the which there is no kingdom; and there is no kingdom in the which there is no space, either a greater or a lesser kingdom. And unto every kingdom is given a law; and unto every law there are certain bounds also and conditions." (D&C 88:36-38). As Job said of man: "Thou hast appointed his bounds that he cannot pass." (Job 14:5). However, when its inhabitants have mastered the bounds and conditions of their particular kingdom, they would merit advancement to a dimensionally superior, or higher, kingdom.

Of our own earth, the Doctrine and Covenants teaches that "in its sanctified and immortal state, (it) will be made like unto crystal and will be a Urim and Thummim to the inhabitants who dwell thereon, whereby all things pertaining to an inferior kingdom, or all kingdoms of a lower order, will be made manifest to those who dwell on it." (D&C 130:9). The next verse suggests that there will be an order of kingdoms higher than the one that will exist on this earth after its sanctification. "The white stones mentioned in Revelation 2:17 will become a Urim and Thummim to each individual who receives one, whereby things pertaining to a higher order of kingdoms will be made known." (D&C 130:10). As Brigham Young stated: "When we have passed into the sphere where Joseph (Smith) is, there is still another department, and then another, and another, and so on to an eternal progression in exaltation and eternal lives." (J.D., 3:375).

The scope of these kingdoms is beyond our comprehension, but prophetic insight provides some clarity. Joseph Smith said: "The great Jehovah contemplated the whole of the events connected with the earth, pertaining to the plan of salvation, before it rolled into existence, or ever 'the morning stars sang together' for joy; the past, the present, and the future were and are, with him, one eternal 'now.'" (Teachings," p. 220). The Savior exists in the present tense, He is "the Great I AM, Alpha and Omega," that are the first and last letters of the Greek alphabet, "the beginning and the end, the same which looked upon the wide expanse of eternity, and all the seraphic hosts of heaven, before the world was made." (D&C 38:1-2). His "course is one eternal round, the same today as yesterday, and forever." (D&C 35:1). In this sense, time itself is a dimension with superior states of being that would allow us to see at once, or perhaps more accurately, from multiple perspectives in time, "the beginning and the end." (D&C 84:120). As Alma explained to Corianton: "All is as one day with God, and time only is measured unto men." (Alma 40:8). Einstein confirmed the truth of that principle. Time, he said, is relative.

Fortunately, the veil keeps us insulated from the other dimensions of reality and solidly grounds us on the familiar bedrock of past, present, and future. For now, the arrow of time moves in only one forward direction. This handy frame of reference allows us to live orderly through a timeline that is woven into the tapestry of three-dimensional space. It reassures us that the sun will come up tomorrow, and that there will be 24 hours in each day. Without the veil, life would be too confusing for most people! When the veil that encloses us in time is no more, time itself will be no more. Truly, this life "is the time for men to prepare to meet God." (Alma 34:32).

When the Lord redeems His people, Satan will be bound and time will no longer exist, because all things will be gathered in one. (Revelation 20:2 & D&C 45:55). Zion will come down from above and up from below at once and at the same time, and the earth will be clothed with the glory of God, who will stand in the midst of His people. (D&C 84:100).

"Even now, time is clearly not our natural dimension," wrote Neal A. Maxwell. "Thus it is that we are never really at home in time. Alternately, we find ourselves impatiently wishing to hasten the passage of time or to hold back the dawn. We can do neither, of course. Whereas the bird is at home in the air, we are clearly not at home in time because we belong to eternity. Time, as much as any one thing, whispers to us that we are strangers here. If time were natural to us, why is it that we have so many clocks, and wear wristwatches?

There are poignant and frequent reminders of the veil," he continued, "adding to our sense of being close but still outside. In our deepest prayers, when our agency encounters the omniscience of God, we sometimes sense, if only momentarily, how very provincial our petitions are; we perceive that there are more good answers than we have good questions; and we realize that we have been taught more than we can tell, for the language used is not that which the tongue can transmit.

We experience this same close separateness when a baby is born," he observed, "but also as we wait with those who are dying - for then we brush against the veil, as goodbyes and greetings are said almost within earshot of each other. In such moments, this resonance with realities on the other side of the veil is so obvious that it can be explained in only one way. No wonder the Savior said that His sheep would recognize His doctrines, that they would know His voice, and that they would follow Him. (John 10:14).

Without the veil," he concluded, "we would lose that precious insulation so necessary for our mortal probation and maturation. Without the veil, our brief mortal walk in a darkening world would lose its meaning, for one would scarcely carry the flashlight of faith at noonday and in the presence of the Light of the world." ("Patience," "B.Y.U. Speeches of The Year," 1979, & "Ensign," 10/1980).

In spite of the veil, those who participate in the ordinances of the gospel understand that there exists a 'second order of mind.' The experiences of the temple, for example, repetitively reinforce the shadow of 'other world' experiences. We are reminded that the endowment, like other gospel ordinances, cannot be exposed to the world, for it is symbolic and is spiritually discerned. In the temple, we institutionally validate the reality of higher spatial and even temporal dimensions in an unseen world. The Pearl of Great Price reinforces the teachings of the temple and confirms that from their superior vantage point in time and space, the Gods organized the heavens and the earth, divided the light from the darkness, created the waters and the earth, and placed all manner of vegetation thereon. Finally, they "watched those things which they had ordered until they obeyed." (Abraham 4:1-18).

What will our faculties be when we are free of the confines and limitations of our mortal bodies? Orson Pratt spoke of the ability to consider many different ideas at the same time, instead of thinking in a single channel only and of following just one course of reasoning. "Suppose He should give us a sixth sense, a seventh, an eighth, a ninth, or a fiftieth? All these different senses would convey to us new ideas, as much so as the senses of tasting, smelling, or seeing communicate different ideas from that of hearing. Do we suppose the five senses of man converse with all the elements of nature? No."

He believed that "knowledge will rush in from all quarters; it will come in like the light which flows from the sun, penetrating every part, informing the Spirit, and giving understanding concerning ten thousand things at the same time; and the mind will be capable of receiving and retaining all. Not one object at a time, but a vast multitude of objects (will) rush before his vision, and are present before his mind, filling him in a moment with the knowledge of worlds more numerous than the sands of the seashore. Will he be able to bear it? Yes, his mind (will be) strengthened in proportion to the amount of information imparted. It is this tabernacle in its present condition that prevents us from a more enlarged understanding.

When this tabernacle is taken off," he continued, "we shall look, not in one direction, but in every direction. This will be calculated to give us new ideas concerning the immensity of the creations of God. This will give us information and knowledge we never can know as long as we dwell in this mortal tabernacle. We shall have other sources of gaining knowledge, besides these inlets called senses. Man will be endowed, after he leaves this tabernacle, with powers and faculties which he now has no knowledge of, by which he may learn what is round about him." ("The Increased Powers of Faculties of Mind in a Future State," Excerpted from "Temples of the Most High," p. 299-312, see also J.D., 2:238-248).

Hugh Nibley has also considered the element of perspective within the gospel setting. He reasoned: "As to taking a calm and deliberate look at more than one thing at a time, that is a gift denied us at present. I cannot imagine what such a view of the world would be like, but it would be more real and correct than the one we have now. Once we can see the possibilities that lie in being able to see more than one thing at a time, the universe takes on new dimensions and God takes over." We should then be as the Brother of Jared, who, when overshadowed by the Spirit, could look upon past, present, and future generations at once. "They all came before him, and there was not a soul that he did not behold." (Mormon 8:35).

Dr. Nibley continued: "Let us remember that quite peculiar to the genius of Mormonism is the doctrine of a God who could preoccupy Himself with countless numbers of things. "The heavens they are many," the scriptures teach, "and they cannot be numbered unto man; but they are numbed unto me, for they are mine." (Moses 1:36). Plainly, we are dealing with a higher order. "For my thoughts are not your thoughts, neither are your ways my ways, saith the Lord. For as the heavens are higher than the earth, so are ... my thoughts than your thoughts." (Isaiah 55:8-9)." ("Zeal Without Knowledge," "Nibley on The Timely and Timeless," p. 263-264).

Brigham Young said: "I long for the time that a point of the finger, or motion of the hand, will express every idea without utterance. When a man is full of the light of eternity, then the eye is not the only medium through which he sees, nor the brain the only means by which he understands. When the whole body is full of the Holy Ghost, he can see behind him with as much ease, without turning his head, as he can see before him. If you have not had that experience, you ought to have. It is not the optic nerve alone that gives the knowledge of surrounding objects to the mind." (J.D., 1:70-71).

When we move into eternity, time will lose all significance, and "See you later," will cease to be in our vocabulary. Time, that we too frequently viewed as a predator that stalked us all our lives, may then be fondly remembered as a companion that accompanied us on our journey through mortality, reminding us to cherish every moment. We will find that our mortal experience was a tiny fraction of a much larger reality, and that our perspective was faulty as long as we believed it to be unique. We may be shocked to learn that mortality was not our natural dimension. We will come to understand why it was that we were never entirely comfortable in our mortal circumstances, and why we felt like "strangers and pilgrims on the earth." (Hebrews 11:13). This will, in turn, explain our innate thrust always toward the future, always beyond the horizon.

We may even find that growing "old" was strictly and uniquely a quality of mortality, and was a brilliant mechanism designed by Heavenly Father that afforded us an opportunity to gauge the approach of our reunion with Him in a higher-dimensional world. We may discover that because we lived in only one dimly lighted corner of reality, it was difficult for us to really appreciate our potential and the power of our position, that we might one day "flourish in immortal youth, unhurt amidst the war of elements, the wreck of matter, and the crash of worlds." (Joseph Addison, "Cato," Act 5, Scene 1). From our very narrow perspective, frozen in time as it were, death seems so distant, and its consequences so remote. We grew complacent in our indifference to the subtle messages reflected in the passage of time, and failed to understand their eternal significance.

When we move into a higher-dimensional reality, however, we will finally realize that time was an artificial and relative dimension in which we could not be completely comfortable, for we are eternal beings, and it was contrived. We shall suddenly realize that time was transitory by definition, and it might have only been our perspective that made it seem that it was we who moved through it, when it was really the other way around. In our youth, it never seemed to pass quickly enough. Perhaps we were so recently removed from the eternal world that we were impatient to return to that more natural environment. In any event, as we approached the terminator line between mortality and immortality, the perception of the passage of time changed again; it seemed to speed up.

If we had been able to view time dispassionately, perhaps we would have realized that when we kill time, we damage our eternal selves, for as the Lord warned, "in an hour when ye think not the summer shall be past, and the harvest ended, and your souls not saved." (D&C 45:2). We would have realized that every second of every day, we were one tick of the clock closer to the higher-dimensional reality of "the undiscovered country, from whose bourne no traveler returns." (Shakespeare, "Hamlet," Act 3, Scene 1).

Ironically, when we make the inevitable move forward into higher temporal and spatial dimensions, we will find that we have come home to a more comfortable and expansive dominion, where free will takes on a new meaning that was beforehand only dimly perceived. As the poet wrote: "Oh, this world has more of coming and of going than I can bear. I guess it's eternity I want, where all things are, and always will be. Where I can hold my loves a little looser. Where, finally, we realize time is the only thing that really dies." (Carol Lynn Pearson, "Optical Illusion," "Beginnings"). In fact, it is only "in the dark recesses of memory, in unbidden suggestions, in trains of thought unwittingly pursued, in multiplied waves and currents all at once flashing and rushing, in dreams that cannot be laid to rest, in the force of instinct, in the obscure, but certain, intuitions of the spiritual life, that we have glimpses of a great tide of life ebbing and flowing, rippling and roiling and beating about where we cannot see it." (E.S. Dallas).

We are fortunate, indeed, if we have shared the experience of the aviator who ecstatically wrote: "Oh, I have slipped the surly bonds of earth and danced the skies on laughter-silvered wings. Sunward I've climbed, and joined the tumbling mirth of sun-split clouds, and done a hundred things you have not dreamed of. I've wheeled and soared and swung high in the sunlit silence. Hovering there, I've chased the shouting wind along, and flung my eager craft through footless halls of air. Up, up the long, delirious, burning blue I've topped the windswept heights with easy grace, where never lark, or even eagle flew. And, while with silent, lifting mind I've trod the high untrespassed sanctity of space, I put out my hand, and touched the face of God." (John G. Magee, Jr., "High Flight").

While we are trapped in time, we can only indirectly appreciate the eternities. As we seek learning, even by study and also by faith, "we can make our lives sublime, and departing, leave behind us footprints on the sands of time." (Henry Wadsworth Longfellow, "A Psalm of Life"). Those footprints might be washed away by the incessant wave action of the unseen temporal and spatial dimensions beating on our shores. "There is a tide (after all) in the affairs of men which, taken at the flood, leads on to fortune." (Shakespeare, "Julius Caesar," Act 4, Scene 2). Our destiny was prepared in the pre-earth existence, is molded in mortality, and will be established in eternity, when the heavens will smile upon us, and we will be clothed with the glory of God in an infinite hierarchy of higher temporal and spatial dimensions.

If we cannot acknowledge the reality of eternity now, however, where will our sanctuary be when the wind blows and the rain beats down? To what safe harbor will we flee when the ocean of life is in turmoil? When we are tossed about as flotsam and jetsam, never coming to a knowledge of what is real, to what source will we look for the stability we so desperately seek, or for the answers to life's greatest questions that continually trouble our spirits? Understanding ourselves from an eternal perspective has many advantages. Not the least of these is that when we raise our sights to the possibility of an expanded view of life, we are up and moving on the pathway to personal re-discovery and self-actualization in the larger arena of higher- dimensional awareness. Perhaps Captain Jean Luc Picard was correct when he declared: "Space is the final frontier."

We shall enter into the temporal and spatial reality of God's Rest when we have gained a perfect knowledge of the divinity of the work, and are liberated from fear, doubt, apprehension of danger, the religious turmoil of the world, and from the vagaries of men. When we have cast off the self-limiting conditions and self-defeating behaviors that blind us to a larger view of life, we will enjoy a settled conviction of the truth in our minds that affords us the peace that follows obedience to celestial principles and brings His reality within our reach. The invitation to follow Him is prefaced by the action verb "come." That journey will carry us beyond an event horizon to an incomprehensively higher dimensional state of being.

After we have kept our second estate, and have glory added upon our heads, what will it be like to be clothed with immortality and eternal life? Will we then more closely resemble our Father in Heaven in image and likeness? If so, we are gods and goddesses in embryo. If our genome is truly divine, it is our destiny to mature to the stature of our Heavenly Parents. C.S. Lewis observed: "It is a serious thing to live in a society of possible Gods and Goddesses - to remember that the dullest and most uninteresting person you talk to may one day be a creature which, if you saw it now, you would be strongly tempted to worship. It is in the light of these overwhelming possibilities and with the awe and the circumspection proper to them, that we should conduct all our dealings with one another. There are no ordinary people. Next to the blessed sacrament itself, your neighbor is the holiest object presented to your senses." ("The Weight of Glory").

The veil is almost transparent in our lives when we are spiritually sensitive and prepared to act. As our powers expand, we experience the glittering facets of the life of the Spirit. "To use the careful preparation and training we receive as a springboard, to be capable of disciplined, controlled procedure and to be receptive to flashes of insight, is what solid Latter-day Saints should have going for them in their inner lives. The gospel sets us free to be creative, and sets us creative to become more free. It is the perfect law of liberty." ("My Religion and Me," Lesson #9). Truly, the gospel amplifies the quiet spiritual stirrings that underlie all mortal experience and is the catalyst designed to propel us into the Presence of God.

"I wish I could remember the days before my birth, and if I knew the Father before I came to earth. In quiet moments when I'm all alone, I close my eyes and try to see my Heavenly home. Although I can't remember and cannot clearly see, I listen to the spirit and so I must believe. But still I wonder, and I hope to find the answer to the question that is on my mind. Where is Heaven? Is it very far? I would like to know if it's beyond the brightest star." (Janice Kapp Perry).

It has been said that it is only when
we stop living that we start dying. In fact, we live
and move and have our being thru sense and perception
that are blended into a refreshing elixir preventing us from
becoming too set in our ways. These will then coalesce into an
unlikely union that by intelligent design was created to expand
our experience to better prepare us to weather our storms and meet
our challenges, ultimately to upset the status-quo. In the end, it
is "by the experiment of this ministration" that we are able to
"glorify God for (our) professed subjection unto the gospel
of Christ." (2 Corinthians 9:13). It was ordained in the
heavens that as we internalize the doctrine and the
principles of The Book of Mormon, we will feel
the exertion of an equalizing influence,
for "all are alike unto God."
(2 Nephi 26:33).

(The) Holy Ghost

It is only when we stop living that we
start dying. We live and move and have our being through
sense and perception that blend into a refreshing elixir preventing us
from becoming too set in our ways. These form an unlikely union, that
by intelligent design has been created to upset the status-quo, expand our
experience, weather our storms, and meet our challenges. At the end of the
day, it is "by the experiment of this ministration" that we are able
to "glorify God for (our) professed subjection unto the gospel
of Christ." (2 Corinthians 9:13). It was ordained in the
heavens that as we internalize the doctrine, we feel
the exertion of an equalizing influence,
for "all are alike unto God."
(2 Nephi 26:33).

Happiness smells like bread baking in the oven, looks like a bright smile, makes us feel warm and cozy inside, sounds like children laughing in the park, and tastes like an ice cream sundae. Apples smell like cider, look like big red balls, feel smooth and hard, sound crunchy when biting into them, and taste sweet and juicy.

Smell, sight, touch, sound, and taste are the passport stamps that attest to our involvement in the world around us. They are critical to our interaction with the environment. Our brains have been created in such a way that they become blenders that take these sensations and whip them up into frothy virgin piña colatas of perception that become our own inimitable windows on the world. Life's experiences create zesty signature specialty drinks complete with little umbrellas that catch our attention, maraschino cherries that hold our interest, and whipped cream that keeps us coming back to the server asking for more, please.

But, as common as our five physical senses are, none of us see things in exactly the same way. Closely associated with intimate experiment, experience testifies to the recognition of our individuality by the Author of the Plan of Salvation. It is within the divinely conceived and ordained process of the marriage of sense and perception that our personalities enjoy their greatest elasticity. The resulting originality allows us to savor the gentle tug of non-conformity. Just as wind and water shape the landscape, the Master Potter takes our pliant mortal clay and fashions His magnum opus, with each piece of the puzzle expressing its own unique character. We are works in progress, stanzas in His unfinished symphony, and are continually evolving in an eternal progression.

It is only when we stop living that we start dying. We live and move and have our being through sense and perception that blend into a refreshing elixir preventing us from becoming too set in our ways. These form an unlikely union, that by intelligent design has been created to upset the status-quo, expand every experience, weather every storm, and meet every challenge. At the end of the day, it is "by the experiment of this ministration" utilizing our senses, that we are able to "glorify God for (our) professed subjection unto the gospel of Christ." (2 Corinthians 9:13). It was ordained in the heavens that as we internalize the doctrine, we feel the exertion of an equalizing influence, for "all are alike unto God." (2 Nephi 26:33). But at the same time, sense and perception flavor a painstakingly crafted formula that enhances the distinctive qualities that make each of us unique.

We have other senses, as well, such as temperature (thermoception), body position (proprioception) pain (nociception), balance (equilibrioception), and time (chronoception). Together, like hormones, they subtly catalyze our environmental awareness. There are other senses that we do not have, or have only in diminished capacity, such as the ability to detect electrical and magnetic fields, polarized and infrared light, water pressure, pheromones, and the ability to utilize sonar. But we do not have a lock on the senses that we do enjoy; they are not uniquely ours. Bears have a better sense of smell, eagles a better sense of sight, catfish (believe it or not) a better sense of touch and taste, and dogs a better sense of sound. But what we do have seems to be in perfect balance and harmony, and is individually tailored to our specific needs.

Roughly 30 percent of the neurons in our cerebral cortex are devoted to vision, 8 percent to touch, 3 percent to hearing, and 0.1% to smell. It is unknown how many of the brain's neurons in the gustatory cortex are related to taste. There are roughly 100 billion neurons in our grey matter with 100 trillion connections (synapses) and a processing capacity of ten trillion instructions per second. The electrical output that would be required to simulate this brain function in a laboratory setting is equivalent to ten megawatts. A phenomenal amount of activity is going on in our brains to accommodate virtually limitless perceptions that take the philosophical supposition "cogito ergo sum" to incomprehensible levels.

Our senses are real, and when our bodies are in homeostasis, or in a state of equilibrium, we experience all of them, often unconsciously. They blend together in harmony to give us all the information we need in order to interact with our environment. But they do more than just that, by magically transforming raw data into perception, and in so doing they enrich our lives. Perception is a good example that the sum is greater than its parts. It sweeps aside the simple math of stimulus and response, nullifying the argument that we simply react to our surroundings, and it introduces the intriguing element of uncertainty that give vitality and vibrancy to life, and new meanings to self-awareness. Perception opens up unknown possibilities of existence that we may have never before considered.

Our senses allow us to communicate, but our perceptions make our lives complete. Take even one sense from us, however, and we may be labeled as handicapped, be thought to have diminished capacity, or made to feel that we are somehow impaired. Our senses are so powerful that it we lose one, by substitution the others will move in with increased acuity to fill the void.

Sometimes, our senses can run wild. Hypersensitivity to auditory, visual, and tactile stimuli comes to mind. We all attempt, with varying levels of success, to compartmentalize endless data streams that unceasingly threaten to overwhelm us. A relentless flood of neural information may so overpower us that we suffer a breakdown of our nervous system. Einstein described sensory overload as a storm that had broken loose in his mind. As a disciplined physicist, he was able to quantify, process, and control the barrage of mathematically complex information to which his brain was subjected. The therapy of his own design was an attempt to wrap his mind around a grand unifying principle that he hoped would harmonize the four fundamental forces of nature. Even with his prodigious mental calisthenics, he was unable to quantify and define that elusive equation, but if the Plan of Salvation is perfect, an equivalent principle must surely exist. It seems certain that God's Plan must hold the key that allows us to create order out of the chaos that is the milieu of mortality.

Some have defined His remedy as a spiritual "sixth sense," like the elusive dark matter that has been postulated to fill the void of space. Some believe that it is intuition, or the ability to take raw data and make sense of it and understand it immediately, without the need for conscious reasoning, interpretive analysis, or cerebral scrutiny. To accommodate the phenomenon of having the strong sensation that a current event has been experienced in the past, we have coined the phrase déjà vu, from French, literally meaning "already seen." The answer could be extrasensory perception, or the reception of information gained with the mind, rather than through the recognized physical senses. Perhaps it is clairvoyance, or the faculty of perceiving things or events in the future or beyond normal contact. Maybe it is premonition, or a strong feeling that something is about to happen. It may be all of the above, and more.

God's whole is surely greater than the sum of His parts, just as our perceptions are more than the sum of the sensory stimulations codified by our cerebral cortices. His spiritual sixth sense must be described by a common denominator that is the elusive theory of everything. Surely, there is a grand unifying principle underlying His Plan, but it probably defies explanation on a chalkboard, cannot be quantified by attaching electrodes to neurons, and will never be explained by dissecting a brain. No matter how far the neural net is cast, it will not be wide enough to catch God's vision for the education and exaltation of His children. His thoughts are not our thoughts, and His ways are not our ways.

The Higgs Boson may be "the God particle" that confirms "the Standard Model," a theory that attempts to harmonize the forces that govern the natural world. But if there is another power that supersedes the discipline of physics, that generates more energy than the Large Hadron Collider, a revision of the basic principles relating to "Philosophiæ Naturalis Principia Mathematica" will be required. (Sir Isaac Newton, July 5, 1687). That revision has always existed, quietly humming along in the background, flying beneath the radar, as it were. We know it as the Plan of Salvation.

Those of us with a strong Judeo-Christian background describe the commanding force the drives the execution of the Plan as the Holy Ghost. We believe that He is real, and that we all experience His influence. We submit that when our bodies are perfectly attuned to celestial rhythms, we often don't even consciously think about Him. We testify that the Holy Ghost has the ability to enrich our lives without dominating or overpowering our interaction with the world, thereby elegantly preserving the principle of free will. Our experience suggests that, with His input, we are given just the right amount of information we need in order to relate more comprehensively with our environment, while at the same time retaining ownership for our actions. And yet, we affirm that He is our fountain of facts and figures, our storehouse of knowledge, our lifetime of learning, our repository of reassurance, our spring of sagacity, our talisman of talents, and our warehouse of wisdom.

He is the author of acumen, the avatar of agency, the architect of aptitude, the benefactor of blessings, the champion of committed Christians, the craftsman of comfort, the designer of our discipleship, the engineer of erudition, the guarantor of gifts, the initiator of insight, the inventor of intelligence, the patron of perception, the provider of praise, the sponsor of scholarship, and the ultimate source of understanding. He testifies of truth, and provides the aether within which we communicate with our Heavenly Father. He makes our lives complete. However, we have also seen that by accident or by intention, we can lose the blessings of His influence. We can find ourselves in a state that is "past feeling," and lose the precious perception that He provides. (Ephesians 4:19).

We do Him little justice if we regard the Holy Ghost as only a spiritual sixth sense. His influence exceeds our ability to understand something immediately, without the need for conscious reasoning; is greater than the gathering of information not gained through the recognized physical senses but grasped with the mind; surpasses a strong feeling that something is about to happen, is superior to the strong sensation that an event has been experienced in the past; and transcends the faculty of perceiving things or events in the future or beyond normal contact.

It is a worthwhile endeavor getting to know the Holy Ghost, "getting to know all about Him, getting to like Him, and getting to hope He like us. Putting it another way, but nicely, He is precisely our cup of tea, getting to feel free and easy when we are with Him. Haven't you noticed, suddenly we're bright and breezy, because of all the beautiful and new things we're learning about Him day by day." (Adapted from "The King and I," "Getting to Know You," lyrics by Lorenz Hart and Richard Rodgers).

The Holy Ghost is real. "We believe in God, the Eternal Father, and in His Son, Jesus Christ, and in the (third member of the Trinity, the) Holy Ghost." (First Article of Faith). The Savior promised: "When he, the Spirit of truth, is come, he will guide you into all truth: for he shall not speak of himself; but whatsoever he shall hear, that shall he speak, and he will shew you things to come." (John 16:13). He is in the form of a man and has a Spirit body. "The Father," said the Prophet Joseph Smith, "has a body of flesh and bones as tangible as man's; the Son also; but the Holy Ghost has not a body of flesh and bones, but is a personage of Spirit." (D&C 130:22). His mission, after bestowing all of the other blessings of which He is capable of providing, is ultimately to bear witness of the Father and the Son. "Wherefore I give you to understand," wrote Paul, "that no man speaking by the Spirit of God ... can say that Jesus is the Lord, but by the Holy Ghost." (1 Corinthians 12:3).

The Holy Ghost manifests truth to the honest in heart. He is a revelator through Whom prophecy comes. By His power we "may know the truth of all things." (Moroni 10:5). "No prophecy of the scripture is of any private interpretation," said Peter. "For the prophecy came not in old time by the will of man: but holy men of God spake as they were moved by the Holy Ghost." (2 Peter 1:20-21). When we, at last, come back into the presence of God our Father, it will be through the tender guidance, concerned supervision, nurturing influence, dizzying inspiration, and powerful witness of the Holy Ghost. His spirit will authoritatively justify us before the throne of God. (Moses 6:60). We will be weighed and measured according to His equitable and unimpeachable testimony.

He is the Holy Spirit of Promise. "Concerning them who shall come forth in the resurrection of the just - They are they who received the testimony of Jesus, and believed on his name and were baptized after the manner of his burial... That by keeping the commandments they might be washed and cleansed from all their sins, and receive the Holy Spirit by the laying on of the hands of him who is ordained and sealed unto this power; And who overcome by faith, and are sealed by the Holy Spirit of promise, which the Father sheds forth upon all those who are just and true." (D&C 76:50-53).

After giving us our physical senses, God paused for a moment, and then also gave us a Divine Companion that we may think of as "the breath of life." (Genesis 2:7). Joseph Fielding Smith (who surely was in a position to know) said the Spirit of God "has power to impart truth with greater effect and understanding than the truth can be imparted by personal contact even with heavenly beings. Through the Holy Ghost, the truth is woven into the very fiber and sinews of the body so that it cannot be forgotten." ("Doctrines of Salvation," 1:47-48). The Holy Ghost weaves golden threads into the tapestry of our lives so that we may take steady steps with the confidence born of its vibrant inner light.

"My life is but a weaving between the Lord and me," wrote the poet. "I cannot choose the colors; He worketh steadily. Oft-times, He weaveth sorrow, and I, in foolish pride, forget that He seeith the upper, and I, the underside. Not 'til the loom is silent, and the shuttles cease to fly, shall God unroll the canvas and explain the reasons why. The dark threads are as needful in the Weaver's skillful hand, as the threads of gold and silver, in the pattern He has planned." (Benjamin Malachi Franklin). If we allow Him to, the Holy Ghost will tailor our lives so that when we present ourselves before the throne of God, our garments will be free of the soil of sin, and we will be neatly dressed in our Sunday best that is a coat of many colors.

In the meantime, one of the principal responsibilities of the Holy Ghost is to anticipate and eliminate the culture shock that we might otherwise feel when we make the inevitable transition from a telestial tenement to a celestial station. We think of Paul's description of a "building fitly framed together (that) groweth unto an holy temple in the Lord." (Ephesians 2:21). C.S. Lewis suggested: "Imagine yourself as a living house. God comes in to rebuild that house. At first, perhaps, you can understand what He is doing. He is getting the drains right and stopping the leaks in the roof and so on. You knew that those jobs needed doing and so you are not surprised. But presently, He starts knocking the house about in a way that hurts abominably and does not seem to make any sense. What on earth is He up to? The explanation is that He is building quite a different house from the one you thought of - throwing out a new wing here, putting on an extra floor there, running up towers, making courtyards. You thought you were being made into a decent little cottage, but He is building a palace." ("Mere Christianity").

We make initial preparations to take up eventual residence in the mansions that have been prepared for us, by submitting ourselves to baptism by water. But that demonstration of faith and obedience only unlatches and nudges open the gate that exposes the pathway leading to the Celestial Kingdom. "For the gate by which ye should enter is repentance and baptism by water; and then cometh a remission of your sins by fire and by the Holy Ghost." (2 Nephi 31:17). Without baptism, we cannot take advantage of the Atonement, but without the gift of the Holy Ghost, we cannot even make the vital distinctions between truth and error. That requires perception on a plane that is more profound that can be provided by our organs working in concert with our central nervous systems. It comes only to those who perceive themselves as acorns of a mighty oak. When we chart the course we would hope our lives might take, we cannot navigate past dangerous shoals and jagged reefs without the assistance of a trustworthy Pilot with unfathomable experience.

The Plan of Salvation cannot operate to our benefit without discernment. Were it not for the gift of the Holy Ghost, the Plan would work to our damnation. Its elements would be thrown into turmoil without the moral element of responsibility that He provides. Joseph Smith was able to enjoy the promptings of the Spirit and exercise his powers of discernment long before he became a member of the church of Jesus Christ. As Peter said: "God is no respecter of persons; but in every nation he that feareth him, and worketh righteousness, is accepted" by him. (Acts 10:34-35).

Today, those who are led by the Light of Christ to seek out the truth may also enjoy the promptings of the Holy Ghost. In the closing chapter of The Book of Mormon, Moroni promised: "And when ye shall receive these things, I would exhort you that ye would ask God, the Eternal Father, in the name of Christ, if these things are not true; and if ye shall ask with a sincere heart, with real intent, having faith in Christ, he will manifest the truth of it unto you, by the power of the Holy Ghost." (Moroni 10:4).

Joseph Fielding Smith said: "We can receive a manifestation of the Holy Ghost, even when we are out of the church, if we are earnestly seeking for the light and for the truth. The Holy Ghost will come and give us the testimony we are seeking, and then withdraw." He continued: "There is no need for anyone to remain in darkness; the light of the everlasting gospel is here; and every sincere investigator on earth can gain a personal witness from the Holy Spirit, of the truth and divine nature of the Lord's work." ("Ensign," 6/1971).

But when we become members of the church, we need the special gift of the Holy Ghost to help us to be true to our blossoming faith. Joseph Fielding Smith said: "We may, after baptism and confirmation, become companions of the Holy Ghost, who will teach us the ways of the Lord, quicken our minds and help us to understand the truth."

("Doctrines of Salvation," 1:42). He can be our ever-faithful companion throughout the course of our mission in mortality, no matter in what areas we might serve, or how surprising our transfers might seem.

We need the gift of the Holy Ghost to eliminate ambiguity in our lives, clarify the elements of the Plan of Happiness, and bring accountability into sharp focus, so we may amend our behavior with the help of the Atonement. Joseph Fielding Smith said: "We are promised that when we are baptized, if we are true and faithful, we will have the guidance of the Holy Ghost. What is the purpose of it? To teach us, to direct us, to bear witness to us of the saving principles of the gospel of Jesus Christ." (C.R., 10/1959).

With the gift of the Holy Ghost, the plain and simple truths of the gospel of Jesus Christ, "even the key of the knowledge of God," will be unfolded to our view. (D&C 84:19). Joseph Fielding Smith said: "What a glorious privilege this is to be guided constantly by the Holy Ghost and to have the mysteries of the kingdom of God made manifest." ("Answers to Gospel Questions," 4:90).

The Holy Ghost orients us toward the celestial kingdom. Joseph Fielding Smith said: "After we are baptized, we are confirmed to make us companions with the Holy Ghost; to give us the privilege of the guidance of the third member of the Godhead, that our minds might be enlightened, and that we might be quickened to seek for knowledge and understanding concerning all that pertains to our exaltation." ("Ensign," 6/1972).

The Holy Ghost endows us with spiritual and priesthood power. Marion G. Romney said: "The gift of the Holy Ghost is an endowment which gives us the right to enjoy the enlightenment, companionship, and guidance of the Spirit, as long as we comply with the commandments of God." He went on to say: "Receiving the Holy Ghost is the therapy which effects forgiveness and heals the sin-sick soul." (C.R., 4/1974).

When we view the gift of the Holy Ghost as an endowment, we can see that only those who are on a path leading to exaltation (through participation in the saving principles of the gospel) need healing at the level and intensity that is provided by intimate association with the third member of the Godhead. After our baptism and confirmation to receive the gift of the Holy Ghost, we receive the priesthood-administered ordinances of the temple. Brigham Young said our endowment of power received there gives us instruction sufficient to lay hold of eternal life, and consists of receiving all those ordinances "which are necessary for you, after you have departed this life, to enable you to walk back to the presence of the Father, passing the angels who stand as sentinels, being enabled to give them the key words, the signs and tokens, pertaining to the Holy Priesthood, and gain your eternal exaltation in spite of earth and hell." (J.D., 2:31).

In a way that presages the endowment in the temple, the gift of the Holy Ghost provides the power to perform whatever work is necessary for us to achieve our exaltation. Joseph Fielding Smith said: "The Holy Ghost is the Messenger, or Comforter, which the Savior promised to send to his disciples after He was crucified. This Comforter is, by His influence, to be a constant companion to every baptized person, and to administer unto the members of the church by revelation and guidance, knowledge of the truth that they may walk in its light. It is the Holy Ghost Who enlightens the mind of the truly baptized member. It is through Him that individual revelation comes, and the light of truth is established in our hearts." ("Answers to Gospel Questions," 2:149-50). He ministers to our needs "with healing in his wings." (Malachi 4:2).

Because the gift of the Holy Ghost is an endowment from on high, it is reserved for the faithful who have entered in at the strait gate of baptism. It is bestowed by those who hold the authority of the priesthood. Joseph Fielding Smith said: "You cannot get the gift of the Holy Ghost by praying for it, by paying your tithing, by keeping the Word of Wisdom, not even by being baptized in water for the remission of sins. You must complete that baptism with the baptism of the Spirit. The Prophet said on one occasion that you might as well baptize a bag of sand as not confirm a man and give him the gift of the Holy Ghost, by the laying on of hands. You cannot get it any other way." ("Doctrines of Salvation," 1:41).

The gift of The Holy Ghost is bestowed under special terms and conditions. Marion G. Romney said the promise that "God shall give unto (us) knowledge by the unspeakable gift of the Holy Ghost" (D&C 121:26) poses the question as to the manner in which we may receive this gift. It is by the laying on of hands following faith in the Lord Jesus Christ, repentance from sin, and baptism by immersion for the remission of sins." (C.R., 4/1974). We receive the gift of the Holy Ghost by obedience to the first principles of the gospel. (See the Fourth Article of Faith).

And yet, there are baptized and confirmed members of the church who do not enjoy "the companionship of the Holy Ghost (because it) is available only to those who prepare themselves to receive it," said Joseph Fielding Smith. "It is my judgment," he continued, "that there are many members of this church who have been baptized for the remission of their sins, and who have had hands laid upon their heads for the gift of the Holy Ghost, but who have never received it. They listen (to heretical teachings) and the first thing you know, they find their way out of the church, because they do not have understanding." ("Seek Ye Earnestly the Best Gifts," p. 3). Without the guidance of the Holy Ghost, "their ears are dull of hearing, and their eyes have they closed." (Acts 28:27). "Noses they have they, but they smell not." (Psalms 115:6).

Our God-given senses cannot replace the influence of the Spirit. "The wind bloweth where it listeth, and thou hearest the sound thereof, but canst not tell whence it cometh, and whither it goeth: so is every one that is born of the Spirit." (John 3:8). Even if we use our physical senses to excess, relying on our intellect and instinct, while ignoring spiritual promptings that are provided in a rarified atmosphere like a refreshing breeze on a hot summer day, we will fall short of our perception potential provided by the pattern of the Plan.

If we do not know, or choose to ignore the Holy Ghost, we become susceptible to three dangers. The first is indifference, or a lack of commitment. If we do not know the Master, how can we be expected to serve Him with all our heart, might, mind, and strength? The second is waywardness, or straying from the gospel standard. If we are unprincipled and believe in nothing, how can we be expected to stand for something? The third is rebellion, or active opposition to the principles of truth. If we extinguish the light, how can we avoid stumbling over the obstacles to our progression in the gathering gloom? King Benjamin cautioned his people: "This much I can tell you, that if ye do not watch yourselves, and your thoughts, and your words, and your deeds, and observe the commandments of God, and continue in the faith of what ye have heard concerning the coming of our Lord, even unto the end of your lives, ye must perish." (Mosiah 4:30).

We may excel in sports, have the I.Q. of a genius, have perfect pitch, receive the accolades of men, spend our days in the heady atmosphere of the ivory towers of academia, jet-set with celebrities, hobnob with princes and potentates, or be the richest person in Babylon, but in the end, if we have not enjoyed the companionship of the Holy Ghost, none of it will be worth the ashes of a rye straw. Perhaps, when the last chapters of our lives are written, teachability and malleability will prevail, rather than sense or sensibility.

Joseph Fielding Smith counseled: "If we find ourselves in a condition of unbelief or unwillingness to seek for the light and the knowledge which the Lord has placed within our reach, then we are in danger of being deceived by evil spirits and the doctrines of devils. When these false influences are presented before us, we will not have the distinguishing understanding" by which we can recognize them for what they are. (C.R., 10/1952). Not only our physical senses, but also our spiritual senses will have failed us in our times of greatest need. Lacking inspiration, we will face eternity short of the breath of the Almighty that might have otherwise sustained our lives. (See Job 33:4). Our final expiration of the celestial aether that filled our lungs at birth will be utterly complete.

Some have received the gift of the Holy Ghost, but then have let it slip between their fingers. Joseph Fielding Smith said: "The Spirit of the Lord will not dwell in unclean tabernacles, and when a person turns from the truth through wickedness, that Spirit does not follow him but departs, and in the stead thereof comes" the overwhelming influence of the physical senses, manifest as the "spirit of error, the spirit of disobedience, the spirit of wickedness, (and) the spirit of eternal destruction." (C.R., 4/1962).

He also taught: "It is the privilege of every member of the church to know the truth, to speak by the truth, to have the inspiration of the Holy Ghost. It is our privilege, individually, to receive the light and to walk in the light; and if we continue in God, that is, keep all of His commandments, we shall receive more light until eventually there shall come to us the perfect day of knowledge." ("Relief Society Magazine," 1/1941).

At that day, "by the power of the Spirit our eyes (will be) opened and our understanding (will be) enlightened, so as to see and understand the things of God." (D&C 76:12). Our physical senses will have finally harmonized with our spirit. We will feel the truth as it swells within our bosom, as it did for the two disciples on the road to Emmaus, who said of the resurrected Lord: "Did not our heart burn within us, while he talked with us by the way, and while he opened to us the scriptures?" (Luke 24:32). We will touch eternity as our cheeks "brush against the veil, as goodbyes and greetings are said almost within earshot of each other. In such moments, this resonance with realities on the other side of the veil is so real that it can be explained in only one way." (Neal A. Maxwell, "(All These Things Shall Give Thee Experience," p. 6-27).

We will smell the sweet fragrance of celestial gardens, and hear the Spirit of truth speak "of things as they really are, and of things as they really will be," and these things will be "manifested unto us plainly, for the salvation of our souls." (Jacob 4:13). We will hear a voice saying: "Well done thou good and faithful servant … enter thou into the joy of the Lord." (Matthew 25:21). At last, we will come back into the presence of God our Father, through the nurturing guidance of the Holy Ghost.

(The) Holy Grail of Religious Doctrine

"O how
great the plan of our God!
... The righteous shall have a perfect
knowledge of their enjoyment and their
righteousness, being clothed with purity, yea,
even with the robe of righteousness ... And assuredly,
as the Lord liveth, for the Lord God hath spoken it, and it
is his eternal word, which cannot pass away, that they who
are righteous shall be righteous still ... O the greatness and
the justice of our God! For he executeth all his words, and
they have gone forth out of his mouth, and his law
must be fulfilled." (2 Nephi 9:13-17).

The Book of Abraham describes "their plan" meaning the plan of the Gods. (Abraham 4:21). Jacob refers to it as: "The plan of our God." (2 Nephi 9:13). Its keystone is the Atonement of Jesus Christ, and so Alma called it "the plan of mercy." (Alma 42:15). Later in the same address, Alma acknowledged its grand nature by calling it "the great plan of mercy." (Alma 42:31).

Its elements predate the organization of worlds without number. It is "the merciful plan of the great Creator" (2 Nephi 9:6), conceived to redeem us from death. Thus, it is "the plan of redemption" (Alma 12:25), even "the great plan of redemption" (Alma 34:31), or "the great and eternal plan of redemption." (Alma 34:16). From our perspective, it is "the plan of redemption, which was prepared from the foundation of the world." (Alma 18:39). It is all-inclusive, inasmuch as it is "the great and eternal plan of deliverance from death." (2 Nephi 11:5).

It is commonly called "the Plan of Salvation." (Alma 24:14). Moses acknowledged the benevolent nature of God when he described it as "the plan of salvation unto all men." (Moses 6:62). It applies to all mankind without exception, so it comes as no surprise that Alma called it "the great plan of salvation." (Alma 42:5). He also called it "the plan of restoration," (Alma 41:2), since its design is to bring us, pure, spotless, and innocent, back into the presence of our Heavenly Father. He knew that with this restoration we would experience indescribable joy, and so he also called it "the great plan of happiness." (Alma 42:8). It is "the plan of happiness, which (is) as eternal also as the life of the soul." (Alma 42:16).

Ultimately, it is "the great plan of the eternal God" (Alma 34:9), that caused us to sing together and shout for joy when its elements were first explained to us. (See Job 38:7).

Because Isaiah's writing style employed types
and shadows, and because his prophecies were dualistic,
in the sense that they had application not only for ancient
Israel, but also for Israel at the time of the mortal ministry of
Christ, for Latter-day Saints, and for millennial Israel, it is
necessary in many cases to dig deeply to ascertain their
true meaning. It is also important to set each chapter
against the backdrop of the historical context
in which it was written, in order to read
between the lines, as it were, to better
understand their importance
and relevancy.

Honesty

"And they were among the people of Nephi, and also numbered among the people who were of the church of God. And they were also distinguished for their zeal towards God, and also towards men; for they were perfectly honest and upright in all things; and they were firm in the faith of Christ."
(Alma 27:27).

The gospel is as much the sum of "Thou shalt" Commandments, as it is "Thou shalt not" Commandments. Its composite principles are the consummate compilation of affirmative actions. For example, "we believe in being honest," because honesty is the mortar that holds together the building blocks of character.(Thirteenth Article of Faith).

"Fame is a vapor, and popularity is an accident. Those who cheer you today may curse you tomorrow. In the end, the only thing that endures is character." (Anonymous). Woven throughout the teachings of the prophets of all ages is the desire to instill in people a sense of integrity, of character, of honesty, that shines like a light through the eyes. George Washington wrote: "I hope I shall always possess firmness and virtue enough to maintain what I consider the most enviable of all titles, the character of an 'Honest Man.'"

The Saints of all ages have been "distinguished for their zeal towards God, and also towards men, for they (are) perfectly honest and upright in all things; and they (are) firm in the faith of Christ." (Alma 27:27). "Surely there could not be a happier people among all the people who (have) been created by the hand of God" than those who have been able to build their society on the foundation of noble character. (4 Nephi 1:16).

Honesty implies being true to the faith of our fathers. "You tell on yourself by the friends you seek, by the very manner in which you speak; by the way you enjoy your leisure time; by the use you make of dollar and dime. You tell who you are by the things you wear, and in the way you wear your hair; by the kinds of things that make you laugh; by the records you play on your phonograph (or MP3 Player).

You tell who you are by the way you walk; by the things in which you delight to talk; by the books you choose from a well filled shelf. In these ways and more, you tell on yourself." (Anonymous)

"God, give us men!" wrote Josiah Gilbert Holland. "A time like this demands strong minds, great hearts, truth, faith, and ready hands. Men and women whom the lust of office does not kill. Men and women whom the spoils of office cannot buy. Men and women who possess opinions and a will. Men and women who have honor. Men and women who will not lie! Men and women who can stand before a demagogue and damn his treacherous flatterings without winking! Tall men and women, sun-crowned, who live above the fog in public duty and in private thinking. For while the rabble, with their thumb-worn creeds, their large professions and their little deeds, mingle in selfish strife, lo! Freedom weeps, Wrong rules the land, and Justice sleeps." ("God, Give us Men!").

Those who are valiant in the testimony of Jesus, and who are honest with themselves, their fellowmen, and the Lord always have a moral and ethical standard upon which their belief system is anchored. Others, who make value judgments based on endocrine secretions, rather than on the unchanging and eternally validated laws of the gospel, have no such foundation, but instead build their houses on the shifting sands of expediency and circumstance. When individuals and society seek to be lights unto themselves, they fail to improve the quality of their disposition, because their intellect can never bridge the gap between rational behavior and faith, nor can it provide the mortar necessary to build character.

Those who are honest will not lie. A prospective employer asked a young man who had applied for a job, "If I hire you, can I count on you to be honest?" The young man replied, "You can count on me to be honest, whether you hire me or not."

Those who are honest will not steal. In church one day, a man gave a sermon on the 8th Commandment. It was a very hard and biting address and after he was finished, he said "I hope we have all learned from this talk, and that we will start now to right our wrongs." Then, he said, "Someone took my umbrella a few weeks ago, and I know it will be very hard for you to return it to me face to face, so I have decided that you can return it tonight after dark, and just leave it on my porch." The next morning there were 45 umbrellas lying on his porch.

We should delight in being honest, and not because we are compelled to be so. Compulsion destroys agency, and those who are repetitively acted upon may ultimately forsake principles of conduct that are consistent with civility. Thus, the Lord instructed the Saints: "He that is compelled in all things, the same is a slothful and not a wise servant … Men should be anxiously engaged in a good cause, and do many things of their own free will, and bring to pass much righteousness. G. For the power is in them, wherein they are agents unto themselves." (D&C 58:26-28).

Agency implies the power and opportunity to choose. "He kept the Ten Commandments until he died. He walked the straight and narrow path and never lied. He never went to the theatres. He never learned to dance. He never once on shapely legs bestowed a wicked glance. He never smoked or kissed another's wife. He never took a bit of liquor in his life. He never let his temper rise. He never called his neighbor a fool. He kept strictly to the Golden Rule. Now you can be assured that he really lived on earth, but he was deaf, and dumb, and blind, and paralyzed from birth." (Anonymous)

Honest individuals will not cheat. Every day, we are faced with choices that scrutinize our values. One examination may well be in math, or history, or economics. The other will be in honesty. If we must fail one test, make sure it is in math, or history, economics. For there are many fine people in the world who are honest and successful and yet know nothing about these other subjects.

Honest individuals do not murmur. Murmuring is the subdued and continually repeated expression of indistinct or inarticulate complaint or grumbling. Like an earthquake, murmuring undermines the foundation of relationships and institutions.

Honest individuals do not gossip. Gossiping is like leaving a feather on the doorsteps of those with whom you share idle thoughts. You cannot go back a day later and gather up the words so loosely spoken. They will have scattered to the four winds, and they cannot be recalled. "Kind words," on the other hand, "can be short and easy to speak but their echoes are truly endless." (Mother Teresa). "There is so much good in the worst of us, and so much bad in the best of us, that it hardly behooves any of us to talk about the rest of us." (Anonymous).

Honest individuals do not find fault with others. They do not pass the buck. Once there were "four people named Everybody, Somebody, Anybody, and Nobody. There was an important job to be done and Everybody was sure that Somebody would do it.

Anybody could have done it, but Nobody did it. Somebody got angry about it because it was Everybody's job. Everybody thought that Anybody could do it, but Nobody realized that Everybody wouldn't do it. It ended up that Everybody blamed Somebody when Nobody did what Anybody could have done." (Anonymous)

We can only excuse our dishonesty for so long. "My father focuses heart-gripping flashes across the wall screen. Family slides. I am small, my brother is smaller, and my sister is smallest. Days now dead re-open like old storybooks from memory's heaped box. Pulling out pictures of cooking in Grandfather's Dutch oven; playing cheetah in our backyard monkey-jungle; being beautifully Easter-bested with my coat buttoned wrong; hugging a mommy minus grey hair. Soberly, I think of another Father, Who someday shall open my mind, and flash reeling remembering of every day's minute across my soul, across the heavens, and kindly ask me to narrate." (Lora Lyn Stucker, "New Era," 8/1973).

We can only stave off the consequences of dishonesty for so long. Ezra Taft Benson declared: "I do not believe the greatest threat to our future is from bombs or missiles. I do not think our civilization will die that way. I think it will die when we no longer care, when the spiritual forces that make us wish to be right and noble die in the hearts of men, when we disregard the importance of law and order, and the basic principles upon which this nation has been built. Great nations are never conquered from outside unless they are rotten inside. Our greatest national problem today is erosion of the national morality." ("The American Challenge").

We can be completely honest as we repent. Dishonesty "leaves a soul scar that only the plastic surgery of repentance can eliminate." (Neal A. Maxwell). Elder Marion D. Hanks observed that "at the banquet of consequences, when we go with our loved ones, there will not be much that is satisfying at the table unless I am able to bow my head in reverence, rather than hang it in shame, in the presence of God who will be there." (B.Y.U. Speeches of The Year, 10/3/1967).

Long ago, Alexis de Tocqueville is purported to have written: "I sought for the greatness and genius of America in her commodious harbors and her ample rivers, and it was not there; in her fertile fields and boundless prairies, and it was not there; in her rich mines and her vast world commerce, and it was not there. Not until I went to the churches of America and heard her pulpits aflame with righteousness did I understand the secret of her genius and her power. America is great because she is good, and if America ever ceases to be good, America will cease to be great. In the words of the Apostle Paul: "Thanks be made for all men ... that we may lead a quiet and peaceful life in all godliness and honesty." (1 Timothy 2:1-2).

The Atonement of Christ was
conceived by our Heavenly Father,
that it might satisfy the demands of
Justice and at the same time mercifully
reclaim His disobedient children from both
physical and spiritual death. The Firstborn
of our Father, Who was the Lamb Slain from
the Foundation of the World, thereby became
the Master of the situation. In His sacrifice,
the debt would be paid, redemption made,
the covenant fulfilled, Justice satisfied,
God's will done, and all power, that
included resurrection's keys,
would be given to His
Only Begotten
Son.

(The) Hourglass of Life

"I also beheld a strait and
narrow path, which came along
by the rod of iron, even to the
tree by which I stood."
(1 Nephi 8:20).

If mortality could be visualized in spatial dimensions, it would take the shape of an hourglass, with the strait gate its narrow midsection. After passing through that constriction, unparalleled vistas would open up to reveal untapped potential and unparalleled opportunity. But initially, many of us would be caught in conceptually confusing cul-de-sacs that would prevent us from comprehending the purpose of the Plan. We would wander to and fro, dazed, and disoriented, like flotsam and jetsam on the sea of life.

Some of us would be stalled in telestial traffic jams that would overheat our engines, foul our lubricants, seize our moving parts, and restrict our access to freely flowing spiritual energy. Others would lack restraint, as if their brake pads were worn, interfering with their ability to slow down as they negotiated the minefields of mortality in order to avoid the sand traps of transgression. Their ability to move forward with purpose might be compromised. They might lose their traction as they tried to move upward, and they might feel as if their gears were grinding, and their clutch plates were slipping.

A few of us might squander scarce resources, as if our thermostats were inoperable, allowing our cooling systems to boil over from the excitement of excessive exertion in the steam plant of sin. All these mechanical issues might combine to overwhelm us in a perfect storm of trial and temptation, forcing, as it were, lifestyle compromises that would make self-control and self-actualization all the more difficult, while making rationalization and self-justification more tempting options.

But for the few of us who were lucky enough to finally reach the constriction in the hourglass, there would come a realization that the time to stand and deliver had arrived. As Brutus observed, we would face that "tide in the affairs of men which, taken at the flood, leads on to fortune. Omitted," we would realize that the voyage of our lives would be condemned to be "bound in shallows and in miseries. On such a full sea," however, we would find ourselves "afloat, and we" would "take the current when it serves, or lose our ventures." (Shakespeare, "Julius Caesar," Act 4, Scene 3).

Those who made it through the strait and narrow way, would be fortunate, indeed, to find that by following the blueprints of the Plan, they were to be given enough wiggle-room to be able to successfully flex their spiritual muscles and exercise their moral agency in a forum of free will that engaged opposition in a vigorous tug-of-war. They would realize that the Plan works best when its participants are able to make excellent choices in the midst of less attractive competing options. They would hope to be sensitive to spiritual promptings, to be stimulated by the light of Christ, to receive the Gift of the Holy Ghost, to be thereby guided, and to be replenished with the high-octane fuel of faith that would ignite the fire of their fortitude and propel them onward.

Those who would seize the moment, thread the eye of the needle, and negotiate the strait and narrow path would realize that what at the outset had felt like a confinement, and a constraint, was in fact a birth canal, or a portal through which all must pass in order to progress eternally. They would feel as if they had been literally born again. Expanding circles of opportunity that had beforehand been hidden from their view would first come into view, and then snap into sharp focus. They would see beyond the limited horizon of their sight, and comprehend a vision in which the perfect law of liberty stretched out before them in a vista of incomprehensible proportion. They would see that God's Plan rests on solid footings that are reinforced with the rebar of our resolve, and that it is upon the foundation of the covenants that we make with Him that celestial sureties are constructed, leading to eternal life in His mansions above.

How Does God Get Things Done?

"Sow a thought, reap an act.
Sow an act, reap a habit. Sow a habit,
reap a character. Sow a character,
reap an eternal destiny."
(David O. McKay)

God "cannot
walk in crooked paths; neither
doth he vary from that which he hath
said; neither hath he a shadow of turning
from the right to the left, or from that which
is right to that which is wrong; therefore,
his course is one eternal round."
(Alma 7:20).

The Savior revealed something about the nature of His Father when He said: "Thy will be done." (Matthew 26:42). In other words, He knew that His Father's resolve would be translated into action, reminiscent of Pharaoh's definitive pronouncement: "So let it be written, so let it be done." In a more profane setting, we recall Michael Crichton's book in which three scientists enter the world of a sphere that gives them the power to manifest their thoughts into reality. Appropriately, the book is entitled "Sphere," recalling a geometrical object that is perfectly round in three-dimensional space, is symmetrical around its center, and represents harmony and beauty that results from balanced proportions without variation of form or substance. Art mimics life, and life mimics eternity. As Alma taught: God "cannot walk in crooked paths; neither doth he vary from that which he hath said; neither hath he a shadow of turning from the right to the left, or fro that which is right to that which is wrong; therefore, his course is one eternal round." (Alma 7:20).

The beginning of the book of Genesis reveals: "God said, Let there be light: and there was light." (Genesis 1:3). "And God said, let the waters under the heaven be gathered together unto one place, and let the dry land appear: and it was so." (Genesis 1:9). "And God said, Let the earth bring forth the living creature after his kind … and it was so." (Genesis 1:24). Quite simply, He gets things done by speaking the word that "is quick, and powerful, and sharper than any two- edged sword, piercing even to the dividing asunder of soul and spirit, and of the joints and marrow." (Hebrews 4:12). It was by the power of His word that Jesus "stood over (Simon's mother) and rebuked the fever, and it left her." (Luke 4:39). It was by the same power that He "rebuked the winds and the sea; and there was a great calm." (Matthew 8:26). In every case, He spoke "with all authority." (Titus 2:15). Thus, He was able to say even "unto the sea, Peace, be still. And the wind ceased, and there was a great calm." (Mark 4:39).

When He cleansed a leper, He needed only to say: "Be thou clean. And immediately the leprosy departed from him." (Luke 5:13). Simeon "came by the Spirit into the temple," and said to Jesus: "Lord, now lettest thy servant depart in peace, according to thy word." (Luke 2:25-32). As had Simeon, the centurion recognized the real source of His authority, when he implored Jesus: "I am not worthy that thou shouldest come under my roof: but speak the word only, and my servant shall be healed." (Matthew 8:8). When the Savior asked the lame man lying beside the pool at Bethesda: "Wilt thou be made whole?" He needed only to say: "Rise, take up thy bed, and walk. And immediately the man was made whole, and took up his bed, and walked." (John 5:6-9).

When the multitudes finally understood the process by which the Son of God gets things done, they were impulsively drawn to Him, and "brought unto him many that were possessed with devils: and he cast out the spirits with his word." (Matthew 8:16). He taught a great grammar lesson when "they brought to him a man sick of the palsy, lying on a bed: and Jesus seeing their faith said unto (him) Son, be of good cheer; thy sins be forgiven thee. And, behold, certain of the scribes said within themselves, This man blasphemeth. And Jesus knowing their thoughts said, Wherefore think ye evil in your hearts? For whether is easier to say, Thy sins be forgiven thee; or to say, Arise, and walk? But that ye may know that the son of man hath power on earth to forgive sins, (then saith he to the sick of the palsy,) Arise, take up thy bed." (Matthew 9:2-6).

Even to raise the dead, it was only necessary that He cry "with a loud voice, Lazarus, come forth. And he that was dead came forth, bound hand and foot with graveclothes: and his face was bound about with a napkin." (John 11:43-44). Fortunately, Jesus identified Lazarus by name, or all heaven and hell might have broken loose at His word. When grieving Jairus brought the Savior to his daughter, He simply said: "Weep not; she is not dead, but sleepeth." Then Jesus "took her by the hand, and called, saying, Maid, arise. And her spirit came again, and she arose straightway." (Luke 8:52 & 54-55).

However, "the kingdom of God is not (so much) in word, (as it is) in power." (1 Corinthians 4:20). Benjamin's simple counsel illustrates the principle: "This much I can tell you." he taught, "that if ye do not watch yourselves, and your thoughts, and your words, and your deeds…ye must perish." (Mosiah 4:30). Ultimately, the power can be traced back to our thoughts. For "as a man thinketh in his heart, so is he." (Proverbs 23:7). Then, translated via our words, the anticipated action is manifest. Mormon recognized this when he observed: "The preaching of the word had a great tendency to lead the people to do that which was just – yea, it had had more powerful effect upon the minds of the people than the sword, or anything else, which had happened unto them – therefore Alma thought it was expedient that they should try the virtue of the word of God." (Alma 31:5). The word had virtue in Mormon's eyes because of its power to effect positive change.

The scriptures teach that it expedient to "turn to the Lord with full purpose of heart." (Mosiah 7:33). This may have something to do with the fact that the Word was "in the beginning…and the Word was with God, and the Word was God." (John 1:1). Of ourselves, our influence over the outcome of events is insignificant, "for there is no power but of God (and) the powers that be are ordained of God." (Romans 13:1). At certain times, though, we may be endowed with "the keys of the power of this priesthood" to act in the name of God according to His word. (D&C 132:59). "Now is the accepted time," taught Paul, wherein all things might be accomplished "by the word of truth, by the power of God, (and) by the armour of righteousness." (2 Corinthians 6:2 & 7). It is by speaking specifically authorized and sanctioned words that we have the power to perform baptisms and other priesthood ordinances such as conferring the gift of the Holy Ghost and blessing the sacrament, and setting apart individuals, dedicating graves, giving priesthood blessings, and casting out evil spirits.

Of priesthood-driven teaching in the church, we are counseled: "The Spirit shall be given unto you by the prayer of faith; and if ye receive not the Spirit ye shall not teach." (D&C 42:14). There is not much we can accomplish without it. When we receive covenants by the power and authority of the priesthood, without the words that are driven by the Spirit the related ordinances are but empty, passive rituals. In fact, the same tongue can give curses as well as blessings. Words can be weapons, but they can also be the Balm of Gilead. Words can initiate action, as when we are enjoined: "Be baptized, every one of you, for a remission of your sins." (D&C 33:11). Words help us to practice what we preach and to make contact with the power of God when we speak in the name of the Lord. We do this when we invoke the Lord's blessings by the power of the priesthood. We do it when we bear our testimonies, by the power of the Holy Ghost. The Lord does it when He looks upon repentant sinners and says: "Thy sins are forgiven thee." (Luke 5:20). He does it when he says: "Go your way and sin no more." (D&C 6:35). We experience His power when He says to us: "Well done thou good and faithful servant: thou hast been faithful over a few things, I will make thee ruler over many things: enter thou into the joy of thy lord." (Matthew 25:21). There are no limitations to the power of spirit-driven words. We can even receive the blessings of exaltation with the spoken word.

At the very end of The Book of Mormon, when Moroni exhorted us to "come unto Christ and be perfected in Him," he did so because he understood that in the Last Days we would be given empowering words as the tools to bring to pass the Restoration. (Moroni 10:32). "Now, what do we hear in the gospel which we have received?" asked Joseph Smith. "A voice of gladness! A voice of mercy from heaven; and a voice of truth out of the earth; glad tidings for the dead; a voice of gladness for the living and the dead; glad tidings of great joy. How beautiful upon the mountains are the feet of those that bring glad tidings of good things, and that say unto Zion: Behold, thy God reigneth! As the dews of Carmel, so shall the knowledge of God descend upon them!" (D&C 128:19).

Little wonder then that "the priest's duty is to preach, teach, expound, and exhort, and baptize, and administer the sacrament." (D&C 20:46). Their responsibility is to speak by the power of the Holy Ghost as if theirs were the Lord's own voice. (See D&C 68:4). Of the power of His words, Isaiah wrote: "The glory of his majesty shall smite them, when he ariseth to shake terribly the earth." (2 Nephi 12:19).

Sometimes, the power of God is so great that words become unnecessary. Robert L. Simpson described his introduction to David O. McKay in 1958. "President McKay extended his firm right hand, and placing his left hand on my shoulder, looked into my eyes and, more than that, into every fiber of my being. After a few seconds, he gave my hand a friendly pump, my shoulder a squeeze, and said, 'Brother Simpson, I am pleased to know you.' Not 'I am pleased to meet you,' but 'pleased to know you.' Three months later, while sitting in my office in Los Angeles, my telephone rang and the voice on the other end of the line said, 'This is David O. McKay speaking.' He said that based on our interview, he had felt impressed to issue a call." ("Improvement Era," 2/1970).

Jacob said: "With one glance of his eye (God) can smite you to the dust!" (Jacob 2:15). In Zarahemla following His crucifixion, the Resurrected Lord told the Nephites how the great destructions in the land had occurred. With terrifying clarity, He revealed that He had "caused" the great city Moroni to be sunk in the depths of the sea, and the inhabitants of the city of Gilgal to be buried in the depths of the earth, and the city Jacobugath to be burned with fire. (See 3 Nephi 9:4-12). The Nephites might have then remembered the awful promise from The Plates of Brass: "I call heaven and earth to record this day against you, that I have set before you life and death, blessing and cursing." (Deuteronomy 30:19).

Under the best of circumstances, the Lord characterized His people as Zion "because they were of one heart and one mind, and dwelt in righteousness." (Moses 7:18). They were pure in heart because their thoughts were focused on the welfare of others and translated seamlessly into words and deeds. The righteousness of Zion typifies the celestial standard by which the Savior shall "judge the poor, and reprove with equity for the meek of the earth: and he shall smite the earth with the rod of his mouth, and with the breath of his lips shall he slay the wicked." (Isaiah 11:4).

The mind-set of Zion is sufficient to "break mountains, to divide the seas, to dry up waters, to turn them out of their course; to put at defiance the armies of nations, to divide the earth, to break every band, to stand in the presence of God" and to manifest thought into reality. (J.S.T. Genesis 14:30-31). Our Heavenly Father gives us the Spirit to test us and to allow us to demonstrate how we would think and act if entrusted with His power, and to speak purposefully as did Nephi, who confirmed: "My God will give me, if I ask not amiss." (2 Nephi 4:35). Passing this verbal exam moves us within the borders of Zion to be "encircled about with the matchless bounty of (God's) love." (Alma 26:15).

King Benjamin understood the generative potential of feelings, and so cautioned the Saints in Zarahemla: "Watch yourselves, and your thoughts, and your words, and your deeds." (Mosiah 4:30). If we do so, we will be assured, as was Joseph Smith: "It shall be given you in the very hour, yea, in the very moment, what ye shall say." (D&C 100:6).

When our relationship with our Father in Heaven is that close, perhaps we will one day be validated as was Nephi the son of Helaman who, when he had entirely proven himself, heard a voice saying: "I will make thee mighty in word and in deed, in faith and in works; yea, even that all things shall be done unto thee according to thy word, for thou shalt not ask that which is contrary to my will." (Helaman 10:5). The voice then revealed Who it was who spoke, and that He had a communicative relationship with His faithful disciple: "Behold, thou art Nephi, and I am God. Behold, I declare it unto thee in the presence of mine angels... I give unto you power, that whatsoever ye shall seal on earth shall be sealed in heaven; and whatsoever ye shall loose on earth shall be loosed in heaven; and thus shall ye have power among this people." (Helaman 10:6-7). Then we will "get things done" in an unrestrained, expansive, interactive, vocal, and even nonverbal way, just as our Heavenly Father does.

Huckleberries and Chokeberries

"I would that ye should
take upon you the name of Christ,
all you that have entered into the covenant
with God, that ye should be obedient unto the end
of your lives. And it shall come to pass that whosoever
doeth this shall be found at the right hand of God, for he
shall know the name by which he is called; for he shall be
called by the name of Christ. And … whosoever shall not
take upon him the name of Christ must be called by
some other name; therefore, he findeth himself
on the left hand of God." (Mosiah 5:8-10).

2009 was a banner year for huckleberries in the North Idaho Panhandle. Our family picked dozens of gallons, and we enjoyed huckleberry ice cream, pancakes, muffins, pies, brownies, and lemon bars, and put berries over fish, steak, and poultry and even in peanut butter sandwiches and mashed potatoes. We froze enough berries to last through the fall, winter, and spring, and hoped that 2010 would produce another great crop.

Picking was a challenge, though, because the bushes were so heavily laden the branches drooped almost to the ground, which made it difficult to see the berries through the leaves. But lifting a branch would reveal twenty or thirty berries in each of several clusters. We sometimes plucked them one-by-one, but more often we just raked them in, as we've seen bears do it in Trapper Creek, north of Upper Priest Lake.

Interspersed with the huckleberry bushes, however, were a fair number of chokeberry bushes, equally endowed with fat berries of a slightly lighter hue than huckleberries, with a very light whitish powder on them, and if you looked very carefully, you could see a characteristic "flare" on the bottom of the berry. But to a casual observer or someone in a hurry to quickly pick as many berries as possible, it would be easy to mistake a chokeberry for a huckleberry. Sometimes in the excitement of the moment, in our eagerness, or maybe because of overzealousness, a fair number of chokeberries inadvertently made it into our buckets.

Those who have salivated over the prospect of gobbling up handfuls of delicious huckleberries, but have instead crunched down on chokeberries, know the feeling. The difference in taste and texture is striking. Whereas a mouthful of huckleberries pops open between the teeth, releasing savory liquid to wash over eager taste buds, a chokeberry is a whole different experience. It is bland, almost bitter, and quite a bit more granular. Anyone who has inadvertently eaten a chokeberry when anticipating a huckleberry will understand the scripture that warns: "I will spue thee out of my mouth." (Revelation 3:26). They will recognize why the Spirit impressed upon Nephi the metaphor of fruit in his vision of eternal life: "And it came to pass that I did go forth and partake of the fruit thereof; and I beheld that it was most sweet, above all that I ever before tasted." (1 Nephi 8:11).

Our life experiences are a lot like picking huckleberries and chokeberries. For example, we may choose our friends the way we pick huckleberries, drawn to them because they are appealing and because they add zest and excitement to our lives. We can't have enough of them, for as Joseph Smith said: "Friendship is one of the grand fundamental principles" that shapes and defines our mortal experience. Because they cement the foundations of relationships, we nurture and protect our friendships as zealously as we would our treasure troves of coveted huckleberries.

Sometimes, we choose our friends because of their exceptional, inimitable, and distinctive qualities. How many times has a particularly appealing huckleberry first caught your attention and then consumed an inordinate amount of your time, as you pushed aside intruding branches and ignored other more easily accessible but less appealing berries so you could concentrate solely on your find? How often are we like the "merchant man, seeking goodly pearls, who, when he had found one" huckleberry "of great price, went and sold all that he had, and bought it." (Matthew 13:45-46). We prize our friends for the same reasons. They are interesting, multifaceted, and add savor to our daily routines. They are fresh and exciting, and we are always exploring new opportunities to interact with them, in spite of the extra expenditure of energy it might take to do so.

The way we spend our time is also related to huckleberries. A bucket full of newly picked berries speaks volumes to others about how we value our time. Our harvest, the tangible representation of our efforts, reveals our priorities. The poet wrote: "You tell on yourself by the friends you seek; by the very manner in which you speak; by the way you enjoy your leisure time; by the use you make of dollar and dime. You tell who you are by the things you wear and in the way you wear your hair; by the kinds of things that make you laugh; by the records you play on your phonograph. You tell who you are by the way you walk; by the things in which you delight to talk; by the books you choose from a well filled shelf." You tell on yourself by the fingers that stain, by the gallons and gallons of berries you gain. You tell on yourself by the pies you can make; by the whipped cream and sugar you add to the cake. You tell on yourself by the pancakes you ate; by the syrup and butter that add to your weight. "In these ways and more, you tell on yourself." (Anonymous).

Anyone who has found a good patch knows how difficult it can be to leave, especially when there are still heavily laden bushes between you and the car. Even as we stop at "just one last bush," we realize that where huckleberries are concerned, picking time is time well spent. When we are gathering gallons and gallons of berries in the newly-found patch we have dubbed "Huckleberry Heaven," we don't need to justify the thought with which we have spent our time, the diligence with which we have made time, the care with which we have found time, or the discipline with which we have taken time. The creative process of time management, expressed in a simple berry patch in the woods, gives us more time to gather the harvest. Idleness is the devil's workshop, and when we don't take advantage of the gift of time we have been given to gather the bounty in the woods, we damage our eternal selves, for "in an hour when ye think not the summer shall be past, and the harvest (of huckleberries) is ended, and your souls (are) not saved." (D&C 45:2).

Those of us who pick huckleberries with a passion have made it a family tradition to do so, and the season brings loved ones together for fellowship and an appreciation of the out-of-doors. Upon arrival at the "secret patch," we first allow fond memories to wash over us, and then we get down to the business of adding new chapters to the book of our life experiences.

But sometimes, when we think we are choosing wisely, we are instead really making poor decisions. We are deceived, in a way, by the chokeberries that lurk among the huckleberry bushes. Their presence should remind us that rather than carelessly or thoughtlessly gulping down whole handfuls of berries, we need to step back, breathe deeply, and make sure we are doing the right thing for the right reasons. If the superficial allure of chokeberries is allowed to overshadow our natural attraction to huckleberries, we might participate in activities that lead to irreversible negative consequences.

Long ago, Aesop warned of "a wolf in sheep's clothing." Had he lived today in the North Idaho Panhandle, his fable might have been entitled: "Huckleberries and Chokeberries." We cannot allow our better judgment to be overcome by our eagerness, or to waste our efforts and squander our resources in the conceptual cul-de-sacs of life. When Alice was in Wonderland, she wondered where the best berry patches might be. "Would you please tell me which way I ought to go from here?" she asked the Cheshire Cat, who responded: "That depends a good deal on where you want to go." Alice acknowledged: "I admit, I don't much care where." To which the cat responded: "Then it doesn't matter which way you go." Alice implored: "Just so I go somewhere!" The cat observed: "Oh, you are sure to do that, if you only walk far enough." If we just don't care, we are likely to wind up with a bucket full of chokeberries, instead of the huckleberries that were our original objective.

Sometimes we settle for chokeberries even though we are fully aware that they are only a substitute for the real thing. We give in to temptation, enticed by the lowest common denominator in the mathematical equations that sooner or later define our character, and consciously do the wrong thing, knowing beforehand the consequences of our actions. We intentionally acquire a taste for the poor imitation of a delicious delicacy, and then we delude ourselves into believing it is the genuine article. Embracing the counterfeit, we engage in mental gymnastics with all its twists and turns, and when we are exhausted by the effort, we claw out of the holes we have dug for ourselves into the light of day, but assuage ourselves with rationalizations so we can face ourselves in the mirror and sleep better when our consciences are later tormented by our own demons as the forgery is exposed.

As creatures of habit, we condition ourselves to no longer care than we are serving ourselves chokeberries instead of huckleberries. In fact, our acclimatization even helps us to enjoy chokeberries. Of such a phenomenon, Alexander Pope wrote: Chokeberries "are of such a frightful mien, as to be hated, need but be seen, but seen too oft, familiar with her face, we first pity, then endure, and then embrace." ("Essay on Man, Epistle 2"). It is only later in the year, when we go to the freezer, that we may pull out a bag full of berries, the evidence of our considerable efforts during the previous summer, oblivious to the fact that, in reality, it is chokeberries that we have so carefully preserved. Opening the bag to pour out its contents, we are starkly reminded of the counsel of our Lord, Who said: "Lay up for yourselves treasures in heaven, where neither moth nor rust (nor chokeberries) doth corrupt, and where thieves do not break through nor steal." (Matthew 6:20).

When we content ourselves with chokeberries, we deny ourselves the unique and wonderful experience of tasting Huckleberry Delight and instead content ourselves with the bitterness of its negative counterpart. We become enthusiastically ignorant as we invent stories that justify our support of the chokeberry culture.

When Isaiah prophesied that in the Last Days "shall the branch of the Lord be beautiful and glorious (and) the fruit of the earth excellent and comely," he was saying that the Lord would provide us with every needful thing, with "every fruit in the season thereof." (Isaiah 4:2 & D&C 89:11). He was promising us gallons and gallons of ripe, plump, purple huckleberries, free of stems, leaves, and those obnoxious, physically damaging and spiritually compromising, chokeberries.

From the perspective of Five Mile Ridge, high above Priest Lake, Joshua declared: "Choose you this day whom ye will serve, but as for me and my house," we will brush aside the chokeberries of life, and instead "serve the Lord" as we pick from the abundance of huckleberries provided by our loving Father. (Joshua 24:15). For we know that we have been "planted in a goodly land, by a pure stream, that yieldeth much precious fruit." (D&C 97:9).

Let' all hope and pray
for sunshine in our souls
"today, more glorious and bright
than glows in any earthly sky, for
Jesus is (our) light. O there's sunshine,
blessed sunshine, when the peaceful,
happy moments roll; when Jesus
shows His smiling face, there
is sunshine in the soul."
(Eliza Hewitt).

Humility

Author's note: As I have read over this essay, I can say with unqualified certainty that it is one of the best I have ever written. ☺

"They did fast and pray oft, and did wax stronger and stronger in their humility, and firmer and firmer in the faith of Christ, unto the filling their souls with joy and consolation, yea, even to the purifying and the sanctification of their hearts, which sanctification cometh because of their yielding their hearts unto God." (Helaman 3:35).

Humility is a feeling of contrition, or the sense that we cannot make progress without the sustaining influence of the Savior. It is characterized by a broken heart that has been touched by the Spirit to seek forgiveness for sins through repentance. It is typified by complete and utter dependence upon the Atonement. It is by our faith in the saving principles of the gospel that we follow this pattern: "Let him that is ignorant learn wisdom by humbling himself and calling upon the Lord his God, that his eyes may be opened that he may see, and his ears opened that he may hear." (D&C 136:32).

The exercise of humility is something that everyone can practice, no matter what their station in life may be. "And whosoever shall exalt himself shall be abased; and he that shall humble himself shall be exalted." (Matthew 23:12). Ultimately, it is "better to be of an humble spirit with the lowly, than to divide the spoil with the proud." (Proverbs 16:19).

When our faith finally convicts us of our sins, and we have come "down into the depths of humility" because our hearts have been softened by the Spirit, we reach the point where we may be "baptized (and) visited with fire and with the Holy Ghost." (3 Nephi 12:2). We develop the companion virtues of "faith, virtue, knowledge, temperance, patience, brotherly kindness, godliness, charity, (and) diligence." (D&C 4:6).

Humility is a recognizable sense of inadequacy that creates a tangible need for the tender mercies of the Lord. It was in this context that Moses exclaimed: "Now, for this cause, I know that man is nothing, which thing I never had supposed." (Moses 1:10). Humility is an outgrowth of meekness, and is a conscious submission to God's will. It leads us, as it did the people of Zarahemla, to exclaim: "The Spirit of the Lord Omnipotent...has wrought a mighty change in us, or in our hearts, that we have no more disposition to do evil, but to do good continually." (Mosiah 5:2). Humility tugs at our heartstrings with resonant chords that harmonize with the words of the hymn "I Need Thee Every Hour." (Lyrics by Annie S. Hawks).

But can we really know when we are humble? Can we put our finger to its pulse to perceive its faint stirrings? Is humility such a tender trait that runs so deeply in our character that it seldom surfaces to be recognized? Can humility have its origins in both the sacred and the secular? Are both weaknesses and strengths intertwined with humility? Does our growth in spiritual stature go hand-in-hand with humility? Is losing ourselves in service an unconscious exercise in humility? Can we gain a testimony of humility by practicing the principle, or is it a characteristic that is gained by observance of other principles? Just what is an "exercise" in humility?

Is the blessing of exaltation in the Celestial Kingdom of God predicated upon humility? Peter counseled: "Humble yourselves therefore under the mighty hand of God, that he may exalt you in due time." (1 Peter 5:6). The Lord said of the Saints: "For behold, I have prepared a great endowment and blessing to be poured out upon them, inasmuch as they are faithful and continue in humility before me." (D&C 105:12). James taught: "Humble yourselves in the sight of the Lord, and he shall lift you up" at the last day. (James 4:10).

Do we feel humility only when we are touched by the better angels of our nature? If we lack humility, can we righteously desire to obtain it? Is it one of those qualities, like greatness, that is thrust upon us? Is humility a tool that awakens in us the remembrance of who we are? Are we being honest with ourselves, and with God, when we pray: "We come to Thee in humility…?"

Clearly, those with humility have embraced a set of standards that runs counter to the world's expectations. The lifestyle of humble disciples may even seem silly to those who would have us believe that good guys finish last, and that you don't get what you deserve, you get what you negotiate. Those who are humble, unpretentious, self-effacing, meek, and lowly can expect to be bullied and taken advantage by the arrogant, the conceited, the egotistical, and the haughty. But as Paul explained: "God hath chosen the foolish things of the world to confound the wise; and God hath chosen the weak things of the world to confound the things which are mighty." (1 Corinthians 1:27). Those with delicate spirits should not expect, and indeed do not deserve, tangible rewards for being humble.

Daddy Warbucks, reflecting on his life in the shark-infested waters of the business world, told Annie: "You don't have to be nice to those you step on or climb over, on your way up the ladder of success, if you don't plan on coming back down again." To put it even more bluntly, from the world's perspective: "He who has the gold makes the rules." But, as Brigham Young taught: "If we go on lusting after the groveling things of this life which perish with the handling, we shall surely remain fixed with a very limited amount of knowledge and like a door upon its hinges, move to and fro from one year to another without any visible advancement or improvement." (J.D. 10:265-274). The Savior was speaking from personal experience when He articulated the celestial principle: "He that is greatest among you shall be your servant." (Matthew 23:11).

Religious history teaches us interesting lessons about humility. Lowly Israel, and not the mighty kingdoms of Assyria, Babylonia, or Egypt, remained the repository of true religion. "Christianity did not go from Rome to Galilee; it was the other way around. In our day, the routing is from Palmyra to Paris, and not the reverse." (Spencer W. Kimball, C.R., 4/1978).

The Little Town of Bethlehem, and not mighty Jerusalem, was the birthplace of the Savior. Bethlehem stands in the shadow of the 6,000-year-old Holy City. Attesting to its strategic importance, Jerusalem has been completely destroyed at least twice, attacked 52 times, besieged 23 times, and captured and recaptured 44 times. Humble Bethlehem, just 6 miles down the road, has been largely ignored in the process. The cave or grotto on the outskirts of the town in which Joseph and Mary took refuge was a far cry from the 5-Star King David Hotel in Jerusalem. It was likely overbooked anyway, when Joseph desperately sought accommodations anywhere in the vicinity of Bethlehem. If only he had flashed a Hilton Honors Frequent Guest card, he might have received more personalized attention!

The Savior was not the lord of a worldly domain, but was the Prince of Peace, a monarch without a kingdom, and a man without a country, so to speak. "Foxes have holes, and birds of the air have nests; but the Son of man hath not where to lay his head." (Luke 9:58). He cared little for the profane emblems of power, because His was a royal priesthood that was not of this world. The kings of the earth, in order to validate their claims to authority, hold in their hands the orb, an emblem of power, usually made of precious metal encrusted with jewels, and consisting of a sphere with a cross on it. The orb symbolizes the universe as a harmonious whole. It hearkens back to Rome and beyond, but the Holy Roman Emperor Henry II was the first to hold it in his hand during his coronation in 1014. From the perspective of the Latter-day Restoration, we view his pomp and circumstance as a feeble attempt to usurp the supreme power and authority of "the blessed and only Potentate, the King of kings, and Lord of lords." (1 Timothy 6:15).

Latter-say Saints are familiar with the Liahona, that was passed from father to son by Lehi's descendants. It was a royal treasure, and probably the prototype of the orb. Critics of The Book of Mormon have ridiculed the Liahona, but of all the symbols of royal authority, it is the most authentic. We do not know exactly what it looked like, although Nephi described it as "a round ball of curious workmanship; and it was of fine brass. And within the ball were two spindles; and the one pointed the way whither we should go into the wilderness." (1 Nephi 16:10).

Similar religious artifacts, royal orbs, spheres of the firmament, crystal balls, and the like have survived in art, although they are stylized almost beyond recognition, and understanding of their underlying power has been completely lost. That power came from Jesus Christ, Who was the Author of Salvation, and not of best-sellers. If He wrote anything at all, it has been lost to the ages. The only tantalizing reference in the scriptures to His writing is John 8:6: "Jesus stooped down, and with his finger wrote on the ground." The gospel narratives relating to His ministry were only written years afterward.

The first Christian father to quote Matthew was Ignatius, who died around 115 A.D. It is generally believed that the Gospel according to Matthew was written before 70 A.D., and perhaps as early as 50 A.D. Mark was not an eyewitness to the Savior's ministry; it is believed that it was Peter's recollections that guided Mark to record his Gospel. His account of the Savior's ministry may be the earliest Gospel to be written, between 55 A.D. and 70 A.D. Nor was Luke an eyewitness of the life of the Savior. He was a Gentile convert and companion to Paul, who likewise was not an eyewitness! But they both had many opportunities to interview disciples who had known Christ and could provide substance to the Gospel and the Book of Acts being written by Luke. The Gospel according to Luke was written around 62 A.D. The Gospel according to John was an eyewitness account of the theological aspects of the ministry of Christ that confirmed His divinity. He wrote his Gospel during his banishment to the Isle of Patmos, around the end of the First Century. So, the four canonical Gospels were written about the Savior, but the New Testament, a narrative of the greatest story ever told, includes nothing written by the Savior Himself. There would be no lucrative book deals for Him!

We know that He was "the firstborn of every creature." (Colossians 1:15). When we view our existence from the gospel's perspective, our humility is enlarged to eternal proportions. We realize that Jesus Christ was not only the first of our Heavenly Father's children, but also the best and the brightest of His offspring. "For by him were all things created, that are in heaven, and that are in earth, visible and invisible, whether they be thrones, or dominions, or principalities, or powers: all things were created by him, and for him: And he is before all things, and by him all things consist. And he is the head of the body, the church: who is the beginning, the firstborn from the dead; that in all things he might have the preeminence." (Colossians 1:16-18). The birthright fell to Him, because He was the Firstborn. If anyone deserved to feel special, it would be Him, and yet, He was the personification of humility.

He has been likened unto a lamb, without spot or blemish. The Lion of Judah is the symbol of the tribe of Judah, originating with the blessing given to Judah by Jacob. (See Genesis 49:9). Isaiah referenced lions, lambs, and a little child. He wrote that in the Millennium, "the wolf also shall dwell with the lamb, and the leopard shall lie down with the kid; and the calf and the young lion and the fatling together; and a little child shall lead them." (Isaiah 11:6).

The Lion of Judah may also represent the Lord. (See Revelation 5:5). However, most Christians prefer to think of Jesus Christ as "the Lamb of God, which taketh away the sin of the world." (John 1:29). What better example could there be of true submissiveness to the will of the Father, than of the One who said: "Father, if thou be willing, remove this cup from me: nevertheless, not my will, but thine, be done." (Luke 22:42).

He was the grand architect of our salvation. We are all familiar with those who focus their worship on "elegant and spacious buildings and fine work of wood, and all manner of precious things." (Mosiah 11:8-11). We remember the Emperor Justinian, who "began a new Santa Sophia. He summoned the best architects to plan and superintend the work. Abandoning the traditional Basilican form, they conceived a design whose center would be a spacious dome resting not on walls but on massive piers, and buttressed by a half dome at either end. Ten thousand workmen were engaged, and 320,000 pounds of gold were spent on the enterprise. In five years and ten months the edifice was complete, and on December 26, 537 A.D., the Emperor led a solemn inaugural procession to the resplendent cathedral. Justinian walked alone to the pulpit, and lifting up his hands, cried out: "Oh Solomon! I have vanquished you!" (Will Durant, "The Lessons of History," 4:130). News flash: Justinian has long since left the great and spacious building, headed for parts unknown.

1,463 years later, writer and director James Cameron stood before the Academy of Motion Picture Arts and Sciences and a television audience of around 40 million viewers, and with an Oscar in each of his raised hands cried out, "I'm the king of the world!" At uncomfortable moments like this, visions of the "Prince of Darkness" loom before us. (John Milton, "Paradise Lost"). We retreat to the sanctuary of the Savior's counsel: "Lay not up for yourselves treasures upon earth, where moth and rust doth corrupt, and where thieves break through and steal." (Matthew 6:19). We acknowledge that humility need not be incompatible with temporal successes, but realize that it cannot co-exist with the raw and ugly feeling of pride that is sometimes associated with that success. Truly, "pride goeth before destruction, and an haughty spirit before a fall." (Proverbs 16:18).

In 1964, John Lennon famously declared: "Christianity will go. It will vanish and shrink. I needn't argue with that; I will be proved right. We're more popular than Jesus now." The Beatles broke up 6 years later, and in 1980, Lennon went the way of all flesh to meet his Maker, "to stand with shame and awful guilt before the bar of God." (Jacob 6:9). Today, by most reports, Christianity is still alive and well. Latter-day Saints are reminded of the more popular part of the Zoramites, who were the rock stars of their day, who "were angry because of the word (of God), for it did destroy their craft," which was The Book of Mormon equivalent to heavy metal music, "therefore they would not hearken unto the words" of eternal life that would have been the key to their salvation. (Alma 35:3). The proud and the haughty, "who undertake to set themselves up as judges of truth and knowledge, are shipwrecked by the laughter of the gods." (Albert Einstein).

Sometimes there is a fine line between a humble and yet confident leader like Jesus Christ and the nattering nabobs of negativism that are so prevalent in the world, and that seek so seductively to subtly influence us. Their defiance provokes fear, while the Savior creates confidence. Their detractions generate resentment, while the Savior promises peace. Their distain leads to apathy, while the example of Jesus Christ breeds enthusiasm. Their denigrations shout "I," while the Lord Omnipotent softly says "We." They decry accountability and assign blame, while our Advocate goes about fixing mistakes. These doubters crave control, while the Lord Jehovah endows us with responsibility. They disregard know-how, even as our Exemplar shows how. Their disparagement reduces work to drudgery, while the Lord of the Vineyard elevates effort to excitement. Their derision drives the masses, while the Prophet of The Highest is out in front of His troops. The real measure of the Man of Holiness is that "when he had sent the multitudes away,' when there was no one left to sustain Him, "he went up into a mountain apart to pray: and when the evening was come, he was there alone." (Matthew 14:23). There was no fanfare, no public display of support, no exclusive interviews by the silver-haired news anchors of an adoring press corps, no merchandising of His celebrity status, just quiet reflection, meditation, contemplation, introspection, and a deep desire to draw near to His Father. Our prayers, both audible and inarticulate, reflect the same conviction. Though our flesh and our hearts fail, God is our strength and our portion forever. (See Psalms 73:26).

There is no evidence that Jesus ever received a gold watch or a brass plaque to commemorate His achievements. Instead, He quietly counseled: "When thou doest thine alms, do not sound a trumpet before thee, as the hypocrites do in the synagogues and in the streets, that they may have glory of men. Verily I say unto you, They have their reward." (Matthew 6:2). "And when thou prayest, thou shalt not be as the hypocrites are. For they love to pray standing in the synagogues and in the corners of the streets, that they may be seen of men." (Matthew 6:5). "Moreover, when ye fast, be not as the hypocrites, of a sad countenance: for they disfigure their faces, that they may appear unto men to fast." (Matthew 6:16).

Too many of us engage in chit-chat that is nothing more than a parody of principles, a distortion of doctrine, a simulation of standards, a caricature of canon, and a façade of faith within crystal cathedrals. If we want to gain a new perspective on humility, we might study the masterful discourse given by the Savior and recorded by Matthew, known as the Sermon on the Mount. (See Matthew 5, 6, & 7). It can be divided into sections: the Beatitudes, new laws, the Lord's Prayer, a discussion of money, and warnings. Nowhere, however, do we find evidence that He used His influence to solicit monetary contributions, that He formed a political action committee, became a media mogul, sought product endorsements, promoted merchandise, inked a book deal, or engaged in a lucrative T.V. ministry. In fact, His polar opposites are characterized by today's televangelists, of whom it has been written: "Someone needs to say this plainly: The faith healers and health-and-wealth preachers who dominate religious television are shameless frauds. Their message is not the true gospel of Jesus Christ. There is nothing spiritual or miraculous about their on-stage chicanery. It is all a devious ruse designed to take advantage of desperate people. They are not godly ministers, but greedy impostors, who corrupt the word of God for money's sake. They are not real pastors who shepherd the flock, but hirelings, whose only design is to fleece the sheep. Their love of money is glaringly obvious in what they say as well as in how they live. They claim to possess great spiritual power, but in reality they are rank materialists and enemies of everything holy." (John MacArthur). The lesson to be learned is that we need to be careful about our motives, and to be sure we are preaching the word for the right reasons. The barometer of humility can be a measure of whether or not we are headed toward "the personality precipice" envisioned by Neal A. Maxwell.

When religion becomes "magical," and when the power by which the church operates is transferred from God to those who profess to be His earthly representatives, but who are instead only fiercely competing for "market share," we are having a problem with humility. When the Bible becomes a fairy tale, conveying power and knowledge without the aid of revelation, we are having a problem with humility. When priesthood acquires the status of an office that automatically bestows power and grace without any regard for the spiritual or moral qualifications of its possessor, we are having a problem with humility. These phenomena, declared Thomas Jefferson, "constitute the power and the profit of the priests. Sweep away their gossamer fabric of factitious religion" he declared," and they would catch no more flies." ("The Writings of Thomas Jefferson," 6:192).

He wrote that "the religion builders (who, in his day, sought to lead the church without humility) have so distorted and deformed the doctrines of Jesus, so muffled them in mysticisms, fancies and falsehoods, have caricatured them into forms so inconceivable, as to shock reasonable thinkers. Happy in the prospect of a restoration of primitive Christianity, I must leave to younger persons to encounter and lop off the false branches which have been engrafted into it by the mythologists of the middle and modern ages." ("Jefferson's Complete Works," V. 7, p. 210 & 257).

Back in the day, Nathanael asked: "Can there any good thing come out of Nazareth?" (John 1:46). Others wondered: "Is not this the carpenter's son?" (Matthew 13:55). Isaiah prophesied: "He hath no form nor comeliness; and when we shall see him, there is no beauty that we should desire him." (Isaiah 53:2). There is no record that His likeness was ever captured on canvas, much less on a theater marquee, or on a boulevard billboard, and no cameo exists that would provide clues to His appearance, but if we desire to know what He looked like, humility could be the passport to our spiritual rebirth, wherein we receive the image of God in our countenances. (See Alma 5:14). With humility, we just might be able to look in the mirror, in order to catch a glimpse of the divine presence.

During His ministry, the Savior used simple and easy to understand examples to teach the doctrine of salvation, such as birds, coins, flowers, leaven, olives, pearls, sowers, talents, travelers, wind, bread and wine, candles under bushels, fig trees, loaves and fishes, mustard seeds, sheep and goats, tax gatherers and sinners, vessels of oil, and wheat and tares. His examples were familiar to his relatively unsophisticated disciples. They were fishermen, husbandmen, hypocrites, lepers, tax collectors, family members, the deaf and dumb, laborers in vineyards, scribes and Pharisees, the blind and lame, the weak and infirm, and widows.

He used no Power Point or Keynote presentations to convey His message, no green screen, no C.G.I., no personal information devices, and no social media. He had no hashtag, no Twitter account, and no Facebook followers. He didn't augment His message with a boost from Industrial Light and Magic, Dolby sound, or IMAX, for that special "pop." He never sent a text message and never sent out an email blast. He never posted on Instagram, and never established a Pinterest board. And yet, through it all, He remains our Exemplar and our Spiritual Rock, Who invited us: "Come unto me, all ye that labour and are heavy laden, and I will give you rest." (Matthew 11:28). He only asks that we be "willing to mourn with those that mourn; yea, and comfort those that stand in need of comfort, and to stand as witnesses of God at all times and in all things, and in all places that (we) may be in." (Mosiah 18:9). He asks for the sacrifice of a heart broken down in humility.

If we follow His example, will we, too, have humility? Only once in the New Testament, and once in The Book of Mormon, is the Savior characterized as being humble, and yet He was its personification. Paul wrote: "And being found in fashion as a man, he humbled himself, and became obedient unto death, even the death of the cross." (Philippians 2:8). Speaking from the dust, Moroni told us: "And then shall ye know that I have seen Jesus, and that he hath talked with me face to face, and that he told me in plain humility, even as a man telleth another in mine own language, concerning these things." (Ether 12:39).

Everything written about the Savior, though, suggests a profound humility that was intrinsic to His nature. John declared: "The Son can do nothing of himself, but what he seeth the Father do." (John 5:19). He urged his disciples: "Be ye, therefore, perfect, even as your Father which is in heaven is perfect." (Matthew 5:48). He taught us how to pray: "Our Father which art in heaven, Hallowed be thy name." (Matthew 6:9-10). In His agony, He declared: "Thy will be done." (Matthew 26:42). He submitted completely to the will of His Father.

If we are anxiously engaged in following His example, humility will be like a butterfly that comes and sits quietly on our shoulder. Because of Him, we can be a little more cheerful, concerned, considerate, faithful, friendly, generous, gentle, grateful, helpful, hopeful, kind, prayerful, and thoughtful. We can be facilitators, intercessors, mediators, and peacemakers. We can be more motivated to be charitable, compassionate, and thankful. We can give ourselves to consecration, forgiveness, quiet contemplation, reconciliation, sacrifice, service, and worship. We can devote ourselves to family, friends and neighbors, our church, community, nation, and the world. We can be less inclined to be concerned about keeping up appearances, less discouraged by influences that are out of our control, less distracted by telestial toys, less focused on a temporal time table, less likely to be puffed up in pride, less pressured by our peers, less prone to criticism, less quick to anger, less susceptible to the siren song of social media, less swayed by carnal, sensual, and devilish desires, and less wrapped up in ourselves and smitten by our seeming successes.

If we are anxiously engaged, we will be a little more like Captain Moroni, of whom Mormon wrote: "Yea, verily, verily I say unto you, if all men had been, and were, and ever would be, like unto Moroni, behold, the very powers of hell would have been shaken forever; yea, the devil would never have power over the hearts of the children of men." (Alma 48:17). We will have humility, but will be so outwardly focused on the peaceable things of the Kingdom that we will scarcely notice.

Perhaps our moment of greatest challenge will come when we are placed in a compromising social situation and are tempted to homogenize our standards. Maybe it will be when we are climbing the ladder of success and are tempted to scramble over those who are supposedly in our way or impeding our progress. It might be that when we are alone with our computer and surfing the web, we are prone to visit sites of questionable value. It may come at the end of the month when we are reconciling our checkbook or balancing our budget, and we have not yet paid our tithing. It may be when we have not engaged in our ministering assignments, or have not attended the temple in a while, and worldly concerns compete for our time and attention.

Hypocrisy

"Thou hypocrite, first cast the
beam out of thine own eye."
(3 Nephi 14:5).

"Woe unto you, scribes and Pharisees, hypocrites! (1st time). For ye pay tithes…and have omitted the weightier matters of the law, judgment, mercy, and faith: these ought ye to have done, and not to leave the other undone. Ye blind guides, which strain at a gnat, and swallow a camel. Woe unto you, scribes and Pharisees, hypocrites! (2nd time). For ye make clean the outside of the cup and of the platter, but within they are full of extortion and excess. Thou blind Pharisee, cleanse first that which is within the cup and platter, that the outside of them may be clean also. Woe unto you, scribes and Pharisees, hypocrites! (3rd time). For ye are like unto whited sepulchres which indeed appear beautiful outward, but are within full of dead men's bones, and of all uncleanness. Even so ye also outwardly appear righteous unto men, but within ye are full of hypocrisy and iniquity." (Matthew 23:23-28).

Jesus really disliked hypocrites! Three times in the above quoted scripture, He condemned them. In Hebrew, to repeat something three times makes it superlative, as in "good," "better," and "best." The scribes and Pharisees, of whom Jesus was so critical, were like many of us today. They paid tithing, gave to the poor, attended worship services, and went regularly to the temple. What was it, then, that caused the Lord to condemn them? The Savior simply said: "All their works they do for to be seen of men." (Matthew 23:5).

On one occasion, "as he returned into the city, he hungered. And when he saw a fig tree in the way, he came to it, and found nothing thereon, but leaves only, and said unto it, Let no fruit grow on thee henceforward for ever. And presently the fig tree withered away." (Matthew 21:18-19). The tree had leaves, and by all intents and purposes, it should have borne much fruit. But its appearance was deceiving; it was, in fact, devoid of figs. By cursing the tree, the Savior emphasized how serious a sin is hypocrisy. He was especially mindful of the Pharisees, who "loved the praise of men more than the praise of God." (John 12:43).

When Jesus triumphantly entered Jerusalem a week before the Passover, "the multitudes that went before, and that followed, cried, saying, Hosanna to the Son of David: Blessed is he that cometh in the name of the Lord; Hosanna in the highest. And when he was come into Jerusalem, all the city was moved, saying, Who is this? And the multitude said, This is Jesus the prophet of Nazareth of Galilee." (Matthew 21:9-11). But just seven days later, this same multitude demanded the death of the Savior, crying: "His blood be on us, and on our children." (Matthew 27:25). How quickly does the pendulum swing!

When Jesus came "into the temple, the chief priests and the elders of the people came unto him as he was teaching, and said, By what authority doest thou these things? and who gave thee this authority?" Faithlessly, they demanded to know by what power He conducted His ministry. The questioned His judgment, and sustained Him by the outward show of an uplifted hand, but not with their actions. "Jesus saith unto them, Did ye never read in the scriptures, The stone which the builders rejected, the same is become the head of the corner: this is the Lord's doing, and it is marvellous in our eyes?" (Matthew 21:42).

Because they summarily rejected Him, He said: "The kingdom of God shall be taken from you, and given to a nation bringing forth the fruits thereof. And whosoever shall fall on this stone shall be broken: but on whomsoever it shall fall, it will grind him to powder." (Matthew 21:43-44).

When Jesus came to Bethany, to the home of Mary and Martha, Mary took "a pound of ointment...very costly, and anointed the feet of Jesus, and wiped his feet with her hair: and the house was filled with the odour of the ointment. Then saith one of his disciples, Judas Iscariot...Why was not this ointment sold for three hundred pence, and given to the poor? This he said, not that he cared for the poor; but because he was a thief." (John 12:3-6). Sometimes, we say things because it is politically correct or expedient, or to our advantage. Likewise, sometimes we do not say things that should be said, because we fear the consequences. But as Abraham Lincoln cautioned: "To sin by silence, when words should be spoken, makes cowards of men." (Original quotation by Ella Wheeler Wilcox).

Modern scribes and Pharisees omit the weightier matters of the law such as faith and mercy. They strain at a gnat, and swallow a camel. They appear to be righteous, but inside are "full of extortion and excess." (Matthew 223:25). Our sincere desire to serve and obey Jesus Christ, motivated by love and faith, brings us closer to Him, leaving no room for hypocrisy to creep into our lives.

I am a Child of God

"Because
of the covenant which ye
have made, ye shall be called the
children of Christ, his sons,
and his daughters."
(Mosiah 5:7).

The lyrics to the song "I am a Child of God" were written in 1957 by Naomi Randall (1908 - 2001). A friend composed the music. It is one of 45 hymns that The Church of Jesus Christ of Latter-day Saints includes in its basic musical curriculum, and it is one of the first hymns that new members learn. It has been translated into over 90 languages, and its lexicon has become a means of teaching a doctrine that is simple and easy to understand. Thus, it is frequently found in church instructional curricula, it is woven into sermons, and it even finds itself the subject of merchandizing and novelties. It is a song that is easy to understand, because it transcends time and space. Its resonant theme has stirred the hearts of countless of God's children, no matter where they may be busily engaged in their mortal curriculum. (For some of our interstellar cousins, it would help to have a Universal Translator handy).

Randall composed the song at the request of the Primary General Board, of which she was a member at the time. Its objective was to have a tune that Primary age children could easily remember and sing, that would reflect doctrinal teaching on the nature of our relationship with our Heavenly Father. Randall described how she went about fulfilling her commission from the Board: "I got down on my knees and prayed aloud, pleading that God would let me know the right words. Around 2:00 a.m., I awakened and began to think again about the song. Words came to my mind, and I immediately got up and began to write them down as they had come to me. Three verses and a chorus were soon formed. I gratefully surveyed the work, drank of the message of the words, and returned to my bedroom, where I knelt before my Father in Heaven to say: Thank you!" In the morning, she mailed the lyrics to her friend Mildred T. Pettit, who immediately wrote the accompanying music.

Sister Randall had been guided by the Spirit, as had Job of old. He described how "in a dream, in a vision of the night, when deep sleep falleth upon (us, and) in slumberings upon the bed. Then he openeth (our) ears, and sealeth (our) instruction." (Job 33:1-16). "I am a Child of God" was first performed at a stake Primary conference in 1957. After hearing it, that same young boy from Thatcher, Spencer W. Kimball, who by then was an Apostle, asked the Primary General Board if the phrase "Teach me all that I must know" could be changed to "Teach me all that I must do." As he later explained, "To know isn't enough. The devils know and tremble. We have to do something." The suggestion was gratefully accepted by Sister Randall, and the change was made.

"I am a Child of God" was first published in the "Sing with Me" songbook for children. (1969). In 1978, Sister Randall composed a fourth verse, but when the song was added to the L.D.S. Hymnal that same year, that verse was excluded because it had not been an official part of the original song. However, in 1989, when a new songbook for children was published, the fourth verse was included.

Today, "I am a Child of God" (with three verses) is selection number 301 in "Hymns of The Church of Jesus Christ of Latter-day Saints," and the song is included in the "Children's Songbook" with the fourth verse included. This brings us to the first verse: "I am a child of God, and He has sent me here; has given me an earthly home, with parents kind and dear." As William Wordsworth wrote: "Our birth is but a sleep and a forgetting. The soul that rises with us, our life's star, hath had elsewhere its setting, and cometh from afar. Not in entire forgetfulness, and not in utter nakedness, but trailing clouds of glory do we come, from God, Who is our Home." (Ode: Intimations of Immortality, from Recollections of Early Childhood).

Our understanding that God's genetic code has been scattered across the galaxy places a high priority on our responsibility here on Earth to teach children correct principles, thereby to nurture their faith in the titular Head of our extended family. "Faith," after all, "cometh by hearing, and hearing by the word of God." (Romans 10:17). "For unto us," wrote Paul, "was the gospel preached, as well as unto them (of ancient Israel); but the word preached did not profit them, not being mixed with faith in them that heard it." (Hebrews 4:3).

In the Book of Moses, we learn that the great lawgiver's sense of identity was based on his eternal relationship with his Father in Heaven. (Moses 1:3-4). He knew that he was God's offspring. In fact, he was inexorably intertwined, in a double helix, with God. That bond was fixed and immovable, and it could not be broken, and when his Father spoke to him, He confirmed: "Behold, I am the Lord God Almighty, and ... Thou art my son. (Moses 1:3-4). Today, we teach our children who they are, and the missionaries cite these same scriptures that resonate with truth. That burgeoning knowledge largely defines our character, and the strength of our conviction firmly establishes our place in the cosmos, shoulder to shoulder, as it were, with all our brothers and sisters who reside upon God's creations.

And then, the chorus: "Lead me, guide me, walk beside me, help me find the way. Teach me all that I must do to live with Him some day." Children learn to be obedient, that one day they may, in turn, teach their own offspring, in an unbroken pattern. But if there are children in Zion whose parents fail to teach them to understand the doctrines of the kingdom. and especially the truth that each of us is a star-child, trailing clouds of glory, as it were, from God, Who is our Home, "the sin be upon the heads of the parents." (D&C 68:25-28).

The second verse reads: "I am a child of God, and so my needs are great. Help me to understand his words before it grows too late." The three most important days of our lives are the day we were born, the day we find out why, and the day we die. With that awakening awareness, we come full circle. "When a baby is born, and as we wait with those who are dying, we brush against the veil, as greetings and goodbyes are said almost within earshot of each other. In such moments, this resonance with realities on the other side of the veil is so obvious that it can be explained in only one way." (Neal A. Maxwell, "B.Y.U. Devotional," 11/1979).

All the children of God will make a giant leap in time, space, and faith, when they return to Him one day. We can almost hear the angelic voices now: "Here you are, home from your mission. It seems like it was such a short time. Think of the people you met, the people you helped. Think of how you have grown spiritually. You were just a child when you left home, not so long ago. There is Mother waiting to embrace you, standing just a bit behind Father, who is bursting with pride. Are those tears of happiness on Mother's cheeks? Father first strikes hands with you, and then pulls you into His embrace. The feelings are resonant, and you know this is where you belong - this is a real homecoming - home to Heavenly Father and Mother." (Anonymous).

The third verse reads: "I am a child of God. Rich blessings are in store. If I but learn to do his will, I'll live with him once more." Alma called God's Plan "The Plan of Happiness." (Alma 42:16). Its design provides a way for us to acknowledge the genetic blueprint of our lives and follow it past solar systems, through star clusters, around nebulae, and beyond galaxies, to find eternal happiness,. God's Rest can be pinpointed at the very center of our star charts, and "is the object and design of our existence and will be the end thereof if we follow the path that leads to it. And this path includes faith, virtue, uprightness, and keeping all the commandments." (Joseph Smith, "Teachings," p. 255-256).

As we engage the curriculum of life's learning laboratory, it helps to have celestial signposts and millennial mile markers to navigate the telestial traffic jams, the conceptual cul-de-sacs, and the doctrinal deviations that threaten to detour us from the strait and narrow way onto telestial turf and the minefields of mortality. The expanding circle of opportunity afforded by obedience to gospel principles, however, assures us of direct experience with the perfect law of liberty. Thus, we trade the uncertain course adopted by individuals bound for the telestial kingdom for the certain reality of celestial surety. That knowledge is as a warning buoy, an aid to navigation for the children of God, no matter in what part of the cosmos they may reside.

In countless episodes of "Star Trek: The Next Generation," Captain Jean Luc Picard sat in his chair on the bridge of the Enterprise-E, raised his right hand, pointed two fingers toward the view screen, and uttered the command: "Engage!" With that, off they went in their starship, inertial dampers online as they almost instantly reached maximum warp. We do something similar when we engage our agency, which is to us as our own personal Quantum Drive propulsion system. Our course is laid in, and the parameters of our journey are defined by our Operations Manual, whose elements can be found within The Plan of Salvation. The only boundaries it recognizes are those the Lord has set. Our navigational deflector shield is Jesus Christ, and our inertial damper is His Atonement. Our willingness to "engage" is determined at the molecular level by our genetic code. Its blueprint will take us to the final frontier of experience at the edge of eternity, where we will encounter strange new worlds, new life, and new civilizations, in regions of space where no one has gone before.

The good decisions we make along the way, during our visionary travels across the galaxy, will take us to intermediate "star bases," and particularly to the Sacrament table. These stops will automatically negate the consequences of poor choices that sometimes creep into our travel itinerary. Our inertial damper will protect us from the spatial distortions of sin, from the negative effects of inertial indecision, and from the buffetings of the gravimetric waves of unlimited freedom that would lead us to the temporal distortions of unrelenting tyranny. On our journey to the far reaches of our imaginations, even without the benefit of a trans-warp conduit, we will be reassured by the knowledge that we are children of God, proven by a heraldry that proclaims our independence in that stage of development to which our decisions have led us. Our divine genome will become an armorial bearing that distinguishes us as members of a royal family. In this, the best of circumstances that are dictated by the principles of The Plan, "the universe itself will become a machine for the making of Gods." (Henri Bergson, "Two Sources of Morality and Religion," p. 306).

There is a fourth authorized verse of "I Am a Child of God" that is included in the Children's Songbook: "I am a child of God. His promises are sure. Celestial glory shall be mine, if I can but endure." To know that we are children of God is enough to kindle a spark within us that ignites our sense of wonder, illuminating our understanding of the depths of eternity. It gets the dilithium crystals in the warp drive of our resolve up to critical mass. But it would be wrong to leave it at that, for to know only would underestimate the magnitude of The Plan and put at risk our relationship with God in such a way that its overarching importance in every aspect of our lives might be diluted or demeaned. The matter / antimatter interaction in our warp core might overload, and our genetic code might be misinterpreted, underutilized, or even ignored.

At the end of the day, we need to know that we are God's children, and then act upon that innervating knowledge. Doing so frees us to keep our finger on our quickening pulse, as we actively monitor our burgeoning relationship with our Heavenly Father. Our faith is founded upon the very points of doctrine that address salvation and exaltation, and upon these elements hinges its correct understanding. "I am a Child of God," as it turns out, is a very good choice of words when describing the intimacy that our Heavenly Father desires to have with us, and with His children everywhere.

I Have Fought a Good Fight

"And now I bid unto all, farewell. I soon go to rest in the paradise of God, until y spirit and body shall again reunite, and I am brought forth triumphant through the air, to meet you before the pleasing bar of the great Jehovah, the Eternal Judge of both quick and dead. Amen."
(Moroni 10:34).

"I have fought a good fight, have finished my course, I have kept the faith." (2 Timothy 4:7) The apostle Paul lived his life in such a way that he could make this wonderful affirmation toward its end. Inherent within his declaration, however, was the message that there is a difference between winning and finishing the race of life. There is only one victor in competitive sports. But in the race of life, everyone finishes, but each of us may be awarded a gold medal as we cross the line with the tape streaming behind us, the thunder of applause resounding in our ears, and the dazzle of a thousand flash bulbs popping furiously before our eyes.

The only things standing in our way are the elements of apostasy and the demons associated with a denial of the faith. These were described by Nephi, who said that in the Last Days churches would be built up to get gain, and that they would contend with each other for market share. He said they would teach after the manner of men and would reject not only the influence of the Spirit, but also of the Lord Jesus Christ Himself. They would plant in our minds the seeds of the heresy that we have somehow legitimately appropriated His power by the sheer force of our collective intellect and the expansion of our abilities. As a result, we risk confirming the worst fears of J. Robert Oppenheimer, the scientific director of the Manhattan Project that developed nuclear weapons during World War II. In reference to the detonation of the first atomic bomb, Oppenheimer recalled the Bhagavad Gita: "Now I am become Death, the destroyer of worlds."

We are all familiar with those who focus their worship on their "elegant and spacious buildings and fine work of wood, and all manner of precious things." (Mosiah 11:8-11). We remember the Emperor Justinian, who "began a new Santa Sophia. He summoned the best architects to plan and superintend the work. Abandoning the traditional Basilican form, they conceived a design whose center would be a spacious dome resting not on walls but on massive piers, and buttressed by a half dome at either end. Ten thousand workmen were engaged, and 320,000 pounds of gold were spent on the enterprise. In five years and ten months the edifice was complete, and on December 26, 537 A.D., the Emperor led a solemn inaugural procession to the resplendent cathedral. Justinian walked alone to the pulpit, and lifting up his hands, cried out: "Oh Solomon! I have vanquished you!" (Will Durant, "The Lessons of History," 4:130).

In like manner, James Cameron stood before the Academy of Motion Picture Arts and Sciences in March 2000, (and a television audience of around 40 million viewers) and with an Oscar in each of his raised hands cried out, "I'm the king of the world!"

In 1964, John Lennon famously said: "Christianity will go. It will vanish and shrink. I needn't argue with that; I will be proved right. We're more popular than Jesus now. I don't know which will go first - rock 'n' roll or Christianity." (The Beatles broke up six years later. Today, by all reports, Christianity is still alive and well).

In the Last Days, the appeal of apostasy would be woven into the persuasively subliminal message that God's miracles have been replaced by technologies that would seduce us to eat, drink, and be merry, without worrying about the inconvenient burden of consequences.

Because apostasy is congenitally short-sighted, it promotes a lifestyle in which its advocates live for the moment, come what may. However, we should all remember the cartoon philosopher Pogo, who said of the disheveled bum sleeping it off in a gutter: "Aha! Here we have someone paying for the sin of excess. The hobnailed boots of indiscretion's marathon dancer tap a rowdy two-step across the terracotta of his consciousness. Excess was his master. Reason was cast into the rumble seat of his libidinous juggernaut. Now the piper must be paid!"

Apostasy appeals to our worldly cravings as well, and to our lust for material possessions, for we "tend to fill space, as if what we have, what we are, is not enough. Being affluent, we strangle ourselves with what we can buy, things whose opacity obstructs our ability see what is really there." (Gretel Erlich, Under Wyoming Skies, Atlantic Magazine).

Apostasy begs Satan's Golden Question: "Do you have any money?" and anticipates his follow-up declaration: "You can have anything in this world for money!" Newsweek Magazine reported that, long ago, "Europeans who investigated the phenomenon of a country without a titled aristocracy discerned that the pursuit of wealth would become the Americans' route to distinction, and that America would eventually develop an ideology founded on money: capitalism."

Because they reject repentance, the advocates of apostasy are deluded into thinking that even if God did exist, He would only punish them lightly and then let them get on with their self-indulgent behavior. Nephi said: "There shall be many which shall teach after this manner, false and vain and foolish doctrines, and shall be puffed up in their hearts." (2 Nephi 28:3-9).

Of such, the Lord said: "They have strayed from mine ordinances, and have broken mine everlasting covenant; They seek not the Lord the establish his righteousness, but every man walketh in his own way, and after the image of his own god, whose image is in the likeness of the world, and whose substance is that of an idol, which waxeth old and shall perish in Babylon, even Babylon the great, which shall fall." (D&C 1:15-16). Because of the reality of apostasy, it is vital to embrace true doctrine to avoid the pitfall of "ever learning, and never (being) able to come to the knowledge of the truth." (2 Timothy 3:7).

In fact, our education is of no worth unless it leads us to the truth, and so we have been admonished: "Continue thou in the things which thou hast learned and hast been assured of, knowing of whom thou hast learned them; And that from a child thou hast known the holy scriptures which are able to make thee wise unto salvation through faith which is in Christ Jesus. All scripture is given by inspiration of God, and is profitable for doctrine, for reproof, for correction, (and) for instruction in righteousness. That the man of God may be perfect, thoroughly furnished unto all good works." (1 Timothy 3:14-17). Paul emphasized to Timothy the importance of learning and teaching true principles, and promised: "If thou put the brethren in remembrance of these things, thou shalt be a good minister of Jesus Christ, nourished up in the words of faith and of good doctrine." (1 Timothy 4:6).

Speaking of its power, Boyd K. Packer said: "True doctrine changes attitudes and behavior. The study of the doctrines of the gospel will improve behavior quicker than a study of behavior will improve behavior." ("Ensign," 11/1986). We can be sure that what we teach is true doctrine if our instruction is founded on the scriptures and the counsel of latter-day prophets. As Mormon observed of Alma: "He commanded them that they should teach nothing save it were the things which he had taught, and which had been spoken by the mouth of the holy prophets. Yea, even he commanded them that they should preach nothing save it were repentance and faith on the Lord." (Mosiah 18:19-20). This basic principle has been reiterated in the Last Days: "Preach none other things than that which the prophets and apostles have written, and that which is taught them by the Comforter through the prayer of faith." (D&C 52:9).

Once we have received true doctrine, Paul said we must "hold fast the form of sound words." (2 Timothy 1:13). To keep the floodgates of apostate practices closed, he knew we must cling to "the faithful word as (we have) been taught, that (we) may be able by sound doctrine both to exhort and to convince the gainsayers." (Titus 1:9). Nephi understood the doctrine as Paul did, observing: "Whoso would hearken unto the word of God, and would hold fast unto it, they would never perish; neither could the temptations and the fiery darts of the adversary overpower them unto blindness, to lead them away to destruction." (1 Nephi 15:23-24). They would "be an example of the believers, in word, in conversation, in charity, in spirit, in faith (and) in purity." (1 Timothy 4:12).

In short, Paul's formula was to follow after righteousness and to deny ungodliness. "For we brought nothing into this world," he observed, "and it is certain we can carry nothing out. And having food and raiment let us be therewith content." We must not "trust in uncertain riches, but in the living God, who giveth us richly all things to enjoy." (1 Timothy 6:7-10 & 17-19). To those whose nature it is to serve without recompense or recognition, Jacob taught that there is responsibility associated with the blessings that accompany the embrace of sound doctrine. He both promised and admonished: "After ye have obtained a hope in Christ ye shall obtain riches, if ye seek them; and ye will seek them for the intent to do good - to clothe the naked, and to feed the hungry, and to liberate the captive, and administer relief to the sick and the afflicted." (Jacob 2:18-19).

In the case of the Apostle Paul, he knew he would suffer martyrdom for his unswerving obedience to the eternal principles embedded within sound doctrine. Therefore, he counseled Timothy to "Fight the good fight of faith," and to "lay hold on to eternal life." (1 Timothy 6:11-12). If we stay on course, we too can say: "I have fought a good fight, I have finished my course, I have kept the faith" (2 Timothy 4:7).

The anniversary of our death is
the birth date of our immortal soul.
It was this philosophical viewpoint that
motivated Socrates, with cup of hemlock
in his hand, to declare: "Look death in the
face with joyful hope and consider this a
lasting truth - The righteous man has
nothing to fear, neither in life, nor
in death, and the gods will
not forsake him."

I Have Overcome the World

"I could remember my pains no more; yea, I was harrowed up by the memory of my sins no more."
(Alma 36:19).

It is a marvelous thing to see how the gospel prepares us to handle the challenges of life. With its principles as our foundation, our perspective may be "fair as the moon, clear as the sun, and terrible as an army with banners." (D&C 109:73). It determines how we handle our weaknesses, limitations, and even sin. Without it, self-defeating behaviors may impede our progress. On the other hand, in partnership with the Savior, we will turn the tables on Satan, and actually use our imperfections as stepping-stones to higher achievement. Negative experiences can be the diamond dust that polishes us to a high luster, or they can be the abrasive that wears us down and grinds us up.

The Lord said: "If men come unto me, I will show unto them their weakness. I give unto men weakness that they may be humble; and my grace is sufficient for all men that humble themselves before me; for if they humble themselves before me, and have faith in me, then will I make weak things strong unto them." (Ether 12:27). This is a startling concept to a world in which weakness is perceived as a liability, and strength and independence are viewed as positive values.

The world gravely underestimates the power of well-founded faith in Jesus Christ. When it does its job and convicts us of our sins, those of us who are on the path of progress take the matter before the Lord. After we have truly repented and received forgiveness (a process that may take some time) He will remember our sins no more in the sense that He will not count them to our detriment. Life is not like military boot camp, where an uncaring drill sergeant assesses demerits for rules infractions until they have amassed to the point that harsh punishment is inevitable.

Instead, the Atonement wipes the slate clean, levels the playing field, and resets our pedometer to zero. We begin our walk anew, brimming with confidence. We believe Isaiah, who said: "Though your sins be as scarlet, they shall be as white as snow; though they be red like crimson, they shall be as wool." (Isaiah 1:18). We remember the wise advice that reminds us that although we cannot go back and make a brand-new start, we can start now and make a brand-new ending.

Because of the Atonement, the sky is the limit, and our expectation of success is 100%. Nevertheless, like a twisted nail that has been pulled from a board, after repentance and forgiveness, the hole created by sin will still be there, and we may pensively run our fingers over it from time to time. Tracing the outline, we may even relive the emotional rush of our brush with the forbidden.

If we do so by habit or if we feel compelled to revisit the damage created by our sin, let us be as Alma the Younger, who confided to Helaman when reflecting on the rebellious years of his youth: "I was racked with eternal torment, for my soul was harrowed up to the greatest degree and racked with all my sins. Yea, I did remember all my sins and iniquities, for which I was tormented with the pains of hell; yea, I saw that I had rebelled against my God, and that I had not kept his holy commandments. Yea, and I had murdered many of his children, or rather led them away unto destruction; yea, and in fine so great had been my iniquities, that the very thought of coming into the presence of my God did rack my soul with inexpressible horror." (Alma 36:12-14). In the midst of such anguish, Alma cast his broken spirit on the altar of the Atonement to find peace. He took hold of the horns of sanctuary and sought the healing balm of Gilead to ease his troubled soul. So exquisite was the peace he found that many years later he told his son: "I could remember my pains no more; yea, I was harrowed up by the memory of my sins no more." (Alma 36:19).

Recollections of our blackest deeds may surface in our memory only to serve the purpose of motivating us to hold steady as we strive to be better in the future. But the pain associated with our former sins will have been swallowed up in the Atonement. Like the people of Zarahemla who were called to repentance by their king, we will exclaim: "Yea, we believe all the words which thou hast spoken unto us; and also, we know of their surety and truth, because of the Spirit of the Lord Omnipotent, which has wrought a mighty change in us, or in our hearts, that we have no more disposition to do evil, but to do good continually." (Mosiah 5:2).

As we heed the counsel of King Benjamin, we will be less inclined to yield to the enticements of Satan and return to our sins. Truly did Solomon observe: "As a dog returneth to his vomit, so a fool returneth to his folly." (Proverbs 26:11). As we turn to the scriptures, to prayer, and to an active discipline-based lifestyle, we will be more likely to make progress along the Rod of Iron toward the Tree of Life. We will remember the word of the Lord to Israel through His prophet Hosea: "I will heal their backsliding, I will "love them freely: for mine anger is turned away." (Hosea 14:4). (It is interesting that Hosea had been commanded by God to marry Gomer, "a wife of whoredoms." (Hosea 1:2). Evidently, "God is no respecter of persons." (Acts 10:34). Instead, He "esteemeth all flesh in one; (and) he that is righteous is favored of God." (1 Nephi 17:35).

We will finish each day and be done with it. "You have done what you could," declared Ralph Waldo Emerson. "Some blunders and absurdities no doubt crept in; forget them as soon as you can. Tomorrow is a new day; you shall begin it well and serenely and with too high a spirit to be encumbered with your old nonsense."

As we move forward, we may loosen our grasp on the Rod with first one hand, and then the other. But we must never let go with both hands at the same time, thinking that we can make more rapid progress on our own by leaping over perceived obstacles. If we do so, we may suffer even as Zeniff, who was "over-zealous to inherit the land of his fathers, therefore (he was) deceived by the cunning and craftiness" of those who valued neither his welfare nor the merits of Jesus Christ.

"Watch yourselves," Benjamin had cautioned, "and your thoughts, and your words, and your deeds, (note the hierarchy of self-determination in the order of these actions) and observe the commandments of God, and continue in the faith of what ye have heard concerning the coming of our Lord, even unto the end of your lives." (Mosiah 4:30). Mormon saw our day, and in his abridgment on The Large Plates of Nephi determined to engrave verbatim the words of King Benjamin's address, because they would be relevant to our circumstances.

We cannot truly overcome the world until we know Christ and hearken to His counsel. The scales that measure strength suggest that spirituality must be inextricably interwoven into our character. If we pattern our lives after the example of the Savior, internalize gospel principles, and are obedient to priesthood covenants, the scales are tipped in our favor, and we can do all things. Our determination to "put on the strength of the Lord" leads to the positive reinforcement of sustainable good works. (Mosiah 10:11).

However, we are not, and can never be, lights unto ourselves. We cannot overcome the world on our own. But when we borrow His strength and His power, we can do all things. Many times, the Lord told disobedient Israel that His "hand is stretched out still." (Isaiah 10:4). If we ignore that helping hand, or if we refuse His invitation to lift us up, we invite disaster. Our behavior must foster humility, for it is the meek who shall inherit the earth.

Heber J. Grant stated: "I do not believe that any man lives up to his ideals, but if we are striving, if we are working, if we are trying, to the best of our ability, to improve day by day, then we are in the line of our duty. If we are seeking to remedy our own defects, if we are so living that we can ask for light, for knowledge, for intelligence, and above all, for His Spirit that we may overcome weakness, then, I can tell you, we are in the straight and narrow path that leads to life eternal." ("Gospel Standards," p. 184-5).

"Even the humblest human beings (observed Pope John Paul II, during an interview with "Time" Magazine, 10/26/1998), are naturally philosophic, asking themselves such questions as: 'Who am I?' 'Where did I come from?' and 'Where am I going?' Religious revelation provides answers to these questions," the Pope acknowledged.

Isaiah in The Book of Mormon

"And now, behold, I say unto
you, that ye ought to search these things.
Yea, a commandment I give unto you that
ye search these things diligently, for
great are the words of Isaiah."
(3 Nephi 23:1).

"The version of Isaiah in the Nephite scripture hews an independent course for itself, as might be expected of a truly ancient and authentic record. It makes additions to the present text in certain places, omits material in others, transposes, makes grammatical changes, finds support at times for its unusual readings in the ancient Greek, Syriac, and Latin Versions, and at other times no support at all. In general, it presents phenomena of great interest to the student of Isaiah." ("Book of Mormon Compendium," p. 512).

"The text of Isaiah in The Book of Mormon is not word for word the same as that of the King James Translation. Of 433 verses of Isaiah in the Nephite record, Joseph Smith modified 234. Some of the changes were slight, others were radical. However, 199 verses are word for word the same as the K.J.T. We, therefore, freely admit that Joseph Smith may have used the K.J.T. when he came to the text of Isaiah on the gold plates. As long as the K.J.T. agreed substantially with the text on the gold plates, he let it pass; when it differed too radically, he translated the Nephite version and dictated the necessary changes." ("Book of Mormon Compendium," p. 507-508, See C.E.S. Manual, p. 90, & Commentary Reference to 2 Nephi 26:15).

As Hugh Nibley has pointed out, "resemblances between the Bible and The Book of Mormon are not hard to explain. Far from being evidence of fraud, they are rather confirmation of authenticity. If The Book of Mormon is what it pretends to be, we should expect to find a strong biblical influence in it. Its prophets sound like those of the Old Testament because they studied and consciously quoted the words of those prophets, and all prophets moreover are programmed to sound alike, being called for the same purpose under much the same conditions." ("Churches in The Wilderness").

Mark E. Petersen wrote: "When the King James translators began their work, they did so with fasting and prayer. For the most part they were pious men who sought the inspiration of the Lord in their work. We believe they received it. The preservation of the Bible thru the ages is itself a miracle. It was accomplished only thru the hand of God. Then why not its translation: The King James translators did everything they knew how to obtain divine inspiration for their task. Knowing the great value of that book to the Gentiles, as Nephi himself said, would God withhold the necessary inspiration: Those humble translators were instruments in the hands of the Almighty to further His purpose among the Gentiles. ("Those Gold Plates!" p. 52 & 56).

Nephi himself revealed why a comprehension of Isaiah is difficult even for biblical scholars. He wrote: "Now I, Nephi, do speak somewhat concerning the words which I have written, which have been spoken by the mouth of Isaiah. For behold, Isaiah spake many things which were hard for many of my people to understand; for they know not concerning the manner of prophesying among the Jews." (2 Nephi 25:1). That is to say, the prophet Isaiah spoke in figures, using types and shadows to illustrate his points. The key to an understanding of the scriptural code employed by Isaiah is somewhat involved, and thus requires a foundation of explanation.

Only Sam and Nephi, and perhaps their wives, had lived "at Jerusalem." Therefore, they alone had a first-hand understanding of their cultural heritage, and the distinctive writing style of the Jews. On the one hand, it would be important that the people of Nephi be comfortable with the contents of the Plates of Brass, because the teachings therein contained many important doctrinal truths. On the other hand, Nephi abhorred that part of the Jewish mindset that was responsible for the persecution of his family, and for their expulsion from their homeland.

Nephi expressed his reluctance to teach the people many things concerning the manner of "the Jews," but at the same time he wrote: "My soul delighteth in the words of Isaiah, for I came out from Jerusalem, and mine eyes hath beheld the things of the Jews, and I know that the Jews do understand the things of the prophets, and there is none other people that understand the things which were spoken unto the Jews like unto them, save it be that they are taught after the manner of the things of the Jews." (2 Nephi 25:6).

Indirectly, Nephi was illustrating the importance of Book of Mormon scholarship, and of studying the Nephites, their culture, and their world. If we do not do that, we cannot understand the manner of prophesying of men like Nephi, Jacob, Alma, Helaman, Mormon, and Moroni, let alone Isaiah. They can be understood, but one must pay the price. Perspiration must precede inspiration. There is no revelation where there is no student.

Because Isaiah's writing style employed types and shadows, and because his prophecies were dualistic, meaning that they had application not only for ancient Israel, but also for Israel at the time of the mortal ministry of Christ, and for Latter-day and Millennial Israel, it is necessary in many cases to analyze nearly every word of a verse in order to ascertain its true meaning. It will also be necessary to set the chapters against the backdrop of the historical context in which they were written, in order to 'read between the lines' and better understand their meaning.

At first, this might seem a bit cumbersome to do, but with a deeper understanding, Isaiah's writings come alive with imagery and metaphor, and loom larger than life, because they were written to transcend the ages.

The Lord declared: "Now behold, a marvelous work is about to come forth among the children of men." (D&C 4:1). "And if thou wilt inquire, thou shalt know mysteries which are great and marvelous." (D&C 6:11). "Now behold, I say unto you, that ye ought to search these things. Yea, a commandment I give unto you that ye search these things diligently; for great are the words of Isaiah." (3 Nephi 23:1).

Only when they have paid the price, will the words of Isaiah flow easily and poetically to the minds of his students. Scriptural fluency will come after practice that is manifested by memorization, recitation, individual and cooperative study, comparison with companion scriptures, expansion of understanding by critical analysis of supportive commentaries, and faith and prayer.

Is Heaven Hotter Than Hell?

"According to the power of justice, for
justice cannot be denied, ye must go away into
that lake of fire and brimstone, whose flames are
unquenchable, and whose smoke ascendeth up
forever and ever, which lake of fire and
brimstone is endless torment."
(Jacob 5:10).

In 1972, an article in Applied Optics (11:14) stated that Heaven must be hotter than Hell. The paper noted that Revelation 21:8 describes a lake in Hell "which burneth with fire and brimstone." For there to be such a lake, the authors reasoned, Hell's temperature must be below the boiling point of sulphur, at 444.6¼° C. At a higher temperature, the lake's contents would simply boil away. Meanwhile, Isaiah 30:26 describes the conditions in Heaven, where "the light of the Moon shall be as the light of the Sun, and the light of the Sun shall be sevenfold, as the light of seven days."

The authors reasoned that if "the light of seven days" is a metaphorical way of describing heaven, then we can determine that heaven receives from the moon as much radiation as we do from the sun, and in addition seven times seven as much as the earth does from the sun, or fifty times as much in all.

Since the light we receive from the moon is just a ten-thousandth of the light we receive from the sun, we can ignore it as insignificant. The radiation falling on heaven will heat it to the point where the heat lost is just equal to the heat received, maintaining a state of equilibrium. Therefore, heaven receives and loses 50 times as much heat as the earth by radiation. Using the Stefan-Boltzmann Fourth Power Law for Radiation, then, the temperature of Heaven was calculated to be a sweltering 525¼° C. Heaven really is hotter than hell!

But then, a letter published in the magazine "Physics Today" said that the "Applied Optics" authors misinterpreted the date in the Isaiah passage, wrongly multiplying seven by seven to make the illumination in Heaven forty-nine times as bright as that experienced by us on earth. Theologians have argued that only a single factor of seven was intended by Isaiah. Consequently, Heaven's temperature was recalculated as only 231° C., blisteringly hot, but probably still cooler than Hell.

The question "How hot is hell?" was thus left open to debate. We do know this. A thermodynamics professor gave his graduate students a take home exam. It had only one question: "Is Hell exothermic (does it give off heat) or is it endothermic (does it absorb heat?)" The answer was to be supported with a proof.

Most of the students wrote proofs of their beliefs using Boyle's Law: Gas cools off when it expands and heats up when it is compressed. But one student wrote the following: "First, we need to know how the mass of Hell is changing in time. So, we need to know the rate at which souls are moving into Hell and the rate at which they are leaving. I think we can safely assume that once a soul gets to Hell, it cannot leave. As for how many souls are entering Hell, consider that most religions state that if you do not believe as they do, you will go to Hell. So, we can assume that nearly everyone is going to Hell. As a matter of fact, we can expect the number of souls in Hell to increase exponentially. This leaves two possibilities according to Boyle's Law.

#1. If Hell is expanding slower than the rate at which souls enter Hell, then the temperature and pressure in Hell will increase until all hell breaks loose.

#2. If Hell is expanding at a rate faster than the increase of souls in Hell, then the temperature and pressure will drop until Hell freezes over.

It's Our Book

The Book of Mormon was preserved for our day because each of us must stand "to be judged of (our) works, whether they be good or evil." It helps us to "believe the gospel of Jesus Christ," and it serves as another witness to "the Jews, the covenant people of the Lord ... that Jesus, whom they slew, was the very Christ and the very God." It helps us to "repent and prepare to stand before the judgment-seat of Christ." (Mormon 3:20-22).

The first reason is so that everyone in the world may know that "every soul who belongs to the whole human family of Adam ... must stand to be judged of (their) works, whether they be good or evil." (Mormon 3:20). Everyone will be redeemed from spiritual death to appear before God at the Judgment Bar of Christ. This reason for the preservation of The Book of Mormon is critically tied to the fourth reason listed below.

The second reason is because the book helps us to "believe the gospel of Jesus Christ." (Mormon 3:21). As Joseph Smith stated: "I told the brethren that The Book of Mormon was the most correct of any book on earth, and the keystone of our religion, and a man would get nearer to God by abiding by its precepts, than by any other book." ("Book of Mormon Introduction").

The third reason is that The Book of Mormon will serve as another witness to "the Jews, the covenant people of the Lord ... that Jesus, whom they slew, was the very Christ and the very God." (Mormon 3:21). The Book of Mormon will be given to the Jews in the Last Days "for the purpose of convincing them of the true Messiah, who was rejected by them; and unto the convincing of them that they need not look forward any more for a Messiah to come ... for there is save one Messiah spoken of by the prophets, and that Messiah is he who should be rejected of the Jews." (2 Nephi 25:18).

The fourth reason for the preservation of The Book of Mormon in the Last Days is that Mormon saw our day, and knew our needs. (Mormon 8:35). The Book of Mormon helps a world in need to "repent and prepare to stand before the judgment-seat of Christ." (Mormon 3:22).

In summary, The Book of Mormon was preserved for our day 1) that it might prepare us for the coming judgment, 2) that it might help us to embrace the gospel, 3) that it might stand as a witness to the Jews that Jesus is the Christ, 4) that it might help us to deal with latter-day challenges.

The light and the life of the world is "Jesus Christ, the Son of God, who was crucified for the sins of the world." (D&C 35:2). As far as we are concerned, His light has always existed. His flawless character focuses and clarifies His light as would a magnifying glass.

Joseph Smith: A Rough Stone Rolling

"Yea, Joseph truly said: Thus saith the Lord unto me: A choice seer will I raise up out of the fruit of thy loins; and he shall be esteemed highly among the fruit of thy loins. And unto him will I give commandment that he shall do a work for the fruit of thy loins, his brethren, which shall be of great worth unto them, even to the bringing of them to the knowledge of the covenants which I have made with thy fathers."
(2 Nephi 3:7).

"In the forepart of September 1827, I went to Rochester on business and returned by Palmyra to be there about the 22nd of September ... That night we all went to bed and in the morning I got up and my horse and carriage were gone ... After a while he (Joseph Smith) came home with the horse. All came into the house to breakfast. But no thing was said about where they had been. After breakfast Joseph called me into the other room ... He set his foot on the bed and leaned his head on his hand and said ... 'It is ten times better than I expected.' Then he went on to tell the length and width and thickness of the plates, and said he, 'They appear to be gold'" (Reminiscences of Joseph Knight, Church History Library, This manuscript, written between 1833 and 1847, has been published in Dean C. Jesse, "Joseph Knight's Recollection of Early Mormon History," BYU Studies, 17:1, p. 30-39).

"I prophesied that the Saints would continue to suffer much affliction and would be driven to the Rocky Mountains, many would apostatize, others would be put to death by our persecutors or lose their lives in consequence of exposure or disease, and some of you will live to go and assist in making settlements and build cities and see the Saints become a mighty people in the midst of the Rocky Mountains." (H.C., 5:85).

"It is my meditation all day, and more than my meat and drink, to know how I shall make the Saints of God comprehend the visions that roll like an overflowing surge before my mind. Oh! how I would delight to bring before you things which you never thought of! But poverty and the cares of the world prevent. ... Hosanna, hosanna, hosanna to Almighty God, that rays of light begin to burst forth upon us even now. I cannot find words in which to express myself. I am not learned, but I have as good feelings as any man. Oh, that I had the language of the archangel to express my feelings once to my friends! But I never expect to in this life." (H.C., 5:362).

"There has been a great difficulty in getting anything into the heads of this generation. It has been like splitting hemlock knots with a corn-dodger [a piece of corn bread] for a wedge, and a pumpkin for a beetle [a wooden mallet]. Even the Saints are slow to understand. I have tried for a number of years to get the minds of the Saints prepared to receive the things of God; but we frequently see some of them, after suffering all they have for the work of God, will fly to pieces like glass as soon as anything comes that is contrary to their traditions: they cannot stand the fire at all. How many will be able to abide a celestial law, and go through and receive their exaltation, I am unable to say, as many are called, but few are chosen. (H.C., 6:184-85).

"I am not like other men. My mind is continually occupied with the business of the day, and I have to depend entirely upon the living God for everything I say on such occasions as these (a funeral) … "Had I inspiration, revelation, and lungs to communicate what my soul has contemplated in times past, there is not a soul in this congregation but would go to their homes and shut their mouths in everlasting silence on religion till they had learned something. Why be so certain that you comprehend the things of God, when all things with you are so uncertain? You are welcome to all the knowledge and intelligence I can impart to you." (H.C., 5:529-30).

"Some people say I am a fallen Prophet because I do not bring forth more of the word of the Lord. Why do I not do it? Are we able to receive it? No! not one in this room." (H.C., 4:478; from a discourse given by Joseph Smith on Dec. 19, 1841, in Nauvoo, Illinois; reported by Wilford Woodruff).

"I will from time to time reveal to you the subjects that are revealed by the Holy Ghost to me. All the lies that are now hatched up against me are of the devil, and the influence of the devil and his servants will be used against the kingdom of God. The servants of God teach nothing but principles of eternal life, by their works ye shall know them. A good man will speak good things and holy principles, and an evil man evil things. I feel, in the name of the Lord, to rebuke all such bad principles, liars, etc., and I warn all of you to look out whom you are going after. I exhort you to give heed to all the virtue and the teachings which I have given you … "I enjoin for your consideration – add to your faith virtue, love, etc. I say, in the name of the Lord, if these things are in you, you shall be fruitful. I testify that no man has power to reveal it but myself—things in heaven, in earth and hell … I commend you all to God, that you may inherit all things; and may God add His blessing." (H.C., 6:366-67; from a discourse given by Joseph Smith on May 12, 1844, in Nauvoo, Illinois; reported by Thomas Bullock).

"I was this morning introduced to a man from the east. After hearing my name, he remarked that I was nothing but a man, indicating by this expression, that he had supposed that a person to whom the Lord should see fit to reveal His will, must be something more than a man. He seemed to have forgotten the saying that fell from the lips of St. James, that (Elijah) was a man subject to like passions as we are, yet he had such power with God, that He, in answer to his prayers, shut the heavens that they gave no rain for the space of three years and six months; and again, in answer to his prayer, the heavens gave forth rain, and the earth gave forth fruit. Indeed, such is the darkness and ignorance of this generation, that they look upon it as incredible that a man should have any [dealings] with his Maker." (H.C., 2:302; from a Joseph Smith journal entry, November 6, 1835, Kirtland, Ohio).

"When did I ever teach anything wrong from this stand? When was I ever confounded? I want to triumph in Israel before I depart hence and am no more seen. I never told you I was perfect; but there is no error in the revelations which I have taught. Must I, then, be thrown away as a thing of naught?" (H.C., 6:366; from a discourse given by Joseph Smith on May 12, 1844, in Nauvoo, Illinois; reported by Thomas Bullock).

"Although I do wrong, I do not the wrongs that I am charged with doing: the wrong that I do is through the frailty of human nature, like other men. No man lives without fault. Do you think that even Jesus, if He were here, would be without fault in your eyes? His enemies said all manner of evil against Him—they all watched for iniquity in Him."

(H.C., 5:140; from a discourse given by Joseph Smith on August 31, 1842, in Nauvoo, Illinois; reported by Eliza R. Snow).

"I ... went over to the store (in Nauvoo), where a number of brethren and sisters were assembled, who had arrived this morning from the neighborhood of New York ... I told them I was but a man, and they must not expect me to be perfect; if they expected perfection from me, I should expect it from them; but if they would bear with my infirmities and the infirmities of the brethren, I would likewise bear with their infirmities." (H.C., 5:181; from a Joseph Smith journal entry, October 29, 1842, Nauvoo, Illinois).

"I speak boldly and faithfully and with authority ... I know what I say; I understand my mission and business. God Almighty is my shield; and what can man do if God is my friend? I shall not be sacrificed until my time comes; then I shall be offered freely. ... I thank God for preserving me from my enemies; I have no enemies but for the truth's sake. I have no desire but to do all men good. I feel to pray for all men." (H.C., 5:257, 259; from a discourse given by Joseph Smith on January 22, 1843, in Nauvoo, Illinois; reported by Wilford Woodruff).

"If I had not actually got into this work and been called of God, I would back out. But I cannot back out: I have no doubt of the truth." (H.C., 5:336; from a discourse given by Joseph Smith on April 6, 1843, in Nauvoo, Illinois; reported by Willard Richards).

"I am a rough stone. The sound of the hammer and chisel was never heard on me until the Lord took me in hand. I desire the learning and wisdom of heaven alone." (H.C., 5:423; from a discourse given by Joseph Smith on June 11, 1843, in Nauvoo, Illinois; reported by Wilford Woodruff and Willard Richards).

"The burdens which roll upon me are very great. My persecutors allow me no rest, and I find that in the midst of business and care the spirit is willing, but the flesh is weak. Although I was called of my Heavenly Father to lay the foundation of this great work and kingdom in this dispensation, and testify of His revealed will to scattered Israel, I am subject to like passions as other men, like the prophets of olden times ... I see no faults in the church, and therefore let me be resurrected with the Saints, whether I ascend to heaven or descend to hell, or go to any other place. And if we go to hell, we will turn the devils out of doors and make a heaven of it. Where this people are, there is good society." (H.C., 5:516-17; from a discourse given by Joseph Smith on July 23, 1843, in Nauvoo, Illinois; reported by Willard Richards).

"The Saints need not think because I am familiar with them and am playful and cheerful, that I am ignorant of what is going on. Iniquity of any kind cannot be sustained in the church, and it will not fare well where I am; for I am determined while I do lead the church, to lead it right." (H.C., 5:411; from instructions given by Joseph Smith on May 27, 1843, in Nauvoo, Illinois; reported by Wilford Woodruff).

"If I am so fortunate as to be the man to comprehend God, and explain or convey the principles to your hearts, so that the Spirit seals them upon you, then let every man and woman henceforth sit in silence, put their hands on their mouths, and never lift their hands or voices, or say anything against the man of God or the servants of God again. ... If I am bringing you to a knowledge of Him, all persecutions against me ought to cease. You will then know that I am His servant; for I speak as one having authority ... I can taste the principles of eternal life, and so can you. They are given to me by the revelations of Jesus Christ; and I know that when I tell you these words of eternal life as they are given to me, you taste them, and I know that you believe them. You say honey is sweet, and so do I. I can also taste the spirit of eternal life. I know that it is good; and when I tell you of these things which were given me by inspiration of the Holy Spirit, you are bound to receive them as sweet, and rejoice more and more ... I have intended my remarks for all, both rich and poor, bond and free, great and small. I have no enmity against any man. I love you all; but I hate some of your deeds. I am your best friend, and if persons miss their mark it is their own fault. If I reprove a man, and he hates me, he is a fool; for I love all men, especially these my brethren and sisters ... You don't know me; you never knew my heart. No man knows my history. I cannot tell it: I shall never undertake it. I don't blame any one for not believing my history. If I had not experienced what I have, I would not have believed it myself. I never did harm any man since I was born in the world. My voice is always for peace. I cannot lie down until all my work is finished. I never think any evil, nor do anything to the harm of my fellow-man. When I am called by the trump of the archangel and weighed in the balance, you will all know me then. I add no more. God bless you all." (H.C., 6:304-5, 312, 317; from a discourse given by Joseph Smith on Apr. 7, 1844, in Nauvoo, Illinois; reported by Wilford Woodruff, Willard Richards, Thomas Bullock, and William Clayton).

Joseph Smith History

"The history of the world is
but the biography of great men."
(Thomas Carlyle).

"Unless a man shall endure to the end,
in following the example of the Son of the
living God, he cannot be saved … and then are ye
in this strait and narrow path which leads to eternal
life'; yea ye have entered in by the gate; ye have done
according to the commandments of the Father and the Son;
and ye have received the Holy Ghost, which witnesses of the
Father and the Son, unto the fulfilling of the promise
which he hath made, that if ye entered in by the way
ye should receive … and by the power of the Holy
Ghost ye may know the truth of all things."
(2 Nephi 31:16 & 18, & Moroni 10:5).

It is important to study the life of Joseph Smith since the three pillars of testimony are that the Lord Jesus Christ visited him in the Sacred Grove, that he subsequently translated The Book of Mormon by the gift and power of God, and that he then fulfilled his divine commission relating to the restoration of the church in the Last Days.

In the Nineteenth Century, the Prophet Joseph Smith was a wonderful guide to those seeking pure and undefiled religion, and even today he is still leading those who lack wisdom to the fountain of all truth. (See James 1:27). That an apostasy within Christianity had taken place was evident to Joseph, who wrote of his early experiences in Palmyra, New York: "There was in the place where we lived an unusual excitement on the subject of religion. It commenced with the Methodists, but soon became general among all the sects in that region of country. Indeed, the whole district of country seemed affected by it, and great multitudes united themselves to the different religious parties, which created no small stir and division amongst the people, some crying, 'Lo, here!' and others, 'Lo, there!' Some were contending for the Methodist faith, some for the Presbyterian, and some for the Baptist. All their good feelings one for another, if they ever had any, were entirely lost in a strife of words and a contest about opinions." (J.S.H. 1:5-6). Certainly, this is still happening in the world, where we see daily evidence of "a war of words and tumult of opinions." (J.S.H. 1:10).

Joseph's only desire at that time was to know "who was right and who was wrong." (J.S.H. 1:8). He searched the scriptures and discovered that the best approach would be to follow the admonition of James. Inherent in that passage was the principle that the key leading to salvation comes from God by revelation. As Paul said of his understanding of the saving principles of the gospel: "For I neither received it of man, neither was I taught it, but by the revelation of

Jesus Christ." (Galatians 1:12). The instruction that Joseph received before his theophany, as he read his Holy Bible, was: "If any of you lack wisdom, let him ask of God, that giveth to all men liberally, and upbraideth not; and it shall be given him." (James 1:5).

"Never did any passage of scripture come with more power to the heart of man that this did at this time to mine," he later reflected. "It seemed to enter with great force into every feeling of my heart. I reflected on it again and again, knowing that if any person needed wisdom from God, I did; for how to act I did not know, and unless I could get more wisdom than I then had, I would never know." (J.S.H. 1:12).

What Joseph next described was completely foreign to everyday experience. "I saw a pillar of light exactly over my head," he later testified, "above the brightness of the sun, which descended gradually until it fell upon me. When the light rested upon me I saw two personages, whose brightness and glory defy all description, standing above me in the air." (J.S.H. 1:16-17). A distinct pillar of light, with defined borders, traveled downward, not at 300,000 kph, but "gradually." Within it, clothed in immortal burnings, were two distinct individuals in anthropomorphic form.

It is remarkable that, under the circumstances, Joseph was able to gather his wits about him and remember why he had prayed to God in the first place. In any event, he wrote: "No sooner, therefore, did I get possession of myself, so as to be able to speak, than I asked the Personages who stood above me in the light, which of all the sects was right?" (J.S.T. 1:18). Conspicuously absent was any hint of an inquiry that was oriented toward the notion that a new church might be in order. Instead, in his innocence and with child-like faith, the young boy found his tongue and humbly asked one of the pivotal questions of all time: "Which church is right? So too, had Newton asked: "Why does an apple fall from the tree," and Einstein had mused, "What would the world look like from a moving streetcar or If one were riding on a beam of light?" Sometimes questions that are stated simply and without embellishment have profound consequences, while in the hushed halls of heaven angels wait in excited anticipation as the fate of mankind hangs in the balance.

"I was answered that I must join none of them, for they were all wrong;" Joseph related, "and the Personage who addressed me said that all their creeds were an abomination in his sight; that those professors were all corrupt; that 'they draw near to me with their lips, but their hearts are far from me, they teach for doctrines the commandments of men, having a form of godliness, but they deny the power thereof.' And many other things did he say unto me, which I cannot write at this time." (J.S.H. 1:19-20).

Of these experiences, Joseph F. Smith declared: "The greatest event that has ever occurred in the world since the resurrection of the Son of God from the tomb and his ascension on high, was the coming of the Father and of the Son to that boy Joseph Smith, to prepare the way for the laying of the foundation of his kingdom. Having accepted that truth, I find it easy to accept every other truth that he enunciated and declared during his mission of fourteen years in the world." ("Gospel Doctrine," p. 495-496). Joseph Smith, said Truman Madsen, was "a prism of the Lord Jesus Christ." ("Defender of the Faith: The B. H. Roberts Story," p. 93). Through him, secular Christianity's gossamer web of entangling tenets was swept aside, while every relevant principle of eternal importance was once again clearly defined, plainly articulated, and seamlessly stitched into the fabric of the restored gospel.

B.H. Roberts was once asked a question about the life and teachings of Joseph Smith. "As he answered, the elders saw their beginning curiosity expanded to vast proportions, and they nodded in grateful admiration" as he unfolded to them his witness of the prophet. All of a sudden Brother Roberts looked up, "raised his hands, and said, 'Brother Joseph, I have fought for you. I have defended you. I have loved you.'" (Truman Madsen, "Defender of The Faith").

The prophet could have this kind of impact on people. One of his greatest contributions "was his knowledge of what is to come after death. He did much to clarify our understanding of heaven and to make it seem worth working for." (Sunday School Manual: "My Religion & Me"). He "holds the keys of this last dispensation, and no man or woman in this dispensation will ever enter into the I of God without the consent of Joseph Smith." (Brigham Young, C.R., 9/10/1859)

His presence dominates our history. From his birth to his martyr's death at the age of thirty-eight, we feel his power and influence. "He emerges the prophet, seer, organizer, lawgiver, promoter, architect, and teacher. His religious concept includes fashioning the kingdom of God upon the earth, changing the lives of men, and preparing everyone who will listen for Christ's advent." (Ivan Barrett, "Joseph Smith & The Restoration").

Nevertheless, the reaction of the ministers of the day to news of his First Vision was predictable. Because he dared to disrupt the status quo, defy conventional wisdom, because he was politically incorrect, and an iconoclast, and because he continued to affirm that (he) had seen a vision, he "suffered severe persecution at the hands of all classes of men, both religious and irreligious." (J.S.H. 1:27). It was generally supposed that he was deluded. (J.S.H. 1:22). When great ideas are presented to the world, in general they are at first ridiculed, then are met with violent opposition, and finally are accepted as self-evident. Perhaps we will yet see the day when the need for a Restoration is widely recognized as patently obvious.

But during the three and a half years following the First Vision, by his own admission, Joseph was on his own. He "was left to all kinds of temptations; and, mingling with all kinds of society, (he) frequently fell into many foolish errors, and displayed the weakness of youth, and the foibles of human nature." He was "guilty of levity, and sometimes associated with jovial company." (J.S.H. 1:28). In fact, he acted much like the teenagers with whom we are all familiar.

Finally, on the evening of September 21, 1823, an event transpired that was the beginning of the ministry of angels in this dispensation. Joseph later wrote that while in the attitude of prayer: "I discovered a light appearing in my room, which continued to increase until the room was lighter than at noonday, when immediately a personage appeared at my bedside, standing in the air, for his feet did not touch the floor." (J.S.H. 1:30).

This was Moroni, "a messenger sent from the presence of God." (J.S.H. 1:33). He told Joseph about "a book deposited, written upon gold plates, giving an account of the former inhabitants of this continent, and the source from whence they sprang. He also said that the fulness of the everlasting gospel was contained in it, as delivered by the Savior to the ancient inhabitants." (V. 34). He recited scripture, and "offered many explanations which cannot be mentioned here." (V. 41). During the next four years, Joseph "received instructions and intelligence from him at each of (their) interviews." (V. 54). We can only imagine how wondrous his learning experiences must have been.

On September 22, 1827, "having gone as usual at the end of another year to the place where they were deposited, the same heavenly messenger" delivered the plates to Joseph with a solemn charge to care for them with the utmost responsibility. (V. 59). At the same time, he was also given the Urim and Thummim and the breastplate that he would physically need in order to commence the inspired translation of the records.

Between December 1827 and February 1828, Joseph was able to copy a considerable number of the characters from the plates, but because of persecution, he was not really able to commence much of a translation. (V. 61-62). Not until April 7, 1829, after the arrival of Oliver Cowdery at the Smith home, did Joseph begin in earnest the translation of The Book of Mormon from the plates he had received from Moroni. (V. 66-67).

The Book of Mormon enlarges our
perspective, and it's grand themes encourage
us to consider light and its contrary of darkness.
In our everyday lives, we are familiar with both light
and its opposite. We take for granted that light can easily
dispel darkness, and we unconsciously witness the miracle
many times a day. But we rarely, if ever, stop to wonder why
darkness cannot dispel light. Why does it work in only one
direction, and not the other way around? Like the arrow of
time, light marches forward to dispel the darkness and
fill the immensity of space. (See D&C 88:44-47).
From every perspective, we can see the shadows
only if we turn our backs to the light.

Jumping Out of Our Skin

"The Spirit cried with a loud voice, saying: Hosanna to the Lord, the most high God; for he is God over all the earth, yea, even above all. And blessed art thou, Nephi, because thou believest in the Son of the most high God; wherefore, thou shalt behold the things which thou hast desired. "And it came to pass that the Spirit said unto me: Look! And I looked and beheld a tree; and it was like unto the tree which my father had seen; and the beauty thereof was far beyond, yea, exceeding of all beauty; and the whiteness thereof did exceed the whiteness of the driven snow."
(1 Nephi 11:6 & 8).

"Though your sins be as scarlet, they shall be as white as snow; though they be red like crimson, they shall be as wool." (Isaiah 1:8)

We read in The Book of Mormon: "And it came to pass that Jesus blessed them as they did pray unto him; and His countenance did smile upon them, and the light of his countenance did shine upon them." (3 Nephi 19:25).

Normally, our red, yellow, brown, black, or white skin fits very well, like a well-tailored Brooks Brothers or Ann Taylor suit. It should, because it has been reported that we annually spend over $55 billion to pamper it with creams, lotions, balms, emollients, astringents, clarifiers, modifiers, oils, ointments, liniments, balsams, salves, gels, and lubricants. Why do we bother? It may be because our skin reflects who we are; ideally, it wraps us up in neat and tidy packages; it is the one organ we have that can make or break a first impression.

We all know that beauty is only skin deep, and that some people get under our skin, or make our skin crawl. We all have escaped calamity by the skin of our teeth, and some of us have breathed deep sighs of relief when we have, perhaps selfishly, saved our own skin. At other times, in spite of our best efforts, we have gotten skinned. We sometimes need to develop a thick skin, because some of us have a thin skin. We just need to learn to be comfortable in our own skin. At the end of the day, we cannot allow others get under our skin.

At times, we have been so frightened that we have almost jumped out of our skin, while at other times, we have become so accustomed to trauma that it is no skin off our nose. However, if we are caught in a downpour, we may get soaked to the skin, or if we fail to maintain adequate nutrition, we may waste away until we are nothing more than skin and bones. Faced with challenges, we may find more than one way to skin a cat.

Our skin is the largest of our organ systems, covering an area of around 22 square feet (2.04 square meters). About 1,000 species of bacteria (around 1 trillion in all) call our skin home. Skin comes in pre-determined colors, although with applications of bleaching crème (e.g. "Porcelana") or spray-tan, some lighter or darker shade adjustments can be made. Our skin is individually crafted for a custom fit, and it uniquely and precisely defines and shapes our physical form. It does an excellent job of covering nearly 100% of our exteriors, no matter that we may be short, tall, fat, or thin, newborn or elderly. It doesn't do quite as well with the aged, however, because it can get very wrinkly, but so can the skin of babies, if they are left in bath water for too long, or if they are really well-fed.

Skin provides tidy cohesiveness, and can be quite esthetic, even eliciting sexual desire. It delicately helps us to maintain our balance and integrity, as well as our temperature. But it can annoyingly expand over time in response to changing circumstances, especially if we habitually overindulge at the dinner table. It is quite elastic, almost instantly transforming its shape by either stretching or contracting. It folds and creases over time, like a roadmap, to reveal our disposition, and it can broadcast to others that we have been consistently happy or sad, or have habitually smiled or frowned. It can be hard and cracked and worn by exposure to weather, or it can feel soft and supple and as smooth as a baby's bottom. It can blister with heat, and be either dry or clammy, or warm or cold to the touch.

The skin covering our fingertips has 2,500 nerve receptors per square inch, which can be a real bonus for safecrackers. It callouses with work, and can develop goose bumps when the weather is nasty or when we are frightened. It turns white with shock, and gets clammy during panic attacks (or when we are going through menopause). It streaks with sweat during exercise, during acts of passion, and when we are nervous. It flushes with embarrassment, and puckers up when we are kissing. It resists tearing, but can uncomfortably blister when exposed to thermal or ultraviolet radiation. It bruises with injury, and leaks blood when it is punctured. It grows hair, which sometimes sprouts in awkward places. It gets dirty easily, but can be cleaned up nicely with the application of warm soapy water. It completely replaces itself every four weeks (about 27 trillion cells, in all). It is a biological clock that unerringly mirrors the inexorable passage of time, in spite of all of our efforts to slow down the process or turn the tide. In general, our skin provides a very accurate indication of how we have interacted with the outside world. Without its organizational ability, we would be hard to recognize; we would be like octopuses on roller skates.

Skin serves our needs for the moment, suits our lifestyle, and provides us with a much neater and tidier appearance than some of the alternatives that come to mind. Think: jellyfish, slugs, seaweed, mucous membranes, tripe, and the movie "Alien." But when all is said and done, as comfortable as we may be in our own skin, it is not our natural element. It is only a fleeting shadow and corruptible approximation of what was provided at the creation. God's declaration: "Let us make man in our image, after our likeness," defines what the covering of our proper and perfect frame should look like under ideal circumstances. (Genesis 1:26). That skin is our ideal, and the economy of the gospel has provided a perfect formula, that we might regain and retain the glow of our former home. It is called "repentance."

In a Garden setting, the skin of Adam and Eve must have shone with the innocence and purity of their former home. We know that the countenances of angels who come from the presence of God to minister among men are as lightning. (See Matthew 28:3, D&C 20:6, & J.S.H. 1:32). When the Savior visited the Kirtland Temple, those who saw Him testified that "His countenance shone above the brightness of the sun." (D&C 110:3). In his dedicatory prayer in that holy house, Joseph Smith implored our Father in Heaven: "Help us by the power of thy Spirit, that we may mingle our voices with those bright, shining seraphs around thy throne, with acclamations of praise, singing Hosanna to God and the Lamb!" (D&C 109:79).

The celestial skin of our first parents was the holy representation of a backstage pass that granted them access to their Father's listening ear. He must have visited the Garden many times, instructing and preparing Adam and Eve for mortality. They were certainly familiar with His form and comfortable with His companionship, as He took them into "His bosom" where they shared many innocent intimacies. (Isaiah 40:11).

Heavenly Father had created the Garden as a learning laboratory with limitations. Adam and Eve were quite comfortable in their celestial skin, right up to the moment when He asked them: "Who told thee that thou wast naked?" (Genesis 3:11). That innocent inquiry redefined their existence and put a sharp point to the purpose of life. Beforehand, they'd had no reason to believe that appearances could be deceiving, but now they had to deal with the consequences of the destroyer's hypocrisy, who had appeared to them in the skin of a serpent. The introduction of the concept of opposition into their peaceful environment negated their naivety, pummeled their purity, and violated their virtue. The scriptures attest to the telestial turmoil that resulted from the disruption of their idyllic existence. But they also describe a transformation from a morally static environment to one filled with the promise of progression through the exercise of free will. Had He not allowed the introduction of opposition into the only world Adam and Eve had ever known, God would have ceased to be God. (See 2 Nephi 2:13). Even as their skin lost a bit of its intrinsic luster, Adam and Eve kept their faces oriented toward heaven, and their cheeks must have glowed in hopeful anticipation of the further light and knowledge their Father had promised to give them.

It was not long after their expulsion from Eden, that nearly every one of their descendants began to walk "in his own way, and after the image of his own god, whose image (was) in the likeness of the world." (D&C 1:16). Agitators for social change probed the limits of their newfound independence, in contrast to their parents' lifestyle of moderation. The restraint that had been taught in the tranquility of the Garden was now being put to the test in the lone and dreary world.

Among the children of men, however, one thing became almost immediately apparent. The image and likeness of God that had been so familiar in the Garden became almost unrecognizable in the urban jungles east of Eden, as nudity became the norm and the string bikini the logo of lasciviousness. In the parlors where the sons of Adam and the daughters of Eve festooned their bodies with tattoos and piercings, and in the absence of repentance, their skin became only a caricature of its former purity.

To put a positive spin on it, though, mortals became the perfect runway models, warts and all, to showcase opposition. We have all witnessed those who have vacationed in Idumea to celebrate the festival of free will and the carnival of carefree living. But we also remember Paul, who shed his telestial trappings in order to experience a greater comprehension of eternity. He must have felt inadequate trying to describe what had happened to him. He simply wrote: "Whether in the body, or out of the body, I cannot tell." (2 Corinthians 12:3). He knew that he had somehow jumped right back into his celestial skin, and sensed that he had been clothed with a finer substance in a spiritual aether that allowed him to gently brush against the veil in order to catch a glimpse of eternity. His later ministry confirms that his repentance for his former sins was comprehensive.

But in the lone and dreary world of unrepentant Babylon, Satan exults in his role as the de-facto god of this earth. (See 2 Corinthians 4:4). In the Garden, He actually believed that he had thwarted the Plan by metaphorically bringing to the attention of Adam and Eve their nakedness. More literally, his nefarious counterfeit was designed to expose their vulnerability by penetrating their celestial skin and contaminating it with the worldly elements of transgression. Satan mistakenly thought that by then calling attention to their nakedness, their embarrassment at having yielded to temptation would require them to forsake forever the celestial skin that God had provided for them. The tempter fancied himself a telestial tailor, who could trick Adam and Eve into thinking that they could hide their nakedness from God. "And the eyes of them both were opened, and they knew that they had been naked. And they sewed fig leaves together and made themselves aprons." (Moses 4:13).

Satan believed that his enticements would irreparably destroy the celestial skin, the spiritual protection of Adam and Eve, and that in the ensuing confusion over a wardrobe change, he could install himself as a puppet ruler, even the god of this world. (See 2 Corinthians 4:4). What he had not counted on, however, was the fact that it was not their celestial skin, but their divine nature, that had been Adam and Eve's protection. He also grossly misjudged the ability of the Savior to redeem all mankind through the Atonement. All that was necessary to restore their purity was the further light and knowledge from God that they had been promised. Satan never saw that one coming.

Satan also believed that by partaking of the forbidden fruit, the natural defense systems of Adam and Eve had been irreparably weakened. But the Lord, who sees the end from the beginning, countered by promising them further light and knowledge even after their expulsion from Eden. "I will give unto you a pattern in all (these) things," He later affirmed, "that ye may not be deceived." (D&C 52:14). That pattern of repentance provided a means for the redemption of not only Adam and Eve, but also of their posterity, all the way down to the present day.

Jesus Christ alluded to the integumentary system that defines heavenly forms and features, and that is common to all of us, with this reassurance: "He that hath seen me hath seen the Father." (John 14:9). The countenance of the Gods is marked by refreshing candor and uncomplicated honesty, and reflects Their divine attributes and Their noble character. Its nature and expression is free of whimsy, confusion, and hypocrisy. The visage of God is "like a jasper stone, clear as crystal." (Revelation 21:11). The Savior's countenance is in the express image of His Father, and what we see is what we get, plain and simple. (See Genesis 1:26). Figuratively and literally, we receive Him at face value. Our undeviating Exemplar is unlike those chameleon-like figures who sell their birthright for a mess of pottage, compromise their standards for stardom, and dilute their discipleship with the values of vulgarity.

Joseph F. Smith, in his Vision of the Redemption of the Dead, described "Abel … and his brother Seth, one of the mighty ones, who was in the express image of his father, Adam." (D&C 138:40). Evidently, patriarchal proclivities extended from father to son. President Smith continued: "From among the righteous, he organized his forces and appointed messengers, clothed with power and authority, and commissioned them to go forth and carry the light of the gospel. (D&C 138:30). When we return to our heavenly home, we may be clothed in tangible trappings, but we will also be arrayed with the power and authority of metaphysical vestments that nurture intrinsic light.

Case in point – the Doctrine & Covenants records: "God ministered unto" Joseph Smith "by an holy angel, whose countenance was as lightning, and whose garments were pure and white above all other whiteness." (D&C 20:6). "Not only was the angel's "robe exceedingly white, but his whole person was glorious beyond description, and his countenance truly like lightning. The room was exceedingly light, but not so very bright as immediately around his person." (J.S.H. 1:32).

God's pattern provides many opportunities during mortality for repentance, that we might put our fingers to the pulse and test the promises of His Plan's guiding principles. He is the quintessential Travel Agent whose side trips and excursions have been arranged to expand our appreciation of life's real purpose, which is to learn from our experiences while interacting with the wonders of the world. In order to accomplish this, we must ultimately take over the responsibility for our own travel plans by organizing ourselves, as we "prepare every needful thing; and establish a house, even a house of prayer, a house of fasting, a house of faith, a house of learning, a house of glory, a house of order, (and) a house of God." (D&C 88:119). Once again, the elegant simplicity of The Plan trumps the deception and confusion of its convoluted and counterfeit alternatives.

The pattern of the Plan works to our benefit when we pay attention to its priorities. Proper prior parental planning on God's part prevents poor priesthood performance on ours. To that end, in our pre-earth existence, a Council was held to pre-emptively obtain our informed consent to endorse the principles of The Plan prior to our coming to earth. During that discussion, God explained His vision for our continuing progression, entertained alternative proposals, and opened up the floor to a frank discussion of the risks we would take by participating in His ordained program. He answered questions, and even anticipated the actions of those who would later foster rebellion. That the meeting came to a successful conclusion is implied by the scripture that asks: "Where wast thou when I laid the foundations of the earth? Declare, if thou hast understanding. When the morning stars sang together, and all the sons of God shouted for joy." (Job 38:4 & 7).

Even then, our Elder Brother, "the good shepherd," anticipated and addressed our concerns. (John 10:11). His nurturing influence during our pre-mortal sojourn helped to settle our minds regarding the uncertainties that lay ahead, and convinced us that He is "not the author of confusion, but of peace." (1 Corinthians 14:33). That peace hinged on His role as our Redeemer, and upon our eagerness to repent.

What happened to us later was akin to "going down a rabbit hole." (See "Alice's Adventures in Wonderland," Chapter 1, by Lewis Carroll). Our travel from our first estate through the birth canal into the breathtaking expanse of the wide, wide world erased the memory of our former life, but new vistas soon opened up to fill in the void. To reinforce our understanding of the principles we had aforetime internalized, religious recognition, a re-cognition, a re-knowing, or an intuitive remembrance of our former glory, came into play. Carefully articulated Articles of Faith had been formulated that would now "ring a bell" and stir our memories. To describe the process, the expression "Deja-vu" was coined.

These ingenious devices were provided to show us how to jump right back into the spiritual skin that had defined our familiar heavenly home from the beginning. For those who would be "born again," that shield would be akin to the barrier protection afforded to health care providers, to safeguard them from the relentless assault of pathogens during critical patient care. With equivalent "barrier protection" shielding our divine center, the likelihood of a return to the full form and stature of our spirit could be maximized.

The Plan has been tested in the crucible of countless classrooms across the cosmos. It is "fair as the moon, clear as the sun, and terrible as an army with banners." (D&C 109:73). Its worth defies argument. Its dedication to proven principles is incontrovertible. Its learning opportunities minimize the risk of succumbing to the wiles of a counterfeit and corruptible curriculum that is only a caricature of canon.

The original "Wile E. Coyote" is the devil, who "is the author of all sin," and the architect of the aforementioned cowardly curriculum. (Helaman 6:30). Even as he gloated in the "nakedness" of Adam and Eve in the Garden, he "knew not the mind of God." (Moses 4:6). The high-fives Satan and his henchmen must have exchanged turned out to be a bit premature. God parlayed his trickery right into the execution of The Plan. "Wo unto them that are deceivers and hypocrites," warned the Savior, for their deceptions will come to naught. (D&C 50:6).

Anciently, a "hypocrite" was the mask worn by the actors of classical Greece in the plays written by Aeschylus, Euripedes, Aristophanes, and others. The term has come to derisively characterize those who make false appearances with the intent to deceive. It describes those who pretend to be something they are not. If we are not careful, hypocrites can get under our skin; they can worm their way right into our hearts, minds, and souls after our barrier protection has been compromised. Unless we are quick to repent, our celestial features can then be distorted into the caricature of a hypocrite's mask.

In the novel "The Picture of Dorian Grey," by Oscar Wilde, a particularly handsome young man's enchanting portrait degenerates over time in response to his moral depravity and self-indulgence, while at the same time his face retains its alabaster innocence. He embraces the philosophy that the only way to eliminate a temptation is to yield to it. After many years of decadence have taken a mighty toll on his character, he loses his mind, grabs a knife, and attacks the picture that with such stark realism and accuracy has reflected his mounting debauchery. The servants of the house awaken to a cry from the locked room of the anguished debaucherer, and break down the door. Before them lies the body of an unrecognizable old man, stabbed in the heart, his face withered and decrepit. Only by the ring on his finger can they identify the disfigured corpse as their master. (The Ring of Gyges comes to mind. See below). Beside the emaciated figure is the picture of Dorian Gray that has reverted to its original loveliness.

In Book 2 of Plato's "The Republic," Glaucon and Adeimantus present the myth of the Ring of Gyges, by means of which Gyges is able to make himself invisible. They then ask Socrates: "If one came into possession of such a ring, why should he act justly?" Socrates replies that although no one could see their body, the soul would be horribly disfigured by the evils that had been committed behind the illusory shield of invisibility.

Thankfully, God has turned the tables on Satan by providing the principle of repentance, that we might jump out of our skin whenever it has become corrupted and contaminated by sin. We need not fear that our spiritual portraits will lose their luster. We need not be like that unfortunate soul who took the Excess Express, and who, when he got to heaven, "saw something that filled him with fright, for his spiritual body was one sorry sight! No more than a skeleton, covered with corruptible skin. He got up to heaven, but didn't get in!" (Anonymous).

God's Plan of Repentance and Mercy gives our bumpy ride through mortality a profoundly positive twist, energizing it with vitality and the ability to re-write its last chapters, and even to alter eternity. We cannot go back and start a new beginning, but we can start today and make a new ending. We can re-boot the system, get rid of bad code, and restore damaged files. We can create enough RAM and additional disk space to write a bedtime story in which we live happily ever after. Hans Christian Anderson said it best: "Our lives are fairy tales written by the finger of God."

He has made it possible for us to be dermatologically transformed, to physically manipulate the makeup of our bodies, to figuratively influence our integumentary systems, and to defeat spiritual death without the need for expensive creams, lotions, balms, emollients, astringents, clarifiers, modifiers, oils, ointments, liniments, balsams, salves, gels, and lubricants. He has provided a prequel to the resurrection, by allowing us to have the experience of jumping out of our corruptible skin. This may be a collective experience, but it is always intensely personal. It was our Exemplar, after all, Who stood beside an empty tomb, and cautioned Mary: "Touch me not; for I am not yet ascended to my Father." (John 20:17). She then went and told the other disciples that she had witnessed a miracle. (John 20:18).

When we present ourselves before God, we too will be uncompromised by corruption. (See Alma 5:14). As the people of Zarahemla exclaimed, so must we: "The Spirit of the Lord Omnipotent … has wrought a mighty change in us, or in our hearts, that we have no more disposition to do evil, but to do good continually." (Mosiah 5:3). Under those circumstances, the last thing we would want to do would be to compromise our spiritual solidarity by failing to throw ourselves on the mercy seat, grasping the horns of sanctuary that are provided by The Great and Eternal Plan of Deliverance from Death (2 Nephi 11:5), or by reverting to a corruptible lifestyle.

The Plan has the inherent power to accomplish the transformation of 27 trillion skin cells, not in four weeks' time, but only after being wrapped in the "clean linen cloth" of the gospel. (Matthew 27:59). If the clothes in which we have gone out to play on terra firma have been soiled by sin, we can forsake our filthiness in favor of clean heavenly vestments. Unlike the clothing made for the Emperor in the tale by Hans Christian Anderson, our celestial garments are tangible; they are real. We need not fear the cries of children in the streets: "But they aren't wearing anything at all!" ("The Emperor's New Clothes").

The scriptures prepare our minds with additional contrasting examples. When Belshazzar of old saw the prophetic writing upon the wall, his "countenance was changed, and his thoughts troubled him, so that the joints of his loins were loosed, and his knees smote one against another." (Daniel 5:6). A fundamental transmutation with intensely personal negative consequences was in the works. Soon thereafter, he was "weighed in the balances, and found wanting." (Daniel 5:27). The celestial skin provided by God to Belshazzar had mutated through apostasy, and without repentance, the resultant 20 pounds or so of dermal and epidermal cells (comprising not only the largest, but also the heaviest organ system in the human body) no longer afforded him protection from the elements of his cankered and cancerous soul.

Things turned out better for leprous Naaman, the captain of the hosts of the king of Syria, who was told by the messenger of Elisha: "Go and wash in Jordan seven times, and thy flesh shall come again to thee, and thou shalt be clean. Then went he down, and dipped himself seven times in Jordan, according to the saying of the man of God: and his flesh came again like unto the flesh of a little child, and he was clean. (2 Kings 5:10 & 14).

The skin of other lepers benefitted from the application of celestial salve, as well. The scriptures record that as Jesus "entered into a certain village, there met him ten men that were lepers, which stood afar off: And they lifted up their voices, and said, Jesus, Master, have mercy on us. And when he saw them, he said unto them, Go shew yourselves unto the priests. And it came to pass, that, as they went, they were cleansed." (Luke 17:12 & 14). But let us not forget that, while Jesus has power to Atone for our sins, in every instance following our repentance, we hear Him say: "Neither do I condemn thee. Go, and sin no more." (John 8:11).

Joseph Smith recorded his impressions from many encounters with the spirit: "Often times it maketh my bones to quake while it maketh manifest." (D&C 85:6). Faithful members of the church have had similar feelings in preparation to receive "health in their navel and marrow to their bones," as they experience the miracle of forgiveness and jump out of telestial trappings into celestial robes. (D&C 89:18). More than a nutritional nuance or a medical marvel, this priesthood transformation insures a metaphorical manipulation through rhetorical analogy: "Though (their) sins be as scarlet, they shall be as white as snow; though they be red like crimson, they shall be as wool." (Isaiah 1:18).

King Benjamin suggested: "The natural man is an enemy to God, and always has been from the beginning," even from that time so long ago when Adam and Eve initially jumped out of carefully crafted and meticulously maintained celestial skin. (Mosiah 3:19). It is clear that each of us must, as Paul suggested, be fitted by the Master Tailor to receive a heavenly vestment, and become "a new creature" in Christ. (2 Corinthians 5:17). "Have ye spiritually been born of God?" Alma asked. "Have ye received his image in your countenances? (Alma 5:14).

When the Spirit has stretched and molded us, its expression will be manifested in an unblemished skin-tone. We will have "the look." Like it or not, by the time we are middle-aged, the record of the conduct of our lives will have been indelibly etched into the unalterable expressions of our countenances. If we have memorized the celestial melodies that move us to "sing the song of redeeming love," our countenances will shine with a radiance from the presence of the Lord that will rest upon us. (Mosiah 5:26, see D&C 138:24).

After his parents' expulsion from the Garden, "Cain was very wroth," and he found himself shedding his celestial skin. (We do not know for sure, but he may have been in those difficult teenage years). In any event, he was in a flat spin from which he could not recover. His "countenance fell." (Genesis 4:5). He could neither overcome his fallen nature nor endure the molting process we all must face when we make 'the leap.' But it is only at that moment that we are able to slough off the telestial trash of dead skin cells, (all 27 trillion of them), so that our "sleeping dust (may be) restored unto its perfect frame." (D&C 138:17). It is only then that "the sinews and the flesh upon them, the spirit and the body (will be) united, never again to be divided." (D&C 138:17). It is only then that "old things shall pass away," (D&C 29:24), "and there shall be a new heaven and a new earth." (Ether 13:9). Only then, will we shed the trappings of our former life, and "every limb and joint shall be restored to its body; yea, even a hair of the head shall not be lost; but all things shall be restored to their proper and perfect frame." (Alma 40:23).

In the meantime, God gives us repetitive opportunities to practice jumping out of our telestial skin, off of complacency plateaus, into the more comfortable and form-fitting celestial silhouette that enables us to leap tall buildings at a single bound. We must repent with measured consideration, testing its claim of protection from the scorching sun in the heat of the day. Sometimes, we must sometimes jump from the frying pan right into the fire. With practice, when we jump we will land on springboards to action that propel us upward, to balance confidently on pinnacles of perfection. We should always look before we leap, but leap we must. Sometimes, we are prompted, or are so intensely invested, so spiritually charged, or so inspired, that we only need to heed the admonition: "Who hath faith to leap shall leap." (D&C 42:51). We must repent, and we must do it now.

At a critical juncture in their trek through the far reaches of the galaxy, Captain Jean Luc Picard of the Star Ship Enterprise urged his crew: "Now, this will put us at risk. Quite frankly, we may not survive. But I want you to believe that I am doing this for a greater purpose, and that what is at stake here is more than any of you can possibly imagine. I know you have your doubts about me, about each other, about this ship. All I can say is that although we have only been together for a short time, I know that you are the finest crew in the fleet. And I would trust each of you with my life. So, I am asking you for a leap of faith, and to trust me." ("All Good Things" 5/23/1994).

If we happen to be startled by our corruptible reflection in the windows of a great and spacious building, we need to jump out of our skin without hesitation, remembering that "the Lord seeth not as man seeth; for man looketh on the outward appearance, but the Lord looketh on the heart." (1 Samuel 16:7). We need to jump without even thinking about it, emulating the Saints who have rejoiced in their resurrection. Of these, Joseph F. Smith observed: "Their countenances shone, and the radiance from the presence of the Lord rested upon them." (D&C 138:24). We need to jump so that our afterglow is so compelling that its lingering effects overshadow any latent images of our reflection in the windows of even the tallest telestial towers.

When Joseph Smith and Oliver Cowdery attended the dedication of the Kirtland Temple, they shed their telestial trappings to enjoy an unprecedented vision of the Savior. "His eyes were as a flame of fire," Joseph recorded, and "the hair of his head was white like the pure snow; his countenance shone above the brightness of the sun." (D&C 110:3). The Lord's appearance was untainted by familiar telestial trauma. He was "Alpha and Omega, the beginning and the ending, the Lord, who is, and who was, and who is to come, the Almighty." (J.S.T. Revelation 1:8). Joseph and Oliver were provided with a preview of the extreme makeover, punctuated by a spiritual change of wardrobe, that awaited them in the I.

Joseph's observations went beyond garments and compelled him to consider the spiritual center of resurrected beings. Of the Angel Moroni, he had recorded: "His hands were naked, and his arms also, a little above the wrist; so, also, were his feet naked, as were his legs, a little above the ankles. His head and neck were also bare. I could discover that he had no other clothing on but this robe, as it was open, so that I could see into his bosom. Not only was his robe exceedingly white, but (also) his whole person was glorious beyond description, and his countenance truly like lightning. The room was exceedingly light, but not so very bright as immediately around his person." (J.S.H. 1:31-32).

But what about those of us who are less sure of ourselves? What happens if we look in the mirror and see the face of a stranger staring back at us? What if our knees wobble at the prospect of a leap that requires an "identity transplant?" This has happened enough times in the scriptures that the "face" is referenced 684 times, "new" 206 times, "image" 166 times, "change" 104 times, and "countenance" 70 times. "Image of God" is mentioned a dozen or so times, and "visage" 4 times. The scriptures provide a lot of counsel regarding the purpose behind our packaging.

Since the first partial face transplant was performed on a woman in France in 2006, psychologists have been asking if such a procedure carries the risk of psychological impairment, or if it might, on the other hand, offer the possibility of enriching the narrative of one's life by giving identity a new look. The jury is still out on that question, but it begs another: What happens under ideal circumstances, when the Lord's witness protection program functions optimally, and Satan can no longer find us, because we have been "born again; yea, born of God," and changed from our "carnal and fallen state, to a state of righteousness, being redeemed of God, becoming his sons and daughters?" (Mosiah 27:25). What happens when we are no longer recognizable as our former selves, when all ties to our past lives have been severed? What positive changes occur when we really take advantage of the Atonement, and jump out of our skin, when "old things are passed away, (and) all things are become new?" (2 Corinthians 5:17).

The simplest answer to these questions might be found in the recorded experiences of those who have had a "heart transplant" when they accepted the gospel. Alma spoke of his own father's conversion: "According to his faith there was a mighty change wrought in his heart." (Alma 5:12). Paul may have been thinking along the same lines, when he described the new gospel-oriented identity that is found in the "fleshy tables of the heart." (2 Corinthians 3:3). Converts often emerge from the refiner's fire having had spiritual open-heart surgical procedures, wherein the dross of their former life has been burned out of their systems by the white-hot fire of God.

The identity crisis of such individuals is mitigated because of God's care and concern relating to these extreme makeover procedures. It turns out that the grass really is greener on the other side of the fence, where a pleasant pastoral environment promises a new perspective. The prophet may have been alluding to this when he wrote: "Say to the prisoners, Go forth; to them that are in darkness, Shew yourselves. They shall feed in the ways, and their pastures shall be in all high places." (Isaiah 49:9).

In any event, of those who have repented, taken their vows, and moved upward to new plateaus that are springboards for affirmative action, their new look is visibly different. Their features are flushed with confidence. They stand out from the crowd. They are enthusiastic, passionate, fervent, eager, animated, excited by life, and get a high from the natural release of endorphins.

These dedicated disciples remind us of Abinadi, of whom the scriptures record: "The Spirit of the Lord was upon him; and his face shone with exceeding luster." (Mosiah 13:5). They stand in sharp contrast or opposition to those whose yoke is a heavy burden because they are mired in sin and bound in iniquity. Of them, Jeremiah wrote: "Their visage is blacker than a coal; they are not known in the streets: their skin cleaveth to their bones; it is withered." (Lamentations 4:8).

Those who have brushed against physical death often describe an "out of body" experience akin to "jumping out of their skin." Today, members of the Lord's church do the same when they are redeemed from spiritual death; when they "walk in newness of life." (Romans 6:4).

Latter-day Saints come full circle, and end where they began, albeit with a wider perspective from a higher vantage point. It is strangely familiar to read about how "the Gods went down to organize (them) in their own image, in the image of the Gods to form (them), male and female to form they them." (Abraham 4:27).

To really take advantage of their temporal travels and put a positive spin on their telestial trials, Latter-day Saints learn to repent, to jump out of their skin, to be restored to their "proper and perfect frame," and ultimately to face their destiny, clothed in glory, immortality, and eternal life. (Alma 40:23). They constantly remind themselves that they are "strangers from a realm of light, who have (nearly) forgotten all – the memory of their former life and the purpose of their call. And so, they must learn why they're here, and who they really are." (See "Saturday's Warrior," lyrics by Doug Stewart).

Just Get Back on The Bike

"The race is not to the swift."
(Ecclesiastes 9:11).

"As the Lord liveth, and as we live, we will not
go down unto our father in the wilderness until we
have accomplished the thing which the Lord hath
commanded us. Wherefore, let us be faithful in
keeping the commandments of the Lord;
therefore, let us go down to the land
of our father's inheritance."
(1 Nephi 3:15-16).

When my grandson Parker Edwards was 10 years old, his interest in dirt bikes reached an almost feverish pitch. For a time, his excitement exceeded his skill, and he consequently took his fair share of spills. Motorcycling can be a lot of work, and for a ten-year-old it can be exhausting, especially in the aftermath of a yard-sale crash. Fortunately, our motorcycling experiences have been (for the most part) free of serious injury, 1) because of Parker's ability to carefully follow instructions, 2) because of attentive parental control, and 3) because of a serious investment in protective equipment.

Nevertheless, after an especially grueling morning at an ORV Park in the Coast Range west of Portland, Oregon, Parker was ready to hang it up right there on the trail, and just walk away from his (upside-down) bike. The only problem was that we were miles from the parking lot, and slinking away to lick his wounds was not really an option. I was impressed with the simple wisdom and broad application of the counsel given to Parker by his father, when he gently said: "Just get back on the bike."

I think dirt biking is similar to our life experiences. Maybe that's why I enjoy it so much. We can be zooming along standing on our foot-pegs without a care in the world, with the wind in our face, and enjoying the freedom of the trail. Then, almost without warning, we might hit a rock that jerks the handlebars sideways, causing us to lose our sure grip, and we suddenly find ourselves one with mother earth. (Maybe that's why they call it "dirt-biking!").

When life throws us a curve, and we go south when the trail goes north, we need to remember to "Just get back on the bike." When we do, and I think of Parker when I say this, we'll find that in no time, we'll forget the spill, as we twist the throttle to get back up to speed, looking with eager anticipation for the next opportunity to get serious air. Then, when the next rock in the trail looms before us, we'll be the wiser for our experiences, we'll be less intimidated, and we'll be better prepared to avoid another close encounter of the dirt kind.

Just as the
water from the spring of Gihon
was vital for the physical survival of
Hezekiah's people during the Assyrian
conflict, living water is essential for our
spiritual survival during our battle with
Satan. In effect, we are under siege
throughout our lives, and our
constant access to living
water is our only hope
of salvation.

Justice

"The meaning of the word restoration is to bring back again evil for evil, or carnal for carnal, or devilish for devilish, good for that which is good; righteous for that which is righteous; just for that which is just; merciful for that which is merciful."
(Alma 41:13).

Even those who have been called to preach the gospel risk falling into transgression in consequence of a shallow understanding of principles and doctrines. As Alma declared to the inhabitants of Ammonihah: "Behold, the scriptures are before you; if ye will wrest them it shall be to your own destruction." (Alma 13:20). Picking apart the scriptures can distort the doctrines into meaningless fragments without any coherent connection.

Alma's son Corianton was an example of one who suffered the ill effects of doctrinal misinterpretation. Until Corianton understood and was committed to the gospel Plan, he could not rebuild his troubled life and could not perform the missionary labor to which he had been called. Therefore, his father sought to remedy the situation by explaining the doctrine of justice that had been troubling him.

The contrasting states of the inhabitants of the Spirit World are typified by happiness or misery. Justice, Alma explained, demands "all things shall be restored to their proper order, everything to its natural frame, raised to endless happiness to inherit the kingdom of God, or to endless misery to inherit the kingdom of the devil." (Alma 41:4).

The mortal mission of the Savior was to "redeem those who will be baptized unto repentance, through faith on his name. (Alma 9:27). The Atonement is for those who enter into the covenants and repent. This is the gospel Plan, that all might have the opportunity to benefit from the Law of Mercy, that the Savior of the world might satisfy the demands of the Law of Justice through the Atonement for sin.

Joseph Smith once declared, "happiness is the object and design of our existence and will be the end thereof, if we pursue the path that leads to it; and this path is virtue, uprightness, faithfulness, holiness, and keeping all the commandments of God." ("Teachings," p. 255). But God will always grant to His children agency to choose their own path, "for behold, they are their own judges, whether to do good or do evil." (Alma 41:7).

We can choose our own actions, but we cannot choose to escape the consequences of those actions. "The decrees of God are unalterable; therefore, the way is prepared that whosoever will, may walk therein and be saved." (Alma 41:8). But we cannot "be restored from sin to happiness." (Alma 41:10).

For emphasis, Alma cited a Hebrew Hokmah: "Wickedness never was happiness." (Alma 41:10). In the words of Samuel the Lamanite: "Ye have sought all the days of your lives for that which ye could not obtain; and ye have sought for happiness in doing iniquity, which thing is contrary to the nature of that righteousness which is in our great and Eternal Head." (Helaman 13:38).

Moroni taught that "despair cometh because of iniquity." (Moroni 10:22). Every law has both a blessing and a punishment affixed to it. When the law is obeyed, a blessing is given that results in happiness, or joy. When that law is disobeyed, punishment is given that results in unhappiness, or misery. Despair is the feeling of hopelessness that accompanies disobedience.

As Alma explained: "All men that are in a state of nature, or I would say, in a carnal state, are in the gall of bitterness and in the bonds of iniquity; they are without God in the world, and they have gone contrary to the nature of God; therefore, they are in a state contrary to the nature of happiness." (Alma 41:11). The Savior taught that if men lack vision, and build "upon the works of men, or upon the works of the devil, verily I say unto you they have joy in their works for a season, and by and by the end cometh, and they are hewn down and cast into the fire, from whence there is no return." (3 Nephi 27:11).

As Corianton listened to his father, he began to understand that "the meaning of the word restoration is to bring back again evil for evil, or carnal for carnal, or devilish for devilish, good for that which is good; righteous for that which is righteous; just for that which is just; merciful for that which is merciful." (Alma 41:13). So important was this principle, that Alma constructed the message in the form of a chiasm that is preserved in verses 13-15.

Sometimes, it is very difficult to tell just what brings happiness. Both poverty and wealth have failed miserably. Neither fame nor anonymity holds the key. Neither sickness nor health has the ability. Both principalities and the absence of worldly influence are inadequate. Neither beauty nor the beast has the advantage.

Sometimes, people forget that when they pray for rain, and their prayers are answered, they are also going to have to deal with some mud. "The dark threads are as needful in the weaver's skillful hand as the threads of gold and silver, in the pattern he has planned." (Anonymous). People can never hope to understand the answers they receive, if they continue to ask the wrong questions, or if they formulate their petitions based on desires and not on needs. In fact, without the symmetry and balance of the Lord's spiritual fitness program, life lacks coherence. This is why Moroni taught that "despair cometh because of iniquity."

Alma closed this portion of his exhortation to Corianton by applying the principle of restoration directly to his son: "Therefore, my son, see that you are merciful unto your brethren; deal justly, judge righteously, and do good continually; and if ye do all these things then shall ye receive your reward; yea, ye shall have mercy restored unto you again; ye shall have justice restored unto you again; ye shall have a righteous judgment restored unto you again; and ye shall have good rewarded unto you again." (Alma 41:14).

The fundamental truth he wanted to emphasize was that restoration in its broad sense is personal and of relevance to every individual, for "that which ye do send out shall return unto you again." (Alma 41:15). Alma wanted Corianton to understand that justice and mercy are inexorably tied to the Golden Rule that should be committed not just to memory, but to life itself. We should be proud of our honesty with ourselves and with our fellow men, true to proven principles, faithful to our covenants, and diligent in doing good to all men, in whatever circumstances we might find ourselves.

Then, as now, we believe in every principle that uplifts, motivates, and inspires mankind to noble behavior. Alma sought to rekindle in his son a bright hope in the future, as the Light of the world beckons us to follow His Shining Example. He knew that Corianton would be comforted in his trials as he endured in righteousness. Alma had tried the virtue of the word of God, and knew that if there is anything at all that is lovely, or of good report or praiseworthy, it would be to his advantage to seek after these things, because light cleaves unto light, and intelligence to intelligence.

An animated religious debate centers around whether it is a constructive use of our time and energies to catalog these Compendia, and then to decide if they should be relegated to apocryphal works, (biblical or related writings that have significant spiritual value, but have not been accepted as part of the canon of scripture), pseudepigraphical works (a loose collection of falsely attributed works that may still have esoteric or historical value), or simply to the large body of profane works that are not sacred and whose study may even be detrimental to our spiritual welfare.

Justice and Mercy

"According to justice, the plan of redemption could not be brought about, only on conditions of repentance of men in this probationary state, yea, this preparatory state, for except it were on these conditions, mercy could not take effect except it would destroy the work of justice .. and the plan of mercy could not be brought about except an atonement should be made. Therefore, God himself atoneth for the sins of the world, to bring about the plan of mercy, to appease the demands of justice, that God might be a perfect, just God, and a merciful God also." (Alma 42:13-15).

Arguably, Alma Chapter 42 contains the best explanation in all scripture regarding the justice and mercy of God. Alma taught his son these principles because Corianton had been excusing wrong behavior, claiming that it was unjust to punish sinners. In fact, justice is the unalterable decree of God that declares that both righteousness and sin dictate their own consequences.

Alma refreshed Corianton's memory, reminding him that at the time of Adam and Eve's transgression, God "placed at the east end of the garden of Eden, cherubim, and a flaming sword which turned every way, to keep the tree of life." (Alma 42:2). He had very effectively used the same illustration 10 years earlier when teaching the people of Ammonihah, explaining to them that eternal life is gained by redemption and not by the overpowering of cherubim. Using the same logic, he had shown that by placing cherubim to guard the tree of eternal life, Heavenly Father had prevented Adam and his posterity from inappropriately partaking of the fruit of the tree of life before being taught the Plan of Salvation, and the power of the Atonement, and thus from living forever in their sins. Thereby, they were prevented from having any basis for justifying sinful behavior.

Antionah had cited Genesis 3:24: God "placed at the east of the garden of Eden cherubims, and a flaming sword which turned every way, to keep the way of the tree of life." He had erroneously concluded that the only way to live forever was to "partake of the fruit of the tree of life." If this were so, Antionah had reasoned, the people would have a justification for sinning. For if the key to immortality were simply partaking of the fruit, then with cherubim guarding the way, there would be "no possible chance that they (could) live forever." (Alma 12:21).

Just as Alma had answered the question posed by Antionah, so did he for his son Corianton. Fortunately, Alma was more familiar with the scriptures and the doctrine of the Kingdom than was his son, and so he was able to explain that there is another way whereby man may live forever, not in sin, but in purity and glory.

One of the foundation teachings of the gospel is that men came into this world to die. "And now behold, I say unto you that if it had been possible for Adam to have partaken of the fruit of the tree of life at that time, there would have been no death, and the word would have been void, making God a liar, for he said: If thou eat thou shalt surely die." (Alma 12:23). It was clearly understood before we came here that our experience would end in the death of the mortal body. It is part of the Merciful Plan of our Father. When Adam was sent into the Garden of Eden, it was with the understanding that he would violate or transgress a law in order to bring to pass mortality.

The Book of Mormon clearly teaches that the purpose of the Fall was to give man the opportunity to come to the earth in order to prepare for a resurrection. "And we see that death comes upon mankind, yea, the death which has been spoken of by Amulek, which is the temporal death; nevertheless there was a space granted unto man in which he might repent; therefore this life became a probationary state; a time to prepare to meet God; a time to prepare for that endless state which has been spoken of by us, which is after the resurrection of the dead." (Alma 12:24). Through the Atonement, men would be raised in that resurrection clothed in exactly the kinds of bodies needed to dwell in the various degrees of glory.

The Plan of Salvation is the Plan of Redemption, the Plan of Mercy, and the Plan of Happiness, because it makes possible the resurrection of otherwise imperfect mortals to an eternal life of glory. "Now, if it had not been for the plan of redemption, which was laid from the foundation of the world, there could have been no resurrection of the dead; but there was a plan of redemption laid, which shall bring to pass the resurrection of the dead." (Alma 12:25).

Alma also taught that in the absence of repentance for one's sins, and without the benefit of the gospel Plan of Salvation, man must ultimately be miserable, living forever in his sins. "And now behold, if it were possible that our first parents could have gone forth and partaken of the tree of life they would have been forever miserable, having no preparatory state; and thus, the plan of redemption would have been frustrated, and the word of God would have been void, taking none effect." (Alma 12:26).

Without redemption from sin, if one were to partake of the fruit of the tree of life, which is eternal life, or the highest expression of the love of God, it would not be possible to sustain a celestial existence, inasmuch as one in that condition would be incapable of obedience to celestial principles. Thus, the Plan of Salvation would be frustrated.

The scenario outlined by Alma to the people of Ammonihah demonstrated that this was not to be the case. Satan, who was a liar from the beginning, attempted to foil the Plan of Salvation by substituting a counterfeit, unworkable plan, but His efforts were thwarted. Instead, mankind was provided with "a probationary time, a time to repent and serve God." (Alma 42:4). Probation is a time of testing, or of putting to the proof some question, which in this case is: "Will men serve God, if given the opportunity? Will they recognize Christ as their Savior, and exercise faith unto repentance?"

The cherubim guaranteed that the Plan of Salvation would no" be frustrated. "For behold, if Adam had put forth his hand immediately, and partaken of the tree of life, he would have lived forever, according to the word of God, having no space for repentance." (Alma 42:5). However, this posed an immediate problem. Because of the transgression in the Garden, justice demanded that "man became lost forever, yea, they became fallen man. And now, ye see by this that our first parents were cut off both temporally and spiritually from the presence of the Lord." (Alma 42:6-7). So it was, that "they became subject to follow after their own will." The crowning principle of agency was to be honored, even if it meant that justice must be served. Therefore, "it was appointed unto man to die" (Alma 42:6), rather than to reclaim him "from this temporal death, for that would destroy the great plan of happiness." (Alma 42:8).

"The fall had brought upon all mankind a spiritual death as well as a temporal (death), that is, they were cut off from the presence of the Lord." The violation of God's commandment had resulted in alienation from His presence, which is spiritual death, and the expulsion from the Garden had resulted in man's mortality, making his eventual temporal death inevitable. (See Moses 5:4). But all was not lost. It was expedient that mankind should be reclaimed from this spiritual death." (Alma 42:9).

Our nature in our fallen state is to be subject to the influences of Satan. When we have no direct or indirect experience with the Divine, when we are alienated from God by spiritual death, we become "carnal, sensual, and devilish." (Alma 42:10). This is why, from the Fall of Adam, God has provided us with the Plan of Salvation, the Plan of Redemption, or the Plan of Happiness, that mortality might be a preparatory state, where we might develop the qualities required for our redemption from spiritual death.

It is for our benefit that we become acquainted with evil as well as with good, with darkness as well as with light, with error as well as with truth, and with punishment for the infraction of eternal laws, as well as with the blessings that follow obedience. Mortality is really our only opportunity to have these experiences.

Ralph Waldo Emerson once asked: "What is the use of immortality to one who cannot wisely use half an hour?" Every minute of mortality is precious. This is why Alma and so many other fathers have invested so much time and energy teaching their children correct principles, and training them in their proper execution.

In Alma Chapter 40, Alma had laid the groundwork for this discussion with Corianton by explaining conditions in the Spirit world. Now he reminded him "if it were not for the plan of redemption, as soon as they were dead their souls were miserable, being cut off from the presence of the Lord." (Alma 42:11). Justice would demand that they suffer eternally the consequences of their own actions. (Alma 42:12). They would be "in the grasp of justice; yea, the justice of God, which consigned them forever to be cut off from his presence." (Alma 42:14).

"According to justice, the plan of redemption could not be brought about" and "mercy could not take effect except it should destroy the work of justice." (Alma 42:13). The beauty of the Plan of Redemption, then, is that it meets the demands of perfect justice through the infinite mercy of a loving Heavenly Father. The Plan allows God to be both just and merciful at the same time.

The Plan of Redemption required that "an atonement should be made; therefore, God Himself atoneth for the sins of the world, to bring about the plan of mercy, to appease the demands of justice, that God might be a perfect, just God, and a merciful God also." (Alma 42:15). The Atonement allowed God to satisfy justice and still mercifully reclaim mankind from physical and spiritual death.

The Savior thus became the Master of the situation. In His sacrifice, the debt would be paid, the redemption made, the covenant fulfilled, justice satisfied, the will of God done, and all power, including the keys of resurrection, now given to the Son.

Alma had certainly studied the counsel of Father Lehi, recorded on the Plates of Lehi that were in his possession, and on it he based the next section of his remarks. He affirmed that "there is a law given, and a punishment affixed, and a repentance granted; which repentance, mercy claimeth." (Alma 42:22). "Is justice dishonored?" asked John Taylor. No, it is satisfied; the debt is paid. Is righteousness forsaken? No, this is a righteous act. All requirements are met. Is judgment violated? No, its demands are fulfilled. Is mercy triumphant? No, she simply claims her own. Justice, judgment, mercy, and truth all harmonize as the attributes of Deity." ("Mediation and Atonement," p. 171-172).

"Mercy claimeth the penitent, and mercy cometh because of the atonement; and the atonement bringeth to pass the resurrection of the dead; and the resurrection of the dead bringeth back men into the presence of God. For behold, justice exerciseth all his demands, and also mercy claimeth all which is her own; and thus, none but the truly penitent are saved." (Alma 42:23-24). Our conscience is a celestial spark that God has put into every man for the purpose of saving his soul.

These "great and eternal purposes were prepared from the foundation of the world." (Alma 42:26). John Taylor taught that "to the Son is given the power of the resurrection, the power of the redemption, the power of salvation, the power to enact laws for the carrying out and accomplishment of the design. Hence, life and immortality are brought to light, the gospel is introduced, and He becomes the Author of eternal life and exaltation." ("Mediation and Atonement," p. 171-172).

Alma reminded Corianton that the only payment required for the gift of salvation is "the heart and a willing mind." (D&C 64:34). The only things that an individual must give up are his sins. (See Alma 22:18). Therefore, Alma counseled his son to "only let your sins trouble you, with that trouble which shall bring you down unto repentance." (Alma 42:29).

The first step in that process is the turning point at which the guilty party consciously recognizes his sin. (See Jeremiah 6:15). Secondly, having clearly defined justice and mercy, and then having explained the relationship and harmony between the two that was effected by the Plan of Redemption, Alma warned Corianton to cease excusing himself in sin. "O my son, I desire that ye should deny the justice of God no more. Do not endeavor to excuse yourself in the least point because of your sins, by denying the justice of God; but do let the justice of God, and his mercy, and his long-suffering have full sway in your heart; and let it bring you down to the dust in humility." (Alma 42:30).

Lastly, he called his son to return to his missionary labors. "And now, O my son, ye are called of God to preach the word unto this people. And now, my son, go thy way, declare the word with truth and soberness, that thou mayest bring souls unto repentance, that the great plan of mercy may have claim upon them." (Alma 42:31).

That Corianton was faithful to his father's counsel is evident from a reference to him in the abridged record of Shiblon. Seventeen years later, Mormon recorded that Shiblon "was a just man, and he did walk uprightly before God; and he did observe to do good continually, to keep the commandments of the Lord his God; and also did his brother (Corianton)." (Alma 63:2).

Keep Smiling

"And when Jesus
had spoken these words he came
again unto his disciples; and behold
they did pray steadfastly, without
ceasing, unto him; and he did
smile upon them again."
(3 Nephi 19:30).

Surprisingly, in the scriptures, there are just four references to "smiling." Three are in The Book of Mormon, and one is in the Pearl of Great Price. Considering that smiling is a universal language that is emotionally understood in much the same way by almost everyone on the planet, I find this perplexing. Maybe the Patriarchs lived in a more austere and somber age. Perhaps they simply used different words to communicate the expression of the human emotion that lies at the very heart of our spirits. Certainly, in the gospel there is a lot to smile about, and one would think that the prophets would openly address and showcase its emotional appeal.

Gordon B. Hinckley was one who did. On more than one occasion, he urged members of the church to light up the world with their smiles, and not to be pickle suckers. On one occasion, he begged students at B.Y.U: "I come this morning with a plea that we stop seeking out the storms and enjoy more fully the sunlight. I am suggesting that we accentuate the positive. I am asking that we look a little deeper for the good, that we still our voices of insult and sarcasm, that we more generously compliment virtue and effort. I am not asking that all criticism be silenced. Growth comes of correction. Strength comes of repentance. Wise is the man who can acknowledge mistakes pointed out by others and change his course. I am not suggesting that our conversation be all honey and blossoms. Clever expression that is sincere and honest is a skill to be sought and cultivated. What I am suggesting and asking is that we turn from the negativism that so permeates our society and look for the remarkable good in the land and times in which we live, that we speak of one another's virtues more than we speak of one another's faults, that optimism replace pessimism, that our faith exceed our fears." (11/29/1974).

Lack of smile references notwithstanding, there are still a lot of scriptural references to emotions whose expression are found in a smile: There are 333 references to "joy," 127 references to "glad," 62 references to "gladness," 40 references to "happy," 37 references to "happiness," 34 references to "merry," and 15 references to "mirth." That is 646 references to the emotional states that should evoke a smile. Interestingly, there are 10 references to "laughter," and 1 to "jovial," but all 11 have negative connotations.

For what it is worth, here are the four references to "smiling" that are found in the scriptures: "And when Jesus had spoken these words he came again unto his disciples; and behold they did pray steadfastly, without ceasing, unto him; and he did smile upon them again; and behold they were white, even as Jesus." (3 Nephi 19:30). "And it came to pass that Jesus blessed them as they did pray unto him; and his countenance did smile upon them, and the light of his countenance did shine upon them." (3 Nephi 19:25). "And the hand of providence hath smiled upon you most pleasingly." (Jacob 2:13). "Wherefore Enoch saw that Noah built an ark; and that the Lord smiled upon it, and held it in his own hand." (Moses 7:43).

Because I want to keep this essay on topic, if we were to pick and choose from among the expressions that are only related to smiling, we might settle upon "countenance," as the one that is most closely aligned. For example, D&C 59:15 speaks of "a glad heart and a cheerful countenance." Psalms 89:15 describes those who "walk in the light of (the Lord's) countenance." Proverbs 15:13 teaches that "a merry heart maketh a cheerful countenance." 1 Samuel 16:12 turns our mind's eye to David, who was "of a beautiful countenance, and goodly to look at." The Savior is described as having such a peaceful appearance that Moses was moved to exclaim: "The Lord lift up His countenance upon thee, and give thee peace." (Number 6:26). David described Him as "the health of my countenance, and my God. (Psalms 42:11). Alma asked his brethren of the church if they had "spiritually been born of God," or if they had "received his image in (their) countenances." (Alma 5:14). Joseph Smith described the Savior as having a "countenance (that) was as lightning" (D&C 20:6), that "shone above the brightness of the sun." (D&C 110:3). The Lord assured him: "Ye shall behold the joy of my countenance." (D&C 88:52). The laborers in the field all received "the light of the countenance of their Lord." (D&C 88:58).

Intriguingly, if we perform a simple exercise, and substitute the word "smile" for the word "work" in selected scriptures, the results almost pop off the page. For example: "Great and marvelous are thy smiles, O Lord God Almighty! (1 Nephi 1:14). "The day should come that they must be judged of their smiles." (1 Nephi 15:32). "If a man bringeth forth good smiles he hearkeneth unto the voice of the good shepherd." (Alma 5:41). "Prepare ye the way of the Lord, for the time is at hand that all men shall reap a reward of their smiles." (Alma 9:28). Therefore, let your light so shine before this people, that they may see your smiles and glorify your Father who is in heaven. (3 Nephi 12:16). "Who can comprehend the marvelous smiles of God?" (Mormon 9:16). "I remember the word of God which saith by their smiles ye shall know them; for if their smiles be good, then they are good also." (Moroni 7:5). "The Lord shall come to recompense unto every man according to his smile." (D&C 1:10). "My smile shall go forth." (D&C 3:16). "By their desires and their smiles you shall know them." (D&C 18:38). "I shall pass upon the inhabitants thereof, judging every man according to his smiles and the deeds which he hath done." (D&C 19:3). "My smiles have no end, neither beginning." (D&C 29:33). "Those that live shall inherit the earth, and those that die shall rest from all their labors, and their smiles shall follow them; and they shall receive a crown in the mansions of my Father." (D&C 59:2). "Pray unto the Lord, call upon his holy name, make known his wonderful smiles among the people." (D&C 65:4). "Great and marvelous are the smiles of the Lord, and the mysteries of his kingdom which he showed unto us, which surpass all understanding in glory, and in might, and in dominion." (D&C 76:114).

I particularly like the following scripture, because smiles seems to lie at the pinnacle of our discipleship: "All those who humble themselves before God, and desire to be baptized, and come forth with broken hearts and contrite spirits, and witness before the church that they have truly repented of all their sins, and are willing to take upon them the name of Jesus Christ, having a determination to serve him to the end, and truly manifest by their smiles that they have received of the Spirit of Christ unto the remission of their sins, shall be received by baptism into his church." (D&C 20:37).

We can achieve the same powerful effect by substituting the word "smile" for the word "endure." "If they smile unto the end, they shall be lifted up at the last day." (1 Nephi 13:37). "I am the law, and the light. Look unto me, and smile to the end." (3 Nephi 15:9). How about the word "perseverance?" "Let your smiles be redoubled, and you shall in nowise lose your reward (D&C 127:4). Try it with the word "faith." "Look forward for the remission of your sins, with an everlasting smile." (Alma 7:6). "As many as are not stiffnecked and have smiles, have communion with the Holy Spirit." (Jarom 1:4). "Hope cometh of smiles." (Ether 12:4). "By smiles, they become the sons of God." (Moroni 7:26). "Without smiles there cannot be any hope." (Moroni 7:42). "Remember that without a smile you can do nothing." (D&C 8:10). "Without smiling no man pleaseth God." (D&C 63:11).

If we tack on the modifier "with a smile upon your face" to certain scriptures, they become even more meaningful. For example: "I command thee that thou shalt pray vocally as well as in thy heart, with a smile upon your face." (D&C 19:28). Or: "And thou shalt declare glad tidings, yea, publish it upon the mountains, and upon every high place, and among every people that thou shalt be permitted to see, with a smile upon your face." (D&C 19:29). Or: "Take upon you the name of Christ, with a smile upon your face." (Alma 34:38). Or: "If thou art merry, praise the Lord with singing, with music, with dancing, and with a prayer of praise and thanksgiving, with a smile upon your face." (D&C 136:28). Smiling can even be a token, as it were, of our covenant relationship with the Lord. "Choose ye this day to serve the Lord God, with a smile upon your face." (Moses 6:33). "If they hold out faithful to the end they are received into heaven, that thereby they may dwell with God in a state of never-ending happiness, with a smile upon their face." (Mosiah 2:41). "This mortal shall put on immortality, and this corruption shall put on incorruption, and shall be brought to stand before the bar of God, with a smile upon their face." (Mosiah 16:10). "And then shall it come to pass, that the spirits of those who are righteous are received into a state of happiness, with smiles upon their faces." (Alma 40:12).

What would the scriptures, or the world for that matter, be like, if there were no smiles to brighten their pages or our lives? "The evil spirit teacheth not a man to pray, but teacheth him that he must not pray, and that he must never smile." (2 Nephi 32:8). "Do not suppose, because it has been spoken concerning restoration, that ye shall be restored from sin to happiness, or from frowns to smiles." (Alma 41:10). "How then can I do this great wickedness, and sin against God, and wipe the smile from my face?" (Genesis 39:9). "And there shall be weeping and wailing among the hosts of men, and there shall be no cause to smile under the heavens." (D&C 29:15).

Fortunately, the scriptures abound with allusions to our smiles that are not only grammatical constructions, but are also curves that set everything straight. Even though it may be raining, the scriptures teach that if we keep smiling, the sun will soon show its face and smile right back at us. Smiles in the scriptures are often concealed, but they cannot be hidden for long. As smiles peak out at us as honest emotions from behind familiar passages, we can almost hear the Spirit challenging us to smile in return; to smile so widely that we could eat a banana sideways.

When we feel happy, we smile with all our heart, and when we're down, we smile with all our might. If we do nothing else, we can still be the smile on the faces of those that mourn, or stand in need of comfort. Our smiles can be a daily exercise that we can do without ever breaking a sweat. The smiles that we wear on the outside tell others what's happening on the inside. Sometimes our joy is the source of our smile, but sometimes our smile may be the source of our joy. As we smile with a determined effort to fight our way through brimming tears, we can take comfort in the fact that at least the corners of our mouths point toward heaven.

Even as the world broadcasts insistent messages that beauty has the advantage, we know that it is a smile that is the absolute guarantee. When we get up in the morning, we are only half-dressed until we put on our smile. We realize that, when it comes to smiling, one size fits all. Our smile is an accessory that never goes out of style. No matter what obstacles may be thrown before us throughout the day, smiling in the face of our challenges makes the tasks that lie ahead seem easier. Somehow, our trials are no match for a confident smile. Others are less likely to notice our imperfections, our shortcomings, or our old and worn-out clothes, when we are wearing a smile. As frugal shoppers, we know that a smile is an inexpensive way to change our look. In fact, every smile makes us a day younger. Our smile is like an instant face-lift. Stubborn frowns bring out wrinkles, but those with dimples are doubly blessed. They have been entrusted with a special role in the universe, and that is to smile.

As we embrace life, we recognize that vibrant color is nature's way of smiling at us. After every storm, we look forward to the dappled rays of sunlight that smile down upon us. Among all the mighty works of man, we realize that a smile is civilization's finest adornment. Of all the creations of God, we acknowledge that a beautiful smile that is flashed for no apparent reason separates us from all other creatures. We have no original facial expressions: We have inherited our smiles from our parents, we borrow them from our friends, and we receive them as gifts from complete strangers. We are drawn to those who make a difference in our lives, to those who make us smile.

Smiling evokes vivid memories of our innermost emotions, just as our vivid memories often evoke a smile. Sometimes, our joy is the source of our smiles, but sometimes it is the other way around. We don't cry because it's over; we smile because it happened. Too often, we underestimate the power of our smile, or forget that it is love that has taught us how to smile. A gentle word, a kind look, and a good-natured smile can work wonders and accomplish miracles, especially when we remember that smiles are meant to be given away. They are the most inexpensive of gifts that should never be in short supply, and yet their power can vanquish kingdoms.

With our smiles, we sign our autographs. They may be the most powerful forces in nature, whose effects may last for eternity. It only takes a split second to smile, and then we may forget about it; and yet, to the one to whom it was given, and who needed it at that exact moment, its positive influence might last a lifetime. When we receive a prompting to smile at a stranger, we might never know that we have changed a life. When we are blessed to see the smiles on the faces of innocent children, we are given a glimpse of the divine nature that is in each of us.

Smiling can be intensely gratifying. It can warm our hearts when others smile, but most of us especially like it when we make them smile. When we carry a smile, one of the many faces of love knocks at our door. Smiles fill our hearts with the joy of life. When we smile, we find that, all along, happiness was right under our nose.

Sometimes we smile to keep from crying, and it can be inexpensive therapy for our wounded souls. When we feel that there is no reason to smile, we try to find one, because we have learned the hard way that nothing can shake a smiling heart. If we have to, we will be the smile on someone else's downcast face, to melt away their fears and their tears. Our smile can replace their despondency with cheerfulness. If need be, with a smile on our face we can climb the steps to the gallows, give a jest to the crowd, a coin to the hangman, and make the drop. Short of that, we pray for opportunities to replace the tears of the downcast and oppressed with smiling faces that point the way to the windows of their souls.

We are ever on the lookout for those who could really use a smile, as therapy for their lonely hearts. When we see others who needs a smile, we give them one of ours. We keep apples in our fruit basket, but we know by experience that it is a smile a day that keeps the pain away. Smiles are the spotlights that shine on our hearts. The simplest gift we can give to another is our smile. We try to so live that we can be someone else's reason to smile. We recognize the incredible power of our smiles to change the world, and so we defend ourselves, that the world might never have the power to change our smiles into frowns. We smile at everyone because it might be the last chance we have to do so, because we, or they, may not be here tomorrow.

Smiling doesn't always mean we are happy. Sometimes, we smile to avoid sadness. A smile may be just the therapy that we need. Or, because our smile may be the only sunlight in the life of a fellow traveler, we are careful to so live that we don't dim that light. Because they are nondiscriminatory, our smiles may be the quickest way to establish communication with strangers. We answer both praise and criticism with a smile. Our smiles can be good icebreakers, because if we've put a smile on the face of someone we barely know, we've done more good than we can imagine.

We smile if for no other reason than that there seem to be so many frowns. Our smile makes a positive statement that squarely addresses the pessimism of a dark and negative world. In fact, the most potent force on earth could be our smile. We smile because we accept hatred with love. Our smiles are the lights of our souls, that can conquer even the coldest souls, because they dance to the rhythm of hearts that are full. We smile as if unborn poems are stirring within us. Our smiles are the bouquet of our joy, the expression of our ecstasy with life, and the God-given manifestation of our love that drive out darkness, which is why our genuine smile is sometimes the best form of communication.

If we need to recharge our batteries, with conscious effort we may take a few steps into the darkness, buoyed up by the sustaining influence of our smiles, which are our spiritual strong searchlights. If we have lost our smiles, we know in which direction we must move to find them again. If we are really desperate, and cannot find a reason to smile, we can always go out and buy a puppy. When we are still, and are seeking quiet spiritual confirmations, the surplus of our hearts will overflow in smiles. When technology threatens our inner peace, we replace the cell phones in our hands with smiles on our faces. There is no other emoticon that can take the place of a genuine smile that is personally given to another human being. Every once in a while, we smile even when life tastes like bitter bile. When thunderstorms roll in, we make a choice to either succumb with fright, or smile and look to see if we can find a rainbow somewhere in the gloomy downpour.

Our smiles release an awesome power within us. We have heard the compliments of others, who say: Your smile becomes you. But perhaps you become you, when you smile. Those who smile while they are alone used to be called insane, until we invented smartphones and social media. A smile is the light in our window that tells others that there is a caring, sharing person inside. In the morning, we drink a glass of sunshine to brighten our hearts and lift our spirits, and then we smile to spread the light of life. As we pleasantly smile, we take control of the moment, and as we persist in smiling, we own it.

Sometimes, when we wish to make particularly significant contributions, we offer our silence with smiles on our faces. We smile at others with such intensity that they feel that they have won a prize, and they have no choice but to smile back at us, in appreciation. Our cheerful conversation tickles our throats and forces our lips into smiles. We can only appreciate the value of a smile when we own the face behind it. But when our smiles become the expressions of the divine center within us, they are easier to give away.

Even simple smiles are rewarded in heaven. Our smiles are the unfathomable gifts of the gods. While others smiled, we cried at birth, and even if others cry, we hope to be able to smile at our death. When we die, we would love to die smiling, because we have already been blessed to see the smiles on the faces of those who are about to complete their journey to the veil. When we cross over the bar to heaven, we hope to go with smiles on our faces. However, should we forget this in the excitement of the moment, we hope there will be someone in eternity waiting to greet us with a smile, and that we will be prompted to respond in kind. In the interim, the biggest reward of our lives will be to have finished each day with smiles on our faces. Someday, we are going to be able to look back on every shared smile, and then quietly smile, one last time.

It's easy to learn to smile. When we smile, our faces light up with a celestial glow. We smile large. Our cheeks may hurt, but it's the cutest thing. We are really in the swing of it, and truly smile, only when our mouths and hearts coordinate with each other. We smile as if we've just been told the best joke on earth. When we smile like the morning sun, our lives are filled with fun. Anyone can smile on their best of days. We want to be able to smile on our worst days. Our genuine smiles come from our hearts, but our healthy smiles need good dental care. We know that life is short, and so we smile while we still have teeth.

We smile like flowers that attract everyone. We are smile-magnets. We smile at others as if it were the last smile they will ever see on earth. When we smile, our ears rise, as well as our listening ability. We decorate our faces with piles of smiles. We smile at perfect strangers, and mean it, because we realize that nearly everyone could use a lift. We look for special opportunities to spoil the day of a grump, by giving him or her our smiles. Sometimes we crack a smile, even though we don't like breaking things. Because it's the worst form of identity theft, we refuse to let anyone steal our smiles.

If we're not using our smiles, we're like the person with a million dollars in the bank and no pen to write a check. If we're not smiling, it's because our hearts must be on vacation. When we wear a smile, we have friends, but when we wear a frown, we have wrinkles. No one is perfect, unless they smile. Our smiles preemptively confuse approaching frowns. While frowns mean nothing, our smiles mean everything. It takes 64 facial muscles to make a frown, and only 13 to make a smile, and so we ask ourselves: "Why work overtime?" (It really does take more muscles to frown than it does to smile, which make sense because yesterday I saw someone who frowned so much they ended up pulling a groin muscle). Before we put on a frown, we need to make absolutely sure there are no smiles available. It's no coincidence that smiles turn up the corners of our mouths, while frowns turn them down. In the economy of nature, it could have just as easily have been the other way around, if it were not for the fact that God has a sense of humor.

We never ask for permission to smile, and never consider ourselves too poor to give one away. One time, I thought I had lost my smile. But then I found it in a daffodil. Life is about the number of faces that smile when they hear our names mentioned. I have been told that I have a winning smile, but I must confess that it's just not true. My grin only won a silver medal at last year's Facial Expression Olympics. We smile and thank God that we are alive. Especially when it's cold outside, we can always bring someone into the warmth of our smile.

We smile so powerfully that it shames the sun itself, because a smile can be even more cheerful. We smile as if the sun had just come out from behind a cloud. The world always looks brighter from behind a smile. Sometimes we feel that if we had a star for every time we smiled, we would be holding the night sky in our hand. If we haven't seen our wives smile at a traffic cop, we haven't seen them smile at their prettiest. For some reason, our children are always on their best behavior when they're smiling. We know by experience that love is a smile that is shared between two people. Our smiles are often the best reaction to life's experiences. Smiles are the twinkle that adds to our happiness, which is probably why each of us has smiles to go before we sleep. All the statistics in the world can't measure the warmth of our smiles. Our enigmatic smiles are worth ten pages of dialog. When we smile, we reflect the face of God.

You want to know who is amazing, and has the best smile ever? Read the first word of this paragraph again. But your smile isn't about you; it's about helping others. A smile doesn't always stand for a perfect life, but a men and women who smile when they fall, give the devil a good slap on the cheek. If we smile, or if we don't smile, everyone around us is affected. Our smile is a perfume that we cannot pour out on someone else without getting a few drops on ourselves. What sunshine is to flowers, smiles are to humanity.

Our smiles are like stress-formula vitamins. When we sulk, we create noise, but when we smile, we create music. If we can win an argument by stretching our lips into a smile, it makes no sense to open our mouths and lose it in the process. If the world appears either abundant in smiles or overwhelmed by scowls, we might ask ourselves if we are responsible. It's hard for someone to stay angry with us when we smile. We keep right on smiling, because it makes people wonder what we're up to. Love and peace can create smiles, but our smiles can also create love and peace. If we disagree with others, our discussions should be punctuated with smiles. Our smiles are evidence that we are on the side of their recipients. Smiles increase our face value. When we lead with a smile, we are more likely to be lucky.

Our smiles are contagious, and they are the only infectious affliction everyone is encouraged to spread. They can start an epidemic, and so we should indiscriminately share them. Most smiles are jump-started by other smiles. The shortest distance between two people is a smile. Our smiles can be the keys that fit the locks on our hearts. One smile probably won't change the world, but it could change ours, and so we smile at everyone. We never know when we're smiling at an angel. Although a laugh can be a smile that has burst its borders, a smile means a lot more, because it is a true reflection of emotion, while laughter is often just a by-product of humor. Unlike gossip, no-one minds if you spread a smile. Our smiles speak a language that even babies understand; think of the smile that flickers on a baby's mouth when it is sleeping, and prepare to be amazed.

Remember to smile the next time you stand before the congregation to bear your testimony, when you are given a service opportunity, when you approach the Recommend Desk at the temple, when you greet your son or daughter who has just returned home from a date, when you are asked about your ministering report by your file leaders, when you meet with the Bishop to discuss a church calling, when you entertain the missionaries with a meal in your home, when a non-member friend asks you a question about the church, or when you are asked by a neighbor to move outside your comfort zone to provide temporal or spiritual assistance.

Remember to smile when things don't go as you have planned, when life throws you a curve, when your best-laid plans go awry, when the baby needs a diaper change, when the car starts making weird noises, when your son throws an errant baseball through the front window, when the new driver in your family has a close encounter with a curb or a tree, when an open container of yoghurt falls upside-down on the kitchen floor, or when someone who has used the bathroom before you has squeezed the toothpaste from the middle of the tube.

Remember to smile when you miss by one day the big sale at the department store, when someone at work who is less deserving gets the promotion, when someone else gets recognition for your achievements, or when a neighbor comes home with the same new car you've been dreaming about.

But also remember to smile when you think about how the Lord has blessed you, and how He has provided for your needs and even granted you a surplus, how you have friends you can trust, how your spouse and children sustain you, how others look to you for counsel, how your dog thinks you can do no wrong, and how fortunate you are to be alive.

We are all familiar with the story of the man who complained because he had no shoes, until he met a man who had no feet. Helen Keller took gratitude to a whole new level when she "asked a friend who had just returned from a long walk in the woods what she had observed. 'Nothing in particular,' he replied. "How was that possible," Helen asked herself? "I, who cannot hear or see, find hundreds of things to interest me through mere touch. I feel the delicate symmetry of a leaf. I pass my hands lovingly about the rough shaggy bark of a pine. Occasionally, if I am very fortunate, I place my hand gently on a small tree and feel the happy quiver of a bird in full song." ("The Atlantic Monthly").

We need to be more like Brigham Young, who testified: "I feel like shouting Hallelujah, all the time, when I think that I ever knew Joseph Smith," or like Parley P. Pratt, who declared: "I have received the holy anointing, and I can never rest till the last enemy is conquered, death destroyed, and truth reigns triumphant." With smiles on our faces, may each of us have the joyful anticipation of a reward both on earth and in heaven. We have all heard the story about the optimistic little boy, who, when faced with the task of shoveling up an enormous pile of manure in the horse stall behind his home, enthusiastically set about his task with the smiling exclamation: "There's got to be a pony in there, somewhere!"

We should be excited to live in a time when smiling is in vogue, with the possible exception of runway models who look like they have been weaned on pickles. There is so much to smile about! From "selfies," to Facebook posts, to Instagram photos, to Pinterest, and even to Snap Chat, it's cool to broadcast a smiling face in cyberspace. But in a disposable world that casts aside interpersonal relationships like empty plastic water bottles, where the counterfeits for happiness can be so easily manufactured, processed, packaged, and promoted, let's make sure we generate daily smiles, and are doing so for the right reasons. Let's not allow gullibility or photoshop to overpower our native common sense. Let's take a lesson from Joseph Smith, who by all accounts was a good-natured and affable soul. But even he admitted: "I was guilty of levity, and sometimes associated with jovial company, not consistent with that character which ought to be maintained by one who was called of God as I had been. But this will not seem very strange to anyone who recollects my youth, and is acquainted with my native cheery temperament." (J.S.H. 1:28).

Let' all hope and pray for sunshine in our souls "today, more glorious and bright than glows in any earthly sky, for Jesus is (our) light. O there's sunshine, blessed sunshine, when the peaceful, happy moments roll; when Jesus shows His smiling face, there is sunshine in the soul." (Eliza Hewitt).

Labels

"Neither were there Lamanites, nor any
manner of -ites, but they were in one,
the children of Christ, and heirs
to the kingdom of God."
(4 Nephi 1:17).

Elder Boyd K. Packer was once asked, "What is the future of the Lamanites in the church?" His immediate response was: "I cannot answer that question. We have no '-ites' in The Church of Jesus Christ of Latter-day Saints." One immediately thinks of the conditions in Zarahemla described by Mormon following the ministry of the Savior among the Nephites. "There were no robbers, nor murderers, neither were there Lamanites, nor any manner of -ites; but they were in one, the children of Christ, and heirs to the kingdom of God." (4 Nephi 1:17). It was an ideal society that had been stripped of the pride and contention that define the distinctions created by selfish individuals.

At roughly the same time, the Apostle Paul similarly counseled the Ephesians: "Now therefore ye are no more strangers and foreigners, but fellowcitizens with the saints, and of the household of God." (Ephesians 2:19). Those to whom he had written his epistle were members of one of the seven churches of Asia, and might have considered themselves privileged individuals and members of an exclusive society. They may have grown accustomed to applying labels to themselves in complimentary terms, and to others in a derogatory way.

Paul might have been saying to the Ephesians that, should strangers, or foreigners from Corinth, Philippi, or Colossae arrive in Ephesus, they should not be labeled as such, but should rather be recognized as fellowcitizens with the saints, and that, in their thinking, the church as a whole should fall within the household of God in the bonds of fellowship.

Ideally, those who today enter into the covenants, are they "who have come out of the world, who have left the loneliness and estrangement of a fallen creation and entered the realm of divine experience. They have forsaken the orphanage of spiritual alienation and been received into the family and household of the Lord Jesus Christ. They have left the ranks of the nameless and taken upon them the blessed name of Jesus Christ. They are Christians. Through their Master, they become, in time, joint heirs to all that the Father has." ("Doctrinal Commentary on The Book of Mormon," 4:202).

We cannot afford to apply labels to others that artificially categorize or compartmentalize them, segregate them from the blessings of the gospel, define and limit their potential, demean their status as children of our Heavenly Father, or communicate mistrust, misunderstanding, or even worse, contempt. Is there really a palpable, perceptible difference between the prince and pauper, those who bask in the limelight and those who hug the shadows, member and non-member, active and inactive individual, adult Aaronic and Melchizedek priesthood bearer, or single, divorced, widowed, and married people? Are saints and sinners so very different?

The Lord God "inviteth them all to come unto him and partake of his goodness; and he denieth none that come unto him, black and white, bond and free, male and female; and he remembereth the heathen; and all are alike unto God, both Jew and Gentile." (2 Nephi 26:33). Nephi could not have put it more emphatically than to say that both Jew and Gentile are the same in the eyes of our Heavenly Father, for the Jews were almost fanatically obsessed with their status as the Chosen People of God. This verse posts a notice for all to see across centuries of prejudice, that God is indeed no respecter of persons, but rather that it is righteousness that is important to Him. (D&C 38:16, see Ephesians 6:9).

Today, members should understand that "while The Church of Jesus Christ of Latter-day Saints is given a prominent part in this great drama of the Last Days, it is not the only force nor the only means that the Lord has employed to bring to pass those things of which His prophets in ancient times have testified." (B.H. Roberts, quoted in "The Mormon Experience," p. 257). More particularly, members living in the U.S. need to remember that there is no United States of America in heaven.

Zion, ultimately, comes in many different colors. Zion speaks Aymara, Afrikaans, Fijian, Polish, Mandarin, and dozens of other languages. It lives in well over 3,500 stakes and in practically every country of the world. It has over 17 million members who are red, yellow, brown, black, and white. With equal comfort, Zion wears a sarong, a grass skirt, a tupeno, a blue collar, and a white shirt. It lives in igloos, thatch cottages, bamboo huts, and condominiums. Most important of all, it shares a common testimony that Jesus is The Christ, and that His love, indeed, makes the world go around. (Adapted from "The Improvement Era," 9/1973).

Lamanites by The Waters of Sebus

Ammon "stood by the waters of Sebus ... and began to cast stones at (the Lamanite ruffians) with his sling; yea, with mighty power he did sling stones amongst them; and thus he slew a certain number of them, insomuch that they began to be astonished at his power." (Alma 17:34 & 36).

In The Book of Mormon account of Ammon by the Water of Sebus, "every man that lifted his club to smite Ammon, he smote off their arms with his sword; for he did withstand their blows by smiting their arms with the edge of his sword, insomuch that they began to be astonished, and began to flee before him; yea, and they were not few in number; and he caused them to flee by the strength of his arm." (Alma 17:37).

Alma may have included this episode in his abridgment because he knew that in our day we would face our own "Lamanites by the Water of Sebus." We all have the same primal needs, and the focus of our concern should be on the potential loss of our energy, vitality, and ultimately our eternal lives.

Perhaps our moment of greatest challenge will come when we are placed in a compromising social situation and are tempted to homogenize our standards. Maybe it will be when we are climbing the ladder of success and are tempted to scramble over those who are supposedly in our way and impeding our progress. It might be that when we are alone with our computer and surfing the web, we are prone to visit sites of questionable value. It may come at the end of the month when we are reconciling our checkbook and balancing our budget, and we have not yet paid our tithing. It may be when we have not engaged in our ministering assignments, or have not attended the temple in a while, and worldly concerns compete for our time and attention.

The Lord said: "That which the Spirit testifies unto you even so I would that ye should do in all holiness of heart, walking uprightly before me, considering the end of your salvation, doing all things with prayer and thanksgiving, that ye may not be seduced by evil spirits, or doctrines of devils, or the commandments of men." (D&C 46:7). The "Lamanites" standing in the way of our progress are those frightful things we see when we take our minds off our goals. They cause us to lose focus. "Lamanites" influence us to lower our sights and achieve our objectives far too easily. If we are gliding smoothly and effortlessly through life with little expenditure of energy, we are probably going downhill, in the company of "Lamanite" pressures. Our own personal progress takes effort as we surmount the obstacles in our path and climb to new heights of achievement.

We have "the power of God unto salvation" and are the architects of our own fate, in a very real sense. (Romans 1:16). We have the skills and the materials to build either a shanty or a temple in which to live our lives. Which one it will be depends on us. The outcome depends largely on our perspective. If we can face the "Lamanites" in our lives "with understanding, faith, and courage, we shall be strengthened and comforted, and spared the torment which accompanies the mistaken idea that all suffering comes as chastisement for transgression." (Marion G. Romney, CR 10/64).

Sometimes bad things happen to good people, and life can be unpredictable. There are uncertainties with which each of us must deal, but if our foundation is solid and our footing secure, we will be able to successfully adapt to every circumstance, and maintain our focus. Fanatics are those who lose sight of their objectives and redouble their efforts. We, on the other hand, remember counsel of Paul, who was familiar with adversity: "Work out your own salvation with fear and trembling." (Philippians 2:12)

As we develop the habit of work, we learn that it is "the most invigorating, satisfying, even relaxing and greatest blessing of our lives. The opportunity to work is God's greatest blessing to mankind and this means six days of each week." (Ernest L. Wilkinson). We develop a testimony of the truth that "Work without vision is drudgery; vision without work is dreamery; but work with vision is destiny!" (Harold B. Lee).

As we face" Lamanites by our own Water of Sebus," we remember that our triumph will come by design, by the strength of our own will, and by our reliance on the Lord. In all our "Lamanite" encounters, we think pro-actively, rather than retroactively. We direct the course of the circumstances in which we find ourselves. We may not be able to control everything that unfolds in our lives, but we can influence outcomes and personal consequences.

Failure to do so is a default, a capitulation of our destiny to forces we believe to be beyond their control. If we roll over and turn belly-up to "Lamanites" when they menacingly surround and threaten us, we have already virtually guaranteed failure. Our flocks will be scattered and our King disappointed. "Now the king will slay us," wailed the servants of Limoni. (Alma 17:28). Our Lord and Master will not take our lives. Instead, it is we who will forfeit our eternal lives if we allow the "Lamanites" to overcome us.

Life is enough of a pressure cooker, as it is, without introducing unneeded additional stress. Many events "remain to (be) overcome through patience (in order to) receive a more exceeding and eternal weight of glory." (D&C 63:66). The Lord told Joseph Smith: "Be patient in afflictions, for thou shalt have many, but endure them, for, lo, I am with thee, even until the end of thy days." (D&C 24:8). Therefore, "In everything (we) give thanks, waiting patiently on the Lord," even in the face of destruction at the hands of fierce "Lamanites." (D&C 98:1-2). We "seek the face of the Lord always, that in patience (we) may possess (our) souls, and... have eternal life." (D&C 101:38).

King Lamoni's people were astonished at Ammon's performance because in the Land of Nephi the Lamanites had not yet learned how to draw upon the power of God. When the king's servants returned to the king and testified to him of the things they had seen Ammon do, "he was astonished exceedingly, and said: Surely, this is more than a man. Behold is this not the Great Spirit?" (Alma 18:1-2). They knew that God was capable of mighty works, but they had never considered that He might transfer His power to man so that he might also perform miracles. They did not know that they were capable of withstanding the onslaughts of even the most formidable bands of "Lamanites" roaming the land and trolling for unsuspecting shepherds tending their flocks.

(The) Last Judgment

"It was appointed unto men
that they must die; and after death,
they must come to judgment."
(Alma 12:27).

How will we be judged? John the Revelator "saw the dead, small and great, stand before God; and the books were opened; and another book was opened, which is the book of life. And the dead were judged out of those things which were written in the books, according to their works." (Revelation 20:12).

There will be a "Final Judgment" that is only the last in a long series of judgments. We were all judged in the pre-mortal existence, and we are judged throughout our mortal lives. Finally, at the Last Judgment, "our words will condemn us, yea, all our works will condemn us ... and our thoughts will also condemn us." (Alma 12:14). For "every idle word that men shall speak, they shall give account thereof in the day of judgment. For by thy words thou shalt be justified, and by thy words thou shalt be condemned." (Matthew 12:36-37).

Many years ago, the popular comedian Groucho Marx sued for 15 million dollars for breach of contract over obscene remarks he made 'off the record' and that were subsequently published. The plaintiff stated that he became ill when he read the final manuscript and needed medical attention because he was so shocked by its contents.

One day Jan received a telephone call from a ward member. After their conversation was completed, Jan replaced the receiver, but it didn't go all the way down, and the line was still open. Later, when the other person picked up the phone to use it again, she had instant access to an uninhibited conversation in our home. Fortunately, our family did not thereafter have to be like "the kings of the earth, and the great men, and the rich men, and the chief captains, and the mighty men, and every bondman, and every free man, [who] hid themselves in the dens and in the rocks of the mountains; and said to the mountains and rocks, Fall on us, and hide us from the face of him that sitteth on the throne and from the wrath of God." (Revelation 6:15-16).

"We are going to be judged out of the things written in books, out of the revelations of God, out of the temple records, out of those things which the Lord has commanded us to keep." (Joseph Fielding Smith, "Doctrines of Salvation," 2:200). Our own bodies will be the most accurate record, for "the work of the law (is) written in (our) hearts." (Romans 2:15). The record of our lives is "written not with ink, but with the Spirit of the living God; not in tables of stone, but in fleshy tables of the heart." (2 Corinthians 3:3). The individual "tells the story himself. That record is written by the man himself in the tablets of his own mind. That record cannot lie and will in that day be unfolded before God and angels, and those who sit as judges." (John Taylor).

"The book of life is the record of the acts of men as such record is written in their own bodies. It is the record engraven in the very bones, sinews, and flesh of the mortal body. That is, every thought, words, and deed has an effect on the human body; all these leave their marks, marks which can be read by Him who is Eternal as easily as the words in a book can be read." (Bruce R. McConkie, "Mormon Doctrine," p. 97).

By divine investiture of authority, Christ is the ultimate Judge, for "the Father judgeth no man, but hath committed all judgment unto the Son." (John 5:22). The Judgment Seat lies in a straight course. The gatekeeper there will not be Saint Peter, but Christ Himself, for "He employeth no servant there." (2 Nephi 9:41).

Today is the Day of Judgment. Continually, we speak, think, and act according to celestial, terrestrial, or telestial law. A barometer can be used to measure the direction in which weather is headed. Our faith in Christ, and the evidence of that faith, or our actions, point in the direction in which we are headed.

Each day of our lives, we are 24 hours closer to the Pleasing Bar of Christ, if we pattern our behavior after the Thirteenth Article of Faith. (See Moroni 10:34). "We believe in being honest, true, chaste, virtuous, and in doing good to all men. Indeed, we may say that we follow the admonition of Paul: We believe all things, we hope all things, we have endured many things, and hope to be able to endure all things. If there is anything that is virtuous, lovely, or of good report or praiseworthy, we seek after these things." "Happiness," after all, "is the object and design of our existence, and will be the end thereof, [at the Last Judgment], if we follow the path that leads to it, and this path is virtue, uprightness, faithfulness, holiness, and keeping all the commandments of God." (Joseph Smith).

"At the banquet of consequences, there will not be much that is satisfying at the table, unless I am able to bow my head (in reverence), not hang it [in shame], in the presence of God, who will be there." (Marion D. Hanks, "B.Y.U. Devotional Address," 10/3/67).

"Blessed is the man that walketh not in the counsel of the ungodly, nor standeth in the way of sinners, nor sitteth in the seat of the scornful. But his delight is in the law of the Lord, and in his law doth he meditate day and night. And he shall be like a tree planted by the rivers of water, that bringeth forth his fruit in his season; his leaf also shall not wither; and whatsoever he doeth shall prosper. The ungodly are not so: but are like the chaff which the wind driveth away. Therefore, the ungodly shall not stand in the judgment, nor sinners in the congregation of the righteous. For the Lord knoweth the way of the righteous: but the way of the ungodly shall perish. (Psalms 1:1-2).

Life is a Three Act Play

*"And this is the manner
after which they were ordained –
being called and prepared from the'
foundation of the world according to the
foreknowledge of God, on account of their
exceeding faith and good works; in the
first place being left to choose good
or evil." (Alma 13:3).*

Truly did Shakespeare observe: "All the world's a stage," for life is a Three Act Play. ("As You Like It," Act 2, Scene 7). We are willing participants in a drama whose script was written eons ago, long before the world was made. The First Act took place in the Pre-earth existence, where our Father nurtured spirit children by His side. The Second Act takes place on the earth, where we have come for a brief sojourn to have experiences that only mortality can offer, to develop faith, and to learn to be obedient. The Third Act will take place after physical death overtakes us and we are carried home.

That we participated in the First Act comes as a complete surprise to most of us, because a veil has been drawn across our memory of those events. We take for granted our participation in the Second Act, because it involves the "here and now." The Third Act fills us with trepidation, because of our inherent fear of the unknown. But when we comprehend the grammar of the gospel, we realize that "death is a mere comma, and not an exclamation point." (Neal A. Maxwell, "Ensign," 5/1983). It is not extinguishing the light, but rather putting out the lamp because the dawn has come, for "life is eternal, love is immortal, and death is only a horizon which is nothing save the limit of our sight." (Raymond W. Rossiter).

In our primeval childhood, as the curtain rose on the First Act, the sons and daughters of the Master Playwright tried out for individual parts with the enthusiasm and energy characteristic of budding actors who are full of confidence and expectation. He, in turn, bestowed upon each of us a role that was ideally matched to our budding talent, and that would maximize the potential to grow and develop as the play unfolded.

From the very beginning, the Master Playwright made each of us "accountable, as a steward over (our) blessings, which (He had) made and prepared for (His) creatures." For He "stretched out the heavens, and built the earth," for it was his handiwork, and all things therein are His. (D&C 104:13-14). Set design, lighting, sound, costuming, and a thousand other details (but no stunt doubles!) were perfectly choreographed so that the production would be ideal from the beginning. Nothing would be left to chance. In the words of one young actor by the name of Einstein, the Master "does not play dice with His creations."

The thespians excelled during that First Act, mastering life's lessons until no more could be learned, and when the curtain fell at its conclusion, so did their profound comprehension of the three acts of the Play. In the light of the morning of a new day, they awakened to the Second Act, and their mortal experience was as fresh and new to them as if it were their first encounter with the Play itself. This time, the wonders of mortality would fill a new stage whose breadth and depth and profundity would continually amaze them.

If they were fortunate enough to be born into homes where the script to the Play was available for careful study, the actors would awaken, as it were, from a dreamless sleep. The provided storyboard would help them to gradually come to an awareness of their divine potential, and it would kindle within them an acknowledgement that they had tools sufficient to the tasks at hand. There would come a point in time when the eyes of their understanding would snap into sharp focus, enlightening them to an expanded vision of themselves as sons and daughters of God, and even as white-hot sparks struck off His divine anvil. The flame of faith would ignite their resolve, define their determination, and focus their power to conduct themselves virtuously, in order to regain the glory of their former home at the conclusion of the Second Act of the Play.

For those who had retained no remembrance of the First Act, and who now saw themselves as strangers in a strange land, cast upon a foreign shore without map, compass, or G.P.S. coordinates to provide orientation, the Second Act would, nevertheless, be breathtaking in scope, and for many, it would simply be enough to enjoy its twists and turns, its nuances, and its capacity for character development. The highways and by-ways they would travel would be stimulating enough.

But those familiar with the script knew of the Master's reputation for theatrical encore, something that critics might mistake for frivolous repetition. In fact, sooner or later, there would be for each participant in the Play their own personal moment in the sun, when the light of understanding would illuminate their mind and confirm to their soul its divine potential.

Victor Hugo articulated this key feature of the play: "The nearer I approach the end," he realized, "the clearer I hear around me the immortal symphonies of the world that invite me. It is marvelous yet simple. For half a century, I have been writing my thoughts in prose, verse, history, drama, romance, tradition, satire, ode, and song. I have tried them all; but I feel that I have not said a thousandth part of that which is in me. The tomb is not a blind alley. It is an open thoroughfare. It closes in the twilight to open in the dawn. My work is only a beginning; my work is hardly above its foundation. I would gladly see it mounting forever."

Thus, every scene during the Second Act was designed to have profound significance. "The earth rolls upon her wings, and the sun giveth his light by day, and the moon giveth her light by night, and the stars also give their light, as they roll upon their wings in their glory, in the midst of the power" of the Master Playwright. "Behold, all these are kingdoms, and any man who hath seen any of the least of these hath seen (him) moving in his majesty and power." (D&C 88:45 & 47).

Thoughtful attention to each scene reveals its intrinsic importance, and when as actors we no longer trivialize outwardly insignificant story lines within the Play, we finally realize the truth of the statement of the Lead Character, Who said "then shall ye know that ye have seen me, that I am, and that I am the true light that is in you, and that you are in me." (D&C 88:50).

Even as that First Act unfolded, the Master Playwright saw that "among all (the players) there were many of the noble and great ones; and (He) saw these souls that they were good. And he stood in the midst of them, and he said: These I will make my rulers." (Abraham 4:22-23). That is to say, some would be given starring roles, while others were to be given less spectacular, but equally supportive, assignments. All would be given the gift to act independently within the sphere of their influence, to see if they would sustain the intent of the Play, its creative purpose, which would be to "bring to pass the immortality and eternal life of man." (Moses 1:39). Every participant would have opportunities to progress within the greater context of the Play itself.

In an evolutionary development of character, then, there came a time when it dawned upon the participants that "they who (kept) their first estate (should) be added upon; and they who (kept) not their first estate (should) not have glory in the same kingdom with those who (kept) their first estate; and they who (kept) their second estate (should) have glory added upon their heads for ever and ever." (Abraham 3:26). It would not be a question of maturation, but rather of generation. Every cast member would become a new creature, born again, as it were, to blossom with rediscovered talent whose vibrancy would contribute significantly to the accomplishment of the objectives of the Second Act.

But there was an unanticipated surprise built into in the storyboard created by the Master Playwright. The curtain that fell after the First Act was more impenetrable than thick fog, for not only was the vision of the players obscured, but also their very memory of the First Act. The memorization of their lines, their dress-rehearsals, their interactions with other cast members, and even the overall objectives of the play had been erased. Nevertheless, flashes of insight would provide tantalizing hints of their former life. As William Henry Wordsworth wrote: "Our birth is a sleep and a forgetting. The soul that rises with us hath had elsewhere its setting, and cometh from afar. Not in entire forgetfulness, and not in utter nakedness, but trailing clouds of glory do we come, from God, who is our Home." ("Ode: Intimations of Immortality").

As we now participate with awakening understanding in the Second of the Three Acts, we realize that no matter our individual circumstances, our lives have meaning and purpose that we can scarcely comprehend. "My life is but a weaving between the Lord and me," wrote the poet. "I cannot choose the colors. He worketh steadily. Oft-times, He weaveth sorrow, and I, in foolish pride, forget that He seeith the upper, and I, the underside. Not 'til the loom is silent, and the shuttles cease to fly, shall the Master Playwright unroll the canvas and explain the reasons why. The dark threads are as needful in the Weaver's skillful hand, as the threads of gold and silver, in the pattern He has planned." (Benjamin Malachi Franklin).

Joseph Smith gave the Three Act Play, a name, calling it The Plan of Salvation. He characterized it as "one of heaven's best gifts to mankind." (H.C. 2:23). Alma variously called it The Merciful Plan of the Father, The Plan of Mercy, The Plan of Redemption, The Plan of Happiness, and the ever-popular Great Plan of Happiness. (Alma 42:8). Whereas the most wildly successful play on Broadway closes its run after 10 or 15 years, the Plan of Salvation has been around since before our first parents attended opening night in the Garden in Eden. Uninterrupted performances will continue beyond mortality, (which is the Second Act), on into the eternities, where the Third Act will engage the attention of its participants forever.

If there were ever a play worthy of a Tony Award, it would be this one, for "the great plan of salvation is a theme which ought to occupy our strict attention." (Joseph Smith, "Teachings," p. 68). In this ultimate sense, it is clear that our "Father knows best!"

As members of the cast, we can better understand our roles if we engage others in the scenes we play, and if we are familiar with the other actors in the drama and empathize with the challenges they face in mastering the nuances of their own parts. In addition, we can better relate to the other participants, and they to us, if we see each other against the milieu of the First, Second, and Third Acts, namely, our pre-mortal (or pre-earth) life, mortality, and life after death. Knowledge of its intricacies, complexities, and sophistication are essential to our understanding of the Play itself, and to a comprehensive focus on its theatrical interpretation.

In clearly written, explicit, and unambiguous language, the script confirms that we are spiritual children of the Master Playwright and are lifetime card-carrying members of His Screen Actor's Guild. We are guaranteed ultimate recognition for our efforts, and within each of our contracts are terms specifying that we may, conditional upon our worthiness, not only receive perpetual royalties for our efforts, but also walk down a red carpet and climb the stairs onto center stage to receive before our friends and colleagues Lifetime Achievement Awards at the conclusion of the Second Act.

After all is said and done, our familiarity with the script answers the questions: "Who are these children coming down like gentle rain through darkened skies, with glory trailing from their feet as they go, and endless promise in their eyes? Who are these young ones growing tall, growing strong, like silver trees against the storm, who will not bend with the wind or the change, but stand to fight the world alone? These are the few, the warriors saved for Saturday; to come the last day of the (Second Act). These are they, of Saturday. These are the strong, the warriors rising in their might to win the battle raging in the hearts of men, on Saturday. Strangers from a realm of light, who have forgotten all - the memory of (the First Act) and the purpose of their call. And so, they must learn why they're here, and who they really are." (Doug Stewart, "Saturday's Warrior").

Annotations within the script shed new light on our relationship with the Master Playwright, Who is therein revealed as our Heavenly Father, for "by him, and through him, and of him, the worlds are and were created, and the inhabitants thereof are begotten sons and daughters of God." (D&C 76:24). Each of us participated "in the beginning with God" in the performance of that First Act. (D&C 93:29).

The Pearl of Great Price provides a glimpse into the cast meeting held before opening night of the Play. The setting was a Grand Council where "there stood one among them that was like unto God, and he said unto those who were with him: We will go down, for there is space there, and we will take of these materials, and we will make an earth whereon these may dwell; And we will prove them herewith, to see if they will do all things whatsoever the Lord their God shall command them." (Abraham 3:24-25). In other words, the members of the cast were to be proven with the earth itself. The stage on which the Second Act was to be choreographed would be part of an experimental theater in which cast members could be tried, tested, and proven.

It was necessary that we be familiar with each of the key participants in the Play. Our comprehension of the role of Lucifer/Satan in the Play had all to do with adversity and opposition, two conditions that would be essential to faithful adherence to the intent and purpose of the Play. These would be new concepts for us, basking as it were in the light of the Play and the Plan, at the very feet of the Master Playwright. Nevertheless, as our dialogue coach Lehi taught: "It must needs be that there is an opposition in all things." (2 Nephi 2:11). Else how could we enjoy happiness, if there were no misery? How could we experience life itself, if there were no death?

Lucifer read for a leading role in the Play, but that he rebelled against the Play itself is undisputed. "And I, the Lord God, spake unto Moses, saying, That Satan, whom thou hast commanded in the name of mine Only Begotten, is the same which was from the beginning, and he came before me, saying, Behold, here am I, send me, for I will be thy son, and I will redeem all mankind, that one soul shall not be lost, and surely I will do it, wherefore give me thine honor." (Moses 4:1).

Lucifer's interpretation of the Play was fundamentally different from that of the Master Playwright. It was a corrupted, pirated version of the play that was a counterfeit copy. Covertly, it was a work of fiction, but like good fiction, it must have been immensely entertaining and somewhat distracting. It was probably a "good read" that touched impressionable young minds with titillation, drawing on sensory experience that could only be imagined by neophyte actors with little stage experience. It was avant-garde, risqué, and trendy, with an allure of unconventionality, innovation, and an exciting sense of experimentation. It was good drama, in the sense that it left questions unanswered and doors ajar. Its Bohemian approach to life may have left its readers with a touch of exhilaration. Lucifer had been a "light bearer," with gaffers and key grips at his beck and call, but those who were dangerously drawn to him were as moths drawn to the fire, flirting with death in a deadly dance with the flickering flame.

As fiction often does, his manuscript flirted with the forbidden, anticipating a future connection to the qualities of carnality and sensuality that are always good selling points and crowd pleasers. His soundbites might have been appealing, but in the larger context they were meaningless poppycock. Exposed as a work of fiction, (for that is what it really was), it was deviously dangerous, fatally foolish, egotistically self-absorbed, nonsensically narcissistic, and it was inoperable to boot. Its fatal flaw was simple: it would not work. That it was, nevertheless, attractive to at least some of the Master Playwright's spirit children attests to the power of its ideology, however blemished it might have been.

Lucifer's hidden agenda was to usurp the power of the Master Playwright, but he lacked both the inherent skill and the requisite patience to step up the plate and pay the performance costs associated with greatness. He wanted the steak without the sizzle, and when he could not have it, he threw a temper tantrum, as gifted yet egocentric artists sometimes do, and became Satan. For the scriptures attest that "the devil was before Adam, for he rebelled against me, saying, Give me thine honor, which is my power; and also a third part of the hosts of heaven turned he away from me because of their agency. And they were thrust down, and thus came the devil and his angels." (D&C 29:36-38).

From this footnote in the Script, we know that as a consequence of Lucifer's disobedience, at least some of the Master Playwright's other spirit children also rebelled while yet in the opening scenes of the First Act of the Three Act Play. The process may have been more like a slow leak rather than a blowout. In their adolescent immaturity, they probably first refused to memorize their lines and then they showed up late for rehearsals. Perhaps they eschewed discipline on the set and were disruptive to the other cast members. They may have questioned the storyboard itself, thinking that it applied to others but not to themselves. They may have envied the roles of other cast members. Their murmuring may have begun with fault-finding that finally blossomed into the conspiratorial machinations of a full-blown rebellion.

Fortunately, their numbers were few. One part of the cast remained valiant in defending the vision of the Master Playwright. Another part did not actively disobey but perhaps with less fervency rallied somewhat abjectly around the Master. It was that disobedient third part of the host, whose preparation and practice during the First Act were of no value or benefit whatsoever, who were dismissed from the party and whose names were removed from the credits that would roll at the conclusion of the Third and Final Act of the Play. As a result, they were given other, less glamorous roles to play in the Second Act.

We know that we responded to the announcement of the Plan and Play with unbridled enthusiasm, for Job later reported we were there when "the foundations of the earth (were laid) ... when the morning stars sang together, and all the sons of (the Master Playwright) shouted for joy." (Job 38:4 & 7). We were present on opening night at the raising of the curtain on the First Act. As the overture played, it was met with our thunderous applause.

All the cast members were surely sitting side-by-side at that council. When assignments were given and temporal roles were allocated, some must have turned to friends seated nearby with pleading in their eyes that said: "Find me! You will find me, won't you?" It would be necessary to do so, because many are now only going through the motions of the Second Act with little or no understanding of the Play itself. They have lost the script, and without its guidance they have no comprehension, but wander to and fro as flotsam and jetsam on the sea of life. Alternative screenplays that are the centerpiece of summer-stock have been created in frantic attempts to explain the mysteries of life, but every wind of doctrine carries their devotees further from the truth. Many of these fictions are nothing more than short-lived sit-coms that will be cancelled after a season or two. Others are devious attempts at misinformation. "For there are many yet on the earth among all sects, parties, and denominations, who are blinded by the subtle craftiness of men, whereby they lie in wait to deceive and who are only kept from the truth because they know not where to find it." (D&C 123:12).

Even when they are at their very best, these self-appointed lights-unto-themselves lack the "star-power" of recognizable stage legend such as "Jesus Christ, whom the prophets testified shall come into the world. And behold, (said He) I am the light and the life of the world; and I have drunk out of that bitter cup which the Father hath given me, and have glorified the Father in taking upon me the sins of the world." (3 Nephi 11:10-11). It was His selflessness and sacrifice that set Him apart from, and above, all other members of the cast.

In mortality, myriad characters in the Play surround us, the Second Act grinds on relentlessly without interruption, and whether we recognize it or not, every social gathering is another cast party. Our earliest experiences are relatively uncluttered and unencumbered by soul-stains that corrupt the script. In fact, "heaven lies about us in our infancy. (But then) shades of the Prison House begin to close upon the growing boy, (even as) he beholds the light from whence it flows. He sees it in his joy. The youth, who daily farther from the east must travel, still is nature's priest, and by the vision splendid, is on his way attended. At length, the man perceives it die away, and fade into the light of common day." (Wordsworth, "Ode: Intimations of Immortality). As we gradually lose our perspective; we forget (if we ever knew in the first place) where we came from, why we are here, and where we are going.

But even that apparent misfortune may be a blessing in disguise. For a fall from grace became a critical and necessary part of our progression through the Second Act and on into the Third. "It came to pass that the devil tempted Adam, and he partook of the forbidden fruit, and transgressed the commandment, wherein he became subject to the will of the devil, because he yielded unto temptation." (D&C 29:40). And thus, it came to pass that, for all the sons and daughters of the Master Playwright, mortality the Second Act of the Three Act Play, became a time for men and women to prepare to meet God.

As the Master Playwright, He knew beforehand that in the day Adam partook of the fruit, his eyes would be opened, and he would possess a balanced perspective, for he would experience both good and evil. (See Moses 4:11). Master became Mentor, and the crucible of mortality became the experimental theater it was designed to be. The stage on which the Second Act would be played out, the universe itself, became "a machine for the making of Gods." (Henri Bergson, "The Two Sources of Morality and Religion").

Because of the Fall, we are subject to physical and spiritual death, the two fundamental certainties integral to the Second Act. So, the Atonement became a critically important component of the Play, allowing us to return to the presence of our Heavenly Father, to fulfill the mandate He gave concerning our participation in the Third Act. The Prophet Joseph Smith said: "We came to this earth that we might have a body and present it pure before God in the Celestial Kingdom." ("Teachings," p. 181). While we are here, we "should be anxiously engaged in a good cause, and do many things of (our) own free will, and bring to pass much righteousness; for the power is in (us), wherein (we) are agents unto (ourselves)." (D&C 58:27-28). We have the power to rely upon the merits of Christ, so that we might be called and chosen to participate fully in the Third Act of the Play.

We know that life does not end with physical death, for 'through the redemption which is made ... is brought to pass the resurrection from the dead. And the spirit and the body are the soul of man. And the resurrection from the dead is the redemption of the soul." (D&C 88:14- 16). For we are "spirit, the elements are eternal, and spirit and element, inseparably connected, receive a fullness of joy." (D&C 93:33). When we finally enter our third estate, when the curtain rises on the Third Act of the Play, we "shall be judged according to (our) works, and (we) shall receive according to (our) own works." (D&C 76:111).

The line in the fairy tale that goes "... and they all lived happily ever after," is not written into the Second Act. It is in the Third Act that it finally takes place. As Boyd Packer said: "Until you have a broad perspective of the eternal nature of the Plan, you won't make much sense out of the inequities of life. (But) when you know the Plan and the purpose of it all, even those things will manifest a loving Father in Heaven." (Kirkland Washington Stake Conference, 5/7/1995). All throughout the Second Act, we will be tested by trials and temptations, and we will make mistakes as a consequence of the Fall. We will be exhausted, at times, by the effort it takes to carry on. We will be bruised, but we will not be beaten. We will rise above our failures because of the love of the Savior and because of His Atonement. It is in the next Act that all the mysteries will be solved, there will be no more loose ends, all the pieces of the puzzle will be put in their proper place, the confusion tormenting us will be put to rest, and everything will be made right.

Even as we pass through mortality, it is the Third Act that competes for our attention, so it helps to have celestial signposts to guide us through the telestial traffic jams and conceptual cul-de-sacs that threaten to detour us from the strait and narrow way. That path leads to a parted veil that will allow us to pass onto the stage where the Third Act will play out. If we are true to eternally valid principles, expanding circles of opportunity will assure us of direct experience with the Master Playwright. We will trade the uncertain course adopted by individuals bound for the Telestial Kingdom for the certain reality of Celestial Surety. Then, the Third Act will be everything for which we have ever hoped and dreamed and worked. Our creative expression will receive ultimate divine fulfillment. Hans Christian Anderson said: "Our lives are fairytales waiting to be written by the hand of God." In the Play and the Plan, fairytales do come true.

When we engage our agency within the bounds the Master Playwright has set, we limit our options. If we choose the better alternative, we automatically have made the decision not to choose less attractive alternatives together with their attendant consequences. Those who suffer from compulsions have reached this condition because of repeated and successive re- acts until a point is reached where, as William James explained, "unlimited freedom leads to unlimited tyranny." Under these circumstances, the Play can morph into a nightmare, even a living hell. Instead, faithful participants in the Play are now and forever independent in that stage of development to which their decisions have led. Poised on the edge of forever, they need little incentive or external warrant to push off into the unknown. Heavy with anticipation, they eagerly look forward to the Third Act of the Three Act Play and to the final page of the script, where they will read of themselves: "Well done, thou good a faithful servant. Thou hast been faithful over a few things. I will make thee ruler over many things. Enter thou into the joy of thy Lord." (Matthew 25:21). And then, they will all live happily ever after.

As the Prophet Joseph
Smith explained to John Wentworth:
"No unhallowed hand can stop the work
from progressing. Persecutions may rage,
mobs may combine, armies may assemble,
and calumny may defame, but the truth
of God will go forth boldly, nobly, and
independently, until it has penetrated
every continent, visited every clime,
swept every country and sounded
in every ear, until the purposes
of God shall be accomplished
and the Great Jehovah shall
say the work is done."
(H.C. 4:540).

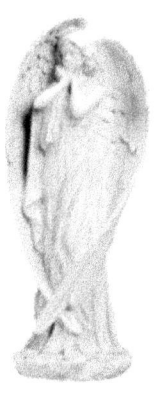

Life or Death: Mutually Exclusive?

(or part of the same process)

God "granteth unto men
according to their desire, whether it be
unto death or unto life; yea, I know that he
alloteth unto men, yea, decreeth unto them
decrees which are unalterable, according
to their wills, whether they be unto
salvation or unto destruction."
(Alma 29:4).

Under the best of circumstances, life is short, and yet all that is required may be accomplished. When the curtain closes on mortality, and one chapter in our lives comes to an end, another is just beginning. The life that begins with death is also essential to the Plan of Happiness. In a larger context, we see that the transgression of Adam and the consequent Fall were integral parts of the Plan, inasmuch as they gave Adam's posterity the opportunity to be born in to this world, to live, and to move on. Mortality, which was the consequence of his transgression, was not a punishment for sin any more than was death. "Adam fell that men might be, and men are that they might have joy." (2 Nephi 2:25).

The difficulty is for those who die in their sins, for "wo unto them, for their death is bitter." (D&C 42:47). Such are unprepared to meet God. (See Alma 48:23). Therefore, Alma gave the following counsel: "Do not procrastinate the day of your repentance until the end, for after this day of life, which is given us to prepare for eternity, behold, if we do not improve our time while in this life, then cometh the night of darkness, wherein there can be no labor performed." (Alma 34:33).

The two most important days of your life are the day you were born, and the day you find out why. When we truly understand the purpose of mortality, our lives will never again be the same. When we comprehend the grammar of the gospel, we realize that "death is a mere comma, and not an exclamation point." (Neal A. Maxwell). It is "not extinguishing the light, but rather putting out the lamp because the dawn has come," (Ramindraneth Tagore) for "life is eternal, love is immortal, and death is only a horizon which is nothing save the limit of our sight." (Raymond W. Rossiter).

The Savior counseled the saints that they should "live together in love, insomuch that thou shalt weep for the loss of them that die, and more especially for those that have not hope of a glorious resurrection." (D&C 42:45). "The only difference between the old and the young dying," taught Joseph Smith, "is one lives longer in heaven and eternal light and glory than the other, and is freed a little sooner from this miserable world."

Grief is good (good grief) when we mourn for those who have died in full faith and fellowship in the church and kingdom of God with the secure hope of eternal life. As Joseph Fielding Smith said: "They shall never die the second death or feel the torment of the wicked, when they come face to face with eternity."

However, mourning also describes the sense of loss that is felt by those who carry with them the burden of sin. When we mourn together, we help our brothers and sisters overcome the negative consequences of sin. To a great extent, our mourning can facilitate the process of repentance, so that the joy of forgiveness may be experienced.

The Savior taught: "Blessed are all they that mourn, for they shall be comforted." (3 Nephi 12:4). In one specific way, those individuals are truly blessed who have been baptized and have received the Holy Ghost, because the heaviest burdens that we have to bear are those that have to do with unresolved sin. Obedience to gospel principles having to do with repentance and forgiveness helps individuals to wash away the soul stains of sin, and to thereby live abundantly. Those who have been forgiven of their sins look forward with unbridled enthusiasm to life's experiences. They have no cause to mourn lost opportunities, the passing of loved ones, or their own proximity to the terminator line between this life and the next.

"If, in the pre-mortal existence, we looked forward to birth, which was the leaving of our Father and our eternal family, how much more we must have looked forward to death, which would be a later and essential step in coming home. Mortality is the prerequisite to immortality. It is by passing the tests and gaining the progress of this world that men obtain eternal life. Thus, death is as important as birth, and both are among the essential transitions in the Father's Plan for our salvation." (Richard Eyre, "The Birth That We Call Death," p. 37). Rightly did Jacob declare: "Death hath passed upon all men, to fulfil the merciful plan of the great Creator." (2 Nephi 9:6).

In fact, the anniversary of our death is the birth date of our immortal soul. It was this philosophical viewpoint that motivated Socrates, with cup of hemlock in hand, to declare: "Look death in the face with joyful hope, and consider this a lasting truth: "The righteous man has nothing to fear, neither in life, nor in death, and the gods will not forsake him."

Since we are spiritual beings having mortal experiences, it could be argued "life actually has no significance except as a preparation for the ultimate goal of death." (Carl Jung). If that is true, then "we ought not measure life by the hopes and enjoyments of this world, but by the preparation it makes for another – looking forward to what you shall be, rather than backward to what you have been." (Munger).

Victor Hugo declared: "The nearer I approach the end, the clearer I hear around me the immortal symphonies of the world which invite me. It is marvelous yet simple. For half a century, I have been writing my thoughts in prose, verse, history, drama, romance, tradition, satire, ode, and song. I have tried them all; but I feel that I have not said a thousandth part of that which is in me. The tomb is not a blind alley. It is an open thoroughfare. It closes in the twilight to open in the dawn. My work is only a beginning; my work is hardly above its foundation. I would gladly see it mounting forever."

"Our birth," wrote Wordsworth, "is but a sleep and a forgetting," while death is an awakening and a remembering. One's mortal life may be but a pre-natal experience, a marvelous prelude and dress rehearsal of a drama to be played out on a far larger stage where we may enjoy a more profound enjoyment of life.

Life's Greatest Questions

*"I know that God will give liberally
to him that asketh. Yea, my God will give me,
if I ask not amiss; therefore I will lift up my voice
unto thee; yea, I will cry unto thee, my God, the
rock of my righteousness. Behold, my voice
shall forever ascend up unto thee, my
rock and mine everlasting God."*
(2 Nephi 4:35).

"Even the humblest human beings, (Pope John Paul II) observed, are naturally philosophic, asking themselves such questions as "Who am I? Where do I come from, and where am I going?" Religious revelation provides answers to these questions, the pope acknowledges." ("Uniting Faith and Reason," "Time" Magazine. 10/26/1998)

Ever since the restoration of guiding principles under priesthood direction in the Last Days, members of the Lord's church have known of their origin and destiny as children of God. This knowledge has acted as a catalyst, inspiring them to be the best that they can. Those without the eternal perspective of the gospel, however, who define themselves only in the present tense, are much less inclined to make the kinds of decisions that reflect the character of the Father of their spirits, or to develop attitudes and habits that bring them into conformity with His nature. "Whenever individuals believe that there are no absolute values, there are, ultimately no sin and no crime. If there is no cosmic yardstick by which we can really measure things, how then can we punish people for falling short by feet or Inches?" (Neal Maxwell, "Freedom: A Hard Doctrine").

When men are caught up in the moment, they tend to be short-sighted, and can be insufferably self-indulgent, if only because they have no parameters to establish a foundation frame of reference, no mentors to monitor progress, no sustaining support of a sympathetic priesthood, no standard to which the may turn, no iron rod running straight and true to which they may hold, and no absolutes in which they can place their implicit trust. Ever learning and never coming to a knowledge of the truth, they grasp at straws, failing to recognize that nothing will keep them out of Zion more surely than that self-assurance that fails to acknowledge the influence of a power greater than themselves. Nothing will kill the guiding Spirit faster than absolute self-confidence that can all too easily mutate into unbridled pride, vanity, selfishness, and haughtiness.

When we build upon the shifting sands of secular humanism, where will our sanctuary be when the wind blows, and the rain beats down? To what safe harbor will we flee when the ocean of life is in turmoil? When we are tossed about as flotsam and jetsam, never coming to a knowledge of what is real, to what source will we look for the stability we so desperately seek, or for the answers to life's greatest questions that continually trouble our spirits?

When we submit to blind guides, we turn our backs to our Father in Heaven, refuse His grace and deny His power to change our lives. We dismiss the sacrifice of His Son, and esteem as a thing of naught His suffering. We close our minds to the soul expanding opportunities afforded by mortality. We decline His offer to experience the abundant life. We ignore His invitation to follow Him. We are deaf to His entreaty to find in Him every good thing. Living for the moment, we die as to the things of the Spirit. We paint ourselves into conceptual corners, limiting our creative talents to a few expressions of a narrow and confusing rational reality. Turning our backs to the light of the gospel, we think we have it all, when all that is before us is an illusion and a shadow and only a caricature of reality.

Understanding ourselves from an eternal perspective has many advantages. The Latter-day Saint view of life is multidimensional. "Whom say ye that I am?" the Savior asked Peter. When he realized that Jesus was in fact the Christ, the Son of the Living God, Peter was up and moving along on the pathway to personal re-discovery and self-actualization.

We live in eternity, as well as in time. The scriptures make a valiant effort to describe God's perspective, but it remains that man, trapped in time, can only indirectly appreciate the eternities. "Even now, time is clearly not our natural dimension," said Elder Neal A. Maxwell. "Thus it is that we are never really at home in time. Alternately, we find ourselves impatiently wishing to hasten the passage of time, or to hold back the dawn. We can do neither, of course. Whereas the bird is at home in the air, we are clearly not at home in time, because we belong to eternity. Time, as much as any one thing, whispers to us that we are strangers here. If time were natural to us, why is it that we have so many clocks and wristwatches?" ("B.Y.U. Speeches of The Year," 1979).

The world, though, would rather focus its attention and energy on "more pressing matters" of immediate urgency. When it prioritizes activities, it engages those tasks that concentrate on building, and obtaining, and accumulating, and securing its temporal well being, while the eternal welfare of the soul hangs in the balance. Wasting the precious time allotted to us, most of us spend our time far less wisely than we spend our money. "Twentieth Century Americans tend to fill space, as if what we have, what we are, is not enough. Being affluent, we strangle ourselves with what we can buy, things whose opacity obstructs our ability to see what is [really] there." (Gretel Erlich, "The Atlantic Magazine").

Ironically, we will ultimately find that time is an artificial measurement and that we come from a better realm where we were taught that success is measured by accomplishment, by the building of character, and by giving service. Religious recognition is just that, a re-knowing of what we have already learned. As Carol Lynn Pearson wrote: "Oh this world has more of coming and of going than I can bear. I guess it's eternity I want, where all things are, and always will be; where I can hold my loves a little looser; where, finally, we realize that Time is the only thing that really dies." (from "Optical Illusion").

Where did we come from?

Insight from the scriptures stirs our spirits and confirms the truth. "I am God," the Lord told Moses. "I made the world, and all men before they were in the flesh." (Moses 6:51). Moses then shared the wonderful news with Israel: "Ye are the children of the Lord your God." (Deuteronomy 14:1). Later, Jehovah explained to Jeremiah that he was a spirit child of God, saying: "Before I formed thee in the belly I knew thee; and before thou camest forth out of the womb I sanctified thee, and I ordained thee a prophet unto the nations." (Jeremiah 1:4-5)

Israel was asked to "remember the days of old ... when the most High divided to the nations their inheritance, when he separated the sons of Adam, he set the bounds of the people according to the number of the children of Israel." (Deuteronomy 32:7-8). Clearly, we lived before we were born, and were nurtured in the household of God. As the

Psalmist said, "all of you are children of the most High." (Psalms 82:6). The Preacher knew that, after mortal life, "shall the dust return to the earth as it was: and the spirit shall return unto God who gave it." (Ecclesiastes 12:7).

Latter-day revelation confirms that we were organized from uncreate intelligence, as spirit children of our Heavenly Father. "Man was also in the beginning with God." (D&C 93:29). He was "created before the world was made." (D&C 49:17). Emphatically, the Lord declared: "I was in the beginning with the Father, and am the Firstborn. Ye were also in the beginning with the Father." (D&C 93:21 & 23). His spirit children "received their first lessons in the world of spirits and were prepared (there) to come forth in the due time of the Lord." (D&C 138:56).

As Eliza R. Snow wrote: "O my Father, thou that dwellest in the high and glorious place. When shall I regain thy presence, and again behold thy face? In thy holy habitation, did my spirit once reside? In my first primeval childhood, was I nurtured near thy side? For a wise and glorious purpose, Thou hast placed me here on earth, and withheld the recollection of my former friends and birth. Yet, oft-times a secret something whispered, 'You're a stranger here,' and I felt that I had wandered from a more exalted sphere. I had learned to call t'ee 'ather, through thy 'pirit from on high, But until the key of knowledge was restored, I knew not 'hy.' In the heavens are parents single? No, the though makes reason stare! Truth is reason, truth eternal tells me I've a mother there. When I leave this frail existence, when I lay this mortal by, Father, Mother, may I meet you in your royal courts on high? Then, at length, when I've completed all you sent me forth to do, with your mutual approbation let me come and dwell with you." (Eliza R. Snow, "O My Father").

"'O My Father' has caused a deep turn in traditional New World Christianity. The concept of a literal Mother in Heaven has no antecedent. It opened up a view of woman's role in the eternities - motherhood on a celestial level. The words express plainly the existence of a mother goddess residing in the highest realms of eternity at the side of a Heavenly Father. Understanding all of the poem's lines has confirmed a greater, more exalted role for all women." ("Eliza," p. 58).

Eliza R. Snow herself explained "when we were first organized as a Relief Society, the Prophet used to attend all our meetings and give us instructions in regard to our present duties and also taught many things that transpired in our Spirit home. I got my inspiration from the Prophet's teachings. All that I was required to do was to use my poetical gift and give that eternal principle in poetry." ("Eliza," p. 58). President Wilford Woodruff declared: "That hymn is a revelation, though it was given unto us by a woman, Eliza R. Snow. There are a great many sisters who have the spirit of revelation. There is no reason why they should not be inspired as well as men." ("Discourses of Wilford Woodruff," p. 62).

Sister Snow drew from the same source that revealed to Abraham all "the intelligences that were organized before the world was; and among all these there were many of the noble and great ones; And God saw these souls that they were good, and he stood in the midst of them." (Abraham 3:22-23). These were counted among those who witnessed the foundation of the earth, and who "sang together [when] all the sons of God shouted for joy" after having the Plan of Salvation explained to them. (Job 38:4 & 7).

The Lord Himself told Joseph Smith how this creative process had taken place: "For by the power of my Spirit created I them; yea, all things both spiritual and temporal; First spiritual, secondly temporal." (D&C 29:31-32). "And every plant of the field before it was in the earth, and every herb of the field before it grew. For I, the Lord God, created all things, of which I have spoken, spiritually, before they were naturally upon the face of the earth." (Moses 3:5). Surely, then, "God [is] the God of the spirits of all flesh." (Numbers 16:22).

Luke understood that in God, "we live, and move, and have our being; as certain also of your own poets have said, For we are also his offspring." (Acts 13:28). Jude saw in vision a portion of Heavenly Father's spirit children, "the angels which kept not their first estate" because as spirit sons and daughters of God, they had been rebellious. They "left their own habitation" in consequence of their disobedience, and so "he hath reserved [them] in everlasting chains under darkness unto the judgment of the great day." (Jude 1:6). The Father of The Faithful confirmed "they who keep their first estate shall be added upon; and they who keep not their first estate shall not have glory in the same kingdom with those who keep their first estate." (Abraham 3:26).

But those who did keep their first estate live now "in the hope of eternal life, which God, that cannot lie, promised [to each of His children] before the world began," (Titus 1:2), "according to the promise of life which is in Christ Jesus." (2 Timothy 1:1). In this verse, Paul explained to Titus that the assurance was given during our pre-earth existence that those who continue an unbroken pattern of obedience during mortality should be saved because of the atoning sacrifice of the Lord Jesus Christ.

And yet, even with the benefit of latter-day revelation and teaching, man only dimly perceives his noble heritage, and sometimes finds it hard to accept the reality that he dwelt among the Gods before his mortal birth. In The Book of Mormon, the great prophet Alma was always ready to acknowledge that there were certain points of doctrine that were not completely clear to him. To Corianton, he declared: "Now these mysteries are not yet fully made known unto me; therefore, I shall forbear." (Alma 37:11). He felt that it was always better to keep one's opinion to oneself, rather than to speculate without the foundation of fact or specific revelation. Sometimes it is better to remain silent and be thought a fool, rather than to speak and remove all doubt. When counseling his son, Alma emphasized "there are many mysteries which are kept, that no one knoweth them save God himself." (Alma 40:3).

Without the spiritual enlightenment that comes from the scriptures and from personal revelation, the world does not understand that in the beginning, "the Gods formed man from the dust of the ground, and took his spirit … and put it into him; and breathed into his nostrils the breath of life, and man became a living soul." (Abraham 5:7). The body is composed of the corruptible elements of the earth, but the spirit comes from God, and quickens, or gives life to, the body. Thus, latter-day revelation confirms, "The spirit (which came from God) and body [which was formed of the earth] are the soul of man." (D&C 88:15).

As William Wordsworth wrote, "Our birth is but a sleep and a forgetting. The Soul that rises with us, our life's Star, hath had elsewhere its setting, and cometh from afar. Not in entire forgetfulness, and not in utter nakedness, but trailing clouds of glory do we come from God, Who is our Home." (Ode: Intimations of Immortality, from Recollections of Early Childhood). These inspiring words are true. We "are the sons of the living God." (Hosea 1:10). "The Spirit itself beareth witness with our spirit, that we are the children of God." (Romans 8:16). Within each breast, is the yearning to know: "Have we not all one father?" Each of us is prompted to ask the same question: "Hath not one God created us?" (Malachi 2:10). The answer rings loud and clear, and resonates within our heart: "In him we live, and move, and have our being [for] we are the offspring of God." (Acts 17:28-29). He is "the Father of all." (Ephesians 4:6).

Why Are We Here?

Knowledge of our pre-mortal existence sanctifies life, dignifies individual effort, rewards achievement, and validates progress as a worthy goal. The Lord opens our eyes to the wonder of creation and to the Plan of Salvation, so "that man should not counsel his fellow man, neither trust in the arm of flesh, but that every man might speak in the name of God the Lord, even the Savior of the world; that faith also might increase in the earth; that (the) everlasting covenant might be established; (and) that the fulness of (the) gospel might be proclaimed by the weak and the simple unto the ends of the world." (D&C 1:19-23).

Viewing life from the gospel perspective empowers parents to teach their children correct principles. "Faith," after all, "cometh by hearing, and hearing by the word of God." (Romans 10:17). In time, children will also have the responsibility to teach their own posterity in an unbroken pattern of obedience. "And again, inasmuch as parents have children in Zion, or in any of her stakes which are organized, that teach them not to understand" the doctrines of the church, "the sin be upon the heads of the parents ... And their children shall be baptized for the remission of their sins when eight years old, and receive the laying on of the hands. And th"y (that is, the children) shall also teach their children to pray, and to walk uprightly before the Lord." (D&C 68:25-28).

Our knowledge of the pre-earth existence and of the Plan of Salvation puts the highest priority on relationships that have been ratified by the authority of the priesthood of God. The Savior Himself explained to His Apostles "whatsoever thou shalt bind on earth shall be bound in heaven." (Matthew 16:19). "What therefore God hath joined together, let not man put asunder." (Mark 10:9). Thus sealed in the bonds of holy matrimony, a man and a woman may be "heirs together of the grace of life." (1 Peter 3:7).

"In the celestial glory," we are taught, "there are three heavens or degrees; And in order to obtain the highest, a man must enter into this order of the priesthood (meaning the new and everlasting covenant of marriage)." (D&C 131:1-2). The scriptures clearly teach that "whatsoever God doeth, it shall be forever." (Ecclesiastes 3:14). Ultimately, "neither is the man without the woman, neither the woman without the man, in the Lord." (1 Corinthians 11:11).

Celestial marriage is the diamond tiara of every family created by the power and authority of God. The gospel of Jesus Christ emphasizes the worth of the family, which is the highest expression of individual life. "No religion in the whole world stresses so much the meaning and worth of the individual. Individuality is the ultimate value; the church is the instrument for its fulfillment, and the family is the highest expression of individual life. This is the hardest for others to understand." ("Gospel Doctrine Lesson Manual").

Those who are familiar with The Church of Jesus Christ of Latter-day Saints, however, should not find it surprising that it teaches that the exaltation of families is the work and glory of God. They understand that our knowledge of the Plan of Happiness as it relates to families is a treasured "principle of intelligence [that] we attain unto in this life, [that] will rise with us in the resurrection." (D&C 130:18). The understanding of the profound significance of the family as a stabilizing influence on society is truly a pearl of great price.

As always, we may wisely exercise our agency, or we may repudiate our noble heritage, deny our birthright, forsake happiness, invite misfortune, and forfeit our potential as we wish. It is Christ's way for men to act for themselves. It is Satan's way for them to be acted upon. The choice is between liberty and eternal life, or captivity and spiritual death. Man is free to behave in ways that are contrary to the gospel and its laws, but unbridled freedom to do so eventually leads to tyranny. Men are free to choose, but they cannot choose to escape the consequences of their poor choices. When we voluntarily give up our agency to Satan, we find ourselves in the grip of bad habits, and sooner or later we will feel the heavy cords around our necks that will ultimately restrict our actions and drag us down to hell. It is very hard to break bad habits, precisely because we have given up our agency in order to acquire them. Heavenly Father operates differently. He always honors the eternal principle of agency. It is riskier this way, but it is the only avenue that will provide the conditions for meaningful progress. The "perfect law of liberty" requires that men be free according to the flesh so that they may be agents unto themselves. (James 1:25).

Rather than enslaving us in good habits, Heavenly Father uses the probationary state of mortality to repeatedly gives us the opportunity to recommit ourselves to covenants of obedience to true and eternal principles that free us from the shackles of sin and expand our opportunities for expression. Probation is a time of testing, or of putting to the proof some question, which in this case is: "Will men serve God, if given the opportunity?" "Will they recognize Christ as their Savior, and exercise faith unto repentance?" "Will they allow Him to help them to reach their potential?" "Will they recognize Him as the Father of their spiritual regeneration?"

Because life is a probation, church membership is vital to our spiritual well being. By demonstrating through the ordinances that we are willing to submit to the authority of Christ, our awareness is expanded and we are magnified as our potential is realized. By developing the qualities and attributes of our Heavenly Father and by "keeping our second estate," we are rewarded with glory after we pass beyond the veil separating mortality from eternity. In this sense, meaningful experiences that lead us to make correct choices on an open stage during mortality are essential to our eternal progression. What we do now does make a difference in regard to what opportunities will be available to us later on.

While we are here, one of the ways God helps us to grow is by providing us with experiences that teach us how to deal positively with the adversity that is a part of life. It would be wrong to assume that the more righteous we are, or just because we are members of the church, the less we will suffer. All suffer. God only promises that the righteous will be blessed with the strength to endure. The difference is that the wicked must suffer the consequences of sin, in addition to the suffering that is a natural part of mortal experience. Marion G. Romney once said: "If we can bear our afflictions with understanding, faith, and courage, we shall be strengthened and comforted and spared the torment which accompanies the mistaken idea that all suffering comes as a chastisement for transgression." (C.R., 10/1964).

Punishment follows sin naturally, but even this type of suffering can be a positive consequence when it is the very thing that brings a person to repentance. Truly, the Lord is merciful to His disobedient children, and His course is one eternal round. All of the experiences of mortality may work to our benefit. Lehi taught: "It must needs be, that there is an opposition in all things. If not so ... righteousness could not be brought to pass, neither wickedness, neither holiness nor misery, neither good nor bad." (2 Nephi 2:11).

Opposition is a necessary element of the mortal experience, and was present from the very beginning, but in the Garden of Eden before the Fall, Adam and Eve did not have true moral agency until after they had yielded to the enticements of Satan. Nevertheless, Adam was not deceived. His decision to partake of the forbidden fruit of the tree of the knowledge of good and evil was intelligently and consciously made, the result of a correct understanding of the requirements of the gospel Plan. One of the basic messages of the Restoration is that "Adam fell that men might be, and men are that they might have joy." (2 Nephi 2:25). The scriptures refer only to his "transgression," and the Second Article of Faith makes the specific distinction between it and man's "sins." Mortality, that was the consequence of his transgression, was not a punishment for sin. It was necessary "that the devil should tempt the children of men, or they could not be agents unto themselves; for if they never should have bitter they could not know the sweet. Wherefore, it came to pass that the devil tempted Adam, and he partook of the forbidden fruit and transgressed the commandment, wherein he became subject to the will of the devil, because he yielded unto temptation." (D&C 29:39-40). Life is short, and yet all that is required may be accomplished. The transgression of Adam gave his posterity the opportunity to be born into a world full of exciting alternatives, with hard choices to be made on a daily basis. In the end, after having had the experience that only mortality could provide, all must die in order to "fulfil the merciful plan of the Great Creator." (2 Nephi 9:6).

Because of the opposition that is integral to our experience, our eternal progression depends upon our willingness to take advantage of the Atonement. When the Fall of Adam is considered in conjunction with the mission of Christ as the Savior and Redeemer, it is clear that both are essential to the successful implementation of God's Plan of Eternal Progression for man. The Atonement was required to make the Plan operable for those who would participate in the theater of mortality. It nullifies the permanent effects of physical death, and gives everyone the opportunity to have the effects of spiritual death removed through repentance. The Atonement saves us from the effects of our sins by activating the Law of Mercy that mitigates for those who conform to its requirements the effects of the first Law that demands Justice.

We can only attain a fulness of joy in a personal, tangible, resurrection of the body that is essential to the successful operation of the Plan of Salvation. After all, "man is spirit, the elements are eternal, and spirit and element, inseparably connected, receive a fulness of joy." (D&C 93:33). Therefore, man was born to die, so that he might enjoy a glorious resurrection and receive a fulness of joy. Viewed from an eternal perspective, then, "death is not extinguishing the light; it is [only] putting out the lamp because the dawn has come." (Rabindraneth Tagore). "To a world spiritually illiterate, [faithful Latter-day Saints] give great lessons in the grammar of the gospel, including this one: death is a mere comma, not an exclamation point." (Neal A. Maxwell). "Life is eternal, love is immortal, and death is only a horizon which is nothing save the limit of our sight." (Raymond Rossiter).

Heavenly Father has seen to it that those who have developed faith unto salvation "shall not taste of death, for it shall be sweet unto them." (D&C 42:47). "Thou shalt live together in love," explained the Savior, to the end that "thou shalt weep for the loss of them that die, [but] more especially for those that have not hope of a glorious resurrection." (D&C 42:45). Under the best of circumstances, when the gospel has defined the course and quality of one's journey through life, "the only difference between the old and the young dying, is one lives longer in he'ven and eternal light an' glory than the other, and is freed a little sooner from this miserable world." (Joseph Smith).

Heavenly Father's disobedient or undisciplined children, however, will be unprepared to be reunited with Him at the conclusion of their mortal sojourn. The Lord said of those who die without the hope of a glorious resurrection, "wo unto them, for their death is bitter." (D&C 42:47). In consequence of their disobedience while they yet live, they have no hope of forgiveness, progression, or salvation. Without hope, they "must needs be in despair, and despair cometh because of iniquity." (Moroni 10:22). When one thus droops in sin, it is like being at the Banquet of Consequences, where, when we go with our loved ones, "there will not be much that is satisfying at the table unless we are able to bow our heads in reverence, and not hang them in shame, in the presence of God Who will be there." (Marion D. Hanks, "Speeches of The Year," 10/3/1967).

The Savior taught: "Blessed are all they that mourn, for they shall be comforted." (3 Nephi 12:4). In one specific way, those individuals are truly blessed who have been baptized and have received the Holy Ghost, for the heaviest burdens of man have to do with unresolved sin. If we are sensitive to our feelings, mourning can help us to overcome the negative consequences of sin by facilitating the process of repentance, so that we may be blessed with the joy of forgiveness. In this way, when life's experiences bring us trials, if we are rooted deeply in gospel soil, the Lord may bless us with emotions that help us to maintain an eternal perspective. This can ennoble even the most difficult moments. Obedience to the gospel principles of repentance and forgiveness helps individuals to break free of those shackles that limit progress, and thwart the chance to live abundantly. Those who have been forgiven of the'r sins may look forward with great enthusiasm to life's experiences. They have no cause to despair when they mourn.

Grief is also good when we mourn for those who have died in full faith and fellowship in the church, with the secure hope of eternal life in the Kingdom of God. As Joseph Fielding Smith said: "They shall never die the second [spiritual] death, and feel the torment of the wicked, when they come face to face with eternity." Death is only bitter for those who are unprepared to meet God.

Spiritual death is alienation from the Spirit of God, and occurs when one dies "as to things pertaining unto righteousness." (Alma 12:16). The first individual spiritual death occurs when one commits sin after the age of accountability. In the scriptures, this is called "the first spiritual death." (D&C 29:41). One can be spiritually born again through the cleansing action of the Holy Ghost, after repentance and baptism of water and the Spirit. Therefore, one of life's greatest obstacles to the enjoyment of eternal life, that of spiritual death, can be overcome by the simple act of baptism which follows faith.

Then there is "the second spiritual death," that is an eternal separation from the presence of God, and that occurs after one passes from mortality without having participated in the ordinances of the Priesthood, and when one then willingly declines the vicarious work performed on one's behalf in the temple of the Lord.

And so, we come full circle. The two most important days of your life are the day you were born, and the day you find out why. "When a baby is born, and as we wait with those who are dying, we brush against the veil, as greetings and goodbyes are said almost within earshot of each other. In such moments, this resonance with realities on the other side of the veil is so obvious that it can be explained in only one way." (Neal Maxwell). Mortality is only one act of the great drama. When we have played out life's experiences, it will be time to move on to the next stage of our eternal development.

One of the most mind and soul expanding messages of the Restoration is that we have potential to become as our Father in Heaven. "When the prophet Enoch was called, he wondered why and said, 'I ... am but a lad, and all the people hate me; for I am slow of speech.' (Moses 6:31). Yet something in Enoch whispered to him that in responding to God the test is not our capacity, but our availability. Consequently, Enoch kept the commandments and trusted in the Lord's vision of his possibilities, going on to become the builder of the greatest city of all time ... And it all began with a young man who was less than sure of himself." (Neal Maxwell, "New Era, 5/81, p. 4).

The gospel gives us the power to make a difference, no matter what our station in life may be. "When we are dead," wrote the Fourteenth Century Sufi poet, "seek not our tomb in the earth, but find it in the hearts of men." "Mormons are like artichokes," observed a latter-day journalist. "At first encounter, you either like them or you don't, but those who have unfavorable first impressions often find that once the outer layers are peeled away, both Mormons and artichokes are most likable. In fact, most people who get to know Mormons become their friends. And a little objective research on Mormon beliefs reveals that, except for a few doctrinal differences, these people who call themselves Latter-day Saints are just like the rest of us ... very human beings." ("The Boston Globe," 1967), But they are human beings with a common vision, motivated by zeal and empowered by the gospel to reach their potential as sons and daughters of God, trailing clouds of glory as they make the journey from their former home through the learning laboratory of mortality.

Where are we going?

Since the family of man has the potential to reach a common eternal destination, the Lord's church is oriented to missionary work so that all might have equal opportunity while yet in mortality. His servants do not preach and teach only to make the lives of people better. They baptize so that all might be saved in the I of God. It may seem that, as we look around, the world has gone mad, but the church remains an island in the storm, and the gospel of Jesus Christ provides a refuge from the uncertainties of life. It speaks a language of stability, direction, and purpose to those who are unsure, uncertain, and hesitant. Of the Lord's children, it might be said: "The stars fade away, the sun himself grows dim with age, and nature sinks in years; But thou shalt flourish in immortal youth, unhurt amidst the war of elements, the wreck of matter, and the crash of worlds." (Joseph Addison, "Cato," Act 5, Scene 1).

Longfellow lamented: "Tell me not, in mournful numbers, life is but an empty dream! For the soul is dead that slumbers, and things are not what they seem. Life is real. Life is earnest! And the grave is not the goal. Dust thou art, to dust thou returnest was not spoken of the soul. Not enjoyment, and not sorrow, is our destined end or way; but to act, that each tomorrow finds us farther than today. Lives of great men all remind us we can make our lives sublime, and departing, leave behind us footprints on the sands of time. Let us then be up and doing, with a heart for any fate; still achieving, still pursuing. Learn to labor, and to wait."

Paul asked the question, "If we are no more servants, but rather sons of God, then does it not follow that we are heirs of all that God has through His Son? (Galatians 4:7). We are "heirs of God, and joint heirs with Christ." (Romans 8:17). The purpose of life is to provide a way for the family of man to find eternal happiness. This, said Joseph Smith, "is the object and design of our existence, and will be the end thereof if we follow the path that leads to it. And this path includes faith, virtue, uprightness, and keeping all the commandments of God."

Paul assured the Corinthian Saints that if they remained steadfast, in no matter what circumstances they might find themselves, no matter what cards they might have been dealt in life, in no matter what twist of fate they might think themselves trapped, ultimately, all things would be theirs, for they were "Christ's, and Christ is God's." (1 Corinthians 3:21-23). Our hope of a glorious resurrection hinges on this truth, however dimly it may be perceived. For, although "it doth not yet appear what we shall be, (nevertheless) we know that, when he shall appear, we shall be like him, for we shall see him as he is." (1 John 3:2).

Joseph Smith taught that "God Himself, finding He was in the midst of spirits and glory, because he was more intelligent, saw proper to institute laws whereby the rest could have a privilege to advance like Himself." ("Teachings," p. 364). Eternal life is not thrust upon those who are unprepared or unacquainted with God and His ways, or who are unwilling to make sacrifices today to secure blessings tomorrow. Mortality was designed to be a life-long project to give everyone the opportunity to mold their nature to more closely resemble God's. When that happens, we shall be "caught up to the third heaven," as was Paul. (2 Corinthians 12:2). Then we shall "sit with [God] in (His) throne." (Revelation 3:21). We shall have assumed both His image and His likeness.

When man receives the image of the Lord in his countenance, his face will reflect the light of Christ. When he experiences a mighty change in his heart, the inner man will be transformed. The world seeks change from the outside, and fails miserably. The gospel changes man from the inside, and succeeds brilliantly. Man is thus created to reach his potential in both the image and likeness of God his Father.

As we pass through mortality and exercise our agency, it helps to have celestial signposts to guide us through the telestial traffic jams and conceptual cul-de-sacs that threaten to detour us from the strait and narrow way. The expanding circle of opportunity afforded by obedience to gospel principles assures us of direct experience with the perfect law of liberty. Thus, we trade the uncertain course adopted by individuals bound for the telestial kingdom for the certain reality of celestial surety.

When we engage our agency within the bounds the Lord has set, we limit our options. If we choose better alternatives, we automatically have made the decision not to accept less attractive consequences. Faithful Latter-day Saints are independent in that stage of development to which their decisions have led. In the best of circumstances, "the universe is a machine for the making of Gods." (Henri Bergson, "The Two Sources of Religion & Moorality"). After the completion of their mortal experiences "shall the righteous shine forth as the sun in the kingdom of their Father." (Matthew 13:43).

The true doctrine of Christ is simply that, in order to be saved in the C*lestial Kingdom, all men, everywhere, must repent and believe in Him. Then they must be baptized according to the ordinance authorized by the Savior Himself, and performed by His servants who have been ordained to that ministry. As Jesus Christ taught the Nephites: "Whoso believeth in me, and is baptized, the same shall be saved; and they are they who shall inherit the kingdom of God." (3 Nephi 11:33).

Those who do not believe in the power of God unto salvation deny His grace, and if they do not yield to His Spirit, they will not be able to continue their eternal progression. Therefore, they will be damned. This is not some arbitrary program established by man, with corollaries, footnotes, and exceptions to the rule. It is the Plan of Salvation, spelled out for man in the Dispensation of The Fulness of Times. It is His ordained Plan. It is a perfect Plan, and is all the more beautiful because of its simplicity. It is clearly established and clarified in the Bible and its companion scriptures so that there will be no disputations among the people concerning its validity or its accessibility.

Life Support and Decisions

(Life's Important Decisions).

"The Lord spake unto my father,
yea, even in a dream, and said unto him:
Blessed art thou Lehi, because of the things which
thou hast done; and because thou hast been faithful and
declared unto this people the things which I commanded tee,
behold, they seek to take away thy life. And it came to pass
that the Lord commanded my father, even in a dream, that
he should take his family and depart into the wilderness.
And it came to pass that he was obedient unto the
word of the Lord, wherefore he did as the Lord
commanded him." (1 Nephi 2:1-3).

The medical term "life support" applies broadly to any therapy that is employed to sustain the life of a patient who is critically ill or injured. Intensive care is often required to provide life support, and sound clinical judgment on the part of primary care providers is critical to its success.

Our spiritual health is also dependent upon life support and decisions. Its maintenance requires that when we are faced with life support and decisions, or life's important decisions, we follow a path that will solidify our well-being. For example, when confronted by a difficult choice, Nephi unhesitatingly declared: "I will go and do the things which the Lord hath commanded." (1 Nephi 3:7). Likewise, Joshua drew a line in the sand and challenged Israel: "Choose you this day whom ye will serve … but as for me and my house, we will serve the Lord." (Joshua 24:15).

Gordon B. Hinckley told the youth of the church how to face Life's Important Decisions. He said that in their hearts, they should be grateful, be smart, be clean, be true, be humble, and be prayerful. ("A Prophet's Counsel and Prayer for Youth," "Ensign," 1/2001). Thus, would they receive the guidance they needed for Life Support and Decisions.

In France in the Middle Ages, the heir to the throne was known as the Dauphin. In the reign of King Louis, unscrupulous and crafty counselors tried every means to corrupt him to thereby render him incapable of inheriting the throne. In all their attempts they were unsuccessful. Finally, in resignation, they asked him: "How is it that with all our enticements we were unable to compromise your high standards?" His reply was simple: "I am a King's son." He had preplayed before he replayed, and had already made Life's Important Decisions.

When Joan of Arc was at the stake, she was given the opportunity to obtain her freedom by denying what she believed. Instead, she declared: "I know this. Every man gives his life for what he believes. Every woman gives her life for what she believes. Sometimes people believe in little or nothing and give their lives for little or nothing. One life is all we have, and we live it as we believe in living it, and then it is gone. But to surrender what you are and live without belief is more terrible than dying, even more terrible than dying young." (Maxwell Anderson, "Joan of Lorraine," Act 2, Interlude 3). Her character provided the Life Support to stand by her Decisions.

Both the Dauphin and Joan of Arc had prepared themselves so that when they met temptation, they automatically turned to the right. They were not about to get stuck in a telestial traffic jam that would detour them from celestial sureties. Neither was the young man who found himself in an interview for employment when his prospective employer asked him: "If I hire you, can I count on you to be honest?" The young man looked him in the eye and quickly replied: "You can count on me to be honest whether you hire me or not!"

Life support and decisions and life's important decisions are best made in an atmosphere free of self-defeating behaviors, those narrowly defined perceptual prisons whose walls are reinforced with the razor-wire of limiting beliefs, those stories we tell ourselves that cause us to sabotage our own best efforts. They can damage our self-esteem, diminish our abilities, compromise our progress, and hold us back from achieving our goals. Although all of us have SDBs and limiting beliefs, everyone has the power to defeat them. We are all children of God, and in the best of circumstances, we have been sent to our earthly homes with kind and loving parents who will teach us to listen to the quiet whisperings of the Spirit to lead us, guide us, and walk beside us to help us to find the way back home. Under ideal circumstances, we may be taught all that we must do to live with God someday. Because we have such great potential, our needs are great. Therefore, we must learn to understand the words of life while we still have the resiliency and capacity to make positive changes. Surely, if we do this, rich blessings are in store. We just need to learn to do the will of God so that we can live with him again, for His promises are sure. Celestial glory will be ours, if we but endure. (Adapted from Naomi Randall, "I am a Child of God," 1957). The gospel will provide the answers we need when life's important decisions need to be made. It is the key to the life support and decisions that lead to happiness.

Light

"There is not enough darkness in
all the world to put out the light
of even one small candle."
(Anonymous).
Graphic
"Whatsoever
is light, is good."
(Alma 32:35).

The Savior taught: "The light of the body is the eye. If, therefore, thine eye be single, thy whole body shall be full of light ... and there shall be no darkness in you, and that body which is filled with light comprehendeth all things." (3 Nephi 13:22 & D&C 88:67). He continued: "But if thine eye be evil, thy whole body shall be full of darkness." (3 Nephi 13:23). Elsewhere, He taught: "That which is of God is light; and he that receiveth light, and continueth in God, receiveth more light; and that light groweth brighter and brighter until the perfect day." (D&C 50:24). Its contrast, such as the influence of Satan that gripped Joseph in the Sacred Grove before his deliverance illustrates just how overwhelming intense darkness can be. He wrote: "I was seized upon by some power which entirely overcame me, and had such an astonishing influence over me as to bind my tongue so that I could not speak. Thick darkness gathered around me, and it seemed to me for a time as if I were doomed to sudden destruction ... I was ready to sink into despair and abandon myself to destruction - not to an imaginary ruin, but to the power of some actual being from the unseen world." (J.S.H. 1:15-16). We are reminded of those who lost their way in mists of spiritual darkness in Lehi's Vision of The Tree of Life. (See 1 Nephi 8:23).

To those Nephites who listened to His voice in the midst of darkness that enveloped the land after the crucifixion, the words of Christ must have been powerful indeed, as He declared: "I am the light and the life of the world." (3 Nephi 9:18). "I have sent mine everlasting covenant into the world," He told Joseph Smith "to be a light to the world." (D&C 45:9). His light is a beacon guiding the faithful with unerring accuracy to the safe haven and sheltering sanctuary of the gospel.

In the cold contrast of darkness, when people refuse the gospel, their "land will eventually become desolate, forlorn, and forsaken," as nature withholds her bounties. (Brigham Young, "Millennial Star." 38:344). If we alienate ourselves from God, all nature becomes our enemy. In the days of Enoch, because of the wickedness of the people, when he spoke the word of the Lord by the power of the priesthood, "the earth trembled, and the mountains fled, even according to his command; and the rivers of water were turned out of their course; and the roar of the lions was heard out of the wilderness." (Moses 7:13).

Joseph Fielding Smith cautioned the Saints: "We should wake up to the realization that it is because of the breaking of covenants, especially the new and everlasting covenant, which is the fulness of the gospel as it has been revealed, that the world is to be consumed by fire and few men left. Since this punishment is to come at the time of the cleansing of the earth when Christ comes again, should not Latter-day Saints take heed unto themselves? We have been given the new and everlasting covenant, and many among us have broken it, and many are now breaking it; therefore, all who are guilty of this offense will aid in bringing to pass the destruction in which they will find themselves swept from the earth when the great and dreadful day of the Lord shall come." ("Deseret News," 10/17/1936).

The light and the life of the world is "Jesus Christ, the Son of God, who was crucified for the sins of the world." (D&C 35:2). He is eternal, and His influence extends from a land before time, through our development as spiritual children of our Heavenly Father, on into mortality, and finally to our reunion with Him in the resurrection. As far as we are concerned, His light has always existed. The attributes that define His flawless character focus and clarify His light as would a magnifying glass. We model our behavior after the faultless and unblemished character of Jesus Christ, who in every quality is One with the Father, and who was the mortal expression of His Divine Parents. Because He brought light into a world enshrouded in spiritual darkness, Mormon was prompted to declare: "In Christ there should come every good thing." (Moroni 7:22).

The Light of the world is a Type of completeness. There exists between Him and His Father a physical and spiritual rapport that only true believers can appreciate. Through a bond that is made possible by the Holy Ghost, we may become one in a spiritual sense that is as real as it is intangible. The Priesthood facilitates this unity by physically administering gospel ordinances in the temple, where we enter into the patriarchal order of celestial marriage and are organized into eternal family units. There, we learn temporal and spiritual principles of government and make covenants to consecrate our time and talents to the church and kingdom, and to lend our efforts to the preparation of the earth for the millennial reign of Jesus Christ.

Without the shining example of the House of the Lord, civilizations become empty shells and structures of custom and convenience only, illuminated by the flickering candlelight of superstition and magic. The luminosity of the Lord encourages us to free ourselves from the bondage of sin The warm glow that emanates from a Zion society that has received the blessing of the temple is simply the result of a spiritual transformation in the lives of those who bask in the celestial light of the Lord.

To make sure that the Saints would be able to "chase darkness from among (them)," the Lord reiterated, "He that is ordained of God and sent forth, the same is appointed to be the greatest, notwithstanding he is the least and the servant of all." (D&C 50:25-26). "Woe shall come unto the inhabitants of the earth," said the Lord, "if they will not hearken unto my words." (D&C 5:5). "Wo" is a condition of deep suffering that is the result of misfortune and affliction, or grief and calamity. Our lives are days of probation that is a time of testing, or of putting to the proof our declared values. The gospel of "Repentance is (always available) unto them that are under condemnation and under the curse of a broken law." (Moroni 8:24). If we successfully negotiate our experiential trials, we will escape the ordained consequences of disobedience. Therefore, the Lord told Joseph Smith that it would be critical that "hereafter, (he should) be ordained and go forth and deliver (His) words unto the children of men," that the gospel might be written in their hearts. (D&C 5:6). The light would come from within, activating an internal moral compass to unerringly guide them home.

They would possess all that was necessary for their progress, and they would have at their disposal "the life and the light, the Spirit and the power, sent forth by the will of the Father through Jesus Christ, his Son." (D&C 50:27). They would be given "dominion, and glory, and a kingdom, that all people, nations, and languages, should serve" them.

(Daniel 7:14). They could attain such spiritual stature only if they were purified and cleansed from all sin in the refining light of the Savior of the world.

If we set the stylus of our compass on the process of purification, within the circle thus scribed will be the Sacrament, the Endowment, and the other ordinances driven by the engine of the priesthood and given vitality by the Light of the world. In these ordinances is His power manifest, and our active participation triggers a cleansing or sanctification that allows us to ask God in complete confidence for our desired blessings. In such a state of innocence and holiness, in the dazzling light of truth, the nature of evil abroad on the earth will be plainly manifest, and we shall be given "power over that spirit." (D&C 50:32). We will be given the means to lay bare their true nature of evil, "not with railing accusation … neither with boasting nor rejoicing," but with the measured response expected of the Lord's anointed. (D&C 50:33).

"Giving heed and doing these things" brings us into harmony with the force that powers celestial glories. When that happens, the dynamos spring into operation with the promises of the omnipotent Lord: "The kingdom is given you of the Father, and power to overcome all things … for your sins are forgiven you." (D&C 50:35-36). With the unlimited energy source of God at his disposal, Parley P. Pratt was thus commanded to "go forth among the churches and strengthen them by the word of exhortation." (D&C 50:37). With not only the authority of the priesthood, but more importantly its power, he was to preach the gospel, which involves introducing the principles, truth, and concepts pertaining to the Plan of Salvation. After this introduction, he was to teach the principles, or bring them into focus, and illustrate them in a meaningful way. Then, he was to expound, or enlarge upon the principles, to expand the understanding of the listener. Next, he was to offer exhortation, to instill in them the desire to incorporate the principles into their own lives, to encourage ownership through personal witness or testimony, and to validate the worth of the principles. They were to be brought into the Light.

The gift of God's grace is granted unto us proportionately by our conformity to a standard of personal righteousness that is part of His Merciful Plan. Thus, we are commanded to "grow in grace" (D&C 50:40), until we have been sanctified and justified "through the grace of our Lord and Savior Jesus Christ." (D&C 20:30-32). It is in this sense that Nephi declared that we are saved by grace only "after all we can do," which is primarily to repent of our sins. (2 Nephi 25:23).

Light and Darkness

"Wo unto them that call
evil good, and good evil, that
put darkness for light, and light
for darkness, that put bitter for
sweet, and sweet for bitter."
(2 Nephi 15:20).

In Judeo-Christian thought, there is a fundamental difference between "light" and "darkness." Perhaps it is easier to relate to these religious metaphors because they are polar opposites. Light and truth, after all, forsake the evil one, and there is something about mists of darkness that leave us with a deep sense of foreboding.

In nature, with very few exceptions (near geo-thermal vents deep in the ocean, for example) life is ultimately and entirely dependent upon light. Photosynthesis is at the foundation of all life on earth and is made possible by sunlight. Growing seasons, harvest times, mating seasons, and mighty migrations are predicated upon the length of days and hours of sunlight. The physical constants of light and darkness determine the very rhythms and cycles of life, and still, we try to squeeze yet another hour or two of light into the days of spring and summer, euphemistically characterizing our artificial manipulation as "daylight savings time," in a feeble attempt to hold back the night.

The alternative is figuratively and literally chilling. Our hearts are troubled at the thought of nuclear winter or volcanic ash blocking out the sunlight for months or years, as we contemplate with dread the terrible consequences of a seemingly endless twilight. For it is only in light that "we live and move and have our being." (Acts 17:28). Conversely, it is only in "the night of darkness, (that) there can be no labor performed." (Alma 34:33).

In everyday life, we are familiar with light and its opposite. We take for granted that light can easily dispel darkness and unconsciously witness the miracle many times a day. But we rarely, if ever, stop to wonder: "Why cannot darkness dispel light?" "Why does it work in only the one direction, and not the other way around?" Like the arrow of time, light marches forward to dispel darkness and fill the immensity of space. From every perspective, we can see the shadows only if we turn our backs to the light.

Perhaps this is why we can bring light into a darkened room, but it is impossible to bring darkness into a lighted room. With a cognitive leap of faith, we realize that happy thoughts and experiences do, in fact, brighten our day, our faces really do light up when we see loved ones, and we really are light upon our feet when we are engaged in enjoyable activities. It is no coincidence that Angel food cake is light in color, as opposed to Devil's food cake, or that we don't feel guilty about eating ice cream, whipped cream, or toppings that are characterized as "light."

When we are expecting a loved one to return home late in the evening, we "leave the light on" for them. When our small children need comforting reassurance at bedtime, we turn on a night-light. When we receive understanding, we are "enlightened." When we manage to reduce our stress level, we have "lightened up." At the other end of the spectrum, and for the same metaphysical reasons, an "enlightened" person can sense spiritual darkness. When evildoers work their dark needs, their benighted countenances reflect a deep sense of foreboding. We know by sad experience that the shadow of sin drives away the spirit of light.

What is it that draws us toward light rather than to darkness? We have learned that Seasonal Affective Disorder (whose acronym is SAD) is best treated by healthy doses of sunlight. Even in nature, flowers protectively close their beautiful petals at nightfall, and then joyously open them again when they are warmed by early morning sunbeams.

Familiar expressions affirming the spiritual security afforded by light consistently find their way into our lexicon and into our collective consciousness. Some expressions roll off our lips: "I see the light!" But we are never prompted to exclaim: "I see the darkness?" We say: "A new dawn has arisen," and not: "A new night has descended upon us." We seek enlightenment with an inner yearning that is at once indescribable and intangible. It begs credulity to think that we could illuminate our minds with negative thoughts and feelings, while it is a given that positive thoughts are sometimes so dazzling that our minds are literally flooded with understanding. It is light that sweeps away the cobwebs of darkness, and not the other way around.

We receive flashes of inspiration, and exclaim: "A light bulb went off in my brain." It would never occur to us to say: "The lights went out in my brain." When Albert Einstein formulated the equations relating to his Theory of Relativity, he was moved to exclaim: "A splendid light has dawned on me." When we are flushed with enthusiasm, it is as if we are inspired by "a thousand points of light." No amount of darkness could ever give us similar encouragement. In fact, when our brains cease to function, all neurological electrical activity grinds to a halt. The reassuring waves of light on the oscilloscope are replaced by a "flat line," a sober reminder of "death, the undiscovered country, from whose bourn no traveler returns." (Shakespeare, "Hamlet," Act 3, Scene 1).

Iniquity itself is correlated with darkness, and evildoers work their deeds under its cover. It is in the shadows that standards are often relaxed, and it is no wonder that the worst crimes against persons and property are often committed in "the dead of night."

Yet, when these felonious acts are so brazen, so offend our sensibilities, and are so counter-intuitive to civility, we characterize them as having been committed in "broad daylight." It is in the light of day that unpardonable sins are committed, when there is no excuse, when contrary feelings so overwhelm the transgressor that he can declare that the sun does not exist while at the same time basking in its noontime brilliance.

In fact, the period of time in the history of the world when individual and collective creative thought was virtually extinguished is even today called "The Dark Ages." William Manchester characterized these times as "the densest of the medieval centuries. The portrait which emerges is a mélange of incessant warfare, corruption, lawlessness, obsession with strange myths, and an almost impenetrable mindlessness." ("A World Lit Only by Fire," p. 3).

For nearly a thousand years, even as the sun rose in the morning and set in the evening, often in spectacular heavenly theatrical encore, as the seasons came and went, as light made every effort to penetrate hearts and minds, there was still an overwhelming and almost universal stupor of thought. Isaiah prophetically foresaw that epoch, when he wrote, "darkness shall cover the earth, and gross darkness the people." (Isaiah 60:2). Paul knew it would end, but cautioned: "Let no man deceive you by any means: for that day (of enlightenment) shall not come, except there come a falling away first" into a period of dark apostasy. (2 Thessalonians 2:3).

When we turn our heads upward, we see in the brightly illuminated stars a trail left behind by God to help us find our way back to our heavenly home. They were set in the sky by our Father to guide us, as sparkling multi-faceted diamonds, to the infinite reaches of eternity. On a moonless night, starlight provides enough visibility for us to maintain our bearings, and as it shines on our hopeful countenances, we remember Bergson's metaphor that "the universe is a machine for the making of Gods." ("Two Sources of Morality and Religion").

The night of darkness that lasted nearly a millennium was followed by the Renaissance, that was a rebirth which paved the way for an Age of Enlightenment. Once again, light banished darkness and the world blossomed with new ideas and unbridled optimism. "The people that walked in darkness have seen a great light," wrote Isaiah. "They that dwell in the land of the shadow of death, upon them hath the light shined." (Isaiah 9:2).

In the Star Wars saga, the study in contrasts between the Jedi and the Sith touched our collective consciousness and instinctive awareness that we are children of light. The motion pictures used the vehicle of polar opposites to influence us viscerally as they played off our familiarity with both light and darkness. The ageless conflict fought long ago in a galaxy far away stirred us at our deepest levels.

The Lightsaber was the weapon of choice of the Jedi Knights, who were entrusted with protection of the Empire. To merit a Lightsaber, a novitiate had to exhibit incredible skill and confidence, dexterity, and attunement to the Force. No one, not even the Sith, who embraced the Dark Side, would have thought to call this weapon a "Darksaber."

Darth Vader was the "Dark Lord of the Sith" and it was only because of his corruption and manipulation of the Force that he was able to exploit the power of the Lightsaber. It is significant that his fraudulent use of this weapon that for so long had been employed only in defense of the Empire, ultimately proved to be impotent.

The appeal of Star Wars draws upon our intuitive awareness that Christ is the Creator of our Earth and the source of all light. As imperfect mortals who are acquainted with evil, we even understand the twisted nature of the Dark Side of the Force. But we admire most the Jedi, whose eyes were drawn to light as fire from heaven. The Jedi were pure in heart, and through their discernment could see things in their true light.

In the form of photons (the elementary quanta of radiant energy in the universe), light is everywhere. Photons not only give us the "colors" of the visible portion of the electromagnetic spectrum, but also the unseen energy that falls in the near, mid, and far infrared portion of the EM spectrum, and in the ionizing ultraviolet portion of the EM spectrum, as well.

Photons expand outward at all times and in all directions and do not require a medium through which to travel. Moving through the vacuum of space, they easily penetrate its immensity. They are immune to external influences, are found everywhere in the universe, and define its borders as it infinitely expands. Similarly, the Creator Who is "the Light of the world," also describes Himself as "Alpha and Omega," and as "the Beginning and the End." He is the eternal "I Am."

We use "Light" as a metaphor for His Presence, in part because it is the most impressive phenomenon in the universe, traveling through its vacuum at 299,792.458 k.p.s. or 186,282 m.p.s. Nothing can move more quickly than light and still obey the laws of physics as we understand them.

It is interesting that the generation of light requires a contribution of energy, whereas darkness renders a negative accounting. In our temporal world, light is produced within atoms when electrons that have been energized to move to higher, less stable, orbits fall back to their natural path around the nucleus. In the process, a photon of energy is given off from the atom in a spontaneous emission of radiation, and if the energy of that photon falls within 500 and 800 nanometers in the electromagnetic spectrum, our eyes perceive it as visible light. Photons represent the elemental particles and forces of nature that permit us to visually interact with our environment.

Every photon in the universe (and there are untold numbers of them) is the tangible result of the "Big Bang," the phenomenon that created our physical world in the first place. That event generated heat on an unimaginable scale, around 4 trillion degrees Celsius, when all the matter in the universe was a "quark soup" whose brilliance was incomprehensible. At that moment of Planck time (the smallest observable unit of time and the time before which the laws of physics are unable to describe the universe – around 10-43 seconds) light in the form of photonic energy was "everywhere." It filled the rapidly expanding physical universe, which today is a spherical shell approximately 15.9 billion light years from the common center. But at that time, it was a "gravitational singularity," or "spacetime singularity," wherein the quantities normally used to measure our three spatial dimensions and one temporal dimension become infinitely small in a way that does not depend upon any coordinate system. Because of the Law of Conservation of Energy, we know that even now, that energy, that light, is still present in our expanding universe as the sum total of the elemental quanta of radiant energy.

Some 15 billion years after The Big Bang, heat is still the best way to stimulate the atoms that were then created. Perhaps it is no coincidence that the Spirit can energize us in similar ways. When we consider the value of a suggestion, we "warm up to the idea." Like the cosmic microwave background radiation of 2.725º Kelvin from the Big Bang that lingers everywhere, the light that washes over God's creations is just waiting to be detected, absorbed, and applied to practical applications. There are spiritual counterparts to physical phenomena. For example, B.H. Roberts counseled that the best way to prepare for a dynamic address was to "read yourself full, think yourself straight, pray yourself hot, and let yourself go." He said on another occasion that those who are full of the enthusiasm of the gospel are "as white-hot sparks struck off the divine anvil of God." Moses wrote, "God is a consuming fire" (Deuteronomy 4:24), and he beheld the glory of God as a "bush (that) burned with fire, and the bush was not consumed." (Exodus 3:2). Isaiah asked, "Who among us shall dwell with the devouring fire? Who among us shall dwell with everlasting burnings?" (Isaiah 33:14). John the Revelator perceived the glory of God, and recorded: "Out of (His) throne proceeded lightnings and thunderings and voices, and there were seven lamps of fire before the throne." (Revelation 4:5).

Jeremiah understood how God's power could make us feel with an intensity that would be difficult to describe, when he declared: "I will make my words in thy mouth fire, and this people wood, and it shall devour them." (Jeremiah 5:14). Isaiah saw the seraphim of God "having a live coal in his hand, which he had taken with the tongs from off the altar; and he laid it upon my mouth, and said: Lo, this has touched thy lips, and thine iniquity is taken away, and thy sin purged." (Isaiah 6:6-7).

Most of us innately respond positively to the source of all light, but it is a shame when we harden our hearts, resist spiritual promptings, and incline our heads toward the shadows. Plato was eerily correct, when he observed: "The real tragedy in life is not children who are afraid of the dark, but men who are afraid of the light."

Helen Keller probably articulated it best when she wrote: "I believe that my (heavenly home) will be beautiful with colour, music, and speech of flowers and faces I love. Without this faith, there would be little meaning in my life. I should be a mere pillar of darkness in the dark. Observers in the full enjoyment of their bodily senses pity me, but it is because they do not see the golden chamber in my life where I dwell delighted; for dark as my path may seem to them, I carry a magic light in my heart. Faith, the spiritual strong searchlight, illuminates the way, and although

sinister doubts lurk in the shadow, I walk unafraid towards the Enchanted Wood where the foliage is always green, where joy abides, where nightingales nest and sing, and where life and death are one in the presence of the Lord."
("Midstream").

If we are ever to obtain our exaltation and eternal life, we must do more than simply acknowledge that Jesus Christ is our Lord. The Book of Mormon makes it abundantly clear that the critical point of conversion, beyond which lie the encircling flames of fire in the Celestial Kingdom of God, rests in making a conscious decision to accept not only Jesus Christ, but also to be obedient to the commandments. This includes the covenants we make with God, beginning with baptism by immersion for the remission of sins.

Light and Truth

"I am the light,
and the life, and the
truth of the world."
(Ether 4:12).

On the one hand, the government (which is, after all, here to help us) has initiated myriad programs to "fix" societal ills. We have programs that focus on educational challenges, health and welfare assistance, unemployment assistance, social service, supplemental nutrition, substance abuse addiction recovery, and the list goes on. Unfortunately, these have proven to be haphazard in their nature, with no coherence. In the cold light of day, as we see government assistance in all its forms imploding from faulty comprehension, misguided stewardship, inept execution, and negligent management, we must come to realize that our problems can only be effectively addressed with priesthood correlation.

As the Restoration continued to evolve, the concept of priesthood correlation was formulated as early as 1908, and the Correlation Department of the church, also called the Correlation Program, or simply Correlation, was officially organized in 1972. The power of these programs focuses on the family. For almost 50 years, it has done a remarkable job maintaining consistency in assisting the family in the understanding and practical application of doctrines and principles, benefitting from the administration of the ordinances of the priesthood, becoming more familiar with the resources of auxiliary organizations, providing access to meetings, including fundamental and continuing education opportunities, and making available materials and other tangible and intangible assets, to name a few.

With the increasingly pressing concerns of a multi-cultural membership, and with the church moving into the Third World, Priesthood Correlation has never been more important. The adversary has mounted unprecedented assaults on the family and family values, and the inspired program of Priesthood Correlation is one of the church's major assets in the arsenal to combat evil. Heavenly Father maintains a steady claim upon His children, and He insures their welfare with priesthood correlation.

The integrity of the family is vitally important, and He takes any assault on family values, such as abortion, immorality, pornography, and spousal and substance abuse, very seriously. In 1969, President Joseph Fielding Smith, Jr. prophetically counseled: "There are many great and real dangers to be reckoned with, and those which concern us more than all others combined have to do with our children. The only real protection or adequate defense can be afforded by the home and its influences." ("Our Children: The Loveliest Flowers from God's Own Garden." "Relief Society Magazine." 1/1969).

It has never been more important than it is now, to bring up our children in light and truth. The light of which we speak is any influence that draws Heavenly Father's children to Jesus Christ, and truth is any belief that is in harmony with gospel principles. Charles Dickens wrote of Victorian England: "It was the best of times," but it was also "the worst of times." ("A Tale of Two Cities"). Because those times are so characteristic of the Last Days, the Lord has provided the following inspired counsel: "In consequence of evils and designs which do and will exist in the hearts of conspiring men in the last days, I have warned you, and forewarn you, by giving unto you this word of wisdom" which is the fulness of the gospel, "by revelation." (D&C 89:4). Today, more than ever before, we need the wisdom of Solomon to negotiate the treacherous minefields of mortality.

I was a teenager between 1959 and 1966, when society in the United States began to undergo seismic change. I was a young adult from 1967 to 1981, and witnessed widespread protest for social justice and equality. I was middle aged between 1982 and 2006, when the foundations of Western society began to be regularly rocked by state supported terrorism. In 2007, I joined the ranks of the elderly, and started drawing social security in 2014. I'm now officially over the hill, but I'm picking up speed!

In my lifetime, the challenges associated with raising children have changed dramatically. We are all experiencing an accelerated pace, in the fast lane of life. There are incessant multi-media assaults on our senses. There are far more influences eroding family values than there were when Ma and Pa were raising their family on Walton's Mountain. Today, even more than we did in 1958, when this counsel was given, we need to "keep our families intact, and keep them under the influence of the Spirit of the Lord, trained in the principles of the gospel, that they may grow up in righteousness and truth." (Joseph Fielding Smith, Jr., C.R., 4/1958).

Today, sophisticated marketing techniques tempt us to indulge in things we didn't realize we craved, do not need, should not have, and cannot afford. "We have confidence in the young and rising generation in the church and plead with them not to follow the fashions and customs of the world, not to partake of a spirit of rebellion, and not to forsake the paths of truth and virtue." (Joseph Fielding Smith, Jr., "C.R., 4/1970). We feel both the positive and the negative effects of global awareness and the consequences of the Butterfly Effect. Moral equivocation is evaporating any semblance of standards that might be left. "Chastity, virtue, and freedom from are and must be basic to our way of life, if we are to realize its full purpose." (Joseph Fielding Smith, Jr., C.R., 4/1970).

Today, political correctness embraces and even celebrates all sorts of deviant behavior, in the name of tolerance and a celebration, even an adoration, of diversity. But it forgets that there is a difference between diversity and divisiveness. Flimflam artists adroitly fleece us of our very identity as children of God, and most of the time, we are not even aware that the theft is taking place. "Vice is a monster of such frightful mien, as to be hated needs but to be seen. Yet seen too oft, familiar with her face, we first endure, then pity, then embrace." (Alexander Pope, "Essay on Man, Epistle 2"). We have come full circle from Eve's temptation in the Garden. We are again beguiled with tinkling cymbals and sounding brass. The difference is that when she asked: "Is there no other way?" she was left with no alternative. We, thanks to her, have a choice.

Today, "we must shelter (our children) from the sins and evils of the world as much as we can." They "will have to be taught to discern between good and evil...and be instructed in the doctrines of the church." (Joseph Fielding Smith, Jr., C.R., 10/1916). Translation: They will need to be taught and become familiar with and comfortable with principles that stand in sharp contrast to the so-called values of society that are continually morphed by the shifting sands of cultural expediency. We cannot rely upon the constantly mutating values of society to provide a solid foundation upon which our children may be reasonably expected to somehow develop independently into responsible adults.

Therefore, our Heavenly Father has offered us timely and relevant guidance to shepherd us through these turbulent times. The Lord's church has stepped up to the plate to help our families. For starters, since the introduction of

Priesthood Correlation, there have been somewhere in the neighborhood of 90 General Conferences (around a thousand addresses by General Authorities). The church and its agencies have become service organizations, as it were, to help families, by providing them with regular bulletins filled with practical advice, and offering solutions to the problems they face on a daily basis.

The Lord has provided us with "The Family - A Proclamation to The World" (1995), echoing Joseph Fielding Smith, Jr., who twenty-five years earlier had said: "The first duty pertaining to the training of the children of the church belongs in the home." We have unprecedented access to church media (books, magazines, pamphlets, television, and internet-based resources). These focus on "solidarity in family relationships as the sure foundation upon which the church and society itself will flourish." (Joseph Fielding Smith, Jr., "Message from the First Presidency, in Family Home Evenings," 1970-71).

We receive daily encouragement from our local priesthood leaders and general authorities. "The Lord has commanded us, one and all, to bring our children up in light and truth. Where this spirit exists, disharmony, disobedience, and neglect of sacred duties cannot succeed." (Joseph Fielding Smith, Jr., C.R., 4/1965).

Since 1915, over 100 years ago, Family Home Evening program has been a resource to sustain family values. "There is no greater legacy that parents can leave to their children than the memory and blessings of a happy, unified, and loving home." (Joseph Fielding Smith, Jr., "Message from the First Presidency," in Family Home Evenings, 1970-71). He continued: "Parents who ignore the great help of (family home evening) are gambling with the future of their children." ("Message from the First Presidency," Ensign, 1/1971).

We all have access to educational opportunities such as seminaries & institutes, higher education, and the Pathway Program. The Church Educational System was established in 1877. "The first released-time seminary program was launched at Granite High School in Salt Lake City, Utah. Begun largely as an experiment by a single stake, the program has since grown into a worldwide system of religious education, bringing gospel instruction to young members of the church. From small beginnings, the seminary program and its collegiate counterpart - institutes of religion - have grown to become the primary educational entities in the church, with a larger enrollment than any other LDS educational venture and a wider reach than almost any educational organization worldwide. Today, the seminary and institute programs teach over 700,000 students in 143 different countries through the efforts of nearly 50,000 full-time, part-time, and volunteer teachers and administrators." (L.D.S. Infobase).

The Priesthood Correlation Program teaches members to help their families without violating the principle of agency. It encourages "teaching children when they are young. No person can begin too early to serve the Lord. Young people follow the teaching of their parents. The child who is taught in righteousness from birth will most likely follow righteousness always. Good habits are easily formed and easily followed." (Joseph Fielding Smith, Jr., "Take Heed to Yourselves!" p. 414).

As David O. McKay observed, from the time a child is born until about their eighth birthday (which just happens to be the age of accountability), we teach the principles of the gospel. From their baptism until about the age of 16, we train our youth in the application of these principles with the goal of ingraining the habits of provident living. After their 16th birthday, by and large, we can only trust them to walk in the ways of the Lord.

And so, we introduce our children at a young age to the scriptures. We "begin by teaching at the cradle-side." (Joseph Fielding Smith, Jr., C.R., 10/1948). We weave gospel principles into family activities, as our children commit the 13 Articles of Faith not only to memory, but also to lifestyle. These articles of faith become the particles of their faith. We find priesthood purposes in activities that are oriented toward conversion to the gospel of Jesus Christ, land we live its teachings, serve faithfully in callings, and dedicate ourselves to the responsibilities entrusted to us, giving meaningful service, living worthily to receive priesthood blessings and temple ordinances, preparing to serve honorable full-time missions, obtaining as much education as possible, preparing for and entering into temple marriage, and giving proper respect to others.

We surround ourselves with uplifting art, good music and literature, and other wholesome influences. We avoid indulging ourselves with telestial toys, and we develop the discipline to focus on celestial sureties rather than telestial trinkets.

When our time comes to pass beyond the veil, we will leave behind with our loved ones legacies of both tangible and intangible remembrances. We will leave them with our testimonies. We will leave them with gratitude for the privilege and blessing it has been to be knit together as families.

In anticipation of that day, we will develop the aforementioned action plan to realize our objectives. We will break that plan down into a sequence of steps that must be taken, and identify activities that must be performed well, for our strategies to succeed. We identify and allocate resources, so that we may understand beforehand the costs required to reach our goals. We recognize specific tasks that must be performed, and by whom, and we have a timeline that allows us to follow through to successful conclusions.

Because our children are the nobility of heaven, a choice and a chosen generation with a divine destiny, we are willing to make any sacrifice necessary to ensure their continuing success. Our children come to us from their Heavenly home, "like gentle rain through darkened skies, with glory trailing from their feet as they go, and endless promise in their eyes." While under our care, they grow tall and strong, "like silver trees against the storm; who will not bend with the wind or the change, but stand to fight the world alone." Our children "are the few, the warriors saved for Saturday; to come the last day of the world. These are they, of Saturday. (They) are the strong, the warriors rising in their might to win the battle raging in the hearts of men, on Saturday." They are "strangers from a realm of light, who have forgotten all - the memory of their former life and the purpose of their call. And so, they must learn why they're here, and who they really are." (Doug Stewart).

(The) Light of Christ

"Wherefore, I beseech
of you, brethren, that ye
should search diligently in the
light of Christ, that ye may
know good from evil."
(Moroni 7:19).

To ensure that your answers might be animated with energy, to have no regrets, and to avoid the fate of the Pharisees, you have been given the Light of Christ. It proceeds from His throne as a powerful influence for good that is intended to groom you to receive the Holy Ghost. It is a gift that miraculously multiplies even as it divides within a universe populated with individuals whose actions are governed by free will. It is given, the Lord revealed, "that every man may act in doctrine and principle pertaining to futurity, according to the moral agency which I have given unto him." (D&C 101:78, see D&C 93:31).

It has been benevolently bestowed upon all of us by One Whom we can be sure "denieth none that come unto him, black and white, bond and free, male and female; and he remembereth the heathen; and all are alike unto (him), both Jew and Gentile." (2 Nephi 26:33). The Light of Christ stimulates our soul-sweat as it works on our conscience, our sense of duty, and our scruples. It provides a shield of protection against the corrosive spatter of perspiration cast off by the destroyer, who is insidiously and persistently working overtime to damage our doctrinal defenses, dull our spiritual sensitivities, diminish our charitable capacity, deplete our bountiful reservoirs of sympathy, and destroy our devotions, even as we labor with an equal but opposite intensity to deify our work on the earth.

The Light of Christ exerts a nurturing influence, as well. Although we must daily travel farther from the East, we are nevertheless oriented toward the radiant glow emanating from that distant horizon. It provides us with the regularly recurring reassurance of a religious recalibration that autocorrects with fortuitous frequency and celestial precision. It envelops us in an intuitive appreciation of where we came from, why we are here, and where we are going. As in a heavenly language that is rhythmical, melodious, soothing to our ears, and calming to our souls, when we hear the Spirit quietly whisper: "You're a stranger here," we are comforted with the realization that it is so, only because we have "wandered from a more exalted sphere." (Eliza R. Snow). The Light of Christ examines what it means to be anxiously engaged, inspires us to plumb the depths of our commitment to the Savior, sensitizes us to the nobility of His work, expands upon the visions of immortality, and makes us more acutely aware of His glory, as it brings eternal life within our purview.

In a way, thinking about the Savior can be likened to a primer on midwifery, because one of its purposes is to facilitate the arduous process of our spiritual rebirth, by contributing to our preparation to answer with conviction the questions that were first posed to the Pharisees so long ago: "What think ye of Christ?" and "Whose son is he?" When we feel the urge to push His agenda, the Light of Christ can be our labor coach, providing us with just the right amount of encouragement to successfully deliver our witness of the Savior without being overbearing.

One exciting element of the manifestation of the Light of Christ is the constant stream of inspiration and revelation that cascades down from above. This ensures that all may walk along illuminated pathways, and that no individual or institution may legitimately claim or have a monopoly on divine guidance. It exerts a leveling influence that is the great equalizer, giving each of us the same privileges to use our faculties of mind, intellect, and spirit to our best advantage, that we might discern between truth and error, no matter upon what spiritual plateau we might be currently relaxing. It permits us to listen with sensitivity and to be receptive to the cries of the downtrodden and oppressed, to see with a lucidity that allows us to be responsive to our environment, and to be benevolently blind to the shortcomings of others.

The Light of Christ provides us with a nurturing influence that makes it easier to have lips that have learned to articulate only positive expressions of speech and never speak guile, shoulders that have developed the strength to bear the burdens of those who have been battered and bruised by the vicissitudes of life and who may be faltering under the heavy weight of sorrow or sin, backs that have become sturdy enough to brace us against the fierce winds of adversity and the subtle wiles of the adversary, hearts that have become the receptacles of pure and virtuous principles upon which we may draw in times of need, bowels that are moved to compassion for those who are struggling with misfortune, hands that have become accustomed to lifting those who are in need of support, and feet that have been conditioned to speedily carry us to those who are imprisoned by poor choices, bad habits, or unfortunate circumstances.

Even now, heavenly messengers who minister by the Light of Christ are nursemaids to the nations of the earth, and use its power as a resource to reach out and caress those who are poor in spirit. Men and women of all persuasions feel that angels are watching over them. Witness countless newlyweds who are certain that their match was made in heaven before the world was. Others sense that they have been assisted by acts of providence, are the beneficiaries of divine intervention, have been touched by angels, are moved to compassion, or have been otherwise blessed to "walk in the light of the Lord." (Isaiah 2:5).

Guidance in the form of spiritual promptings and impressions are more common that many would suspect. Powerful intuitive communicators strongly influence nearly all of us to move in the direction of our dreams, toward a greater appreciation of the majesty and power of our Creator. Truly, He "is no respecter of persons" Who causes the sun to shine on the wicked, as well as on the just. (Acts 10:34). Therefore, we must venture forth out of the shadows, even beyond the direction we receive from the Light of Christ and the ministration of angels, if we want to begin to appreciate the special familiarity that the Lord enjoys with those whom He has characterized as "the children of light." (John 12:36). The more we think about Christ, the easier it is to craft with words the sensations that naturally flow to each of us as a result of the stirrings of those feelings of intimacy.

As we think about Christ, we realize how heavily we have borrowed from the towering examples of those who, over the years, have been our mystical mentors, our sensible chaperones, our spiritual guides, our surrogate Saviors, as well as our compassionate critics. They are our avatars, who have shown us the way, strengthened our testimonies, taught us humility, been there to steady and nurture us, applied the Balm of Gilead and bound up our wounds, provided both tangible and immaterial support, emboldened us with words of encouragement, and cheered us on with wise counsel. When we think of this multitude of angels thinly disguised as our family, friends, and peers, we remember the words of Sir Isaac Newton, who, when pressed to reveal the great secret behind his accomplishments, simply replied: "I stood on the shoulders of giants."

If we are fortunate, we are privileged to do so, as well. As we think about our Savior, we draw upon the faith, testimony, and spiritual insight of the General Authorities and lay members of The Church of Jesus Christ of Latter-day Saints, as well as playwrights and poets, philosophers and humanitarians, authors, journalists, essayists, classicists, religious scholars of all persuasions, statesmen, sages, mystics, stoics, and the composers and lyricists with whom we are familiar. Our friends and family are often more influential than they could ever imagine. We are fortunate if we have been blessed with such wonderful traveling companions during our journey through mortality. Such gurus, guides, and governors can profoundly touch our lives with influences that help us to shape tender feelings as we think about the Savior.

In the end, however, we sometimes need to ask for the pardon of our traveling companions when they are confronted by the literal and figurative blemishes, the idiosyncratic foibles, and the objective and subjective imperfections that too often subtly work their way into our character, if we are not vigilant. Whenever we have taken poetic license with foundation principles, or have added needless ecclesiastical embroidery to gospel truths, we beseech the indulgence, and the forgiveness, of our peers. If our passion has clouded our vision or has overpowered our zealous intentions, if the syntax of our speech has, at times, seemed tortuous, too bland, or too spicy, if our feelings have been understated or if we have been given over to hyperbole, or even if we have appeared to drift over the line separating true doctrine from baseless speculation, we beg for the forbearance of our contemporaries, that they might take a step back and allow our expressions to simmer for a while before returning to sample anew their flavor. The reduction sauce of time may enhance the palatability of our perspective.

In any case, as the congealed distillate of our life experiences, our feelings relating to the Savior stand revealed as our innocent attempts to yoke our emotions to language. We hope that others will find them refreshing, and that they too will rely upon the Light of Christ before we consume them as food for thought.

We dream that we might feel the gentle caress of the touch of the Master Potter, as our lives turn with the passage of time. We want Him to mold us and shape us as the Artisan of our destinies. "As the clay is in the potter's hand, so are ye in mine hand," said the Lord to His prophet. (Jeremiah 18:6). As Isaiah declared: "O Lord, thou art our father; we are the clay, and thou our potter; and we all are the work of thy hand." (Isaiah 64:8). We hope and pray that as our thoughts to turn to the Savior, we may remain pliable and impressionable to the Light of Christ.

As His key grips, foley artists, gaffers, and stagehands, all of us need to learn to utilize the divinely designed accouterments of the matchless and multi-talented Carpenter of Nazareth, Who will help us to construct the sets upon which will be enacted the drama of our lives. We can imagine that our efforts will be validated by appreciative applause from the audience, and by the occasional bouquets of red roses that are thrown at our feet. But it will be even more satisfying to remain as His poor understudies, and to give our best efforts to supporting roles in off-Broadway performances that count for more than mere entertainment.

His Plan does not require that we be the stars of the show. Our path of progress to perfection is a process, and not a point. We do not need top billing to fulfill our destiny. We do not seek to garner a People's Choice Award. Rather than becoming the objects of attention of an adoring paparazzi, we foresee ourselves being enveloped instead in a dazzling cloud of divinely directed diamond dust that glitters with thousands of points of light, and becoming the participants in daily dramas that far surpass the pomp and circumstance of any "American Idol" production. Ours will be performances exhibiting displays of celestial energy worthy of notice from above. As fire in the sky, the air in the theater of life will be charged with an electricity that represents the inevitable merger of the universal encouragement of the Light of Christ with the pointed and providential guidance provided by the Holy Ghost. When these influences streak in tandem across the heavens, their trajectories will coalesce to trace a flaming trail that sparkles over a vast cosmic ocean of thought. Over the ebb and flow of its tide, the Spirit will create an effectual bridge of understanding that is buttressed by the cohesive influence of the mighty foundation of faith.

The Book of Mormon addresses themes
of self-denial, meekness, and charity, and it
asks that we surrender to the greater good our desire
for self-actualization, self-renewal, self-determination,
self-fulfillment, self-aggrandizement, and self-control.
It asks us to concentrate our efforts on behaviors that
honor God's design, rather than patronizing the
twisted temporal theories of emotional or
spiritual well-being that lack
an upward thrust.

(The) Light of The World

"I am Jesus Christ, whom
the prophets testified shall come
into the world. And behold, I am the
light and the life of the world."
(3 Nephi 11:10-11).

Without light, life as we know it would not exist. It is in light that we carry out most of our activities. We even call them "daily" routines instead of "nightly" routines, and those who work in the dark before dawn toil in the graveyard shift.

Because of its beneficial physical characteristics, light is used as a symbol to powerful effect. When an idea explodes in our minds, it is as if a light bulb has turned on. Glimmers of truth enlighten us as they illuminate the dark recesses of our thoughts. When the equations of relativity jelled in his brain, Albert Einstein said of the experience: "A splendid light dawned on me." When we research a question, our focused efforts shed light on the problem. As we endure hardship, we are comforted because we can see the light at the end of the tunnel. When stark reality sets in, our shortcomings are seen in the light of day. As the pop tune suggests, a special someone has the power to light up our lives.

In the scriptures, light has been used as a symbol of Jesus Christ. At the Feast of Tabernacles commemorating the Lord's blessings to the children of Israel during their travels in the wilderness, the flames from four enormous candelabra that illuminated the temple could be seen throughout Jerusalem. How appropriate that this was the setting for Jesus to announce: I am the light of the world: he that followeth me shall not walk in darkness, but shall have the light of life." (John 8:12).

Jesus is "the light of truth; Which truth shineth. This is the light of Christ. As also he is in the sun, and the light of the sun, and the power thereof by which it was made. As also he is in the moon, and is the light of the moon, and the power thereof by which it was made; As also the light of the stars, and the power thereof by which they were made; And the earth also, and the power thereof, even the earth upon which you stand. And the light which shineth, which giveth you light, is through him who enlighteneth your eyes, which is the same light that quickeneth your understandings, Which light proceedeth forth from the presence of God to fill the immensity of space— The light which is in all things, which giveth life to all things, which is the law by which all things are governed, even the power of God who sitteth upon his throne, who is in the bosom of eternity, who is in the midst of all things." (D&C 88:6-13).

As we strive to be like Jesus, we reflect His light and become, with Him, "the light of the world." (Matthew 5:14). It is in this sense that the Savior urged: "Let your light so shine before men, that they may see your good works and glorify your Father which is in heaven." (Matthew 5:16). "People are like stained glass windows. They sparkle and shine when the sun is out, but when the darkness sets in their true beauty is revealed only if there is a light from within." (Elizabeth Kubler-Ross).

Limiting Beliefs

"But the worst enemy thou
canst meet, wilt thou thyself always be."
(Friedrich Nietzsche, "Thus Spake Zarathustra").

"They have cast us out of our
synagogues which we have labored
abundantly to build with our own hands;
and they have cast us out because of our
exceeding poverty; and we have no
place to worship our God; and
behold, what shall we do?"
(Alma 32:5).

In a very real sense, each of us is confined to the world of our own making, and most of us are trapped within the narrowly defined perceptual prisons we have created for ourselves. Its walls are reinforced with the razor-wire of limiting beliefs, those stories we tell ourselves that cause us to sabotage our own best efforts. They can damage and even cripple our lives, diminish our abilities, compromise our progress, and hold us back from attaining our goals. Although all of us have limiting beliefs, everyone has the power to change them. Most people, however, don't realize it's possible, and for that matter, aren't even aware that they have made conscious decisions about what they choose to believe and not to believe.

Limiting beliefs exert tremendous pressure on us to resist change and remain short-sighted, as we become caught up in the moment and continue in insufferable self-indulgence. They blind us to foundation frames of reference based on unchanging principles, deafen us to mentors who might otherwise help us to monitor our progress, and foster insensitivity to the standards to which we would otherwise turn. They corrode the iron rods running straight and true which are ever before us, and they weaken the absolutes in which we would normally place our implicit trust. Ever learning but never coming to a knowledge of the truth that would make us free, we grasp at straws, failing to recognize that nothing will kill our creativity more surely than the self-assurance that poisons our ability to recognize the influence of a power greater than ourselves. Nothing will kill the guiding Spirit faster than stubborn self-confidence mutated into unbridled pride, vanity, selfishness, and haughtiness.

Our limiting beliefs provide no sanctuary when the wind blows and the rain beats down. They offer no safe harbor to which we may flee. When the ocean of life is in turmoil and we are tossed about as flotsam and jetsam, never coming to a knowledge of what is real, our limiting beliefs cloud the path back to the source to which we would in other circumstances look for the stability we so desperately seek. Our limiting beliefs conceal the answers to life's greatest questions that continually trouble our spirits.

When we submit to the blind guides of limiting beliefs, we close our minds to the soul expanding opportunities that would otherwise be afforded by mortality, Because the forces of subtraction, rather than addition, are in effect, we decline the offer to experience life abundantly. Living for the moment, we paint ourselves into conceptual corners and telestial traffic jams, limiting our creative talents to a few expressions within a narrow and confusing rational reality. Turning our backs to the light of inspiration and creativity, we think we have it all, when all that is before us is only an illusion and a shadow and a caricature of reality.

Limiting beliefs can be so strong, vivid, and prominent that we cannot even imagine other possibilities. Not so long ago, we convinced ourselves that the earth was flat, and that if we were to sail west, we would fall off its edge. We looked at birds in flight but told ourselves as recently as 1895 that "heavier than air flying machines are impossible." (Lord Kelvin, President of The Royal Society). In 1903, the President of the Michigan Savings Bank refused to back The Ford Motor Company, telling Henry Ford: "The horse is here to stay." "Drill for oil?" said the drillers whom Edwin L. Drake tried to enlist to his project to drill for oil in 1859, in Titusville, Pennsylvania. "You mean drill into the ground to try and find oil? You're crazy!"

Limiting beliefs are strongly influenced by "conventional wisdom." "Computers in the future may weigh no more than 1.5 tons." (Popular Mechanics, 1949). "I think there is a world market for maybe five computers." (Thomas Watson, chairman of IBM, 1943). "Data processing is a fad that won't last out the year." (The editors at Prentice Hall, 1957). "But what (is the microchip) good for?" (I.B.M. engineer, 1968). "The telephone is inherently of no value to us." (Western Union memo, 1876). "The wireless music box has no imaginable commercial value. Who would pay for a message sent to nobody in particular?" (David Sarnoff's associates, 1920). "Who would want to hear actors talk?" (Harry Warner, Warner Brothers Studios, 1927). "People will soon get tired of staring at a plywood box every night." (Darryl Zanuck, head of Twentieth Century Fox, 1946). "Louis Pasteur's theory of germs is ridiculous fiction." (Professor of Physiology at Toulouse, 1872). "The abdomen, the chest, and the brain will forever be shut from the intrusion of the wise and humane surgeon." (Sir John Ericksen, British surgeon to Queen Victoria, 1873).

Limiting beliefs are also influenced by the views of authority figures who all too easily dismiss innovation by saying: "Are you crazy? We've always done it that way. It's too hard to change. No-one would accept it. It's too expensive. It would take too much time. It's too risky. People will laugh at you."

Religious leaders are not immune to limiting beliefs: "There is no scripture other than the Bible. The heavens are closed. Revelation has ceased. Ordinances are unnecessary. God no longer speaks to man. The Church of Jesus Christ no longer exists on the earth. It is impossible to know God's will."

When great ideas are presented to the world, because they fly in the face of limiting beliefs that have imprisoned the minds of entire cultures, they are often met defensively, first with ridicule, and then with active opposition. Finally, though, as they penetrate the darkness clouding stubborn minds, they are acknowledged as self-evident. It would be a good exercise for each of us to look at the way we do things by looking them over carefully. We should be even and objective in our consideration of our perceptions,. After a while, we should regard our pre-conceived ideas and attitudes with suspicion. We should dig deeper into our prejudices and our self-defeating behaviors. And finally, we will recognize that there are many of those behaviors that we should abandon in favor of new approaches.

Understanding ourselves from a perspective free of limiting beliefs has many advantages. It permits a multidimensional view of life. "Whom say ye that I am?" the Savior asked Peter. When he realized that Jesus was in fact the Christ, the Son of the Living God, Peter was up and moving along on the pathway to personal re-discovery. Self-actualization germinates innovation, which is the antithesis of limiting beliefs. It spawns creativity. Innovation can be incremental or revolutionary, but its end result is always positive change. The economics of innovation increase value. However, we should focus on the process itself, rather than on its end point. As we pass through mortality and exercise our agency, it helps to have celestial signposts to guide us through the telestial traffic jams and conceptual cul-de-sacs created by limiting beliefs that threaten to detour us from the strait and narrow way. The expanding circle of opportunity created when we shed our limiting beliefs allows us to trade the uncertain course adopted by individuals bound for mediocrity for the certain reality of celestial-bound individuals.

How can we break away from our limiting beliefs? When we first brush up against the stars, we just might awaken to a new vision that is blinding at first, but as our eyes adjust we might be surprised to see the world, for the first time, as it really is. As we begin to feel the creative expression of the power within us, we realize it is this very energy that makes us more like God. We can feel the divine potential within us. We feel the confidence to as seemingly simple questions that can have profound answers and implications that shake our world, spreading like the ripples radiating outward from a rock thrown into the still water of a pond. In spite of their broad application, these questions are intensely personal. Jacob Bronowski observed of Einstein that he was a man who could ask immensely simple questions from whose answers he could hear God thinking.

Sometimes, the answers we receive resonate with enlightenment; when both scientific and philosophical lines of inquiry lead to mutual illumination. "Is the earth really the center of the universe?" "Why does an apple fall from a tree?" "What would the world look like if I were riding on a beam of light?" "Can I reach the Far East by sailing west?" "What would happen if you fell into a black hole?" As we ask these questions, "poised at the edge of forever," we just might jump off into a stream of revelation and be carried along in the quickening currents of direct experience with God. As George Bernard Shaw so famously put it: "Some men see things as they are and ask why? I dream things that never were, and ask why not?"

Sometimes, our questions cut through to the core of our being. "Am I my brother's keeper?" (Genesis 4:9). "If a man die, shall he live again?" (Job 14:14). "Does God love me?" "Does my existence make a difference?" "Even the humblest human beings, (Pope John Paul II) observes, are naturally philosophic, asking themselves such questions as "Who and I? Where do I come from and where am I going?" Religious revelation provides answers to these questions, the pope acknowledges." ("Uniting Faith and Reason," Time Magazine, 10/26/1998). Such child-like questions ultimately lead to the granddaddy of them all that is at the foundation of the principle of eternal progress: "Which church is right?"

And so, we come to the experience of Joseph Smith and the counsel of James: "If any of you lack wisdom, let him ask of God, that giveth to all men liberally, and upbraideth not, and it shall be given him, But let him ask in faith, nothing wavering." (James 1:5-6). Of this, Joseph Smith said: "Never did any passage of scripture come with more power to the heart of man than this did at this time to mine. It seemed to enter with great force into every feeling of my heart. I reflected on it again and again, knowing that if any person needed wisdom from God, I did; for how to act I did not know, and unless I could get more wisdom than I then had, I would never know; for the teachers of religion of the different sects understood the same passages of scripture so differently as to destroy all confidence in settling the question by an appeal to the Bible. At length, I came to the conclusion that I must either remain in darkness and confusion, or else I must do as James directs, that is, ask of God. I at length came to the determination to 'ask of God,' concluding that if he gave wisdom to them that lacked wisdom, and would give liberally, and not upbraid, I might venture." (Joseph Smith History 1:12-13).

In similar fashion, Alma urged the poor Zoramites: "Awake and arouse your faculties, even to an experiment upon my words, and exercise a particle of faith, yea, even if ye can no more than desire to believe, let this desire work in you, even until ye believe." (Alma 32:27). His suggestion was to study, pray, and commit to a plan of action. The Lord counseled: "Study it out in your mind; then you must ask me if it be right, and if it is right I will cause that your bosom shall burn within you; therefore, you shall feel that it is right." (D&C 9:8).

In essence, He was saying: "Get a "bright idea!" We all learn by experience that "it is impossible to advance in the principles of truth, to increase in heavenly knowledge, except we exercise our reasoning faculties and exert ourselves … to the utmost of our ability." (Lorenzo Snow). Then, after we have received these things, we would do well to follow the counsel of Moroni: "I would exhort you that ye would ask God, the Eternal Father, in the name of Christ, if these things are not true; and if ye shall ask with a sincere heart, with real intent, having faith in Christ, he will manifest the truth of it unto you, by the power of the Holy Ghost. And by the power of the Holy Ghost ye may know the truth of all things." (Moroni 10:4-5).

Breaking free from limiting beliefs unleashes the power of our potential. Spencer W. Kimball taught: "Make no small plans, for they have not the power to stir the souls of men." At the end of the day, the universe is full of magical things patiently waiting for our wits to grow sharper, so that we can appreciate them. (Anonymous). More specifically, "the universe is a machine for the making of Gods." (Henri Bergson).

It behooves us all to sit back and evaluate our own attitudes to see if we have limiting beliefs slinking around in the recesses of our consciousness. Because limiting beliefs often fuel the engine that drives us, the Lord explained: "If men come unto me I will show unto them their weakness. I give unto men weakness that they may be humble; and my grace is sufficient for all men that humble themselves before me; for if they humble themselves before me, and have faith in me, then will I make weak things become strong unto them." (Ether 12:27).

Then, "if your eye be single to my glory," said the Lord, "your whole bodies shall be filled with light, and there shall be no darkness in you; and that body which is filled with light comprehendth all things." (D&C 88:67). "Therefore," He said, "sanctify yourselves that your minds become single to God, and the days will come that you shall see him; for he will unveil his face unto you." (D&C 88:68). Then, we will be hobbled no more by limiting beliefs, "for now we see through a glass, darkly; but then face to face; now I know in part; but then shall I know even as also I am known." (1 Corinthinans 13:12).

Living Water

*"It came to pass that I beheld that the rod of iron,
which my father had seen, was the word of God, which
led to the fountain of living waters, or to the tree of life,
which waters are a representation of the love of God;
and I also beheld that the tree of life was a
representation of the love of God."*
(1 Nephi 11:25).

To help defend Jerusalem against attacks by the Assyrians, King Hezekiah ordered that the fountains of the spring of Gihon outside the city walls of Jerusalem be covered, to provide easy access to the water. The spring was then diverted to the pool of Siloam, inside the city walls. This was done by digging a tunnel through about 1770 feet of limestone rock. Without this water inside the walls of the city, the people of Jerusalem would not have survived the subsequent siege by the Assyrians.

Just as the water from the spring of Gihon was vital for the physical survival of Hezekiah's people during the Assyrian conflict, living water is essential for our spiritual survival during our battles with Satan. In effect, we are under siege throughout our mortal lives, and our constant access to living water is our only hope of salvation.

What is this living water? Jesus said to the woman at the well: "Whosoever drinketh of this water shall thirst again: But whosoever drinketh of the water that I shall give him shall never thirst; but the water that I shall give him shall be in him a well of water springing up into everlasting life." (John 4:10-14). The living water that spiritually sustains us is the doctrine of the gospel of Jesus Christ.

Living water is so crucial to our well-being, that the Lord has provided a conduit that can penetrate solid limestone, as it were, so that it may freely flow into our lives. With great effort, this conduit is chiseled through our rough exterior and stony nature with the tools of faith, obedience, study, prayer, good works, and other healthy lifestyle choices. The conduit to living water is created when we not only believe, but also act on our belief, in being honest, pure, chaste, benevolent, kind, and in doing good to all men. Living water has the power to sustain our lives when we are not just hearers of the word, but doers of the word, as well. (See James 1:22).

We receive living water in the House of the Lord, where we receive instruction, are endowed with power and understanding, and feel peace and joy. We receive living water when we are washed clean from the blood and sins of our generation, through our faithfulness. Worship in the temple was an important protective strategy for the Israelites in Hezekiah's time, and it can be an important weapon in our own arsenal of protection, as well.

The scriptures teach us that we should seek living water "diligently, and teach (each other) words of wisdom; yea, seek ... out of the best books words of wisdom; seek learning, even by study and also by faith. (We must) organize (ourselves and) prepare every needful thing; and establish a house, even a house of prayer, a house of fasting, a house of faith, a house of learning, a house of glory, a house of order, (and) a house of God, that (our) incomings may be in the name of the Lord; that (our) outgoings may be in the name of the Lord; (and) that all (our) salutations may be in the name of the Lord, with uplifted hands unto the Most High. Therefore, (in order to be refreshed with living water, it would be well to) cease from all (our) light speeches, from all laughter, from all (our) lustful desires, from all (our) pride and light-mindedness, and from all (our) wicked doings." (D&C 88:118-121).

In ancient Israel, Hezekiah's father, Ahaz, was a wicked king who had desecrated the temple of the Lord and "shut up (its) doors" (2 Chronicles 28:24). When Hezekiah became king of the Southern Kingdom of Judah in 715 B.C., one of the first things he did was open the doors of the temple and order the priests and Levites to cleanse the Lord's holy house. He realized that the temple first needed to be sanctified in order for his people to enjoy the refreshment of its living water. "For our fathers have trespassed, and done that which was evil in the eyes of the Lord our God, and have forsaken him, and have turned away their faces from the habitation of the Lord, and turned their backs. Also, they have shut up the doors of the porch, and put out the lamps, and have not burned incense nor offered burnt offerings in the holy place unto the God of Israel." (2 Chronicles 29:6-7).

If we disregard the blessings to be found in temple worship, we may be equally guilty of turning away our faces from the habitation of the Lord. Because the people of Judah disregarded the temple, "the wrath of the Lord was upon Judah and Jerusalem, and he...delivered them to trouble, to astonishment, and to hissing.... For, lo, (their) fathers (had) fallen by the sword, and (their) sons and (their) daughters and (their) wives (were) in captivity for this." (2 Chronicles 29:8-9).

Hezekiah hoped to re-establish the Covenant with the Lord by cleansing the temple and preparing it for worship again. The scriptures record that he declared: "Now it is in mine heart to make a covenant with the Lord God of Israel, that his fierce wrath may turn away from us." (2 Chronicles 29:10). He wanted to keep unclean things out of the temple.

Through Joseph Smith, the Lord has promised once again to provide living water in the temples that are found throughout the world, declaring: "Inasmuch as my people build a house unto me in the name of the Lord, and do not suffer any unclean thing to come into it, that it be not defiled, my glory shall rest upon it; Yea, and my presence shall be there, for I will come into it, and all the pure in heart that shall come into it shall see God. But if it be defiled I will not come into it, and my glory shall not be there; for I will not come into unholy temples." (D&C 97:15-17).

If we do not qualify because of uncleanliness to partake of the living water found in the temple, the Lord has made it possible for us to follow the example of the people of Hezekiah. The conduit to living water is accessible if we do as Joseph Smith implored at the dedication of the Kirtland Temple: He prayed that "no unclean clean thing (should) be permitted to come into (the House of the Lord) to pollute it." He prayed that when the "people transgress, (that they might) speedily repent and return unto (God), and find favor in (His) sight, and be restored to the blessings which (He) ordained to be poured out upon those who (should) reverence (Him) in (His) house." (D&C 109:20-21).

Anciently, when the temple had been cleansed, Hezekiah and the people of Jerusalem "made an end of offering, the king and all that were present with him. (And they) bowed themselves, and worshipped. Moreover, Hezekiah the king and the princes commanded the Levites to sing praise unto the Lord with the words of David, and of Asaph the seer. And they sang praises with gladness, and they bowed their heads and worshipped. Then Hezekiah answered and said, Now ye have consecrated yourselves unto the Lord, come near and bring sacrifices and thank offerings into the house of the Lord. And the congregation brought in sacrifices and thank offerings; and as many as were of a free heart, burnt offerings." (2 Chronicles 29:29-31).

In our day, Jesus Christ has promised unimpeded access to living water with this instruction: "Thou shalt offer a sacrifice unto the Lord thy God in righteousness, even that of a broken heart and a contrite spirit." (D&C 59:8). Elsewhere, He said: "Verily I say unto you, all among them who know their hearts are honest, and are broken, and their spirits contrite, and are willing to observe their covenants by sacrifice - yea, every sacrifice which I, the Lord, shall command – they are accepted of me." (D&C 97:8).

Anciently, Hezekiah invited the Ten Tribes of the Northern kingdom of Israel to come to the house of the Lord for the celebration of the Passover. "And Hezekiah sent to all Israel and Judah, and wrote letters also to Ephraim and Manasseh, that they should come to the house of the Lord at Jerusalem, to keep the Passover unto the Lord God of Israel." (2 Chronicles 30:1).

By the time of Hezekiah's reign, much of the kingdom of Israel (the Northern Kingdom) had already been taken captive by the Assyrians. Hezekiah promised the remaining Israelites that if they would "turn again unto the Lord," the captives would be released. Instead, most of the people of Israel rejected Hezekiah's invitation. Because of the wickedness of the people, the remainder of the kingdom of Israel was taken captive within several years, and became the Lost Ten Tribes.

In order to avoid spiritual captivity, Moroni urged us, in the last verses of The Book of Mormon: "I would exhort you that ye would come unto Christ, and lay hold upon every good gift, and touch not the evil gift, nor the unclean thing. And awake, and arise from the dust, O Jerusalem; yea, and put on thy beautiful garments, O daughter of Zion; and strengthen thy stakes and enlarge thy borders forever, that thou mayest no more be confounded, that the covenants of the Eternal Father which he hath made unto thee, O house of Israel, may be fulfilled. Yea, come unto Christ, and be perfected in him, and deny yourselves of all ungodliness; and if ye shall deny yourselves of all ungodliness, and love God with all your might, mind, and strength, then is his grace sufficient for you, that by his grace ye may be perfect in Christ; and if by the grace of God ye are perfect in Christ, ye can in nowise deny the power of God." (Moroni 10:30-32).

Nephi had earlier expressed a common theme of The Book of Mormon: "Inasmuch as those whom the Lord God shall bring out of the land of Jerusalem shall keep his commandments, they shall prosper upon the face of this land; and they shall be kept from all other nations." (2 Nephi 1:9).

When the Assyrians finally did invade the kingdom of Judah, the prophet Isaiah and King Hezekiah prayed for help, and an angel of the Lord destroyed much of the invading army. Isaiah dualistically prophesied: "No weapon that is formed against thee shall prosper; and every tongue that shall rise against thee in judgment thou shalt condemn." (Isaiah 54:17).

In our day, the Savior has promised us similar protection, if only we will nourish ourselves with living water: "Let my army become very great, and let it be sanctified before me, that it may become fair as the sun, and clear as the moon, and that her banners may be terrible unto all nations. That the kingdoms of this world may be constrained to acknowledge that the kingdom of Zion is in very deed the kingdom of God and his Christ; therefore, let us become subject unto her laws." (D&C 105:31-32).

Hezekiah and his people received the Lord's protection because of their repentance and their righteousness, which was demonstrated by their worship in the temple. In the Dedicatory Prayer at the Kirtland Temple, Joseph Smith asked our

Father in Heaven to establish with the nourishment of living water "the people that shall worship, and honorably hold a name and standing in this thy house, to all generations and for eternity; That no weapon formed against them shall prosper; that he who diggeth a pit for them shall fall into the same himself; That no combination of wickedness shall have power to rise up and prevail over thy people upon whom thy name shall be put in this house; And if any people shall rise against this people, that thine anger be kindled against them; And if they shall smite this people thou wilt smite them; thou wilt fight for thy people as thou didst in the day of battle, that they may be delivered from the hands of all their enemies." (D&C 109:24-28). Little wonder that President Howard W. Hunter encouraged: "Let us be a temple-attending people. Attend the temple as frequently as personal circumstances allow."

Hezekiah was succeeded as king by his son Manasseh, and then by his grandson Amon, and then by his great-grandson Josiah, who was made king of Judah when he was just eight years old. He became a righteous king who ruled in Israel from 641 to 610 B.C., at the very time Lehi was growing up in the land of Jerusalem.

Josiah sought the true God, destroyed idolatry in the kingdom, and employed craftsmen to repair the temple. During its renovation, Hilkiah the high priest "found a book of the law of the Lord (the scriptures) given by Moses." (2 Chronicles 34:14). By this time in Judah's history, the written law apparently had been lost and was virtually unknown. This is surely why Lehi felt that it was so important for his sons to return to Jerusalem, at great personal risk, to retrieve the Plates of Brass, which would be to them as living water. As Nephi wrote: "And behold, it is wisdom in God that we should obtain these records, that we may preserve unto our children the language of our fathers; and also that we may preserve unto them the words which have been spoken by the mouth of all the holy prophets, which have been delivered unto them by the Spirit and power of God, since the world began, even down unto this present time." (1 Nephi 3:19-20).

When he read the book of the law, Josiah "rent his clothes." (2 Chronicles 34:19). He was distressed to discover what the book of the law contained. The scriptures record his words: "Great is the wrath of the Lord that is poured out upon us, because our fathers have not kept the word of the Lord, to do after all that is written in this book." (2 Chronicles 34:21). He realized that Israel had polluted the living water that had been provided to sustain her during her greatest trials.

President Ezra Taft Benson said: "In 1829, the Lord warned the Saints that they were not to trifle with sacred things. Surely The Book of Mormon is a sacred thing, and yet many take it lightly, and treat it as though it is of little importance. In 1832, as some early missionaries returned from their fields of labor, the Lord reproved them for treating The Book of Mormon lightly. As a result of that attitude, he said, their minds had been darkened. Not only had treating this sacred book lightly brought a loss of light to themselves, but it had also brought the whole church under condemnation, even all the children of Zion. And then the Lord said: "And they shall remain under this condemnation until they repent and remember the new covenant, even The Book of Mormon."' (D&C 84:54-57). If the early Saints were rebuked for treating The Book of Mormon lightly, are we under any less condemnation if we do the same?" Have members of the church jeopardized their standing before the Lord, because of their pollution of living water?

After Josiah found out that his people would be condemned because they had not done as the scriptures instructed, he called all the people to the temple and read to them out of the book of the law. (2 Chronicles 34:29-30). President Spencer W. Kimball said: "Access to (the scriptures) means responsibility for them. We must study the scriptures according to the Lord's commandment, and we must let them govern our lives." As the Lord taught regarding living water: "These words are given unto you, and they are pure before me; wherefore, beware how you hold them, for they are to be answered upon your souls in the day of judgment." (D&C 41:12).

Because they understood that living water would save their very lives, while Josiah and his people were at the temple, they made sacred promises with the Lord. "And the king stood in his place, and made a covenant before the Lord, to walk after the Lord, and to keep his commandments, and his testimonies, and his statutes, with all his heart, and with all his soul, to perform the words of the covenant which are written in this book. And he caused all that were present in Jerusalem and Benjamin to stand to it. And the inhabitants of Jerusalem did according to the covenant of God, the God of their fathers. And Josiah took away all the abominations out of all the countries that pertained to the children of Israel, and made all that were present in Israel to serve, even to serve the Lord their God. And all his days, they departed not from following the Lord, the God of their fathers." (2 Chronicles 34:31-33).

Just so, today we make sacred covenants with the Lord, the fulfillment of which will bring us earthly blessings and eternal exaltation. As we focus our attention on obeying the Lord's commandments and being worthy to enter the temple, our thirst will be quenched with the living water provided by the gospel of Jesus Christ.

Sir Walter Scott may have been thinking of eternal blessings, as well as to the contrasting element of the stark reality of living month to month, paycheck to paycheck, in the lone and dreary world, when he wrote: "Breathes there the man, with soul so dead, who never to himself hath said, 'This is my own, my native land!' Whose heart hath ne'er within him burned, as home his footsteps he hath turned from wandering on a foreign strand". In The Book of Mormon, we find our way home.

Look Who's Coming to Town

(It isn't Santa Claus)

"Those who gain this divine witness
from the Holy Spirit will also come to know
by the same power that Jesus Christ is the Savior
of the world, that Joseph Smith is His revelator and
prophet in these last days and that The Church of
Jesus Christ of Latter-day Saints is the Lord's
kingdom once again established on the
earth, preparatory to the Second
Coming of the Messiah."
(Introduction).

You better watch out, for ye know not when the master of the house cometh." (Matthew 13:35). You better not cry, or be "as the hypocrites, of a sad countenance." (Matthew 6:16). You better not pout, for "a wrathful man stirreth up strife (Proverbs 15:18), and "whosoever is angry with his brother without a cause shall be in danger of the judgment." (Matthew 5:22). I'm telling you why, so pay attention when I ask you to "listen to the words of Christ" (Moroni 8:8), because the Savior, disguised as Santa Claus, is coming to town "to redeem his people." (Alma 11:40).

He's making a list, and when He does so "another book (shall be) opened, which is the book of life." (D&C 128:6). He's checking it twice, for "in the mouth of two...witnesses shall every word be established." (D&C 6:28). And when He does, He's gonna find out who's naughty or nice, for the Lord "is a discerner of the thoughts and intents of the heart." (Hebrews 4:12). So, around the Christmas season, remember that the Savior, disguised as Santa Claus, is coming to town "to redeem his people." (Alma 11:40).

He sees you when you're sleeping, and softly encourages: "Lift up thine eyes now the way toward the north." (Ezekiel 8:5). He knows when you're awake and longs to "go forth into the north country." (Zechariah 6:6). He knows if you've been bad or good, for "our transgressions are multiplied before (Him), and our sins testify against us." (Isaiah 59:12). So be good for goodness sake, that you "might rejoice and be filled with love towards God and all men." (Mosiah 2:4).

With little tin horns, we will "make a long blast" (Joshua 6:5), and our little toy drums will be as rooty toot toots, or "as sounding brass, or a tinkling cymbal." (1 Corinthians 13:1). Our rummy tum tums, will fill the air with "the sound of the cornet, flute, harp, sackbut, psaltery, and all kinds of musick, (Daniel 3:7), and we will rejoice that we have put Christ back into Christmas and understand the hidden meaning in the lyrics of "Santa Claus is Coming to Town." (Haven Gillespie).

The reason that God has given The Book of Mormon to the world is to show His children how they might qualify to regain the glory of their former home. For now, we remain "at work with our hands to the plough and our faces to the future," reflected Sir William Mulock. "The shadows of evening lengthen about us, but morning is in our hearts. My testimony is this: The castle of enchantment is not yet behind me, but is before me still, and daily I catch glimpses of its battlements and towers. The best of life is always further on. Its real lure is hidden from our eyes, somewhere beyond the hills of time."

Lost Books of The Bible

The "great and abominable
church, which is most abominable
above all other churches, (has) taken away
from the gospel of the Lamb many parts
which are plain and most precious;
and also many covenants of the '
Lord have they taken away."
(1 Nephi 13:26).

As it has come down to us, the Bible is of great worth: "Knowest thou the meaning of the book?" the angel asked Nephi. "The book that thou beholdest is a record of the Jews, which contains the covenants of the Lord, which he hath made unto the house of Israel, and it also containeth many of the prophecies of the holy prophets ... wherefore they are of great worth unto the Gentiles. (For) when it proceeded forth from the mouth of a Jew it contained the fulness of the gospel of the Lord." (1 Nephi 21-24). In older editions of The Book of Mormon, this verse was rendered "the plainness of the gospel of the Lord." But the fulness of the gospel is the plan of Salvation, and that is a more accurate description of the Bible before its plain and most precious parts had been deleted.

What is it that has been removed from our K.J.V. of the Bible? The "great and abominable church, which is most abominable above all other churches, (has) taken away from the gospel of the Lamb many parts which are plain and most precious; and also, many covenants of the Lord have they taken away." (1 Nephi 13:26). Sometimes knowingly, and at other times unwittingly, it has changed the covenant, and has effectively eliminated the Old Testament as a witness for Christ. This is an abomination because such actions stop the potential progression of those caught in their snares, and destroy the purpose of mortality in the great Plan of Salvation. With this in mind, the "Church News" reported" "The witness for Christ was the most important thing in that ancient record." (January 1966). Without the testimony of Christ, the Old Testament loses much of its purpose and power. In consequence of the removal of these things, "an exceedingly great many do stumble, yea, insomuch that Satan hath great power over them." (1 Nephi 13:29).

Clearly, additional scripture is important. Nephi wrote: "I beheld the book of the Lamb of God, which had proceeded forth from the mouth of the Jew, that it came forth from the Gentiles unto the remnant of the seed of my brethren. And after it had come forth unto them I beheld other books, which came forth by the power of the Lamb." (1 Nephi 13:38-39).

Then he addressed the importance of "these last records, which thou hast seen among the Gentiles." They "shall establish the truth of the first, which are of the twelve apostles of the Lamb, and shall make known the plain and precious things which have been taken away from them, and shall make known to all kindreds, tongues, and people, that the Lamb of God is the Son of the Eternal Father, and the Savior of the world; and that all men must come unto him, or they cannot be saved." (1 Nephi 13:40).

Additional scripture is valuable, in spite of the protestations of "many of the Gentiles (who) shall say: A Bible! A Bible! We have got a Bible, and there cannot be any more Bible." (2 Nephi 29:3). God is interested in other nations, besides the Jews: "Know ye not that there are more nations than one?" asked his prophet. "Know ye not that I, the Lord your God, have created all men, and that I remember those who are upon the isles of the sea; and that I rule in the heavens above and in the earth beneath; and I bring forth my word unto the children of men, yea, even upon all the nations of the earth?" (2 Nephi 29:7).

Additional scriptures become a second witness of Christ: "Know ye not that the testimony of two nations is a witness unto you that I am God, that I remember one nation like unto another. Wherefore, I speak the same words unto one nation like unto another. And when the two nations shall run together the testimony of these two nations shall run together also." (2 Nephi 29:8).

The body of scripture is the basis upon which God shall judge the world: "For I command all men, both in the east and in the west, and in the north, and in the south, and in the islands of the sea, that they shall write the words which I speak unto them; for out of the books which shall be written I will judge the world, every man according to their works, according to that which is written." (2 Nephi 29:11).

Latter-day Saints are absolutely certain that there is scripture that has been either purposely deleted, or unintentionally lost, from the King James Version of the Bible. As the aforementioned verses from The Book of Mormon illustrate, this missing scripture could be invaluable in eliminating the confusion that currently exists among Christians in matters relating to doctrine.

The debate with those of other faiths centers on whether it is a constructive use of time to discover these writings, and then to decide if they should be considered canonical, or if they should be relegated to apocryphal works (biblical or related writings that have significant spiritual value, but have not been accepted as part of the canon of scripture), Pseudepigraphical works (a loose collection of falsely attributed works that may have esoteric or historical value) or simply profane works (that are not sacred and may even be detrimental to one's spiritual welfare).

This is arguably a moot point, inasmuch as there are currently over a hundred different translations of the Bible, that collectively incorporate into some 31,102 verses tens of thousands of textual variants, many of which twist the meaning of individual passages or messages. Ultimately, the question "What is the Bible?" might never be answered with finality. To add to the confusion, the King James Version of the Bible has 66 books, while the Catholic version has 73 books. The additional books in the Catholic version are Tobit, Judith, Wisdom, Sirach, Baruch, and 1 & 2 Maccabees.

What adds interest to the discussion are the nearly two dozen biblical references to sources that are nowhere to be found, either in that sacred record or elsewhere. The interesting thing is that these authors found these sources to be relevant to their message, so much so, that they pointedly identified them. These include:

The Book of The Covenant (Exodus 24:7). "And he took the book of the covenant, and read in the audience of the people: and they said, All that the Lord hath said will we do, and be obedient." The term "covenant" is usually taken to refer to the legal, moral, and cultic corpus of literature found in Exodus 20:22-23:33.

The Book of The Wars of the Lord (Numbers 21:14). "Wherefore it is said in the book of the wars of the Lord, What he did in the Red Sea, and in the brooks of Arnon." "The Book of The Wars of the Lord, mentioned only once in the Bible, apparently contained an anthology of poems describing the victories of the Lord over the enemies of Israel. This is the complete title of a book which, like several other literary works, has not been preserved." ("Jewish Virtual Library").

The Book of Jasher (Joshua 10:13). "And the sun stood still, and the moon stayed, until the people had avenged themselves upon their enemies. Is not this written in the book of Jasher? So, the sun stood still in the midst of heaven, and hasted not to go down about a whole day." The translation "Book of the Just Man" is the traditional Greek and Latin translation, while the transliterated form "Jasher" is found in the King James Bible.

The Book of The Acts of Solomon (1 Kings 11:41). "And the rest of the acts of Solomon, and all that he did, and his wisdom, are they not written in the book of the acts of Solomon?" "The Acts of Solomon may have been written by the Biblical prophet Iddo, who was the author of other lost texts.

The Book of the Chronicles of the Kings of Israel (1 Kings 14:19). "And the rest of the acts of Jeroboam, how he warred, and how he reigned, behold, they are written in the book of the chronicles of the kings of Israel." "The Chronicles of the Kings of Israel is a book that gives a more detailed account of the reigns of the kings of ancient Kingdom of Israel than that presented in the Hebrew Bible, and may have been the source from which parts of the biblical account were drawn. The book was likely compiled by or derived from the kings of Israel's own scribes, and is likely the source for the basic facts presented in the Bible, though the compiler(s) of the biblical text clearly made selective use of it and added commentaries and judgments. The book is referred to several times in the Hebrew Bible, but was either not included in the corpus of the biblical text or was removed from it at some stage. The book is counted as one of the Lost books of the Old Testament. This text is sometimes called The Book of the Chronicles of the Kings of Israel or The Book of the Annals of the Kings of Israel." ("Wikipedia").

The Book of the Chronicles of the Kings of Judah (1 Kings 14:29). "Now the rest of the acts of Rehoboam, and all that he did, are they not written in the book of the chronicles of the kings of Judah?" "The Chronicles of the Kings of Judah is a book that gives a more detailed account of the reigns of the kings of ancient Kingdom of Judah than that presented in the Hebrew Bible, and may have been the source from which parts of the biblical account was drawn. It is one of the Lost books of the Old Testament. No copies of this book are likely to still exist." ("Wikipedia").

The Chronicles of King David (1 Chronicles 27:24). "Joab the son of Zeruiah began to number, but he finished not, because there fell wrath for it against Israel; neither was the number put in the account of the chronicles of king David." "It may have been written by the biblical prophet Nathan, who was one of King David's contemporaries." ("Wikipedia").

The Books of Nathan and Gad (1 Chronicles 29:29). "Now the acts of David the king, first and last, behold, they are written in the book of Samuel the seer, and in the book of Nathan the prophet, and in the book of Gad the seer." The Book of Gad the Seer is a presumed lost text, supposed to have been written by the Biblical prophet Gad. These writings of Nathan and Gad may have been incorporated into 1 and 2 Samuel. This text is sometimes called Gad the Seer or The Acts of Gad the Seer.

The Prophecy of Ahijah and Visions of Iddo (2 Chronicles 9:29). "Now the rest of the acts of Solomon, first and last, are they not written in the book of Nathan the prophet, and in the prophecy of Ahijah the Shilonite, and in the visions of Iddo the seer against Jeroboam the son of Nebat?" "The book called the Visions of Iddo the Seer is a lost text that was probably written by the Biblical Prophet Iddo, who lived at the time of Rehoboam." ("Wikipedia").

The Book of Shemaiah (2 Chronicles 12:15). "Now the acts of Rehoboam, first and last, are they not written in the book of Shemaiah the prophet, and of Iddo the seer concerning genealogies? And there were wars between Rehoboam and Jeroboam continually." "It was probably written by the Biblical Prophet Shemaiah, who lived at the time of Rehoboam." ("Wikipedia").

The Book of the Kings of Judah and Israel (2 Chronicles 16:11). "And, behold, the acts of Asa, first and last, lo, they are written in the book of the kings of Judah and Israel."

The Book of Jehu (2 Chronicles 20:34). "Now the rest of the acts of Jehoshaphat, first and last, behold, they are written in the book of Jehu the son of Hanani." "The Book of Jehu is a lost text that may have been written by the Biblical prophet Jehu ben Hanani, who was one of King Baasha's contemporaries." ("Wikipedia").

The Story of the Book of the Kings (2 Chronicles 24:27). "Now concerning his sons, and the greatness of the burdens laid upon him, and the repairing of the house of God, behold, they are written in the story of the book of the kings." "The book is found nowhere in the Old Testament, so it is presumed to have been lost or removed from the earlier texts." ("Wikipedia").

The Acts of Uzziah (2 Chronicles 26:22). "Now the rest of the acts of Uzziah, first and last, did Isaiah the prophet, the son of Amoz, write." "The Acts of Uziah is a lost text that may have been written by Isaiah, who was one of King Uzziah's contemporaries. This manuscript is sometimes called Second Isaiah or The Book by the prophet Isaiah." ("Wikipedia").

The Vision of Isaiah (2 Chronicles 32:32). "Now the rest of the acts of Hezekiah, and his goodness, behold, they are written in the vision of Isaiah the prophet, the son of Amoz, and in the book of the kings of Judah and Israel." "The Vision of Isaiah is known to be part of a larger compilation of texts collectively called the Ascension of Isaiah." ("The Gnostic Society Library").

The Book of the Kings of Israel (2 Chronicles 33:18). "Now the rest of the acts of Manasseh, and his prayer unto his God, and the words of the seers that spake to him in the name of the Lord God of Israel, behold, they are written in the book of the kings of Israel." "The book may be identical with the Books of Kings in the Old Testament, or it may have been lost or removed from the earlier texts." ("Wikipedia").

The Sayings of The Seers (2 Chronicles 33:19). "His prayer also, and how God was entreated of him, and all his sin, and his trespass, and the places wherein he built high places, and set up groves and graven images, before he was humbled: behold, they are written among the sayings of the seers." The Sayings of the Seers is referred to as the Sayings of Hozai, in the Masoretic Text.

The Book of the Chronicles before the King (Esther 2:23). "And when inquisition was made of the matter, it was found out; therefore, they were both hanged on a tree: and it was written in the book of the chronicles before the king." "The Chronicles of the Kings of Israel is a book that gives a more detailed account of the reigns of the kings of ancient Kingdom of Israel than that presented in the Hebrew Bible, and may have been the source from which parts of the biblical account were drawn. The book was likely compiled by or derived from the kings of Israel's own scribes, and is likely the source for the basic facts presented in the Bible, though the compiler(s) of the biblical text clearly made selective use of it and added commentaries and judgments." ("Wikipedia").

A reference to an earlier Epistle of Paul to the Ephesians (Ephesians 3:3). "How that by revelation he made known unto me the mystery; (as I wrote afore in few words)."

A reference to an epistle of Paul from Laodicea (Colossians 4:16). "And when this epistle is read among you, cause that it be read also in the church of the Laodiceans; and that ye likewise read the epistle from Laodicea." "The Epistle to the Laodiceans is a possible lost letter of Paul the Apostle, the original existence of which is inferred from an instruction to the church in Colossae to send their letter to the church in Laodicea, and likewise obtain a copy of the letter "from Laodicea." Several ancient texts purporting to be the missing "Epistle to the Laodiceans" have been known to have existed, most of which are now lost. A Latin "Epistle to the Laodiceans" is actually a short compilation of verses from other Pauline epistles, principally Philippians, and on which scholarly opinion is divided as to whether it is the lost Marcionite forgery or alternatively an orthodox replacement of the Marcionite text." ("Wikipedia").

A former Epistle of Jude (Jude 3). "Beloved, when I gave all diligence to write unto you of the common salvation, it was needful for me to write unto you, and exhort you that ye should earnestly contend for the faith which was once delivered unto the saints."

Prophecies of Enoch (Jude 14). "And Enoch also, the seventh from Adam, prophesied of these, saying, Behold, the Lord cometh with ten thousands of his saints." "Where did Jude get his quotation? It is useless to speculate, for the record does not say. He may have received it directly from the Spirit. He may have quoted from some earlier source to which the writer of the Book of Enoch also had access. No conclusion can be drawn in the absence of more precise information." ("Wikipedia").

As we initially turn our attention to 1 Nephi Chapter 1, and we reach out to touch the face of God, the real journey to Christ has only just begun. We must press forward with complete dedication and steadfastness, with confidence and firm determination, having a perfect brightness of hope and a love of God and of all men. We feast upon the word of Christ, receiving scriptural strength and nourishment, and endure to the end in righteousness. We receive His grace and the hope of eternal life, which is the greatest of all His gifts.
(See 2 Nephi 31:20).

(The) Lost Manuscript

(D&C Section 3)

"The Lord hath commanded
me to make these plates for a wise purpose
in him, which purpose I know not. But the Lord
knoweth all things from the beginning; wherefore, he
prepareth a way to accomplish all his works among the
children of men; for behold, he hath all power
unto the fulfilling of all his words."
(1 Nephi 9:5-6).

At least 8 sections of the Doctrine & Covenants were received by the means of the Urim and Thummim. (Sections 3, 6, 7, 11, 14, 15, 16, 17). It seems that the interpreters were not used after Joseph received the Melchizedek Priesthood, around June 1829. The added endowment of the priesthood, combined with Joseph's greater experience in receiving revelation through the channel of the Holy Ghost, may explain why they were unnecessary.

This revelation was "given to Joseph Smith the Prophet, at Harmony, Pennsylvania, July 1828, relating to the loss of 116 pages of manuscript translated from the first part of the Cumorah record that was called the 'Book of Lehi.' The Prophet had reluctantly allowed these pages to pass from his custody to that of Martin Harris, who had served for a brief period as scribe in the translation of The Book of Mormon." (Superscript to Section 3). Those who thoughtfully study this revelation recognize that it stands as a monument to the basic honesty of Joseph Smith.

Speaking of the loss of the pages of translation, Joseph later said: "They have never been recovered unto this day." (H.C. 1:21). His mother recalled in her journal: "I well remember that day of darkness," when it became evident that the manuscript was gone for good. "The heavens seemed clothed with blackness and the earth shrouded with gloom." But "the works, and the designs, and the purposes of God cannot be frustrated, neither can they come to naught." (V. 1). God knows all everything. (See 2 Nephi 9:20). He knows the end from the beginning. (See 1 Nephi 9:6). He is the same yesterday, today and forever. (See 1 Nephi 10:18). Past, present, and future are ever before His eyes. (See 130:7). He can prepare for any eventuality, and certainly for the loss of a simple manuscript, since He is omniscient.

As Joseph Smith explained to John Wentworth: "No unhallowed hand can stop the work from progressing. Persecutions may rage, mobs may combine, armies may assemble, calumny may defame, but the truth of God will go forth boldly, nobly, and independent, until it has penetrated every continent, visited every clime, swept every country, and sounded in every ear, until the purposes of God shall be accomplished, and the Great Jehovah shall say the work is done." (H.C. 4:540). "For God doth not walk in crooked paths, neither doth he turn to the right hand nor to the left, neither doth he vary from that which he hath said, therefore, his paths are straight, and his course is one eternal round." (V. 2). "No power on earth or hell can overthrow or defeat that which God has decreed. Every plan of the adversary will fail, for the Lord knows the secret thoughts of men, and sees the future with a vision clear and perfect, even as though it were in the past." (Joseph Fielding Smith, Jr., "Church History & Modern Revelation," 1:26). "O how great the holiness of our God! For he knoweth all things, and there is not anything save he knows it." (2 Nephi 9:20). If this were not so, "he would cease to be God, and man could not have faith in him." (Joseph Fielding Smith, Jr., "Doctrines of Salvation," 1:7-10).

God is in every sense perfect and so, it is not His work "that is frustrated, but the work of men. For although a man may have many revelations, and have power to do many mighty works, yet if he boasts in his own strength, and sets at naught the counsels of God, and follows after the dictates of his own will and carnal desires, he must fall and incur the vengeance of a just God upon him." (V. 3-4). Because an appeal to our vanity is the devil's way of turning our minds against the Plan of Salvation, Jacob warned against the pitfalls of intellectual apostasy. (2 Nephi 9:28-29 & 42, & Colossians 2:8). To drive the point home, He employed a Hokmah: "But to be learned is good, if they hearken unto the counsels of God." (2 Nephi 9:29).

In Joseph's first interview with Moroni, his mother said he had been told: "You are but a man. Therefore, you will have to be watchful and faithful to your trust or you will be overpowered by wicked men; for they will lay every plan and scheme to get the plates away from you, and if you do not take heed continually, they will succeed." (Lucy Mack Smith, "History of Joseph Smith," p. 110). Now the Lord reminded Joseph: "How strict were your commandments; and remember also the promises which were made to you, if you did not transgress them." (V. 5). "And behold, how oft you have transgressed the commandments and the laws of God, and have gone on in the persuasions of men." (V. 6). Joseph was only 24 years of age when he lost the manuscript. By his own admission, in his youth he had been "left to all kinds of temptations" and had mingled "with all kinds of society" and "frequently fell into many foolish errors, and displayed the weakness of youth, and the foibles of human nature" that led him "into divers temptations, offensive in the sight of God." (J.S.H. 1:28).

But recently, he had been particularly susceptible to the influences of Martin Harris, who was "23 years his senior, a prominent and wealthy farmer, and one of the few who believed his story and supported him with both money and labor. There would have been tremendous inner pressure for Joseph to want to show his appreciation to Martin Harris. His faith in God was absolutely firm, but he lacked experience in trusting his untried friend in his constant pleadings." (Hyrum M. Smith, Janne M. Sjodahl, "Doctrine & Covenants Commentary," p. 19).

The Lord gently chastened Joseph: "For, behold, you should not have feared man more than God. Although men set at naught the counsels of God, and despise his words, yet you should have been faithful, and he would have extended his arm and supported you against all the fiery darts of the adversary; and he would have been with you in every time of trouble. " (V. 7-8). James E. Talmage taught: "Our Heavenly Father has a full knowledge of the nature and dispositions of each of His children, a knowledge gained by long observation and experience in the past eternity of our primeval childhood; a knowledge compared with which that gained by earthly parents through mortal experience with their children is infinitesimally small. By reason of that surpassing knowledge, God reads the future of men individually and collectively. He knows what each will do under given conditions, and sees the end from the beginning. His foreknowledge is based on intelligence and reason; He foresees the future as a state which naturally and surely will be; not as one which must be because He has arbitrarily willed that it should be." ("The Great Apostasy," p. 20).

Therefore, the Lord softly declared: "Thou art Joseph and thou wast chosen to do the work of the Lord, but because of transgression, if thou art not aware thou wilt fall." (V. 9). God only conditionally pre-ordains our fate. (See D&C 130:20). To bring Joseph to a heightened state of awareness of his transgression, the Lord told him: "Repent of that which thou hast done which is contrary to the commandment which I gave you, and thou art still chosen, and art again called to the work." (V. 10).

The only payment required for his gift of forgiveness would be his "heart and a willing mind." (D&C 64:34). The only thing that he would need to surrender would be his sins. As Alma counseled his son Corianton: "Only let your sins trouble you, with that trouble which shall bring you down unto repentance." Through a trying ordeal, Joseph learned to give himself completely to the Lord. Never again would he be persuaded by men to deviate even slightly from his course. The point was driven home when the Lord said: "Except thou do this, thou shalt be delivered up and become as other men, and have no more gift." (V. 11).

Joseph had committed a serious sin. He had delivered the sacred record "into the hands of a wicked man who (had) set at naught the counsels of God, and (had) broken the most sacred promises which were made before God, and (had) depended upon his own judgment and boasted in his own wisdom." (V. 12-13). Martin Harris had become a victim of his own pride that would become a crippling character flaw. By association, Joseph was in peril as well. But the Lord had confidence in his abilities, and knew that through adversity Joseph would yet develop strong spiritual muscles and fulfill his calling as the Prophet of The Restoration.

The work of the Lord would not be frustrated; as the He explained: "For this very purpose are these plates preserved, which contain these records - that the promises of the Lord might be fulfilled, which he made to his people; and that the Lamanites might come to the knowledge of their fathers, and that they might know the promises of the Lord, and that they may believe the gospel and rely upon the merits of Jesus Christ, and be glorified through faith in his name, and that through their repentance they might be saved." (V. 19-20).

"The truth remains that after" the loss of the manuscript, and after "the thousands of attacks and scores of books that have been published, not one attack or criticism has survived, and thousands have borne witness that the Lord has revealed to them the truth of this marvelous work." (Joseph Fielding Smith, Jr., "Church History & Modern Revelation," 1:28-29).

Following the disappearance of the manuscript, the translation of The Book of Mormon was completed, and it was published as a gift "unto the remnant of the House of Israel." (Title Page to The Book of Mormon). It became a blessing to "the Nephites, and the Jacobites, and the Josephites, and the Zoramites, through the testimony of their fathers. And this testimony (would also) come to the knowledge of the Lamanites, and the Lemuelites, and the Ishmaelites." (V. 17-18). The people would yet be called "Zion, because they (would be) of one heart and one mind, and (would dwell) in righteousness; and there (would be) no poor among them." (Moses 7:18).

"For thou art an holy people unto the Lord thy God, and the Lord hath chosen thee to be a peculiar people unto himself, above all the nations that are upon the earth." (Deuteronomy 14:2). We're unique because we enjoy a special, covenant relationship with heaven. Hence, Peter characterized the Saints as "a chosen generation, a royal priesthood, an holy nation, (and) a peculiar people." (1 Peter 2:9). We privately bear the sacred emblems of that covenant, and publicly testify that God lives. We share the witness of those pre-Christian believers among the Nephites in the New World, and at Qumran in the Old World: "Our sins are forgiven us and in the humility of our souls we are for all the Laws of God. Our flesh is cleansed shining bright in the waters of purification, even in the waters of baptism, and we will be given a new name in due time to walk perfectly in all the ways of God." (The Serek Scroll).

(The) Lost Ten Tribes

"I go unto the
Father, and also to show
myself unto the lost tribes of
Israel, for they are not lost unto the
Father, for he knoweth whither he hath
taken them." (3 Nephi 17:4).

Nephi said: "There are many who are already lost from the knowledge of those who are at Jerusalem. Yea, the more part of all the tribes have been led away; and they are scattered to and fro upon the isles of the sea; and whither they are none of us knoweth, save that we know that they have been led away." (1 Nephi 22:4-5).

Nevertheless, he prophesied: "The Lord God will proceed to make bare his arm in the eyes of all the nations, in bringing about his covenants and his gospel unto those who are of the house of Israel. Wherefore, he will bring them again out of captivity, and they shall be gathered together to the lands of their inheritance; and they shall be brought out of obscurity and out of darkness; and they shall know that the Lord is their Savior and their Redeemer, the Mighty One of Israel." (1 Nephi 22:11-12).

In order to accomplish this: "the Lord shall utterly destroy the tongue of the Egyptian sea; and with his mighty wind he shall shake his hand over the river, and shall smite it in the seven streams, and make men go over dry shod." (2 Nephi 27:15).

The Lord revealed to Joseph Smith: "And they who are in the north countries shall come in remembrance before the Lord; and their prophets shall hear his voice, and shall no longer stay themselves; and they shall smite the rocks, and the ice shall flow down at their presence. And an highway shall be cast up in the midst of the great deep. (D&C 133:26-27).

When speaking of Israel, most people think of the Jews, and when referring to the Gathering of Israel, they have in mind the return of the Jews to the land of Jerusalem. It should be remembered, however, that the Jews represent but one of the twelve tribes of the house of Israel. "For lo ... I will sift the house of Israel among all nations." (Amos 9:9).

Isaiah spoke of the Last Days, when the Lord would set His Hand a second time to gather His people. The first time was either during the Exodus from Egypt, or during Israel's return from the Babylonian captivity, depending upon one's point of view. As he saw it, the house of Israel would return from the seven known countries of his day; "from Assyria, and from Egypt, and from Pathros (or upper Egypt), and from Cush (or Ethiopia), and from Elam (east of Babylonia), and from Hamath (Northern Syria), and from the isles of the sea (the rest of the world)." (2 Nephi 21:11).

The apocryphal writer Esdras recorded this version of the escape of the Ten Tribes from Assyria: "Those are the ten tribes, which were carried away prisoners out of their own land in the time of Hosea the king whom Shalmaneser the king of Assyria led away captive, and he carried them over the waters, and so came they into another land. But they took this counsel among themselves, that they would leave the multitude of the heathen, and go forth unto a further country, where never mankind dwelt, that they might there keep their statutes, which they never kept in their own land. And they entered into Euphrates by the narrow passage of the river. For the most High then shewed signs for them, and held still the flood, till they were passed over. For through that country there was a great way to go, namely, of a year and a half: and the same region is called Arsareth. Then dwelt they there until the latter times; and now when they shall begin to come, The Highest shall stay the stream again, that they may go through." (Apocrypha, 2 Esdras 13:40-47).

Interestingly, Esdras declared that the Ten Tribes determined to keep the statutes of the Lord, even though they had not kept them when they were living in the Northern Kingdom. Other scriptures attest to the facts that these tribes were led away by the Lord, have since been continually preserved by Him, have had their own prophets minister among them, had the Savior Himself visit them after His resurrection, have kept their own scriptures and records, keep the statutes of God, and will be led out of the North Country by His power to help build the New Jerusalem.

Lucifer

"How art thou
fallen from heaven, O
Lucifer, son of the morning!
Art thou cut down to the ground,
which did weaken the nations!
(2 Nephi 24:12).

We can learn as much about Lucifer in The Pearl of Great Price as we can anywhere else in scripture. Much of this book was revealed to Joseph Smith when he was engaged in his translation of the Bible, and so it clarifies themes that are only superficially addressed in the King James Translation.

"And I, the Lord God, spake unto Moses, saying: That Satan, whom thou hast commanded in the name of mine Only Begotten, is the same which was from the beginning, and he came before me, saying - Behold, here am I, send me, I will be thy son, and I will redeem all mankind, that one soul shall not be lost, and surely I will do it; wherefore give me thine honor." (Moses 4:1).

Lucifer was very influential in the pre-mortal world of spirits. The name means "bright morning star" in Hebrew and has also been translated as "Light Bearer." In the Great Council he offered to redeem all mankind. (Abraham 3:22-26). But even then, he lacked the faith necessary to allow free will to rule. He was so obsessed by his quest for power and prestige that he concocted a plan that was, in fact, an inoperable counterfeit. It would not work because it would not permit its participants to exercise agency. This is why Satan is called "the father of lies," and "a liar from the beginning." He promoted a bogus plan that, if embraced by a majority of God's spirit children, was calculated to elevate its author to a position of prestige and power.

2 Nephi 24:12-14 and the corresponding verses in Isaiah 14:12-14 are the only places in the Bible and The Book of Mormon where the name "Lucifer" is used. Commentators believe it is a reference to the King of Babylon, since it comes in the midst of a prophecy about Babylon, but latter-day scripture confirms that "Lucifer" was the pre-mortal name of Satan, who is the king, or head, of Spiritual Babylon. (D&C 76:25-27). Dualistic prophecy is at work here.

In a glorious and panoramic vision of the events transpiring in the pre-mortal, mortal, and post-mortal worlds, and of the degrees of glory, Joseph Smith recorded the following: "And this we saw also, and bear record, that an angel of God who was in authority in the presence of God, who rebelled against the Only Begotten Son whom the Father loved and who was in the bosom of the Father, was thrust down from the presence of God and the Son, And was called Perdition for the heavens wept over him - he was Lucifer, a son of the morning. And we beheld, and lo, he is fallen! is fallen, even a son of the morning!" (D&C 76:25-27).

It is possible that Isaiah had access to the writings of Moses that concern Lucifer and his role in the pre-earth existence, because in the Book of Genesis translation found in The Pearl of Great Price, we read: "Wherefore, because that Satan rebelled against me, and sought to destroy the agency of man, which I, the Lord God, had given him, and also, that I should give unto him mine own power; by the power of mine Only Begotten, I caused that he should be cast down; And he became Satan, yea, even the devil, the father of all lies, to deceive and to blind men, and to lead them captive at his will, even as many as would not hearken unto my voice." (Moses 4:3-4).

In 2 Nephi 24:12, Lucifer is called "a son of the morning" who was "cut down to the ground" because he sought personal power and glory. In verse 13, he claimed: "I will ascend into heaven, I will exalt my throne above the stars of God; I will sit also upon the mount of the congregation," that is also translated "in the assembly of Gods" or "upon the Mount of Assembly, where the Gods meet." "In broad terms of ancient near eastern mythology, the divine council was considered to meet on a "cosmic mountain," that place where the gods lived, where heaven and earth intersected, divine decrees were given, kingship was exercised, and from which the cosmic waters of fertility flowed." (E. Theodore Mullen, "The Divine Council," p. 128-74, and Richard J. Clifford, "The Cosmic Mountain in Canaan and the Old Testament," p. 34-176).

In verse 14, Lucifer boasted, "I will ascend above the heights of the clouds; I will be like the Most High." These verses fit very neatly into the L.D.S. theology that concerns the pre-mortal role of Lucifer at the Grand Council in Heaven, (Abraham 3:22-26) where God introduced His Plan of Salvation to His assembled spirit children, when the "foundation of the earth" was laid, and "the morning stars sang together, and all the sons of God shouted for joy." (Job 38:7-8).

Ideological war in heaven soon raged over the principle of agency. The spirit children of our Father were allowed to choose between His Plan and that of the adversary. However, the consequences of choosing unwisely would be eternally damaging.

Unwittingly, Lucifer became a key player in the Plan of Salvation that invited us to live by obedience and by faith. He "became Satan, yea, even the devil, the father of all lies, to deceive and to blind men, and to lead them captive at his will, even as many as would not hearken unto (the Savior's) voice." (Moses 1:4). Lucifer became Perdition, that means "utter disaster, ruin, or destruction." (Archaic). His progression was halted, because he used his agency in the most inappropriate way, by rebelling against the light, while basking in its warmth, and blaspheming the name of God while yet in His presence.

He was, and continues to be, a principal participant and key player in the Plan by providing the opposition that is necessary in all things, as evidenced by his insatiable quest to bolster the numbers of the host of heaven who have fallen from grace.

Observations

We can lose our focus of faith in The Book of Mormon gradually, just as the acuity of our vision may be lost over time. Whether it's the letter of the law or an eye chart that is beyond our comprehension, in either case, we become legally blind. Having eyes, we can no longer see what the Lord has clearly placed before us.

It is only the Atonement of Christ, that has been so powerfully described by the prophets in The Book of Mormon, that has the power to unshackle us from the unpleasant demands that, in the absence of Mercy, would have otherwise been imposed upon all of us by Justice. While darkness is the conjoined twin of misery, the obedience of faith frees us to embrace the truth, to make intelligent choices, to perform purposefully, to carry on convincingly, and to progress persistently. In short, we may rise above all of the cares of the world through the Savior's sacrifice for our sins of both omission and commission, and all of our shortcomings that lie in between those extremes.

As we read and
study The Book of Mormon,
the Holy Ghost will touch our heart
strings to remind us that we were once
fluent in the heavenly language that was
spoken in our pre-mortal home. Even now, His
voice is rhythmical and melodious, soothing to
our ears, and calming to our souls. When we hear
the Spirit whisper: "You're a stranger here," we are
comforted with the reassurance that all of us have
"wandered from a more exalted sphere." (Eliza R.
Snow). The Holy Ghost helps us to examine what
it means to be anxiously engaged and inspires
us to plumb the depth of our commitment to our
Lord Jesus Christ, sensitizes us to the nobility
of His work, and expands upon the visions of
immortality. The Spirit helps us to retain
an awareness of our close proximity to
heaven, whose glory we only recently
left when the time came for it to
be our turn on earth.

Book of
Mormon prophets from
Nephi to Moroni extended to
their people the chance to preview
the ambiance of the divine domicile
where they hoped to return to the warm
embrace of their Father in Heaven, His
Son Jesus Christ, and the Holy Ghost,
Who together would carry them to the
edge of eternity, to the very portals
of heaven, where Forever would be
revealed to them in a mind-
bending panorama.

Beelzebub, the prince of the power of the air, who is a roaring lion, the angel of the bottomless pit, and a ruler of darkness, was always prodding and probing the Nephites' defenses for signs of weakness in the fortress that was their spiritual security. His temptations of pleasure and advantage were adroit, and they were insidious. And then, when they capitulated to his influences and succumbed to their old habits of sin, they felt increasingly uncomfortable in the company of the more righteous members of their communities. At the same time, as they spiraled inevitably downward into the abyss of apostasy, their free will and power to change slipped away. The gates of hell loomed large, while the weight of the chains of Satan became oppressive to bear for the Nephites, who became thoroughly entrenched in self defeating behaviors.

When cataracts that were created by the Nephites' concessions to sin clouded their sight, their narrow perspective forced them into making comfortless compromises, leaving the landscapes of their lives as nothing but empty shells. Whenever they failed to take advantage of the therapy offered by the Holy Ghost, their prognosis remained poor, for He is a heavenly optometrist for eyes that have lost the ability to see clearly, and that can no longer make the distinction between good and evil and between light and darkness, and even between pleasure and pain. Only He can restore our vision to the 20:20 acuity we enjoyed before we came to earth.

Sometimes all too quickly, and at other times agonizingly slowly, the Nephites who had sold their souls to the Devil for a mess of pottage were dragged down to a veritable hell on earth that was of their own construction. Their bad habits were the result of repetitively impulsive behaviors that, in a rising tide of wickedness, continually eroded away at the foundations of agency. They were fettered by the chains of compulsions. They realized too late that unlimited freedom leads to tyranny. The Holy Ghost had the power, however, to lead them back on the path of safety to the law of liberty that they enjoyed in their heavenly home before their births.

In The Book of Mormon, we're taught that our Heavenly Father is the Grand Architect of a divine design that establishes our familial roots and confirms His fatherhood, that we might enjoy a witness that it is in Him alone that "we live, and move, and have our being; as certain also of (our) poets have said. For we are also his offspring." (Acts 17:28). If we will only seek to understand ourselves from an eternal perspective, we will raise our sights to the possibility of an expanded view of life, and we will be up and moving forward on the pathway to personal re-discovery as well as religious re-cognition.

Life in Zarahemla was made up of an endless chain of spiritual experiences that were offset by a constant counterpoint of worldliness. At first blush, there appears to have been a wide gulf between the spiritual and the temporal, that one would think might have made things easier for the righteous Nephites. The contrasting sides of their nature seem to have been incompatible. Without a working knowledge of the principles of the Plan, it would have been much more difficult to reconcile the two and enjoy a state of holiness as their natural habitat, richer for having had their mortal experiences. The Nephites were not meant to be worn down by life, or to be overcome by evil influences. Rather, they were destined to be refined and purified by adversity, by danger, by misfortune, and by unforeseen challenges.

If, through our study, we are able to learn anything from the experiences of the Nephites, it's that both great and terrible judgments are on the horizon, not at some hazy point in the future, but today. We speak, think, and act according to either celestial, terrestrial, or telestial laws. We've been blessed with a moral compass, and faith in Christ with its evidence in action clearly defines the path that we have chosen to follow. Each day that we live, we are 24 hours closer to the Pleasing Bar of Christ. If we've committed the 13th Article of Faith to practice as well as to memory, its principles will have become the particles of our faith.

Murmuring is the subdued and continually repeated expression of indistinct or inarticulate complaining or grumbling. Like earth tremors, murmuring can build into harmonic waves and undermine the foundations of relationships and institutions. It is an act of cowardice, because those who murmur expect results without responsibility. While it is often conducted anonymously or in the cloak of secrecy, its effect is felt publicly. Those who murmur want a tangible return without having made a legitimate initial investment. "Laman and Lemuel and the sons of Ishmael did begin to murmur exceedingly, because of their sufferings and afflictions in the wilderness; and also, my father began to murmur against the Lord his God; yea, and they were all exceedingly sorrowful, even that they did murmur against the Lord. (1 Nephi 16:20).

Every time that the Nephites turned their backs on the Law, their temporal preparation proved to be of no benefit in avoiding the pitfalls to progression and inevitable disasters that rained down upon them. Their calamities have been symbolized by the burning of both stubble and chaff (see 2 Nephi 15:24), that are very quickly engulfed, and then consumed, by fire.

Untested potential is antithetical to the principles of the Plan. The Lord said: "I will try the faith of my people." (3 Nephi 26:11). The Book of Mormon's been given to the church members as a self-administered examination. They are compelled to read it in order to nurture independent testimonies of the book's divine authenticity and to be able to answer God's test questions. If they don't wholeheartedly embrace the doctrine of Christ contained therein, and if they fail to live up to their covenants, they will be in the power of Satan. The inquisition that accompanied the grand experiment posited by Alma to the poor Zoramites foreshadowed an ominous consequence. (See Alma 32). None of us will receive a witness until after our faith has been tried. Only after having passed through the refiner's fire will we become as tempered steel in our devotion to the Savior. "I have refined thee," said the Lord, "but not with silver; I have chosen thee in the furnace of affliction." (Isaiah 48:10). Tom Paine rightly observed: "What we obtain too cheap, we will esteem too lightly. 'Tis dearness alone that gives everything its value. Heaven knows how to put a proper price on its goods."

The Apostle Paul echoed the teaching of Nephi, writing that it is by grace that we are saved, through faith, and that not of ourselves. "It is the gift of God." (Ephesians 2:8).

It's abundantly clear that the efforts of the Nephites were most profitably expended when they resulted in spiritual fitness. Their testimonies of the gospel and its exalting principles never came as unearned gifts. The Savior said: "Behold, you have not understood," for "you have supposed that I would give it unto you, when you took no thought save it was to ask me, But, behold, I say unto you, that you must study it out in your mind." (D&C 9:7-8). Agency was at its best when it gave the Nephites the power to make correct choices, but it was not free. It was purchased at a substantial cost. Perhaps it would be better to characterize agency as free will, or even as freedom of expression, rather than as 'free agency,' which is a misnomer.

It is beyond the comprehension of the faithless that each of us came into the world that we might die. (See Alma 12:24). Surely, before we left our pre-mortal home, we must have clearly understood that the Plan of Salvation would require the death of our bodies. Adam was sent to Eden to dwell with Eve with the understanding that they would violate or transgress a law, that they might really live, and then mercifully go the way of all flesh. (See 1 Kings 2:2, & 2 Nephi 9:6).

Ultimately, it was for their own good that Adam and Eve were driven from a morally static environment in the Garden into an unfamiliar and dangerous territory filled with unimaginable opportunity. In the lone and dreary world, even when it became a Land of Promise for Lehi's descendants who had become a fruitful bough who grew over the wall, living by the sweat of their brow was not a punishment, but instead was a celebratory experience.

Within the parameters of our Heavenly Father's "Great and Eternal Plan of Deliverance from Death," (2 Nephi 11:5), there is no latitude in the provision that states that He "cannot look upon sin with the least degree of allowance." (D&C 1:31). Thus, there is no alternative to baptism; it typifies the portal through which we must all pass on our journey home to the celestial courts of God. Faith and repentance lead us to that narrow gate, on whose far side lie the remission of sins, membership in the church, as well as sanctification through receipt of the Holy Ghost. The way is strait and the standard undeviating, with no room for rationalization or compromise. There can be no allowance made for the indifferent substitution of less rigorous stipulations that attempt to homogenize the requirement for forgiveness of our sins.

The logical and measured rational thought processes
of secular humanism that govern "our age is retrospective,
building on the sepulchers of the fathers. It writes biographies,
history, and criticism. The foregoing generations beheld God and
nature face to face; we, thru their eyes. But why should we not also
enjoy an original relation to the universe? Why should we not have
a poetry and philosophy of insight and not only of tradition, and
a religion by revelation to us, and not just the history of theirs?"
Ralph Waldo Emerson). If we will recommit ourselves to study
the revealed word of God, we will find that Alma's promise
is true; that it will have a great tendency to lead us to do
what is right. In fact, it will exert a more powerful
effect upon us than the sword, or anything
else which could have wrought upon
us, to amend our behavior.
(See Alma 31:5).

We will never be able to partake
of the cornucopia of fruit that hangs from the
branches of the Tree of Life unless we have first
accepted the fact that perspiration must precede
inspiration. (See Alma 32:40). If we choose
mediocrity, rationalization, things of the
world, selfish pleasures, the honors of
men, or disobedience, our priorities
are out of order. As long as we
remain in this state, we lose
the power to make even
hesitant progress on
the path leading
to the tree.

The
prophet Zenos
foresaw that Israel,
represented by the leafy
branches of an olive tree that
had grown wild, would be grafted
in to the natural tree, representing a
spiritual rebirth. The roots and branches
would be equal in strength, as they were
nourished by the word of God. They would
embrace each line upon line and precept
upon precept. Covenant Israel, who are
the Gentiles, would grow up beside
Blood Israel, with testimonies of
the Lord. In the millennial day,
it will no longer be as it had
been, when the branches
had grown at a faster
rate than the roots
could bear.

Just as the Lord Jehovah
had made an oath to Noah that He would never
again destroy the earth by a flood (see 3 Nephi 22:9, &
Genesis 9:12-17) so too did He swear to the Nephites that
He would not be angry with the children of Israel: "For the
mountains shall depart and the hills be removed, but my
kindness shall not depart from thee, neither shall
the covenant of my peace be removed, saith
the Lord that hath mercy on thee."
(3 Nephi 22:10).

It should come as no
surprise to learn that there
still exist doctrines relating to
the expansive scope of the Plan of
Salvation that simply have not yet been
made clear, either in the scriptures, or in the
teachings of the prophets. Alma felt that it was
always better to keep his opinion to himself, rather
than to speculate without a foundation of revelation.
It is prudent, he suggested, that one remain silent and
be thought a fool, than to speak, and remove all doubt
in the matter. When counseling his son Corianton, he
underscored this point: "There are many mysteries,"
he explained, "which are kept, that no one knoweth
them, save God himself." (Alma 40:3). He taught
that when God withholds understanding from
His children, it is "for a wise purpose," and
there has been no intent to mislead or to
deceive. We can always be certain
that "his paths are straight."
(Alma 40:12).

When they have unexpectedly found
themselves bathed in the stunning clarity
of light that comes streaming down from above,
those who are reading The Book of Mormon for the
first time will often stare in wide-eyed wonder at
the simplicity of the interwoven threads found
within the pattern of gospel principles that
make up the tapestry of the Plan of
Salvation that is described
in the book.

Alma taught the poor
Zoramites only the first
principles and basic doctrines
of the gospel, in order to strengthen
their faith. The question on his mind as
he approached his assignment must have
gone something like this: "Am I providing
them with skim milk, 2% milk, or with
milk whose shelf life has passed the
expiration date? Or, am I instead
giving them the whole, fresh,
nutritionally fortified and
organically certified
milk that they
need?"

When
we accept The
Book of Mormon
as holy scripture, we
choose liberty and eternal
life, instead of captivity and
spiritual death. We choose to live
our lives in accordance with the laws
of the gospel. Without them, unbridled
freedom to choose might lead to tyranny.
We are free to choose whether or not we wish
to embrace the book, but we cannot escape
the consequences if we've unwisely
chosen to summarily dismiss
its merits.

With only a few clicks of a mouse, or with just one or two keystrokes, even those with few computer skills can be transported directly "into enemy territory without having to first go through passport control." (Neal Maxwell). The acquisition of knowledge can be a treacherous process if it is not accompanied by the Spirit of God. "O that cunning plan of the evil one! O the vainness, and the frailties, and the foolishness of men! When they are learned they think they are wise, and they hearken not unto the counsel of God, for they set it aside, supposing they know of themselves, wherefore, their wisdom is foolishness and it profiteth them not." (2 Nephi 9:29).

To dung a plant (see Jacob Chapters 5 & 6), or to spread manure around its base, is symbolic of the nourishing of gathered Israel with the restored gospel. This careful attention will cause her to grow, or to increase in her righteousness, as God prepares the earth one last time for the glorious return and millennial reign of its rightful King.

Each of us
is subjected to a
constant stream of
insight and intuition,
as well as of inspiration
and of revelation flowing
from heaven in a cascade of
creativity. Celestial direction
prescribes that we walk along
illuminated pathways where
we'll implement our faculties
of mind and spirit, to better
understand how The Book
of Mormon satisfies our
craving for spiritual
understanding.

The plain and simple teachings
of our Savior Jesus Christ may be even more
clearly understood in The Book of Mormon than they
are in the biblical record, which is one of the reasons why an
angel of the Lord told Nephi "they both shall both be established
in one." (1 Nephi 13:41). Thus, thru the Law of Witnesses would
these two books confirm the divinity of our Redeemer. "That which
shall be written (in the Bible and The Book of Mormon) shall grow
together, unto the confounding of false doctrines and laying
down of contentions, and establishing peace among
the (inhabitants of the House of Israel), and
bringing them to a knowledge of my
covenants, saith the Lord."
(2 Nephi 3:12).

Gandhi, "the great soul," proclaimed a simple statement of belief that has forever changed how we look at both ourselves and the world: "My life is my message." The same could be said of Captain Moroni, who was ever faithful to his principles that, as moral and ethical constants, were as guiding stars that led him to safety. The Savior, Who was his Exemplar, was as a Prototype of the perfection that was within the reach of Moroni. He knew that without divine intervention, his efforts would be doomed to failure. His obedience was the key element that broke down every barrier that stood in the way of his personal progress. It was the law of liberty in a world where attacks on freedom were common.

Following Adam's fall from grace, cherubim were instructed by God to prevent him from inappropriately partaking of the fruit of the Tree of Life before first being taught the principles of the Plan of Happiness. (See Alma 42:3). Had he done so without first learning how rely upon the merits of Christ thru the Atonement, he and Eve, as well their posterity, would have lived forever in their sins.

We
are all subject
to the unassailable
law of cause and effect.
As long as those who bear
the burden of sin find it within
themselves to focus their faith on the
Atonement of Christ, which is the only
mechanism that is capable of nullifying the
consequences of their poor choices, and if they
also muster the fortitude to do whatever needs to
be done to draw His power into their own lives, they
will uncover the gifts of the Spirit. All who have faith in
the ability of Christ to save them from their sins will have a
profound motivation to live in accordance with His will. They
will enjoy an eternal perspective because they see with the eye of
faith. They'll not only believe in Christ, but they'll also believe
Christ when He says that they can inherit celestial glories. The
striking manifestation of spiritual gifts will provide dramatic
validation of their persistent efforts to conform their lives to
His nature. They will raise their voices to testify that they
have experienced a change in their hearts, and that
within themselves they have felt the urge to join
with the angels in the praise of God, and to
sing the song of redeeming love.
(See Alma 5:26).

Faithful disciples declare God's truth
as it has been delivered to the world in The Book of
Mormon, with their hands uplifted unto the Most High,
and their incomings, outgoings, salutations, and
hallelujahs in the name of the Lord.
(See D&C 109:17-18.

We
are reinvigorated
to share the gospel with our
friends and neighbors when we
read the account in the Book of Alma
wherein Ammon metaphorically described
a harvest, that he might illustrate how thousands
and thousands of wicked Lamanites had been gathered
through the missionary efforts of his brethren, known as
the Sons of Mosiah. "Behold, the field was ripe," he said, "and
blessed are ye, for ye did thrust in the sickle, and did reap with
your might, yea, all the day long did ye labor; and behold the
number of your sheaves!" (Alma 26:5). His party had come
up out of the Land of Zarahemla into the highlands of
Nephi to bring a message of love to the Lamanites.
In its absence, their kinsmen "would still have
been racked with hatred (against their
brethren the Nephites), and they
would also have (remained)
strangers to God."
(Alma 26:9).

The Book of Mormon remains
as one of God's greatest gifts to
a world that lies groaning under the
massive burden of unresolved sin. It is
an invaluable aid as it brings the riches of
eternity within our grasp by expanding our
vision beyond physical laws that pertain only
to the telestial world, toward an appreciation
of gospel principles that relate to heaven.
The book invites us to reach out and
touch the face of God.

Those who have
become enslaved by
their selfish indulgences
to the point that they "regard
not the work of the Lord, neither
consider the operation of his hands,"
must ultimately drink of the wine of the
wrath of the indignation of God. (2 Nephi
15:12). Without knowledge of heaven, they are
as those who are "famished, and their multitude
dried up with thirst. Therefore, hell hath enlarged
herself, and opened her mouth without measure;
and their glory, and their multitude, and their
pomp, and he that rejoiceth, shall descend
into it (even as) God that is holy (is)
sanctified in righteousness."
(2 Nephi 15:13-16).

We learn from
The Book of Mormon
that following the ministry
of the Savior among the Nephites,
their love for Him, and for each other,
was so great that they were the happiest
people of all those who had ever been
created by the hand of God.
(See 4 Nephi 1:15-16).

The Old Testament prophet Ezra revealed something about his character, that we find reminiscent of the behavior of the righteous Nephites and Lamanites that we read about in The Book of Mormon, when he acknowledged: "At the evening sacrifice, I arose up from my heaviness, and rent my garment and my mantle. I fell upon my knees, and spread out my hands unto the Lord my God, and said I am ashamed and blush to lift up my face to thee, for our iniquities are increased over our head, and our trespass is grown up unto the heavens." (Ezra 9:5-6). "Then Ezra rose up from before the house of God ... and he did eat no bread, nor drink water." (Ezra 10:6).

"They that wait upon the Lord shall renew their strength, they shall mount up with wings as eagles, they shall run, and not be weary, and they shall walk, and not faint." (Isaiah 40:31, see Mosiah 4:27, & Ecclesiastes 9:11). The ancients recognized the relationship that exists between obedience to the commandments and physical well-being; that when we consciously and deliberately adopt lifestyles that lead to poor physical health, "wisdom cannot reveal itself, culture cannot become manifest, strength cannot fight, wealth becomes useless, and intelligence cannot be applied." (Heraclitus).

Lucifer was the quintessential drug
dealer who was particularly successful
among Lamanite addicts, who were often his
best customers. He'd been "a son of the morning,"
whose powerful influence over our Heavenly Father's
children was genuinely impressive. His name meant
"Light Bearer," and so he was. In the Great Council,
he offered to redeem all mankind. But even then, he
lacked the faith necessary to allow agency to rule.
He concocted an inoperable counterfeit plan that
would have denied its participants the powers
to exercise free will in order to create positive
change. Because of his passionate, and yet
misguided, promotion of this spurious
proposal, the scriptures refer to him
as Satan, the father of lies, and
as a liar from the beginning,
meaning from before the
foundation of the
world.

In Book of Mormon times
as well as in our day, God has laid
bare His arm and has shown His power
in order to lead His chosen people Israel out
of captivity, to bring her out of obscurity
and darkness, and to gather her to the
lands of her inheritance, that she
might know that the Lord
is her Redeemer.

Astute observers of The Book of Mormon view its doctrine as the key that unlocks a portal leading to the ordinances and covenants that enable us to be sanctified, to be worthy to live again in a state of holiness in the presence of our Heavenly Father. If we use the book as it was intended, we may all "continue in the supplicating of (God's) grace," to one day stand blameless before Him at His Pleasing Bar. (See Alma 7:3).

We learn by reading the Book of Mormon that the 'rod' is often a symbol of the active engagement of priesthood power. (See 1 Nephi 3:29). The Lord has revealed His battle plan for the Last Days, when a missionary army will engage the worldly, whose corruptible ideology will be overwhelmed. They'll be reborn spiritually in the face of the bombardment of love unfeigned, the onslaught of priesthood principles, and by the crushing clout that is characteristic of the powerful covenants that the penitent have always embraced after their faith has convicted them of their sins.

With our fasting, the temporal and the spiritual sides of our nature are slowly harmonized until they reach an equilibrium. (See Alma 5:46). Our physical desires begin to be tempered by a spiritual awareness that will gradually strengthen our resolve to discipline our carnal nature. We transcend forces that pull us one way or the other, as we enter a metaphysical state of euphoria. (See 4 Nephi 1:12). Virtue begins to garnish our thoughts as the doctrine of the priesthood distills upon our souls as the dews from heaven, and our confidence begins to wax strong in the presence of God. (See Alma 17:9). As this process unfolds, the Holy Ghost will become our constant companion, and our scepter an unchanging scepter of righteousness and truth. Our dominion will be a God centered and focused province of protection. (See Moroni 6:5). When these conditions govern our lives, all that is good will begin to freely flow unto us in a stream that has no end and will exist for all of eternity. (See D&C 121:45-46).

The image and likeness of God (see Ether 3:17), is a reflection of His divine attributes and His noble character. It is marked by uncomplicated simplicity, refreshing candor, unblemished honesty, and undisputed holiness. These qualities are emphasized in The Book of Mormon, in the lives of prophets like Nephi, Jacob, Benjamin, Alma, and Samuel the Lamanite.

Since Nephite times, it has been the vision quest of the righteous that they might obtain the Rest of the Lord. That spiritually stable state of equilibrium is as a steady beacon of hope to the faithful, standing in sharp contrast to the telestial trauma inflicted by wars and rumors of wars that are so commonplace today. Peace of mind and spirit is born of a settled conviction of the truth in our hearts. Today, even in the midst of adversity, and as the order of our society crumbles around us, we enter God's Rest by coming to an understanding of the truths of the gospel, and then by living our lives in harmony with celestial principles. His peace is "the peace born of the righteous life, the peace that lifts the soul, that day by day brings us closer to the home of Eternal Peace, that is the dwelling place of our Father." (J. Reuben Clark, Jr.).

Amidst his attempts to denigrate the significance of the Savior's efforts, the Devil has grossly misjudged His capacity to bless the world with The Book of Mormon. As it turns out, all that's ever been necessary to restore our purity is the further light and knowledge that He has promised to give us. Satan did see that one coming, but he was powerless to intervene or change the outcome.

Moroni
exhibited no hesitation when
prophesying that latter-day Israel
would be brought out of captivity and
obscurity and gathered to the lands of her
inheritance as well as to an awareness that
the Lord Jesus Christ was her Redeemer. (See
Moroni 10:31). The followers of Satan don't
understand that, particularly in the Last
Days, it is the arm of the Lord that is our
real source of strength and support, in
contrast to the arm of flesh which is
unstable, volatile, and subject
to senseless outbursts
of violence.

There is a clear
and unambiguous choice that
every child of God has been blessed to face
in this life, regardless of their circumstances. It
doesn't matter if they are Jews or Gentiles, Nephites or
Lamanites, Muslim or Christian, or believers or heathen.
The choice is not between poverty and wealth, nor is it between
sickness and health, or happiness and misery, or between fame and
obscurity. The choice is between good and evil. And so, when Jesus comes
again, His glory will be like that of a fire purging from blemished lives all
of their accumulated impurities. An analogy comes from the process of
purification: If there are imperfections that remain in metal (or in
character) after the refiner's fire, it will have little or no value,
and must be cast upon the scrap heap. Only if it has been
cleansed of contamination can it be fashioned into
something of worth that will stand up under
punishing use and give years of
consistently reliable service.

In the scriptures, the phrase "Isles of the sea" is a Semitic idiom reflecting the practice of sailing away to far off locations throughout the world. (See 1 Nephi 19:16, 21:8, 22:4, 2 Nephi 10:2 & 29:7). The continents of Asia and Africa, by contrast, were "the earth" because they had access to them by land. Idioms are expressions that are peculiar to a given culture, and we would expect Semitic examples throughout The Book of Mormon. The ease with which idioms have been sprinkled into the narrative suggests that they were utilized by Israelite authors. It begs our credulity to think that Joseph Smith would have been clever enough to employ them on his own and in perfect context.

Alma described God's divine design as a Plan of Salvation and of Redemption, Mercy, and Happiness, because it has made possible the resurrection of otherwise imperfect mortals to an eternal life of joy and glory. These "great and eternal purposes were prepared from the foundation of the world." (Alma 42:26). "To the Son is given the power of the resurrection, the power of the redemption, the power of salvation, the power to enact laws for the carrying out and accomplishment of the design. Hence, life and immortality are brought to light, the gospel is introduced, and He becomes the Author of eternal life and exaltation." (John Taylor).

The psalmist wrote: "But as for me .....
my clothing was sackcloth: I humbled my soul
with fasting." (Psalms 35:13). This is good counsel that
the Nephites could have taken from the Plates of Brass. When
the law is written upon our hearts, and we feel the forgiveness of
God, we must seize the opportunity at that very moment to forgive
others, focusing spiritual power on our efforts, precisely because it
is so contrary to our human nature to do so. (See 3 Nephi 12:44).
The opportunity to forgive others should never be wasted, because
it awakens within our hearts spiritual sensitivity that is far
greater than ourselves. Brigham Young echoed Confucius
when he cautioned the Saints: "He who takes offense
when no offense was intended is a fool, and he
who takes offense when it was intended
is usually a fool."

The Book of Mormon illustrates
how we are all influenced by Satan's
bribes. But it is precisely because the Plan
requires opposition that the earth has become
an astonishing learning laboratory, a majestic
clockwork, and a perfect 'machine for the making
of Gods.' (Henri Bergson). But without the principles,
the ordinances, and the covenants of the gospel that are
designed to hold evil in check, mortality would've become
nothing more than a malicious trap or a snare of Satan;
and if he were to be given free-reign to attack the fold,
his ravenous wolves would first scatter, then isolate,
and finally devour at will every single member
of the flock of the Good Shepherd. Thank God,
or hallelujah, for such a supportive
community of the faithful!

Nephite and Lamanite
prophets provided their people
with celestial sign posts to guide
them thru the telestial traffic jams
that threatened to detour them from the
strait and narrow way. At the same time,
widening circles of opportunity were made
accessible by obedience to gospel principles,
assuring them that they would have direct
exposure to the law of liberty. Thereby, they
abandoned the tortuous route thru Idumea
that was being taken by Lamanites who
were bound for telestial glory. Instead,
the righteous descendants of Lehi
followed an unmistakable track
that led to celestial surety in
a heavenly setting.

"You ought to ask Mr. Mephistopheles, the
original conjuring cat. The greatest magicians have
something to learn from Mr. Mephistopheles' conjuring turn.
And you'll all say: Oh! Well I never! Was there ever a cat so clever
as magical Mr. Mephistopheles?" Mephistopheles, the prince of the power
of the air, is a roaring lion, the angel of the bottomless pit, and a ruler of
darkness. He was always probing Nephite defenses for signs of weakness
in the fortress of their spiritual security. When they finally capitulated
to his wiles and became entrenched in the habit pattern of sin, they felt
uncomfortable associating with the more righteous members of their
communities. At the same time, as they spiraled downward into
the abyss of apostasy, their free will and power to change
slowly slipped away. The gates of hell loomed large,
and the weight of the chains of Satan became
oppressive for them to bear.

The prophet Abinadi cautioned wicked King Noah and his advisors that rather than consolidating power, they should instead listen to the Holy Ghost, Who generates cooperation. When men and women "are carnal," he warned, "the devil has power over them; yea, even that old serpent that did beguile our first parents, which was the cause of their fall; which was the cause all mankind becoming carnal, sensual, devilish, knowing evil from good, subjecting themselves to the devil." (Mosiah 16:3).

When Lamanite ruffians came to scatter the flocks of King Lamoni by the waters of Sebus (see Alma Chapter 17), Ammon maintained unbridled confidence in the power of God unto the deliverance the faithful. Therefore, he anticipated with joy a situation that, at the same time, must have caused palpitations in the hearts of his fearful companions. Today, we too must face our own 'Lamanites by the Waters of Sebus.' All of us have similar needs, but the primary focus of our shared concern should be on the preservation of our eternal lives. In truth, proper prior preparation, and abiding confidence in God's omnipotence, will prevent our poor performance in the very hour of our greatest need.

We share the Good News in
a hierarchy that is first based on
understanding, next on acceptance, then
on commitment, and finally on recommitment.
Our preaching is akin to understanding, teaching to
acceptance, expounding to commitment, and exhortation
to re-commitment. Our testimonies are expression of action
that follow the internalization of principles. They are borne with
strenuous effort that reflects the price we have paid to understand
the voice of the Lord concerning those principles. Testimony is a
reflection of the value that we place on direct experience with the
Spirit as it teaches us about those principles. Testimony isn't
free, but is purchased at a considerable expense. Testimony
releases the power of principles and empowers us to bind
ourselves to those principles by covenants of action
that increase our strength and endurance as
we learn to rely upon the Lord in all that
we say and everything that we do.
He completes us. He is at once
the Author and Finisher
of our faith.

One of the
basic messages of
The Book of Mormon
is that Adam and Eve
fell that they might have
joy during mortality and
in heaven, thru repentance
that had been activated by
their faith in the power of
the Atonement to save
them from, and not
in, their sins.

One of the greatest blessings that we can receive from our Father in Heaven as we devour The Book of Mormon is that when we digest its teachings "all the petty trials, sorrows, and sufferings of life will fade away as temporary, harmless visions seen in a dream." (David O. McKay). Our reverence for the Savior will move beyond an association with the profane. Our standard of reverence will be so high that we will have a desire to be defenders of the faith when the line is crossed by those who find fault with the principles of the gospel or the Author of Salvation. As the Sons of Mosiah, we will never hesitate to venture out of the fold to within a hundred yards of hell, to rescue the lost sheep who cross our paths.

The experiences that we have in mortality are the active ingredients of a fertile matrix that has been carefully prepared by our Father to vitalize the personalized petri dish that is best suited to our individual circumstances. This rich culture medium will become just the agar we need in order to nurture our metamorphosis, to be transformed not by maturation but by generation into the full stature of our spirits. The infusion of a heavenly element readies us to receive with equanimity whatever might come our way during an incubation process that was initiated by divine design to be equally challenging and rewarding.

The flowing river of filthy
water beheld in vision by Lehi was as
"an awful gulf which separated the wicked
from the tree of life, and also from the saints
of God." (1 Nephi 12:16). The Plan of Salvation
requires that there always exist a barrier between
the spirits of the righteous and the unrighteous,
as both await the resurrection. That barrier is
nothing more than the justice of God "and
the brightness thereof (will be) like unto
the brightness of a flaming fire,
which ascendeth up unto
God forever and ever."
(1 Nephi 15:30).

Anciently, the prophet Zenos
likened Israel to an olive tree with
many branches that would be broken
off and "scattered upon all the face of the
earth." (1 Nephi 10:12). Lehi learned from
the Spirit that his family group would be
one of those branches that would leave
their home in the land of Jerusalem,
and would be led to a land of
promise, where they would
constitute the fruitful
bough prophesied
by Joseph.

With only a handful of striking exceptions, the Lamanites seldom wanted to hear the good news. It seems that some things never change. But we need to remind ourselves that when the world rejected the Mortal Messiah, He didn't retreat with His tail between His legs to His home in Galilee. The Lord wants us to know what it's like to feel the Spirit; not only the happiness of seeing our friends and neighbors enter in at the fold and be born again, but also to feel the pain and frustration of rejection. In strange and mysterious ways, these are contraries that work together for our good in the refiner's fire.

Whenever Latter-day Saints cannot find the resources within the church to sustain their connection to Deity that has been established by their study of The Book of Mormon, they will be at risk of sliding into marginalized relationships that may even brand them as less active, or inactive. Fundamentally, they'll lose direction, power, and purpose, because they have lost the means to nourish, support, and sustain the networks that were powered by principles that had, at one time, been their guiding lights.

Early-on in The Book of Mormon's narrative, we discover a verse that explains why a comprehension of Isaiah is so difficult, even for biblical scholars. Nephi said: I "speak somewhat concerning the words which I have written, which have been spoken by the mouth of Isaiah. For behold, Isaiah spake many things which were hard for many of my people to understand; for they know not concerning the manner of prophesying among the Jews." (2 Nephi 25:1). That is to say, the prophet Isaiah spoke in figures, using types and shadows to illustrate his points. Thus, the key to an understanding of his scriptural code requires some elucidation.

Moroni saw that in our day, "religion builders would deform the doctrines of Jesus, muffle them in mysticisms, fancies, and falsehoods, and caricature them into forms so inconceivable as to shock reasonable thinkers. Happy in the prospect of a restoration of primitive Christianity, I must leave it to younger persons to encounter and lop off the false branches which have been grafted into it by the mythologists of the middle and modern ages." (Thomas Jefferson).

"Jesus Christ (is) the Son of God, the Father of heaven and earth, the Creator of all things." (Mosiah 3:8). Reverently, then, we take His name upon ourselves, and when we do so we are called by His name in a familial way. "For this day He hath spiritually begotten you," taught Benjamin. (Mosiah 5:7). A special relationship is reserved for the faithful that is in addition to the reality that we are all the spiritually begotten children of our Father Who lives in Heaven.

If we only superficially understand the guiding principles, or the grammar of the gospel that is taught in The Book of Mormon, we are at risk of falling into transgression, and then suffering from the inevitable consequences of our spiritual illiteracy. We've all witnessed how picking apart the scriptures has a tendency to distort doctrine into meaningless fragments with little or no coherent connection. As Alma counseled the inhabitants of Ammonihah: "The scriptures are before you (and) if ye will wrest them, it shall be to your own destruction." (Alma 13:20).

The Devil's enticements
were hard for Nephites to resist.
He attracted those of weak will with
the offer of pleasure or advantage, and
as a seducer and tempter, he insidiously
deceived them. But because the Plan requires
opposition, their mortal classroom became their
learning laboratory and a majestic clockwork,
and even "a machine for the making of Gods."
(Henri Bergson). But without the principles, the
ordinances, and doctrines of the gospel to hold
Satan in check, for both Nephites and latter
day Christians of convenience, mortality
would have become nothing more than an
evil trap and a Satanic snare, and if
he were given free-reign to attack
the fold, his ravenous wolves
would scatter and then
devour the flock.

It is our firm, abiding, steadfast,
and unshakeable testimonies of our Father
in Heaven's design that has been planned in our
behalf that will forever govern ignorance and become the
catalyst to purposeful action. As we seek to gain knowledge
of both earthly and heavenly things, we will develop the power to
exercise true moral agency. Understanding will come "line upon
line and precept upon precept." (2 Nephi 28:30). It will stay with
us, and will rise with us in the resurrection, bringing us some
advantage in the life to come. (See D&C 130:18-19). If it does
not come as we wish it would, according to our impatient
timetable, at least we have this consolation: The next
life holds the promise of "perfect knowledge" or
understanding. (2 Nephi 9:13-14).

Those
who've brushed
up against the face
of death and have lived to
tell about it, will sometimes
describe it as if it were an "out
of body" experience. Members of
the Lord's church feel the same
when they have been redeemed
from spiritual death and have
been permitted to enjoy a
'peaceable walk with the
children of men."
(Moroni 7:4).

The deadly sins of vanity and pride
that so often distracted the Nephites from focusing
their undivided attention on eternal principles, created a
conundrum of cosmic proportion. They could not concentrate
simultaneously on two different things that were of contrasting
value. Whenever they prayed, their faith competed with timidity; first
blessing, and then cursing escaped the same tongue, and their devotion
to God clashed with allegiance to Babylon. Then, as now, Zion embodied
substance. Babylon was transparent. Zion preached repentance; Babylon
whined with rationalization. Zion changed from the inside; Babylon only
from the outside. Zion acted, while Babylon was acted upon. Conflicting
thought processes illustrated how Zion was grounded on a bedrock of
principle, while Babylon confused values for principles. Vanity
and pride gave the Nephites a false sense of carnal security.
They often thought that all was well in Zion, even as the
world came crashing down around them like a
train wreck in slow motion.

One of
the basic messages
of the Restoration that is
found in The Book of Mormon
is that the grass actually is more
vibrantly green on the other side of
the pasture. That pleasant pastoral
environment extends the promise
of a refreshingly new perspective
on life that follows the strait
and narrow way past the
principle of repentance
all the way to the
greenhouse of
the Lord.

There is a terrifying and
menacing jungle of worldliness
encroaching upon the borders of Zion,
and as we read The Book of Mormon, we
frequently witness Nephites who compromise
their standards as they yield their hearts to the
siren song of Satan's seductive sentinels. All too
often, they lose sight of the undeviating discipline
of the celestial bound individual. Vigilance should
have been their watch-word, since "vice is a monster
of so frightful mien, as to be hated needs but to
be seen. Yet seen too oft, familiar with her
face, we first endure, then pity, then
embrace." (Alexander Pope).

Isaiah may have been referring to the repentant faithful, when he exhorted all Israel: "Say to the prisoners, go forth (and) to them that are in darkness, shew yourselves … Their pastures shall be in all high places." (1 Nephi 21:9).

Angels are sent from the heavens to administer the oil of gladness. It is like having spiritual angioplasty, facilitating the free flow of communication between us and God. It is inspired treatment for sclerosis of the spirit. Mormon recounted that Ammon, one of the Sons of Mosiah, had "reason to rejoice," for he had been given a second chance to fulfill his life's potential after he had been born again. He must have considered himself very fortunate that God had looked beyond the behavior of his rebellious youth, and had been able to see into his heart. His rough exterior had been no more than a façade. His true character was only revealed when, through a spiritual rebirth, he became a new creature in Christ who had been released from bondage to fulfill his destiny.

In The Book of Mormon, we are asked to make room in our homes and our hearts for the Children of the Covenant, for they have awakened, and have arisen from the dust, and have put on their beautiful garments, and have strengthened her stakes, and have enlarged their borders. (See Moroni 10:31). "And (the Lord) shall set up an ensign (or the church in the Last Days) for the nations." (2 Nephi 21:12). As He said to Joseph Smith: "I have sent mine everlasting covenant into the world to be a light to the world, (as well as) to be a standard for my people, and for the Gentiles to seek to it, and to be a messenger before my face, to prepare the way before me." (D&C 45:9).

In Nephite communities, wickedness was sometimes legislated, which is a situation to which we can easily relate today. With its legal adoption, it was clothed in a legitimacy it had neither earned nor deserved. Since it could not be summarily eliminated, we see among the more righteous Nephites efforts to initiate damage control protocols as quickly as possible, to try to contain the problem. (See Helaman 6:37). A stiff dose of gospel principles clothed in the virtue of the word of God was always the best remedy (see Alma 31:5), together with a dash of sackcloth and ashes, and a slice of humble pie.

Because the word of God is superior to the paltry efforts of the adversary, the Lamanites, lacking spiritual strength, characteristically resorted to violence in a vain attempt to strengthen their position. But power and violence are mutually exclusive; where one is present the other is absent. Those who are least prepared for positions of trust and responsibility seem to be most inclined to abuse, authority. By the standard of heaven, violence is also a poor substitute for leadership, and is antithetical to real power. It is a violation of the law of the Celestial Kingdom when we engage in hostility by subjugating the rights of others, especially during our supposed exercise of priesthood authority.

The Savior Jesus Christ changed forever how we look at both ourselves and the world. His life was his message, and His prophets, whose lives are showcased in The Book of Mormon, were equally true to its doctrines and principles, the moral and ethical constants that were created to be guiding stars that would lead them to safe haven. The Savior held Himself up as a Prototype of the perfection that is within our reach. Without His divine intervention, though, we would be doomed to failure in our efforts to be as He is. His gospel is the key that breaks down every barrier that lies in the way of our progress.

Those who bear the vessels of the Lord must be clean. The ark was an unmistakable symbol the presence of God, His throne and His glory, and His supernal majesty. Only the High Priest, a type of Christ, could approach it, and then only after going through an elaborate ritual of personal cleansing and propitiation for his sins. This level of holiness is unambiguously illustrated in The Book of Mormon. No-one that is unclean can endure His glory, for it will be to them as if it were a consuming fire.

It is in the Last Days,

Isaiah tells us from the pages of The Book of Mormon, that the Lord will raise the gospel standard, and after the manner of the electronic media, the summons will come from afar. (See 2 Nephi 15:26-30). The pure in heart will respond to that call, and will hasten to Zion with such speed that before they have had time to become tired, they will have arrived at their destination. "None shall slumber nor sleep; neither shall the girdle of their loins be loosed, nor the latchet of their shoes be broken." (2 Nephi 15:27). During their travels, they will require neither rest nor even a change of clothing. Isaiah further described the sparking and flashing of "their horses' hoofs" and the great noise that iron-wheeled vehicles make.

Whenever
the Nephites found
themselves in anguish,
in light of their recognition
that they had not been valiant in
their testimony of Jesus, it actually
became easier for them to negotiate the
path to complete repentance. Their broken
hearts were softened to receive the Spirit.
They were teachable because their faith
had convicted them of their sins and
as they plunged headlong into the
depths of humility, they were set
free. They were released from
bondage, because they had
received forgiveness.
(See Isaiah
1:18).

The final details of the
Atonement were hammered
out during a negotiation that was
conducted between Justice and Mercy
from before the foundation of the world.
Confident in His ability to muster His
spiritual reserves to save mankind, Jesus
Christ led the way for all who would take
up their cross (see Jacob 1:8) and follow
Him along the path leading through
the Garden of Gethsemane, to the
court of Pilate, along the Via
Dolorosa, to Calvary, to an
empty tomb, and on to
eternal life in the
Kingdom of
God.

Those who have gained a testimony of the truth that is found in The Book of Mormon have a visibly different look about them. They've taken their vows, and have moved upward in the direction of higher plateaus that have become launchpads for affirmative action. Their features are flushed with confidence. They stand out from the crowd. They are enthusiastic, zealous, fervent, eager, animated, thrilled by life, and get high from the natural release of the endorphins that flush their systems with excitement.

The repentant faithful remind us of Abinadi, of whom the scriptures record: "The Spirit of the Lord was upon him and his face shone with exceeding luster." (Mosiah 13:5). They stand out, and are in sharp contrast to the unrepentant, whose sullen and downcast eyes betray the fact that they have become mired in sin and are bound in iniquity.

Anyone who has
feasted upon the scriptures
and particularly upon The Book
of Mormon, and has really sunk their
teeth in and savored them, has prayed for
help in digesting them, and has then pleaded
to receive a witness that what they've devoured is
true, knows what spiritual reality is. It is when the
powers of heaven and earth amplify each other and
carry us on their harmonic waves. When we've had
moments like this, it was as though someone had
given us gospel glasses. Everything resonated
clearly and we felt as if we had been given
the eternal perspective that our eyes
had for so long been craving.

To really
take advantage of
their temporal travels and
to put a positive spin on their
telestial trials, Latter-day Saints
have learned to repent, that they might
in a coming day be restored to their proper
and perfect frame (see Alma 40:23), to face
the future at a destination that has been
clothed in glory, immortality, and
eternal life.

Nephi clearly taught that "it is by grace that we are saved, after all we can do." (2 Nephi 25:23). Latter-day Saints, however, sometimes emphasize their works to the point that it may seem to others that the grace of God takes a back seat to their own efforts to somehow earn salvation without the need for a Savior.

Within the scriptures, many parts of the human anatomy have been linked to behavior. We read of strong backs, eyes, ears, hearts, hands, and bridled tongues. When President Spencer W. Kimball said: "I am like an old shoe, to be worn out in the service of the Lord," he was utilizing vivid imagery relating to the feet, but about themes to which we can all relate.

The grace of
God cannot save
those who stubbornly
determine to ignore His
entreaties to commit by a
covenant to an undeviating
standard of righteousness. (See
2 Nephi 29:3). If we were to believe
that He would do so, or that He would
extend His grace to those who had only
professed to know His name without
the discipline of faith, would be
delusional, at best. (See
2 Nephi 27:5).

We can
do nothing
that puts God in
our debt. His grace is
completely beyond our
ability to pay. (See Mosiah
4:19). But He never demands
that we settle our account with
Him; He only asks us to keep
His commandments.

The
Book of Mormon
allows us to see beyond the
limited horizon of our sight as
we are touched by the virtue of the
word of God. (See Alma 5:7 & 13). It
is our faith that empowers us to savor
revealed truth with a discriminating
taste that empowers us to discern
the distinct flavor of eternal
worlds.

The Book of Mormon
gently soothes our spirits
with the inexplicable images of
religious recognition, touching our
heartstrings and creating harmonic
chords whose music remind us of
our noble birthright.

There's a pathway to heaven that's illuminated by principles of conversion that are described in The Book of Mormon and that point us in the direction of the recognition of our iniquity and then to a deep godly sorrow for our sins. Next comes inescapable suffering and torment that stimulates an appeal to the Savior, with an awakening understanding of the Atonement. With our baptism, comes a remission of our sins, spiritual enlightenment, and great joy. This encourages us to embrace a lifestyle of service and righteousness. Every time this happens, the loop cycles again, but calibrated to a higher plane.

"Be ye therefore perfect" taught the Lord during his mortal ministry," even as your Father in Heaven is perfect." (Matthew 5:48). Or, as The Book of Mormon more comprehensively executes this well-known verse, the resurrected Lord declared: "I would that ye should be perfect, even as I, or your Father who is in heaven is perfect. (3 Nephi 12:48).

In the Last Days,
a casual, or an indifferent,
unattached recognition of the Lord
Jesus Christ will never qualify apostate
Nephite or Lamanite squatters on the world
stage to receive an inheritance of celestial glory.
These Christians of convenience lack the fire in the
belly that is characterized by discipleship. Honorable
people whose faith in the Savior is uncommitted will, at
least initially, qualify by the grace of God to inherit
terrestrial glory as their eternal reward, inasmuch as
in this life they "received not the gospel, neither the
testimony of Jesus, neither the prophets, neither
the everlasting covenant. Last of all, these are
all they who will not be gathered with the
saints, to be caught up unto the church
of the Firstborn, and received into
the cloud." (D&C 76:101-102).

If we follow the
counsel in The Book of
Mormon., and we embrace
the Atonement, we'll embark
upon a journey that is as old as
time. Faith will introduce us to a
procedure with which we may not be
familiar, even that of a spiritual heart
transplant. As we face a bright future
after we have been born again into a
newness of life, carefully prescribed
anti-rejection protocols will need to
be followed, that we might protect
and preserve the steady beat of
the new organs that God has
placed in our chests.

The journey that was taken by Lehi and Sariah with their family through the wilderness to a Land of Promise followed a well-established pattern. "In the Hellenistic age," observed Abba Eban, "the Jews were dispersed over the entire Greek world. As early as 140 B.C.E., the author of the Sibylline Oracles testified that the whole land and seas were full of Jews. A contemporary of Herod said it would have been hard to find a place in the world where there were no Jews. And Josephus added: "There are no people in the world among whom part of our brethren is not to be found." Philo spoke of the wide expansion of the Jews throughout the world, and of Jerusalem as the center of the scattered nation."

"Happiness is the object and design of our existence, and it will be the end thereof, if we follow the path that leads to it." (Joseph Smith). On the other hand, "wickedness never was happiness." (See Alma Chapter 41). For those who have turned their backs on their testimony of God's Great Plan of Redemption and of The Book of Mormon, who are no longer obedient or faithful to the covenants they've made, who treat the Atonement of Christ as a thing of naught, it will not be an easy thing to obtain forgiveness. Those who will no longer allow Him into their lives will die in their sins. Without repentance, they will not receive "a fulness of joy" in the Kingdom of God.
(3 Nephi 28:10).

Throughout the entire Book of Mormon, its prophets repeatedly urged us to persevere in our obedience to our covenants, and to develop strong testimonies of the principles they taught that illuminated great and eternal purposes that were prepared from the foundation of the world. We trace our obedience back to our baptisms, that testify of our desire to participate in every ordinance that pertains to God's great Plan.

A cognate accusative is a device that arises from the similarity between related Hebrew words. For example, the words Jershon, inheritance, and possession, that are found in Alma Chapter 27. "And they went down into the land of Jershon, and took possession (YRS) of the land of Jershon" (yarsôn) "for an inheritance" (yarsôn, Alma 27:22). This is a remarkable example of the cognate accusative in the underlying Hebrew text of The Book of Mormon.

Iago rightly observed: "Who steals my purse steals trash; 'tis something, nothing; 'twas mine, 'tis his, and has been slave to thousands. But he that filches from me my good name robs me of that which not enriches him and makes me poor indeed." (Shakespeare, "Othello"). The formidable fortification of The Book of Mormon protects us from Satan's snares that exist to steal that which is most precious to us: even our spiritual identity as children of God.

Those who have willfully chosen to remain ignorant of the prophetic teachings that may easily be discerned by even a casual reading of The Book of Mormon, Another Testament of Jesus Christ, will at some point in time uncomfortably discover that it is very difficult to continue their progression. For them, and for others who might not even be aware that there is a wedding feast in progress, the foundation principles of the Plan have, at least temporarily, been suspended. However, the earth is even now being flooded with copies of the book. Invitations to come unto Christ have been sent out across the heavens by our Father, Who even now waits for each of us to respond with an R.S.V.P. that declares our intention to participate in the preordained festivities.

The Book
of Mormon illustrates that
life is an endless chain of spiritual
experiences existing in balance with the
counterpoint of worldliness. At first, there
seems to be a gulf separating our spiritual
and temporal nature, that one would think
might make things easier for the righteous.
These contrasting sides of our nature seem
to be incompatible. But without a working
knowledge of the principles of the Plan, it
would be much more difficult to reconcile
the two and enjoy a state of holiness as
our natural habitat, richer for having
had our mortal experiences. We are
not to be worn down by life, or to
be overcome by evil influences,
but rather to be refined and
purified by adversity, by
danger, by misfortune,
by challenges, and
by contraries.

Heavenly Father
is "mighty to save" (Alma
34:18), and is ready to forgive
those who walk in darkness, and
who know not where to find gospel
truth. He is anxious to reach out to
those who have helplessly endured
the night and have suffered
the pain of spiritual
blindness.

Our pre-arranged rendezvous with the Judgment won't come at some hazy point down the road. (See Mormon 7:6). It is happening today, and we speak, think, and act in concert with either celestial, terrestrial, or telestial law. We are blessed with a moral compass. Our faith in Christ, with its evidence in action, clearly defines the path that we have chosen to follow. Every day that we live, we are 24 hours closer to the Pleasing Bar of Christ. If we have committed the 13th Article of Faith to practice as well as to memory, its principles will have become the particles of our faith. We believe in being honest, true, chaste, benevolent, and in doing good to all men. Indeed, we may say that we follow the admonition of Paul. If there is anything virtuous, lovely, or of good report or praiseworthy, we seek after these things. (See Philippians 4:8).

The Book of Mormon permits us to brush up against the face of God to "gentle our condition," as Shakespeare's King Henry V would say.

Book of Mormon prophets intimate that we who have come to earth to fight the battle that is raging in the hearts of men on Saturday were counted as the valiant in the pre-earth existence and that during the propaganda war that was waged by Satan to gain control of the minds of his brothers and sisters we were passionate in our defense of agency. (See 2 Nephi 24:12). Following that struggle, free will prevailed, and when it was time for the victorious spirits to come to the earth, they did so with a passion for their hard-won freedom to choose their own destiny. Therefore, when those spirits are now controlled by compulsion in any degree of unrighteousness dominion, their ingrained tendency is to resist. Therefore, we need to be very cautious when we are interacting with our youth, when questions arise that involve the exercise of their hard-fought divine right of free will.

Ralph Waldo Emerson once observed: "If the stars in heaven should appear but one night in a thousand years, how would men believe and adore, and preserve for many generations, their remembrance of the city of God which had been revealed." In The Book of Mormon, we read of such an event, unprecedented in the history of the world: "And it came to pass also that a new star did appear, according to the word." (3 Nephi 1:21).

The Lord admonishes us to love our enemies, and to do good to them; and to lend, hoping for nothing again; and our reward shall be great. (See 3 Nephi 12:44 & Luke 6:35). The 'get even' mentality of revenge that is so popularized in books and films and reinforced in everyday interpersonal relationships, in commerce and social settings, is antithetical to the gospel of Jesus Christ. It may be that in business, we don't get what we deserve; we get what we negotiate. But when the earth has been cleansed to receive its paradisiacal glory, a much higher standard will prevail. Before that happens, the earth will need to be prepared for the millennial reign of the Savior, when the lion and the lamb will lie down together in harmony "and there shall be no night there, and they (will) need no candle, neither light of the sun; for the Lord God (will give) them light." (Revelation 22:5).

When we read The Book of Mormon with a sincere attitude, we discover for ourselves a vitally important key to our spiritual revitalization. The more we engage its doctrine, the greater is our happiness and joy, the more fully is God able to help us to fulfil our divine destiny, and the more will the Holy Ghost infuse us with a desire to be valiant in the cause of Zion.

Lehi taught that without redemption from sin, if they were to have partaken of the fruit of the Tree of Life, which is eternal life, or the highest expression of the love of God, it would not have been possible for Adam and Eve to sustain a celestial existence, inasmuch as in their current condition they wouldn't have been capable of obedience to the laws that govern those who inherit the glory of heaven. (See 2 Nephi 2:25). Without the Atonement the Plan of Salvation would have been frustrated, not only for them, but also for all of the children of God who would follow after them.

It is when we read in The Book of Mormon about the ideological war in heaven that we learn how a 'third part' of our Father's children forfeit their privilege to obtain a body. (See 2 Nephi 24:12-16). For those who remained faithful, however, there came humbling liabilities, for the Plan required our Creator to die for our sins to mercifully satisfy the demands of Justice, in an act of Atonement that would be conditional only upon our repentance.

May we so live that we
are never more than a day away
from the last time we have read The
Book of Mormon, so that when it is
time for heaven to reach out and
sweep us up into its embrace, we
will be prepared to respond in
kind, with open arms and
an engaging smile on
our face.

The
people of Nephi
were drawn to Eastern
mysticism just as moths
are attracted to fire, and they
were mesmerized by its worldly
manifestations, even though it was
only an illusion and a caricature of the
awesome power that was symbolized by a
burning bush. Sinai, after all is said, is
an attitude more than it is a place. The
faithful and true loose the latchets of
their sandals because they realize
that holy sanctuaries have been
designed to be a part of their
daily experience, and are
ever before their face,
if they will listen
to the Spirit.

When we have
been privileged to reach
out and touch the face of God,
as we do when we read The Book of
Mormon, the Spirit that is present can
be augmented by the medium of music.
Even before the foundations of the earth
were laid, a celestial harmony floated
in the air, when "the morning stars
sang together, and all the sons
of God shouted for joy."
(Job 38:7).

As
we read The
Book of Mormon,
let us remember that
the Savior is our life-line,
providing security when our
footing is unsure and the foaming
sea is streaming across the deck. He is
our compass, showing us the way, especially
when the course before us is unclear. He is our
chart that warns us of hidden dangers. He is our
barometer, alerting us to impending storms. He is
our lookout, standing as our sentinel when we've been
distracted by trivial concerns. He holds the line that
trails in our wake, offering safety should we lose
our footing and fall overboard. He is the wind
that fills our sails, that we may more
easily find our way home.

There
is no fanfare in
the narratives within
The Book of Mormon; just
quiet reflection, meditation,
contemplation, introspection,
and a deep desire to draw near
to our Father. Though our flesh
and our hearts may fail, God
is our strength and our
portion forever.

One
of the blessings
that we receive when we
read The Book of Mormon
is that by doing so there may
be inflicted upon us a benevolent
blindness that actually helps us to
see more clearly than those with 20:20
vision. Those who immerse themselves in
the book often 'feel' with a vibrancy that
is both incorporeal and indefinable. It
kindles a light within their hearts
that supersedes any and all of
their somatic senses, and it
is far more valuable
to them.

Our engagement with The Book of Mormon helps us to see things as they really are, and at the same time, it encourages us to be benevolently blind to the shortcomings of others. Just so, Heavenly Father is blind to our own failures when we come to Him having accomplished the laborious process of repentance.

The living water that spiritually sustains us is the doctrine of the gospel of Christ, including the covenant we make with God at the waters of baptism. (See Mosiah Chapter 18). Later, we symbolically renew that covenant in the ordinance of the Sacrament. (See Moroni Chapters 4 & 5).

It is in
The Book of Mormon
where we learn how to make
sacred covenants with the Savior,
the fulfillment of which will bring us
earthly blessings and eternal exaltation.
As we focus our attention on obedience to
His commandments, our thirst for the
truth will be quenched by the living
water that is provided by the
gospel of Jesus Christ.

If we ignore
The Book of Mormon,
we will be found guilty of
turning our faces away from
the habitation of the Lord. Because
the people of Judah disregarded both
the temple and its related ordinances,
2 Chronicles 29:8 reveals how the wrath
of the Lord Jehovah was upon them and
upon Jerusalem, and how He "delivered
them to trouble, to astonishment,
and to hissing."

The Book
of Mormon must surely
be the prototypical example of the
absolute genius behind God's Plan of
Salvation as it focuses our minds and
our spirits on our covenants, the Savior,
His Atonement, and the commandments.
Our discipline to study that book expands
the capacity of our understanding, and
allows us to experience firsthand how
a gospel-centered life can be greater
than the sum of its parts.

The
Book of Mormon
teaches us how to move
beyond a learner's permit
and to engage the gears of the
engine that will drive us toward
the achievement of our goals. It will
also prevent us from remaining at a
stand-still with our transmission
idling in neutral, and being left
to wonder why we are not being
magically propelled forward
with little or no effort on
our own part.

We are not, and we never
wish to be, lights unto ourselves.
We know that we cannot overcome the
world on our own. But when, with the help
of The Book of Mormon, we borrow the Lord's
power, we can do all things. Repeatedly, He told
disobedient Israel that His hand is stretched out
still. (See Isaiah 10:4). If we ignore it, or if
we refuse His invitation to lift us up, we
invite disaster. Our behavior must
foster the power of humility, for
it is the meek who shall
inherit the earth.

The Book of Mormon
is like a scale that measures
the influence of our discipleship
and the weight of our integrity. It is a
barometer that assesses how spirituality
can be inextricably interwoven into our
character. It beckons us to pattern our
lives after the example of the Savior,
that we might internalize gospel
principles, and demonstrate
obedience to priesthood
covenants.

As we consistently turn our attention to The Book of Mormon, to fasting, to prayer, to the Sacrament, and to an active discipline-based lifestyle, we are more likely to make progress as we follow the Rod of Iron toward the Tree of Life. If we falter in our faith during the journey, we fall back on the reassurance that the Lord gave to Israel: "I will heal their backsliding, I will "love them freely: for mine anger is turned away." (Hosea 14:4).

The arduous road that leads to a testimony of The Book of Mormon is sometimes not well defined, but in the end it will take us thru a portal of personal preparedness to accountability and responsibility, always in the direction of celestial sureties that are encompassed about by an expanding circle of opportunity and embraced by the perfect law of liberty. The covenant that lies at the end of that journey will make us feel as if we have been born again, even though we may also feel that we have passed thru a spiritual birth canal. But all's well that ends well. We will have been delivered into the Rest of the Lord.

How we embrace The Book of Mormon determines how we'll handle our weaknesses, our imperfections, and sin. Without it, self-defeating behaviors will always threaten to impede our progress. Because the book establishes a partnership with our Heavenly Father, the Savior, and the Holy Ghost, we have a tool to turn the tables on Satan, and actually use inadequacies, blemishes, and even transgression, as stepping-stones to higher achievement.

The faithful need not fear, although they "see signs and wonders, for they shall be shown forth in the heavens above, and in the earth beneath. And they shall behold blood, and fire, and vapors of smoke." (D&C 45:40-41). Although the spiritual equivalents of lightning may strike all around them, they will be shielded from harm by the copper grid of The Book of Mormon that surrounds them and grounds them to the Savior.

As we endure to the
end in righteousness, The Book
of Mormon will guide us toward our
eternal destiny in the Kingdom of God.
It's after we've obtained a testimony that the
Spirit will qualify us for the blessings that
are related to the covenants of salvation,
sanctification, justification, and
finally, exaltation.

Perhaps it is because it is so
easy for our vision to get out of focus, to
lose our grip on the iron rod, and to wander
from strict obedience to our covenants, that we
are encouraged to regularly ponder the messages
that are found in The Book of Mormon. We do so,
not in vain repetition, but rather with theatrical
encore. As we immerse ourselves in the book,
we discover that we've become intimately
engaged in the drama of our lives.

One of the best explanations we have been given for The Book of Mormon is that it catalyzes our resolve to bear testimony to the world of the things we have learned by the power of the Spirit, so that our experience can be as it was on the Day of Pentecost, when the witness of Peter and the other apostles carried the day as it penetrated the hearts of all who listened, and instilled within them the desire to inquire: "What must we do if it is our hope to inherit eternal life?"

The Book of Mormon helps initialize both the temporal and the spiritual implementations of God's Plan. It assists us in the monitoring of our relationship with Him during our engagement with mortality. The book illustrates various points of doctrine that focus on salvation, and upon these elements hinges its correct understanding.

We incorporate
into our lives the lessons
we've learned from The Book of
Mormon, that we might overcome our
spiritual death by entering the presence
of our Father and His Son, by way of the
Holy Ghost. His Spirit dazzles us with an
endless reserve of revelation, illuminating
every corner of our minds and our spirits.
Our anticipated blessings proffered by the
combined capacity of the intrinsic light
that radiates from all three members of
the Godhead are beyond description.
Binding covenants bridge the gulf
between the secular and the divine
that, in other circumstances,
might exist for us.

As
we read
The Book
of Mormon,
we understand
that we might have
opportunities to bear
each other's burdens. We
do not consider the merits
of the petitions of the weak
and impoverished who need
our aid and we turn a blind
eye to prejudices that might
threaten to influence the
depth and breadth of
our compassion.

The Book of Mormon asks that we comfort all those who are poor in spirit and to "mourn with those that mourn." (Mosiah 18:9). We smile with all our heart and with all our might. If we do nothing else, we can be the smile on the faces of those who feel as if there is not much going on in their lives to make them happy.

The Book of Mormon's inspirational design is to influence what would be virtually impossible for us to do on our own: to make saints out of sinners. It asks that we hate our former worldly selves. We strive to be better than we have ever been before. We find compassionate ways to minister to the needs of others. The book pushes us out of our comfort zones, and also nudges us away from complacency and indifference, that can be suffocating to our spirits.

The Book of Mormon stimulates within our hearts an awakening dawn of recognition. It teaches that we are the "elect according to the foreknowledge of God … thru sanctification of the Spirit, unto obedience and sprinkling of the blood of Jesus Christ."
(1 Peter 1:2).

The Book of Mormon speaks through the Holy Ghost to our own spirits, for every gospel principle carries within itself a witness that it is true. Its language is universal, and when the Spirit illuminates our minds, we enjoy a fluency and a familiarity that puts us at ease with principles and doctrine. We are more comfortable with the revealed word of God, and we look forward to the vistas of eternal opportunity that we are certain will open up before our eyes.

When we read
The Book of Mormon, we feel not only
the spiritual intensity, but also the tangible
significance, of the narrative. We feel a palpable
connection with the Spirit that washes over us
in concentric waves with a ripple effect
that influences everything
within its path.

When we engage The
Book of Mormon, we press
forward with steadfastness,
having a perfect brightness of
hope and a love of God and of
our brothers and sisters. We
feast upon the word, as we
endure to the end in
righteousness.

When we go
the second mile
while lengthening
our stride during our
Book of Mormon study,
we experience a freedom we
hadn't known before. We're
freed from the shackles that
had limited the expression of
our potential and we receive a
gift of spiritual independence
that disperses the darkness,
while removing the veil of
insensitivity to our
destiny.

The Book
of Mormon equips
us with the tools to forge
relationships on earth
that will endure
in heaven.

As we study
The Book of Mormon,
we take time during quiet
moments of reflection to listen
for the voice of the Lord that is unto
all, for "there is none to escape; and
there is no eye that shall not see,
neither ear that shall not hear,
neither heart that shall
not be penetrated."
(D&C 1:2).

We
study
the scriptures
that we might "be
full of the knowledge
of the Lord, as the waters
cover the sea." (2 Nephi 21:9).
The Book of Mormon promises
that it will leave the world a
better place than it had
been beforehand.

The Book
of Mormon shows
us how to cast ourselves
upon an altar of faith whose
foundation has been buttressed
by a display of supernal direction.
It drives us forward with the confidence
that God's power to save will be unleashed
in our behalf to flow over our wounds as a
healing balm, that we might one day be
able to meet His penetrating gaze
with unencumbered hearts
and clear eyes.

It is in
The Book of
Mormon where
we experience the
excitement of being
spiritually begotten of
God, and of having our
hearts changed through
faith on His name. We
turn our thoughts to
Him, as we feel His
energy building
within us.

The Book of Mormon
provides us with the tools we need
to lengthen our stride. In the sometimes
violent confrontation between principles and
values that will tear at the fabric of our world, the
Savior asks us to exert ourselves with actions that
will stretch the limits of our ability. But in the
process, we will find in the gift of the Holy
Ghost unlimited reserves of spiritual
strength to carry us forward on
the path of progress.

The Book of Mormon
will clothe us in spiritual
chain-mail as protection against
the fiery darts of the adversary. The
telestial turf is Satan's home ground,
and the swamp of secular humanism
and other false ideologies lies ready to
suck the unwary into the underworld
of Beelzebub, but no power on earth
or hell can defeat that which God
has decreed in that body of
holy scripture.

To
activate
the Plan of
God on earth,
there must needs
be opposition; light
and darkness, pleasure
and pain, good and evil,
and happiness and misery,
which makes Book of Mormon
teachings essential. Many of us
don't have the spiritual horsepower
to consistently choose the right, and
we certainly lack the means to save
ourselves. It is safe to say that we
need Him every hour of every
day of our lives.

We receive
the teachings of
The Book of Mormon
in a dramatic validation
of the influence of the Light
of Christ, and of the power of the
Holy Ghost. They will labor in tandem
among us "till we all come in the unity of
the faith, and of the knowledge of the Son of
God, unto a perfect man, unto the measure
of the stature of the fulness of Christ."
(Ephesians 4:13).

As Alma
thought about the
sins for which he had
repented, he realized that
he remembered them only in
the sense that they strengthened
his testimony and consolidated his
resolve to refrain from repeating them,
but he would longer feel the guilt
that had been associated with
the transgression. (See
Alma 36:19).

Moroni knew that
our progress now and in
eternity would hinge largely
upon what we would do with
the Sacrament, and upon
what the Atonement
would do for us.

The Book
of Mormon will help
us to first redefine and
then to redesign what had
heretofore been our stumbling
blocks, repurposing them into
the stepping stones that would
be needed to conquer our fears,
reinvigorate our confidence,
and overcome the obstacles
that are always strewn
about on the paths
of progression.

The Nephites'
repentance culminated
with their partaking of the
Sacrament, when the Holy Ghost
filled their hearts with joy. With the
renewal of their covenant of baptism,
they enjoyed a peace of conscience
that defied explanation.

In a heavenly tongue that is at the same time melodious, rhythmical, and soothing to our ears, it is calming to our souls as we hear the Spirit whisper: "You're a stranger here." We are quickly encouraged by the realization that we have "wandered from a more exalted sphere." Such a road from glory, and our pathway back to God's Celestial Kingdom, are illuminated by stories from The Book of Mormon. It teaches that our discipleship is linked to our faith that the heavens are not closed, and that our Father continues to speak to us.

The faithful view The Book of Mormon a revelatory rapture permeating its narrative. It is as an "enchanted wood where the foliage is always green, where joy abides, where nightingales nest and sing, and where life and death are one in the presence of the Lord Jesus." (Helen Keller).

In The Book of Mormon, the fold will find mentors whom they can emulate, instead of scapegoats that are easy to blame. Instead of looking for easier answers, they dig deeply in its revelations and uncover salubrious resolutions to the challenges they encounter.

We will never thirst if we will anchor ourselves thru the topsoil of the gospel into the Source of living water, and if we will then accept the revelation of The Book of Mormon as one of the defining expressions of honesty with ourselves, with Heavenly Father, with the Savior, and with the Holy Ghost.

The
Book
of Mormon
is a celestial
interpretation
of the truth that
will transport the
righteous past the
vicissitudes of life
all the way to the
steadiness of the
kingdom of God
that is found in
revelation, and
lies above the
confusion of
the world's
turmoil.

The
faithful
know how to
turn stumbling
blocks into stepping
stones. Crisis becomes
opportunity, as victory
is snatched from the jaws
of defeat. They believe that
illumination from The Book
of Mormon will appear as "a
flash of lightning and a clap
of thunder. At first we might
shrink in fear, but after the
the storm, flowers will
bloom." ("I Ching").

Our
faith is that
there is enough
room and adequate
time thru the eternities
for each one of us develop
the ability to see beyond
the limited horizon of our
vision all the way to the
heavens by the power of
the revelations of God
that are found on the
pages of The Book of
Mormon. It is our
golden ticket that
will insure our
safe passage
home.

Some
recognize
the anchor of
faith in the Book of
Mormon as intuition.
It enlarges our capacity to
comprehend the truth without
the stipulation of our conscious
reasoning. It draws upon insight
and is the precursor to inspiration
and revelation that can be both seen
and heard as vivid lightning and
resounding thunder from
heaven.

We turn
to The Book of
Mormon, because
we wouldn't want to
be spiritually starved,
doctrinally dehydrated,
or intellectually inhibited
while only inches from the
living bread that could have
satisfied our hunger, or from
fountains of living water that,
in other circumstances, might
have slaked our thirst, both of
which could have healed our
blemishes and sins.

In the telestial world in which we
live, there is an ever-present negative energy
that influences us, and the promptings that come
to us from the Holy Ghost in the form of revelations
such as are found in The Book of Mormon are its only
possible countermeasures. The only stipulations are
that we confess when we have, in any magnitude,
embraced the opposites that lie before us, and
that we immediately undertake the safety
protocols required by repentance to
bring us back into a state of
harmony with God and
angels in heaven.

The Book of
Mormon explains
that the Atonement
can change the chemical
nature of sin by detoxifying
us from the homogenization of
our standards and the cares of the
world when we are subjected to the
vicissitudes of life. It allows us to
return to the hallowed halls of
the Spirit, to be re-vitalized
as we are re-introduced to
the magical kingdom
of God where dreams
really do come
true.

Our experiences are the
dynamically active ingredients of a
fertile matrix that was carefully created
by God during His preparation of the petri
dish that has been personalized to match our
individual circumstances in the learning
laboratory of life. But He doesn't expect
us to conduct our experiments alone,
but to use The Book of Mormon as
a teaching tutorial to help us to
avoid accidents that could
otherwise occur when we
mix ingredients that
tend to explosively
react with each
other.

Allowing the Book of Mormon to release us from captivity through faith permits us to see things as they really are, and enjoy a lucidity that will come more from our hearts than our heads. From its vantage point we see things more clearly, as we escape the confining limitations of our mortal clay that tend to twist our attention inward toward worldliness and grossly disfigure our perspective of heaven.

At first, it may just be the easier wrong that looks as if it were more convenient, but that is only because it harmonizes with the values of Babylon. Worldliness surrounds us, and without The Book of Mormon's stabilizing influence, moral equivocation can far too easily appear to be the easier way out, and become the habitual pattern of our conduct.

When
we deny The
Book of Mormon,
it can be traced back
to the fact that we have
sold our birthright to the
lowest bidder for a mess of
pottage. Once we have made
the exchange, we may far too
easily be dragged down to hell
on earth, where we realize that
the prison into which we have
been unceremoniously cast is
our own construction. When
there is no vision, and if we
refuse God's invitation to
embrace His word, we'll
surely perish.

The Book of
Mormon gives each
thread in the fabric of
our own faith a vitality,
vim, vigor, and vivacity
unique to holy vestments.
Their steadfast colors will
never fade, save it be thru
neglect or unbelief. They
will remain impervious
to blemishes, except
for the stain of
unresolved
sin.

With
the angels in
heaven, the Holy
Ghost holds His breath
in hopeful anticipation, as
He waits upon our initiative to
open our hearts and embrace the
messages of The Book of Mormon,
that are clothed in holy vestments
that hint of a revelatory
rapture.

Disorder
and progression
must be in balance
with each other. In fact,
The Book of Mormon tells
us that it was ordained in
heaven that there must be a
juxtaposition of opposing
forces for faith to prevail
as the first principle in
revealed religion, and
for revelation to fall
as stardust on
its heels.

We can be
fully committed to
God's merciful Plan and
still have special moments of
reconfirmation, especially if we
are reading The Book of Mormon.
The Holy Ghost will so powerfully
move us that we will say that our
hearts have been changed through
faith on the name of Christ and
that we've been born of Him. No
longer will we be disposed to
do evil, but to do good
continually.

Its
failure to accept
The Book of Mormon
has plunged our society
into a self-destruct mode.
D&C 1:16 cautions us that it
seeks "not the Lord to establish
his righteousness, but every man
walketh in his own way, and after
the image of his own god, whose
image is in the likeness of the
world, and whose substance is
that of an idol, which waxeth
old and shall perish in
Babylon."

Adam and
Eve fell so that they and
their posterity might then be
taught to nurture the moral fiber
that we possess today as the spirit of
revelation, which has carried through
many generations to bless us, among
other things with an appreciation of
The Book of Mormon. After all that
time, the Holy Ghost continues to
extend the invitation to enjoy
the happiness that, from the
very beginning, has been
prepared for the
Saints.

It may be entropy, which is the
fragmentation of order, that creates
the friction that is required to ignite the
fire of revelation that warms the world. One
could argue that opposition drives us to receive
communication from the heavens. As we learn to
deal with what appear to be heightened trials and
temptations in the Last Days, our capacity for
decisive action when we first encounter The
Book of Mormon may actually increase
over time, as it is supervised by the
discipline of revelation. God
works in mysterious
ways.

Those of faint heart, weak will, and indifferent character don't even realize that they are stumbling right past communication that comes from God. They are as the blind leading the blind. They need to tap their way to the strait and narrow path if they ever hope to reach the point in their journey thru life where they emerge from darkness into the light of life and their eyes are finally opened to experience His revelatory thunder and The Book of Mormon.

Our connection with eternity as we read The Book of Mormon may be déjà vu, from the French, meaning 'already seen.' How else could we emotionally explain the phenomenon of feeling that we have somehow taken part in the events that we are reading about. Another way of looking at it, however, would be to characterize our emotions as religious recognition, or an after-image of the lessons we learned during our pre-mortal life.

Cosmic microwave background radiation (that can be visualized as the 'snow' on your television screen) is a footnote of creation, and physicists see in it nothing more remarkable than evidence of the Big Bang, but The Book of Mormon teaches us that our blood runs hot because we are part of God's universe. "The very molecules that make up our bodies are traceable to the crucibles that were once the centers of high-mass stars that exploded into the galaxy, seeding pristine gas clouds with the chemistry of life. We are all connected to each other biologically, to the earth chemically, to the rest of the universe atomically", and to God eternally. (Neil deGrasse Tyson).

One of the reasons that The Book of Mormon was given to the world was to help stem the advancing tide of evil. 200 million copies of the book have been published, trailing only the Bible, the Qur'an, "Quotations from Chairman Mao Tse-tung," "Don Quixote" and (believe it or not) "A Tale of Two Cities." That might not seem like a lot, but it is always better to light a candle than curse the darkness. A sage observation has never been more timely, and that is "to sin by silence, when words should be spoken, makes cowards of men." The Book of Mormon was courageously published, that we might follow up our thoughts and words with purposeful action.

The Book of Mormon gives us the opportunity to recognize that we all live on a kind of spiritual credit, and that one day, our account will be closed and a settlement will be required. "My father focuses heart-gripping flashes across the wall screen. Family slides. I am small, my brother is smaller, and my sister is smallest. Days now dead re-open like old storybooks from memory's heaped box. Soberly, I think of another Father, Who someday shall open my mind, and flash reeling remembering of every day's minute across my soul and across the heavens, and kindly ask me to narrate." (Lora Lyn Stucker).

Because of its unyielding standard in the face of the world's homogenizing influences, the gospel, including The Book of Mormon, is the 'Good News' to those who embrace it, providing all the principles, ordinances, and covenants that enable us to become sanctified so that we may be worthy to live once again in a state of holiness in the presence of our Heavenly Father. Because of the gospel, we may all come unto Christ, "lay hold upon every good gift ... and be perfected in him." (Moroni 10:32). If we "continue in the supplicating of his grace," we will one day stand blameless before Him at His Pleasing Bar. (Alma 7:3).

The Book of Mormon turns the focus of our attention to the Banquet of Consequences, where there will not be much at the table that is satisfying, unless we are able to bow our heads in reverence, and not hang them in shame, in the presence of Christ, Who will be there, to kindly serve us our just desserts. (Marion D. Hanks). Even when we have been blessed to fill our tummies with nourishing food, we need to remember the counsel of Nephi, who said that we should press forward, and not forget to feast upon the word of Christ. (See 2 Nephi 31:20).

Early on Christmas morning, as we excitedly dump out the contents of our stockings that had been hung on the mantle with care, and a cornucopia of treats cascades onto the floor, it strikes us that our Father has promised to open for us "the windows of heaven, and pour out a blessing that there shall not be room enough to receive it." (2 Nephi 24:10). The manifestation of that blessing begins with the greatest Gift of all, not only on Christmas morning, but also every other day throughout the year.

The Book of
Mormon encourages us
to engage in random acts of
kindness that have received the
divine approbation of our Father
in Heaven. These are shining
examples of our firm belief
in the concept of quiet
Christianity in
action.

The Book
of Mormon asks us to draw
from a fountain of living waters, and
to drink copiously from the account of the
ministry of the Savior, which is really the
story of our own personal belonging.
Its currents are possessions worth
sharing, and its joy belongs
to the world.

The Book of Mormon asks us to measure the quality of our experiences,
not by the hopes and enjoyments of this world, but rather by the preparations
we are making for a different journey, looking forward to what we shall become,
rather than backward to what we have been. If we incorporate into our lives the vision
of the book, we will see that "the past is prologue." The phrase, written by Shakespeare for
his play "The Tempest," was intended to imply that our past is merely a prologue, or an
introduction to the great adventure upon which we will embark if we follow through on
His Plan. This interpretation teaches that what has come before doesn't matter in
the grand scheme of things, because a new future lies before us, subject to the
choices we make. However, the way the phrase is commonly used today, it
means the exact opposite, that, because the past defines the present, it
determines the future. And that is why our Heavenly Father
has promised us the companionship of the Holy Ghost,
to shepherd us through the experimentation of our
experiences toward the Light in the East,
which is where our destiny lies.

It is in the pages of The Book of
Mormon where we witness the evidence of
prophets who teach the body of known truth,
seers who see with spiritual eyes and teach
hidden truth, and revelators who bring to
the attention of the world truth that
has never before been revealed.
(See Mosiah 8:13).

The Book of Mormon helps us to deal with the wonderful gift of adversity; when there seems to be no vacancy in the tightly shuttered sanctuaries where we would normally seek shelter from the storms of life.

The Book of Mormon illustrates that "tribulation for righteousness is not a blessing only, but also a gift that God giveth unto none save his special friends." (William Tyndall, "Obedience," p. 9). At the very least, when we endure such trials, we will find ourselves in good company.

King Benjamin related his "nothingness" to our debt to God and taught that if his people praised Him and served Him "with all (their) whole souls, yet (they) would be unprofitable servants." (Mosiah 2:20-21). This is because our debt is completely beyond our ability to pay, and we can do nothing that obliges God to us. But He does not ask us to settle our account with Him; He asks only that we keep His commandments and regularly repent.

We light up the world with our witness of The Book of Mormon, Another Testament of Jesus Christ, precisely because, without it, testimony of His divinity would be only dimly perceived and hesitantly believed by many of our friends and neighbors.

The prophets of The Book
of Mormon remind us that we
are "as white-hot sparks struck off the
divine anvil of God." (B.H. Roberts). Our
flashes of faith ignite the flame of our
resolve. That refiner's fire will then
become a process of purification,
as the dross is burned out
of our nature.

It is because of The Book of Mormon
that we are blessed with the gift of energy to move
forward with renewed purpose on the path of progress.
The bedrock of God's revealed word provides a more sure
footing than does the uncertain and precarious path in
the world of everyday that is congested with telestial
traffic, raked by temporal trauma, compromised
by conceptual cul-de-sacs, pockmarked by
personality precipices and potholes,
and damaged by doctrinal
dilemmas.

The Savior encouraged his disciples to focus their attention on their less fortunate brethren and to lose themselves in their service. He knew that, by doing so, they would be brought into a state of harmony with the attributes of their Heavenly Father. Conforming their lives to His character traits, their nature would be transformed as they assumed both His image and the likeness. "And ye shall be even as I am," He promised, "and I am even as the Father, and the Father and I are one." (3 Nephi 28:10).

The Book of Mormon blesses us with the clarity of spiritual understanding that allows us to pierce the mists of time to see the Star that shone brightly above a manger on the outskirts of the little town of Bethlehem.

One of the greatest tragedies
that we read about in The Book of Mormon was
not when we learned about children "who were afraid of the
dark, but where we witnessed grown men and women who were
afraid of the light." (Plato). As we read The Book of Mormon, what
a heartbreak it is to see what died in the Nephites while they were yet
alive. Still, at times and with child-like faith, they said "to the man
who stood at the gate of the year, 'Give me a light, that I may tread
safely into the unknown.' And his unswerving reply was:
'Go out into the darkness, and put your hand in the
hand of God. That shall be to you better than a
light, and safer than the known way.'"
(Minnie Louise Haskins).

If we are looking for them, The Book of
Mormon will send us messages of sweet memory,
so we might have roses in December. Within its pages,
we will find the love of the prophets, and expressions that
carried with them the same level of determination as that of
Joseph Smith, who wrote to his companions that his resolve
was "fixed, immovable, and unchangeable, to be (their)
friend and brother ... in the bonds of love, to walk in
all the commandments of God blameless, in
thanksgiving, forever and ever."
(D&C 88:133).

God is no
respecter of persons, and
won't draw up sides, nor will
He pick and choose which of His
children to favor, and which to ignore.
His impartiality is eminently fair. We're
all "the children of (our) Father who is in
heaven; (Who) maketh his sun to rise
on the evil and on the good."
(3 Nephi 12:45).

We follow the admonitions given to us
by the Savior in The Book of Mormon to turn the
other cheek (3 Nephi 12:39), to go the second mile (3
Nephi 12:41), and to take up our cross to follow Him to
Calvary and beyond. (See 3 Nephi 12:30). This is not
a doctrine of passive resistance against the forces of
iniquity, but of our active cooperation with powers
far superior to evil. Preparation for the adversity
that is part of life endows us with the power to
conquer opposition of every description,
even if it appears in the insidiously
wicked form of the Devil, and come
away from the experience
wearing the laurel
crown of the
victor.

The Book of Mormon
catches us in concentric waves
of the Spirit as the powers of heaven
sweep across the face of the earth. When
all our trappings and pretenses have been shorn
away, when outward observances and phylacteries
have been stripped from the ritual of our worship, when
the raw sores and ugly stains of worldly influences have
been healed by the Balm of Gilead, when we have given
ourselves completely and without reservation to Jesus
Christ, when we are without guile, and when only
our true feelings remain, we can sense God's
heavenly grace as it is expressed in
The Book of Mormon.

Peacemakers are the children of
God. They are the spiritually begotten
sons and daughters of Christ who actively
seek peace and are its fashioners, whose behavior
models that of the Savior, who was the Prince of Peace.
(See 3 Nephi 12:9). "Theirs is not the peace of this world, of
ease, of luxury, idleness, absence of turmoil and strife, but the
peace born of a righteous life, the peace that lifts the soul, that day
by day brings us closer to the home of Eternal Peace, the dwelling
place of our Father." (J. Reuben Clark, Jr.). Theirs is the peace
that surpasses understanding, the peace that comes from
obedience to the gospel principles that are taught in
The Book of Mormon.

Someone once facetiously said that they very much regretted their inability to preach the gospel with such power that it would result in mob violence. The point is, that in the Last Days, when The Book of Mormon is measured against the shifting sands of secularism, our discipleship will be lived in crescendo. As a result, the Saints will at times come under fire from those who are silhouetted against the shining example of the Savior, of whom the book testifies.

The Book of Mormon empowers our minds to burst free of their fetters with the realization that we have been given gifts that are sufficient to reach out and touch the stars. When we're up and moving along that celestial highway, the Savior will bless us with an awareness of our vested interest in the welfare of others, and with the moral obligation to lift them heavenward, as well.

In The Book of Mormon, we witness the spectacle of Babylon crumbling into dust. We see that force and compulsion have always failed miserably, as they have tried in vain to establish an ideal society. Peace on earth and good will "can only come through transformation of individual souls, and with lives redeemed from sin and brought into harmony with Divine will." (David O. McKay).

It is in The Book of Mormon where we see that Christ's ministry will continue as "long as time shall last, or the earth shall stand, or there shall be one man upon the face thereof to be saved." (Moroni 7:36).

Book of Mormon prophets had the gift of teaching us how to adjust our eyes to the light of the stars in heaven springing, and of attuning our ears to hear the angels singing hosanna to His name. In that book, "still is sung, in every tongue, the angels' song of glory." ("In Wondering Awe").

Revelation is a letter from God that wonderfully expresses His love. "Thou hast had signs enough," Alma counseled Korihor. You "have the testimony of all these thy brethren, and also all the holy prophets. The scriptures are laid before thee, yea, and all things that are upon the face of it … do witness that there is a Supreme Creator." (Alma 30:44). As Ralph Waldo Emerson observed: "How does nature deify us with a few and cheap elements! Give me health and a day, and I will make the pomp of emperors ridiculous."

Christian nations
no longer condemn those
who secularize God's holy day,
and yet we put a halt to our eternal
progression and we die spiritually when,
in consequence of our profane behavior on the
Sabbath, we alienate ourselves from His influence.
God has blessed us with time and to spare to read The
Book of Mormon. That study time is as a work-release
program, and not a vacation, for He wants to see how
we will behave when we are left on our own, after
having received instruction regarding
what we ought to be doing.
(See Alma 26:8).

The Book of Mormon
encourages us "come up on mount
Zion" to clasp our hands with others and
bring them into the warmth of our fellowship.
We are "set to be a light unto the world, and to be
the saviors of men," and so we are determined to
make the journey to the Lord by way of that
book in the good company of our loved
ones and our friends, as well as
our neighbors. (D&C
103:9).

Reading and studying The Book of Mormon will help us to religiously and repetitively recalibrate our moral compasses with celestial precision. The standard that is thereby set will help to soften the trauma we have all experienced as a result of our having been dumped somewhat unceremoniously onto the world stage.

To those living after the manner of happiness in the Last Days, Moroni extended an invitation to come unto Christ and be perfected in Him. (See Moroni 10:30). The problem is that the understanding and behavior of those who've taken pleasure in sin harmonizes with worldly standards, and so as long as they are able to shut out the light of Christ, they may live under the illusion that they are already happy. But sooner or later, the discrepancy between their marginalized behavior and gospel ideals will become so great that their short-lived pleasure in their worldly ways will be destroyed by the realization that their experiences were counterfeit, and that wickedness never was happiness. The Book of Mormon extends to every one of us an invitation to come in from the cold, from their alienation from their God.

We read in The
Book of Mormon the glad
message of "glory to God in the
highest, and on earth, peace, good
will toward men." (Luke 2:14). It is heard
far more clearly than any tumult of opinion
or war of words. "I see the stars; I hear the rolling
thunder; thy power throughout the universe displayed.
Then sings my soul, my Savior God, to thee, How great
thou art." ("How Great Thou Art"). Since the restoration of
the gospel and the publication of The Book of Mormon, a
glorious morning has broken for the people of His
choice, who retreat from the world, and
for a defense set watchmen
on their walls.

We seek
out holy places where
we can read The Book of
Mormon, for we know that
their solitude will stimulate
reflection that only occurs if we
are far from the madding crowd.
These stand in sharp contrast to the
frenzied commotion on the trading
floors of commerce, and the tumult
of the world's opinions that are so
often a part of our everyday
lives.

If we make the time to plumb the depths of The Book of Mormon, our lives will take on a new meaning. We will be compelled to cry out "blessed be the name of He that cometh in the name of the Lord; thou art my God and I will bless thee; thou art my God and I will exalt thee." (Psalms 118:28).

Because of the Savior of the world, "the soul shall be restored to the body, and the body to the soul; yea, and every limb and joint shall be restored to its body; yea, even a hair of the head shall not be lost; but all things shall be restored to their proper and perfect frame." (Alma 40:23). Joseph Fielding Smith, Jr. taught: "All deformities and imperfections will be removed, and the body will conform to the likeness of the spirit." ("Doctrines of Salvation," 2:289). Joseph F. Smith said: "From the day of the resurrection, the body will develop until it reaches the full measure of the stature of its spirit." ("Gospel Doctrine," p. 23).

It is in the Christ Child that we see the purity of the spirit that we all possessed at our births. (See 2 Nephi 19:6). As we grow older, the unrelenting wave action of the world that laps away at our footings may undermine and short circuit our spiritual power grid and cause us to lose the intrinsic light with which our Heavenly Father has blessed us. The Book of Mormon provides a gentle reminder that we must safeguard the illumination that glows from within.

"Come, follow me," said the Lord, who then issued the mind-boggling command to be perfect, even as He and His Father were perfect. (See 3 Nephi 12:48). Thus did the Lord divulge that it is our destiny to develop both the image and the likeness of our Heavenly Father until we become a reflection of both His countenance and His character.

Secularists who worship the virtues of the intellect by demanding tangible proof will always be at odds with The Book of Mormon and the Holy Ghost. They divert us from abiding by the Plan, whose successful execution hinges upon our nourishing the seeds of faith in the word of God. As Sir Walter Scott warned: "Better had they ne'er been born, who read to doubt, or read to scorn."

Far too many of us, by seeking the approbation of the world, allow ourselves to be tossed about as flotsam and jetsam upon the sea of life, never to enjoy the sweet blessing of spiritual centricity that flows out of The Book of Mormon.

The Book of Mormon is a pulsing arpeggio entitled 'Faith to Believe' that ignites our souls with passion. It is this catalyzing influence that spurs our revelatory zeal, but that was conspicuously missing from the pedantic charade of righteous behavior that was embraced by the Pharisees of old, and that is absent in so many circles even today.

As we rehearse in our minds the verbal expression of our witness that The Book of Mormon is Another Testament of Jesus Christ, it is with a zealous rapture that we'll hear the music of a revelatory symphony that has been scored for every imaginable instrument. We have the faith to believe that God's voice can be heard.

We "labor for feeling, knowledge, and understanding, and we beware superstition and persuasion of worldly wisdom, philosophy, hypocrisy, and ceremonies." As the Lord graciously enlightens our minds with The Book of Mormon, "we walk in the plain and open truth." (William Tyndall).

At least for the time being, the truth that is found in The Book of Mormon blazes brightly, liberated from the intensity of martyr's fires. We pray that never again will the church of the devil "suffer no man to know God's word, but burn it and make heresy of it." (William Tyndall).

Every day of the year, there are many of us who continually struggle with vision that too often is obscured by doubt and confusion, and by feelings of hopelessness, that no one seems to know what to believe. Tensions rise, the pace of life is hectic, vulgarity eats away at the borders of our spiritual symmetry, and righteousness is an unpopular faith-based lifestyle. Our sponge has been wrung nearly dry as we have sought to cool our feverish foreheads, and those of others, with living water. What a blessing it is to know that there is light at the end of a long tunnel of darkness; that in The Book of Mormon there is a haven and a place of refuge from the turmoil of the world. Its message reaffirms that life has purpose and direction, and encourages us to quietly rededicate ourselves to the Savior.

When we read and study The Book of Mormon and the veil is removed from our eyes, we will find ourselves awash in a panoramic comprehension of spiritual certainty. Gone will be the inconsistent glimmers of light that we'd aforetime enjoyed. With crystal clarity, we will see from the time we were uncreated intelligence, through our development as spirit children of our Heavenly Father, on to mortality, and finally to our reunion with Him in the resurrection. "Knowledge will rush in from all quarters; it will come to us like the light that flows from the sun, penetrating every part, informing the Spirit, and giving understanding concerning ten thousand things at the same time; and our minds will be capable of receiving and retaining all."
(Orson Pratt).

As we ascend a ladder reaching all the way to heaven, The Book of Mormon will be our antidote to vertigo. From our vantage point in the spiritual stratosphere, we will look down at what we had thought were stumbling-blocks. When we mentally unwrap these gifts from God, we will discover that they are stepping-stones. As we hop from one to another, we will ultimately reach the stability of a far shore where we will find our Heavenly Father waiting to welcome us Home.

The Book of Mormon is a lens that focuses our perspective. It is our Tai Chi; we embrace its teachings with a series of gentle exercises and stretch ourselves physically, mentally, and spiritually. Each position will flow seamlessly into the next in a constant motion. But with the books' focus on the Savior, we'll retain fluidity with nature and harmony with the unseen world.

We express our
appreciation to our Father in
Heaven for the wonderful gift of The
Book of Mormon. Instead of sending
text messages or an email, tagging
Him in a Facebook post, mentioning
Him on Twitter, or even dropping a
thank you note in the mail, He
values simple expressions of
gratitude that are woven
into the fabric of our
heart-felt prayers.

With a little practice,
our spoken testimony of The
Book of Mormon flows easily
from our lips and leaves us
with the taste of honey
on the tips of our
tongues.

Without the Spirit to guide us, we must remain as the "very cautious man who never laughed or played, who never risked, who never tried, who never sang or prayed. And when, one day, he passed away, his insurance was denied, for since he never really lived, they claimed he never died." (Mark Barsouna). However, when we do have the Spirit to be with us, we pour ourselves into the task so that we can be lifesavers. When we teach from The Book of Mormon, we focus on the doctrine of Christ. We have such a passion for our message that those whom we teach find it hard to resist our invitation to action. We bear personal testimony that is based upon our own experiences relating to the anticipated blessings, and make them seem worth working and fighting for. We can be as saviors on Mount Zion through our teaching of key doctrine. (See Obadiah 1:21).

Satan has hired assassins on his payroll whose sole mission is to destroy faith, particularly of those who have initiated a study of The Book of Mormon. The powerful antidote to the telestial trauma caused by the venom of Satan's snake bites is found within its pages. The danger in doing nothing is that we don't know when we are finished. It may be that our good intentions are noble, but the hallmark of progress is based on action.

Commentary, Compendia, & Observations Index

As we read The Book of Mormon, when we've stockpiled ample reserves of revelation from our Heavenly Father in our spiritual bank accounts, it will be as if we had received pennies from heaven, or the currency of faith in its myriad forms.

Commentary Volume One
Born in The Wilderness

- 1 Nephi
- 2 Nephi
- Jacob
- Enos
- Jarom
- Omni
- Words of Mormon
- Observations
- Author's Note
- Addendum – A Sampling of Scriptures

Commentary Volume Two
Voices From The Dust

- Mosiah
- Alma
- Observations
- Author's Note
- Addendum – A Sampling of Scriptures

Commentary Volume Three
Journey to Cumorah

- Helaman
- 3 Nephi
- 4 Nephi
- Mormon
- Ether
- Moroni
- Observations
- Author's Note
- Addendum – A Sampling of Scriptures

Faith
asks a lot of us, but it also
emboldens us with hope, and it blesses
us with the fortitude to be able to endure. It
motivates us to seek after everything that is
lovely, or of good report or praiseworthy. It is
catalyzed to do this when we first open
The Book of Mormon, and read:
"I Nephi, having been born of
goodly parents...".
(1 Nephi 1:1).

Compendium
Volume One

- Introduction
- Questions Answered by The Book of Mormon
- Topical Index
- Observations
- A few of my favorite things
- Familiar Scriptures
- Commentary & Compendium Index

Compendium
Volume Two

- Introduction
- Questions Answered by The Book of Mormon
- Topical Index
- Without The Book of Mormon
- Observations
- Introduction to the Isaiah Chapters
- "And it came to pass in The Book of Mormon
- "Ad thus we see" in The Book of Mormon
- "Behold" in The Book of Mormon
- "Wherefore" and "Therefore in The Book of Mormon
- The Appearance of Gold
- The Use of The Name of Christ
- Pragmatism in The Book of Mormon
- Dry Humor in The Book of Mormon
- A Book of Mormon Timeline
- Commentary and Compendium Index

Compendium
Volume Three

- Compendia Index
- Essays That Relate to Teachings in The Book of Mormon
- Observations
- Commentary, Compendium, & Observations Index

Compendium
Volume Four

- Compendia Index
- Essays That Relate to Teachings in The Book of Mormon
- Observations
- Commentary, Compendium, & Observations Index

Compendium
Volume Five

- Compendia Index
- Essays That Relate to Teachings in The Book of Mormon
- Observations
- Commentary, Compendium, & Observations Index

Those who have become
enamored with their own wit
and wisdom, who think themselves a
gift to the world, wrap themselves up in
very small packages. As a result, they
may never be able to enjoy the soul
expanding epiphanies that could
have been theirs when they were
first exposed to the burning
bush that light up each
page of The Book
of Mormon.

Compendium
Volume Six

- Compendia Index
- Essays That Relate to Teachings in The Book of Mormon
- Observations
- Commentary, Compendium, & Observations Index

Compendium
Volume Seven

- Compendia Index
- Essays That Relate to Teachings in The Book of Mormon
- Observations
- Commentary, Compendium, & Observation Index

Compendium
Volume Eight

- Introduction
- Hebrew Poetry in The Book of Mormon
- Synonymous Parallelism
- Antithetical Parallelism
- Synthetic Parallelism
- Climactic Parallelism
- Chiasmus
- Book of Mormon Scriptures Illustrating

Observations
Volume One

- 550 Observations

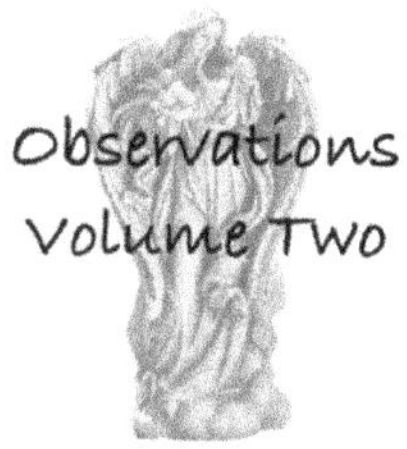

Observations
Volume Two

- 550 Observations

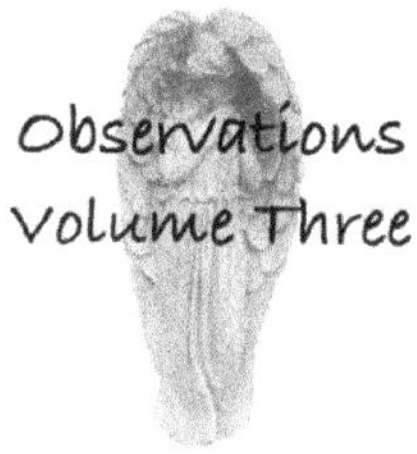

Observations
Volume Three

- 550 Observations

Observations
Volume Four

- 550 Observations

We
glory in revelation, particularly
when it expresses the Book of Mormon
perspective of a pattern of heaven that has
been traced by the finger of God upon the
fabric of our telestial tapestries. It has
neither temporal, nor spatial, nor
even spiritual boundaries. It
can be experienced at one
and the same time in the
past, the present, and
the future; now
and forever.

Observations Volume 5

- 550 Observations
- Commentary, Compendium, & Observations Index

Observations Volume 6

- 550 Observations
- Commentary, Compendium, & Observations Index

if we want to know God's will as it relates to our relationship with The Book of Mormon, we must nurture the development of a lively intercourse between the heavens and the earth. "Behold, I stand at the door, and knock. If any man hear my voice, and open the door, I will come in to him, and will sup with him, and he with me." (Revelation 3:20).

A Book of Mormon Commentary
Volumes One - Three

Compendia
Volumes One - Eight

Observations
Volumes One - Six

www.ingramcontent.com/pod-product-compliance
Lightning Source LLC
Chambersburg PA
CBHW061400010526
44107CB00012B/1000